# Solutions to Social Problems
## From the Top Down:
## The Role of Government

# Solutions to Social Problems

## From the Top Down:
## The Role of Government

**D. STANLEY EITZEN**

**GEORGE H. SAGE**

Boston • New York • San Francisco
Mexico City • Montreal • Toronto • London • Madrid • Munich • Paris
Hong Kong • Singapore • Tokyo • Cape Town • Sydney

**Senior Series Editor:** *Jeff Lasser*
**Series Editorial Assistant:** *Erikka Adams*
**Senior Marketing Manager:** *Kelly May*
**Editorial-Production Service:** *Omegatype Typography, Inc.*
**Composition Buyer:** *Linda Cox*
**Manufacturing Buyer:** *JoAnne Sweeney*
**Electronic Composition:** *Omegatype Typography, Inc.*
**Cover Administrator:** *Elena Sidorova*

For related titles and support materials, visit our online catalog at www.ablongman.com.

Between the time website information is gathered and then published, it is not unusual for some sites to have closed. Also, the transcription of URLs can result in typographical errors. The publisher would appreciate notification where these errors occur so that they may be corrected in subsequent editions.

**Library of Congress Cataloging-in-Publication Data**

Solutions to social problems from the top down : the role of government / [edited by] D. Stanley Eitzen, George H. Sage.—1st ed.
    p.  cm.
  Includes bibliographical references.
  ISBN 0-205-46885-3 (pbk.)
  1. Social problems—Government policy—United States—History.  2. United States—Social policy.  I. Eitzen, D. Stanley.  II. Sage, George Harvey.
  HN57.S64 2007
  361.6'10973—dc22

2005056458

Printed in the United States of America

10  9  8  7  6  5  4  3  2  1     11  10  09  08  07  06

# CONTENTS

# PREFACE

This book is part of a series published by Allyn and Bacon on solutions to U.S. social problems. The first volume, *Solutions to Social Problems: Lessons from Other Societies,* provides examples of how other advanced industrial societies have dealt with social problems with relative success, implying that their strategies may be applicable in the United States as well. The present volume, *Solutions to Social Problems from the Top Down: The Role of Government,* examines U.S. history to assess the role of government in tackling its social problems. The third volume in this series, *Solutions to Social Problems from the Bottom Up: Social Movements,* focuses on how solutions to social problems have emerged from people's social movements.

The focus of this book is on the clash between conservatives and progressives throughout the past 125 years or so over the role of the federal government in solving social problems. For conservatives, big government is the problem, not the solution. For progressives, the federal government is the people's instrument for promoting the welfare of all of the citizens. The question: What has been and continues to be the role of the government in ameliorating social problems?

We want to make clear that when we use the words *conservative* and *progressive* that these words are not synonymous with the Republican and Democratic parties, respectively. Although there is a tendency in the popular discourse to portray the Republican party as the conservative party and the Democratic party as the progressive party, such a simple labeling blurs the political reality of these two heterogeneous parties. Over the history of the United States, both Republican and Democratic parties have elected members with progressive and conservative inclinations. There have been Republican presidents who have initiated progressive policies and there have been Democratic presidents with conservative agendas. Each of the 108 Congresses has had progressive as well as conservative members who were at odds with the dominant political view of their party at that time. In this book, then, we intend to describe and illustrate how progressive practices and policies advance the greater good for the largest number of U.S. citizens and thus promote the good society. In doing so, we endorse progressivism, not a particular political party.

Virtually every major piece of federal legislation and every public policy on behalf of protecting human rights, promoting equal opportunity, ameliorating poverty, aiding the needy, eliminating discrimination, and reducing entrenched privilege has been a progressive initiative that was opposed by conservative interests. Having said that, we recognize that the federal government is by no means perfect. Throughout history there have been corrupt governments; there have been governments that were more concerned with bowing to the power of wealthy interests than in providing for the common good; and sometimes governmental policies have simply been wrong, thus exacerbating social problems rather than solving them. The U.S. government, for example, has supported slavery, limited voting to white males only, and validated segregation, and sometimes corrupt and incompetent administrators of good progressive government programs have wasted taxpayers' money. But that is only half of the story. The federal government has also acted positively, overturning slavery, giving racial minorities and women the right to vote, and ending segregation in the schools, military, and public facilities. The lesson here is that the government, although not a perfect instrument, can work for the common good. The task of this book is to provide examples of how the government has helped the disadvantaged, redistributed income and wealth, provided for racial and gender equity, promoted public education, established and maintained public spaces, and protected the environment.

A final caveat: because we favor progressive social policies does not mean that we endorse an ever larger role for government. The assumption that progressives favor big government is far too simple. As Robert Reich (*Reason,* New York: Vintage, 2004:15) states: "The government's size or reach isn't the issue. . . . It's what it does, and for whom." We, along with Reich, do not want a big government monitoring our behaviors, dictating personal morality, doing the bidding of the wealthy and powerful, or mounting "preemptive" wars without international backing.

The format of this book is that of a text/reader. That is, we have provided rather lengthy introductions for each of the nine sections. In these sections, we have selected three or four readings to highlight government actions in the specified area. These readings may provide a case history of a particular piece of legislation (e.g., the GI Bill) or government program (e.g., Head Start), or they might describe the history of a government agency (e.g., the Environmental Protection Agency) or make the argument to retain a government program that is threatened currently (e.g., Social Security).

This book is intended to supplement traditional social problems textbooks, which typically are long on descriptive content of social problems but short on solutions. Other sociology courses that will find this text useful are political sociology, social policy, and social change. There is also a fit with other disciplines, especially political science, history, and social welfare.

## ACKNOWLEDGMENTS

We are indebted to the sociology editor at Allyn and Bacon, Jeff Lasser, whose idea sparked this project. Others who have had an indirect influence on this project are Maxine Baca Zinn, Craig Leedham, Bill Morgan, Kenneth Stewart, Kathryn Talley, and Doug Timmer. Our ongoing thanks to them for their insights and inspiration.

D. S. E.
G. H. S.

# Time Line of Progressive Social Policies

1862  Homestead Act
      Pacific Railroad Act
      Morrill Act
1863  Emancipation Proclamation
1868  14th Amendment conferring
      citizenship to blacks
1870  15th Amendment gives blacks the
      right to vote
1872  Yellowstone became the first
      National Park

**Progressive Era**

1906  Antiquities Act
      Food and Drug Act
1908  Federal Workman's Compensation
      Law
1912  Children's Bureau established
1913  16th Amendment establishes the
      federal income tax
1914  Smith-Lever Act
1916  Estate tax established
      Creation of the National Park
      Service
1917  Smith-Hughes Act to foster
      vocational education
1920  19th Amendment gives women the
      right to vote
1921  First authorization of Indian Health
      Service

**New Deal Era**

1933  Establishment of Tennessee Valley
      Authority
      Civilian Conservation Corps
      Federal Emergency Relief for
      medically indigent
1934  National Housing Act establishes the
      Federal Housing Administration
1935  Social Security Act (retirement,
      unemployment insurance, AFDC)
      Works Project Administration

1938  Establishment of minimum wage
1939  Social Security Act amendments for
      dependent and survivor benefits
1944  GI Bill of Rights
1946  School Lunch Program
      Hospital Survey and Construction Act
1947  Desegregation of Armed Forces
1954  *Brown v. Board of Education*
      overturns segregated schools
1956  Social Security Act amendments
      for disability benefits
      Segregation in public facilities
      ruled unconstitutional
1957  Civil Rights Act
1958  National Defense Education Act
1961  Food Stamp pilot program
1962  Migrant Health Act
1963  Equal Pay Act
      Clear Air Act

**Great Society Era**

1964  Civil Rights Act of 1964
      Economic Opportunity Act of 1964
      Job Corps
      Food Stamp Act
1965  Voting Rights Act
      Medicare and Medicaid
      Elementary and Secondary
      Education Act
      Higher Education Act
      Head Start initiated
      Appalachian Regional
      Development Act
1966  Child Nutrition Act retaining
      school lunch and milk programs
1968  Fair Housing Act
1969  Head Start authorized as legislation
1970  Occupational Safety and Health
      Administration
1972  Supplemental Security Income and
      Social Security Disability Insurance

Nutrition Program for Women,
  Infants, and Children (WIC)
Title IX
Basic Grant Program (Pell Grants)
1973 *Roe v. Wade* invalidates all state
  laws against abortion
1974 Food Stamp Program and WIC
  authorized as legislation
Child Abuse Prevention and
  Treatment Act
Housing and Community
  Development Act
1975 Education for All Handicapped
  Children Act
Earned Income Tax Credit
Child Support Enforcement Program
Voting Rights Act extended to
  include language minorities

1976 Dependent Care Tax Credit
Adoption Assistance and Child
  Welfare Act
Creation of Superfund
National Consumer Health
  Information and Health
  Promotion Act
1982 Job Training Partnership Act
1987 Homeless Assistance Act
1990 Americans with Disabilities Act
Comprehensive AIDS Resource
  Emergency Act
1997 State Children's Health Insurance
  Program (CHIP)
2001 Economic Growth and Tax Relief
  Reconciliation Act
No Child Left Behind Act

Copyright © David Horsey. Reprinted with permission.

# PART ONE

# The Government and Reform

**Section 1: Progressive Policies: A Persistent Force for the Common Good in the United States**

# Progressive Policies

## A Persistent Force for the Common Good in the United States

*It is the job of government to promote and, if possible, provide sufficient protection, greater democracy, more freedom, a better environment, broader prosperity, better health, greater fulfillment in life, less violence, and the building and maintaining of public infrastructure.*

—Wikipedia

Liberalism and conservativism are two political philosophies that have contended with each other throughout modern times. Both perspectives arose as competing models of social order as part of the Enlightenment in the latter eighteenth century. Liberal thought was associated with a belief in the essential goodness of humans and individual freedom and rights against the arbitrary power of the state and church. It developed as a movement for individual liberty in the political, economic, and social realms, and it endeavored to increase equality and democratic participation in governance. Liberal ideology was committed to transforming the social order through the use of government to aid individuals and groups, thus reducing social injustices and making the human condition better for all.

On the other hand, conservatism arose as an anguished attack on democracy because conservatives viewed the emerging liberal democratic ideas as destroying the old structures of authority. As a result, they mounted a defense of traditional society and values, grounding them in what they considered the wisdom of institutions such as the church, royalty, and propertied social class. Conservativism emphasized the values of the status quo, a social hierarchy over equality, and the support of the existing distribution of power, wealth, and social standing. According to conservative ideology, the mass of people, because of their inherent qualities, such as ignorance and selfishness, is unlikely to create a satisfactory social order by its own efforts (Herzog, 1998).

In terms of U.S. conservative political economic thought over the past two centuries, it has converged into a broad consensus promoting powerful restraints on government while endorsing economic individualism. In brief, conservatism has advocated laissez-faire capitalism unconstrained from government regulation or controls.

## PROGRESSIVISM: A VARIATION OF LIBERALISM

Beginning in the early twentieth century the word *progressivism* came into use to portray a variety of liberal social reform efforts, and when Theodore Roosevelt became president in 1901, his dramatizing of social and political issues needing government leadership launched a popular social reform movement that became known as the Progressive Era in American history. For several decades after the Progressive Era ended around 1920, the word *progressive* was not prominent in the popular discourse, but in the last quarter century it has again come into popular usage.

There are two general reasons for this rise in progressive terminology and commitment. One reason is that many Americans have wanted to move beyond traditional liberal versus conservative ideological debates and are committed to active involvement in social reforms and social movements, which they view as progressive activity. Thus, they believe the word *progressive* is more fitting for their political, economic, and social views and plans of action. A second reason for the renewed use of the progressive label is that the conservative movement initiated a campaign to demonize liberals through a variety of misleading, demeaning, and inaccurate ways, so many liberals have felt it necessary to distance themselves from the word *liberal* by using the word *progressive* as a rhetorical device, and the word *progressive* connotes progress, which has both a positive implication and is unencumbered by the negative portrayals that were given liberals by conservatives. We prefer the concept of progressive, and we shall use it throughout this book, but we acknowledge its philosophical foundations in liberalism.

Today, progressivism is closely related to the liberal concept, but it is an umbrella under which a variety of reform and communitarian groups and champions of liberalism gather. A general spirit of reform with diverse goals typifies progressivism. What unites progressives is the belief that the government should have an active role in solving social problems. George Lakoff (2004), a world renowned cognitive linguistics scholar whose focus in this discipline has been on the study of politics, summarizes progressives' convictions about government in this way: "It is the job of government to promote and, if possible, provide sufficient protection, greater democracy, more freedom, a better environment, broader prosperity, better health, greater fulfillment in life, less violence, and the building and maintaining of public infrastructure" (p. 91). However, progressives are not a totally unified group with a single objective or set of objectives.

## EARLY PROGRESSIVE INITIATIVES FACE
## CONSERVATIVE OPPOSITION

The beginnings of the United States are found in a progressive document, the Declaration of Independence, which described a new kind of liberty and a commitment to the rights of every individual. Eleven years later the Constitutional Convention in Philadelphia formulated what became the Constitution of the United States, creating a central government that was not controlled by a monarchy or a church.

Despite the progressive features of the U.S. Constitution, there were several aspects of the Constitution that were decidedly not progressive, such as the denial of full citizenship to African Americans. But the most reactionary feature of the original Constitution was that there was preciously little about individual civil rights. Consequently, a progressive

movement emerged among small farmers, laborers, those who did not own extensive property, and those who wanted a more democratic federal government. They were dissatisfied
because the Constitution had no "bill of rights" to protect individual liberty. This progressive impetus made possible the adoption of the first ten amendments to the Constitution.
The amendments have become known as the Bill of Rights. Over the ensuing years, many
of the amendments to the U.S. Constitution extending individual rights and liberties have
been the result of progressive movements. Without these progressive campaigns, there
would be far less democracy and personal liberties in the Constitution.

Conservative politics was the prevailing moral force before the Civil War. Alexander
Hamilton, one of the Framers of the Constitution, became the leader of a political party
called the Federalists, a staunchly conservative party. Hamilton wanted political power
vested in wealthy people. He had little faith in the ability of average citizens to govern
themselves; indeed, he called common people "a great beast." Another Federalist, John
Jay, a man who became the first Chief Justice of the Supreme Court, articulated his view of
government this way: "The people who own the country ought to govern it." John Adams,
the second U.S. president, and a Federalist, said that Federalists represented "the rich, the
well-born, and the able."

This is not to say that progressivism was absent. Of the progressive initiatives in the
early nineteenth century, none was more directly related to the progression of democracy
than the movement for free public schools. Another of the many progressive reforms in
which U.S. citizens were engaged during the antebellum period was a more important
place for women in U.S. life. Women's suffrage protests and demonstrations for voting
rights, educational opportunities, equitable legal status, and improved working rights gradually opened opportunities for women. Slavery produced the most violent public agitation
of the first six decades of the nineteenth century. Abolition of slavery was a multifaceted
progressive movement during the first half of the nineteenth century that reached a climax
with the Civil War.

Beyond the ratification of the Thirteenth Amendment in 1865, abolishing slavery in
the United States, the Fourteenth Amendment in 1868, expanding citizen rights, and the
Fifteenth Amendment in 1870, extending the voting rights and giving African Americans
the rights and privileges of other citizens, the years between 1870 and 1900 were bleak
for progressive initiatives. On nearly all essential issues the major differences between
the leadership of the two political parties was muted. All were eager to support the
growing influence of the new industrialists and financiers around them. The pioneers of
industrialism—"robber barons," as some of the most notable of them were called, such
as Cornelius Vanderbilt, Andrew Carnegie, J. P. Morgan, and John D. Rockefeller—were
staunch conservatives who shared the ideal of self-reliant individualism, and they had an
enormous influence on steering the political and social affairs of the nation in a decidedly
conservative manner.

## THE PROGRESSIVE ERA: PROGRESSIVISM
## BECOMES A NATIONAL MOVEMENT

In the early 1890s a progressive movement emerged, and from an unlikely source—farmers.
For the largest occupation, farming, the period between the Civil War and the beginning
of the twentieth century brought many problems, and most of the nation's farmers found

themselves in serious financial trouble. As years went by with no resolution to these problems, and with a sharp decline in farmers' income at a time when their living and operating costs were increasing, in 1891 an agrarian progressive initiative materialized as the Populist movement. This new progressive impulse of farmers became a strong voice for reform. The Populist movement had enough strength to form a national political party in 1892 and take part in the presidential elections in that year and in 1896, but it was unsuccessful at electing a candidate, and the party faded steadily from the political scene in the first few years of the twentieth century.

Just as the Populist movement was losing its momentum, a new and progressive movement was beginning to form. Its first elements were seen in what became known as the Social Gospel. The champions of the Social Gospel felt that religious leaders and congregations—Protestant, Roman Catholic, Jewish—should become more involved in the plight of the poor and needy in the United States, and that the church would be the instrument for a new, humane, and religious society. These moral, even religious, convictions framed a mindset that set the stage for more comprehensive initiatives, which cut across political party lines, and ultimately had important consequences for U.S. political, economic, educational, and social institutions. The movement became such a prominent feature of life in the first two decades of the twentieth century that this period is known as the Progressive Era in U.S. history.

Broadly, the progressive initiatives that gave the Progressive Era its name were attempts to solve many of the problems of society that had surfaced during the enormous expansion of industrialization and urbanization during the last half of the nineteenth century. Large corporate empires were built in conjunction with industrial expansion. Large fortunes were made, and a small percentage of people owned a large proportion of the country's wealth. Thriving cities and businesses grew and proliferated, but most of the growing wage labor force required to sustain this corporate and industrial society did not share in the new wealth. Wages could hardly sustain life. Work weeks of sixty to eighty hours were common, and working conditions were often miserable and dangerous; indeed, poverty was widespread. An aristocracy of wealth and power existed in the midst of a desperately poor and exploited mass of citizens. Furthermore, child labor was widespread, and in many factories children worked the same long hours as adults. By 1907 progressive efforts had led thirty states to abolish child labor.

Unlike many progressive movements, three presidents of the United States were leading progressive advocates: Theodore Roosevelt, Howard Taft, and Woodrow Wilson. Of the three, Theodore Roosevelt is the most noted for the founding of the Progressive Era. Roosevelt, who became president when William McKinley was assassinated in 1901, was elected president on his own in 1904 by a resounding victory at the polls and did much to launch the Progressive Era. His immense popularity, his gifts as a speaker, and his position as president enabled him to endorse a number of the movement's first notable social reforms. During his presidency, he gave the progressive initiatives dramatic national leadership, promising a "Square Deal" to the mass of people struggling for financial security and hoping to experience the personal freedom, liberty, and opportunity they heard so much about (Burt, 2004; Diner, 1998).

Roosevelt's brand of progressivism was rooted in the conviction that citizens who have the wherewithal have an obligation to help improve the human condition of all people within society, especially those in need of collective assistance. During the Progressive

Era, national leaders embraced many types of progressive reform and had specific aims. One major goal was to end political corruption and reform government to give greater control to the rank and file of people. Curbing corporate power by eliminating business monopolies and strengthening antitrust laws was another goal. Progressives also struggled diligently to correct the abuses and injustices that had crept into U.S. life in the age of corporate industrialism. They wanted to bridge the gap between social classes by increasing equality of economic opportunity for the expanding industrial work force, and they wished to restore the lost sense of communitarian-mindedness they believed was being lost with industrialization and urbanization. One writer noted that progressive reforms were helping Americans to understand that the government should stand "for the protection of the weak against the encroachments of the strong" and acted as a forum for "the contest between the strong and the weak, the powerful and the helpless, the many and the few, between the general and the special interests" (Gould, 1992: p. 26; also see Gould, 2001).

The Progressive Era was not merely social reform from above—from political and business leaders—it was mobilized by a broad spectrum of reformers from a wide variety of walks of life. Starting with Roosevelt, politicians in the U.S. Congress and state-level politicians made contributions. Intellectuals, social workers, clergy, and even business leaders who shared common values all helped shape many of the progressive initiatives. Journalists and freelance writers helped shape a climate favorable to reform through their sensational exposés about government corruption, business greed, the horrors of poverty and city slums, dangerous working conditions, child labor, and widespread social injustices. Perhaps the most famous of these writers was Upton Sinclair, whose book *The Jungle* horrified readers with vivid descriptions of atrocious working and sanitary conditions in Chicago's meat-packing plants. The book led to support for remedial legislation. The label *muckrakers* was applied to writers who exposed the corruption in politics and the corporate world. Although the word *muckraker* was used as an unflattering moniker, writers accepted it with pride, and it ultimately came to have a favorable connotation (Weinberg and Weinberg, 2001).

Progressivism was not just a national phenomenon. In many states and municipalities of the country, governors, state legislatures, and city councils were devoted to progressive reforms. The direct primary, the secret ballot, the referendum, and the recall were all important reforms toward democratizing electoral procedures and allowing people to have a more direct role in the political process. Removing corruption and undue influence from government through getting rid of bosses and political machines was a strong initiative for progressives.

The settlement movement administered by social workers who managed settlement houses to protect the poor and improve the prospects for newly arrived immigrants was an impressive progressive force for reform in cities throughout the nation. In 1900 there were fewer than one hundred settlement houses, in 1905 there were some two hundred, and in 1910 there were four hundred. The provision of nurseries, adult education classes, health services, and recreational facilities for children and adults were some of the main features of the settlement houses.

Progressives working at the grassroots level organized support for the 17th Amendment, ratified in 1913, establishing the direct election of U.S. senators by voters in the various states, rather than indirectly by state legislatures. Likewise the struggle for women's rights won vigorous progressive support. Women were not included in the U.S. Constitution and they were largely left out of public life throughout the nineteenth century. In

1890 several suffrage groups formed the National American Woman Suffrage Association, which pursued right-to-vote legislation in earnest. By 1909, women had secured the right to vote in four states (Wyoming, Utah, Idaho, and Colorado), but they could see that fighting legislation on a state-by-state basis was slow and frustrating, so they began to use more aggressive tactics. They organized parades, rallies, and marches, gaining supporters wherever they were active. Finally, in 1920 they won the key prize for which they had been struggling for over a century—the passage of the 19th Amendment, extending the vote to all women in the United States.

In 1908 Roosevelt chose not to run for reelection. His successor, William Howard Taft, despite being more conservative than Roosevelt, accepted the mood of the progressive movement, but he was unable to mediate between the demand for aggressive progressive policy and influential conservative resistance to it. He did support several important anti-trust corporation tax reforms, but he could not project a forceful image and was ousted from the presidency by Woodrow Wilson in 1912. Wilson promised to continue the progressive movement under a slogan he called a "New Freedom," the duty of which, he said, was "to cleanse, to reconsider, to restore . . . every process of our common life." Progressivism continued to define the political agenda after Wilson was elected. He did carry out significant progressive reforms to laws governing tariffs, trusts, labor, agriculture, and banking during his two terms as president. Unfortunately, Wilson's administration was confronted with U.S. engagement in World War I, and progressive initiatives had to take a back seat to national security issues (Chambers, 2000).

The Progressive Era was not just a smooth ride of progressive reforms. Conservative voices in government and business opposed many of the reform initiatives and used what influence they could muster to defeat them. Roosevelt's progressive activities while president were constantly under attack. Conservative voices gradually pulled Taft toward conservative interests. By the end of his term, the conflict between the progressives and conservatives split the Republican party, tilting the influence of the party toward conservative positions throughout the two terms of Woodrow Wilson.

Despite the persistence of conservative opposition to progressive initiatives during the Progressive Era, the zeal for progressive actions was pervasive and sustained for almost two decades. Progressivism made significant positive differences in the political, economic, educational, and social reforms that it won. Many of these progressive measures can still be seen in the U.S. society of the twenty-first century. So in the end, the Progressive Era gave rise to a progressive tradition that left a lasting legacy on the nation's history.

The Progressive Era ended with the United States' involvement in World War I. During the 1920s the United States enjoyed an economic boom and the decade became known as the "Golden Twenties." Although it was a period of international peace and enormous wealth for segments of the population, it was also a decade of hard times for many, especially minorities and immigrants, who suffered widespread social injustices. It was also a period of government scandals and conservative policies endorsed by both political parties; the period ended with the stock market crash of 1929, sending the nation into a deep economic depression.

## A PROGRESSIVE REBIRTH AS THE NEW DEAL

By 1932 people had lost confidence in President Herbert Hoover's ability to reverse the economic depression. As the 1932 presidential election approached, Franklin Delano

Roosevelt (FDR), taking a page from his distant cousin Theodore Roosevelt, who had promised a Square Deal of progressive social policies, promised a "New Deal" in a dramatic speech to the Democratic Convention. He was overwhelmingly elected president, and his New Deal became the domestic policies through which the federal government became more directly involved in the nation's political, economic, and social affairs than ever before, introducing sweeping reforms that have been the bedrock of progressive policies for the past seventy years.

Franklin D. Roosevelt was, at heart, a social reformer. As president, Roosevelt launched the New Deal because, as he said, he wanted to help the average person, whom he called the "forgotten man." That progressive spirit was energized and reinforced by congressional progressives who were committed to the promotion of personal freedom and social progress but who had been frustrated throughout the 1920s by conservative politicians who opposed involving the government in social reforms.

The Great Depression was at its worst as Roosevelt became president in March 1933. Nearly 25 percent of the workers in the United States were unemployed, and many men and women had been out of work for a year or more. Following up on his nomination speech, President Roosevelt established the New Deal to address unemployment and other problems accompanying the Great Depression. The basic legislation for the initiatives that later generations associate with the New Deal had three aims: relief, recovery, and reform.

Roosevelt quickly established the Works Progress Administration (WPA), a work relief program that put nine million people to work on various public works projects: constructing or renovating schools, sewage plants, secondary roads, recreation facilities, and many other public improvements. Other New Deal relief programs aided millions of young people to get an education who were being forced to drop out of high school and college because of desperate economic conditions in their families. Federal money was distributed to needy students who performed useful tasks in and around their schools and colleges. Many other relief and recovery initiatives became law, but the focus here will be on the progressive reform measures that Roosevelt was able to accomplish (McJimsey, 2000).

Within a month after becoming president, Roosevelt sent a bill to Congress authorizing creation of the Tennessee Valley Authority (TVA). Roosevelt and an ally in the Senate, progressive Republican George W. Norris of Nebraska, were advocates of public ownership and operation of public utilities such as power and water services. Roosevelt also saw the possibilities of the TVA for the conservation of natural and human resources. Without a doubt, the TVA was one of the boldest and most sweeping progressive reforms of the New Deal; it was an experiment that had no parallel in U.S. history. For more about the TVA, see Section 6.

The TVA came under persistent legal assault from private power companies, who viewed it as a direct threat. They argued that the TVA was an illegal intervention of the federal government into the rightful domain of private industry. Conservative interests in both government and business charged that the inexpensive electricity generated by the TVA was an unfair gift to the people of that region by the taxpayers of the entire nation—a form of socialism. The influence of the powerful corporations, and their representatives in Congress, was so strong that no project of its kind was initiated elsewhere.

The most comprehensive progressive reform initiative of the New Deal was the Social Security Act of 1935. It tackled one of the most pressing social needs that accompanied modern industrialization: the problem of individual personal security, especially in old age.

It had three main goals. (1) It provided unemployment insurance for workers who lost their jobs; it was set up as a joint federal–state program to be financed by a federal payroll tax paid equally by employers and employees. (2) It provided old-age pensions for persons over 65 years of age; this pension system was to be administered by the federal government and financed by taxes on both employers and employees. (3) It provided help for the disabled (e.g., the blind) and aid to dependent children; government funds were made available to the needy who met the requirements, provided that the states paid an equal amount to protect the welfare of the disabled and dependent children. Shortly after passage of the Social Security Act, Roosevelt's commitment to progressive ideals as exemplified by this Act was articulately expressed in his second inaugural address when he said, "The test of our progress is not whether we add more to the abundance of those who have much; it is whether we provide enough for those who have too little."

Little did anyone realize at the time that this progressive legislation, and subsequent amendments to it, would extend coverage to nearly all gainfully employed workers, including farmers, and would become the foundation for the safety net of economic protection and security for all succeeding generations of citizens who were laid off from work, reached old-age, or were disabled or dependent as children (Edsforth, 2000).

Not everyone supported the Social Security Act. Soon after President Roosevelt signed this legislation, several lawsuits were filed by conservative members of the business establishment challenging Social Security's constitutionality. Also, in 1934, when FDR sent Congress a set of recommendations designed to make the Social Security system more comprehensive by including millions of the poorest workers and their families as well as widows and surviving children, a conservative coalition in Congress blocked FDR's proposals.

One of the last major progressive actions of FDR was overseeing passage of the Serviceman's Readjustment Act of 1944. The G.I. Bill, as it came to be known, provided veterans with educational funding for tuition, books, and partial living expenses while they attended school or college. It also provided government loans to help veterans establish businesses or farms, loans to buy homes, and pensions and hospital care. This legislation created a sea change in U.S. society like no other progressive initiative. It remains a monument to Roosevelt's New Deal and the commitment of his supporters in Congress to progressive goals.

The G.I. Bill became known as the best progressive policy ever enacted in U.S. history, but it was not without its critics when it was first proposed. Although President Roosevelt was a key supporter of this legislation, it was the American Legion that was the major force for its enactment, pressuring staunch conservative members of Congress to come together with New Deal Congressmen and support the G.I. Bill. Social historian Theda Skocpol (1997) summarized the success of the American Legion's efforts in this way: "The usual mold of U.S. federal social provision was broken," meaning conservative objection to progressive reform, "and the result was one of the best-loved and most successful social programs ever sponsored by the American national government" (p. 109).

## PROGRESSIVE POLICIES AND THE GREAT SOCIETY

The next, and most recent, great surge of progressive legislation and policies came under President Lyndon Johnson, who became president when John F. Kennedy was assassinated in the fall of 1963. Johnson gave top priority to three issues: a civil rights law, a tax cut, and an "unconditional war on poverty." In pursuing these goals, he invited people to build what he called the "Great Society." Congress responded to his leadership and within one year had achieved an impressive record of progressive actions. Two of the most notable were the Civil Rights Act of 1964, which outlawed racial discrimination in employment and in public accommodations, and the Economic Opportunity Act of 1964, which marked a significant attempt to "break the cycle of poverty." In addition, to carry out the policies of this act, the Office of Economic Opportunity (OEO) was funded to begin the war against poverty. The OEO launched twelve programs, and most of them are still working in 2005: Head Start, Job Corps, Community Health Centers, Foster Grandparents, Upward Bound, Green Thumb (now Senior Community Service Employment), Indian Opportunities (now in the Labor Department), and Migrant Opportunities (now Seasonal Worker Training and Migrant Education). They were all created to do what they continue to do: provide individuals with economic opportunities they would not have otherwise had (Kotz, 2005).

After his election in 1964, Johnson immediately began other progressive initiatives, and by the fall of 1965 Congress had adopted most of the president's major recommendations. One of the most significant was Voting Rights Act of 1965, which legalized a way for blacks to strengthen their voice at every level of government. The Elementary and Secondary Education Act of 1965 for the first time committed the federal government to helping local public school districts. Subsequent Great Society education legislation helped colleges and universities, bilingual education, and special education. The creation of Medicare was the jewel of the Great Society legislation. Prior to 1965 most of the elderly had no health insurance, and the poor had little access to medical care until they were in critical condition. The Medicare bill also provided for federal grants to states that wished to create health care programs for the needy. Such programs became known as Medicaid. To assist those who lived in low-income regions, Congress authorized a large sum of money to improve the nation's housing (Dallek, 2003).

Joseph A. Califano Jr. (1999), former Secretary of Health, Education, and Welfare, has summarized the Great Society programs engineered by President Johnson in this way: "Johnson converted the federal government into a far more energetic, proactive force for social justice, striking down discriminatory practices and offering a hand up with education, health care, and job training. . . . In numbers of Americans helped, the Great Society exceeds in domestic impact even the New Deal" (7–8).

Conservative opposition to Johnson's Great Society programs was persistent and vociferous, and it gradually began to erode Johnson's popularity. So between conservative hostility to increasing federal spending and what conservatives saw as inappropriate government involvement in citizens' individual lives, plus the growing national resistance to the Vietnam War, Johnson's progressive momentum was brought to a standstill. But the legacy of his Great Society initiatives still exists in many government programs and policies.

## CONCLUSION

There have been three waves of progressive government action since 1900: The Progressive Era, the New Deal, and the Great Society. The social programs from the last two have been under increasing attacks by conservatives for the past twenty-five years, and they have actually accelerated in the past five years. Our book will highlight progressive social policies focusing on social welfare, income and wealth inequality, race and gender equity, education, public spaces, and environmental protections. The book ends with an account of the ascent of the conservative assaults on progressive policies and programs and an analysis of the potential consequences of this trend on the role of government in achieving the good society.

## REFERENCES

Burt, Elizabeth V. (2004). *The Progressive Era: Primary Documents on Events From 1890 to 1914.* Westport, CT: Greenwood Press.

Califano, Joseph A. (1999). "What Was Really Great about The Great Society?": www. washingtonmonthly.com/features/1999/9910.califan.html.

Chambers, John W. (2000). *The Tyranny of Change: America in the Progressive Era, 1890–1920.* New Brunswick, NJ: Rutgers University Press.

Dallek, Robert. (2003). *Lyndon B. Johnson: Portrait of a President.* New York: Oxford University Press.

Diner, Steven J. (1998). *A Very Different Age: Americans of the Progressive Era.* New York: Hill and Wang.

Edsforth, Ronald. (2000). *The New Deal: America's Response to the Great Depression.* Malden, MA: Blackwell Publishers.

Gould, Lewis L. (2001). *America in the Progressive Era, 1890–1914.* New York: Longman.

Gould, Lewis L. (1992). *Progressives and Prohibitionists: Texas Democrats in the Wilson Era.* Austin: Texas State Historical Association.

Herzog, Don. (1998). *Poisoning the Minds of the Lower Orders.* Princeton, NJ: Princeton University Press.

Kotz, Nick. (2005). *Judgment Days: Lyndon Baines Johnson, Martin Luther King, Jr., and the Laws That Changed America.* Boston: Houghton Mifflin.

Lakoff, George. (2004). *Don't Think Like an Elephant.* White Water Junction, VT: Chelsea Green.

McJimsey, George. (2000). *The Presidency of Franklin Delano Roosevelt.* Lawrence: University of Kansas Press.

Skocpol, Theda. (1997). "The G.I. Bill and U.S. Social Policy, Past and Future." *Social Philosophy and Policy* 14 (2):95–115.

Weinberg, Arthur, and Weinberg, Lila Shaffer (eds.). (2001). *The Muckrakers.* Champaign: University of Illinois Press.

# 1

# The Real World of Liberalism

*DAVID SPITZ*

*In this reading, the author poses the question of whether there is a collection of policies and thoughts that tend to correspond to and appear associated with liberalism and with conservatism. David Spitz believes that there is such a unity or tradition for each of these two views of the social order, and he articulates the differences and cleavages between them.*

If we are to talk sensibly of liberalism and conservatism, we must probe somehow to a common core of meaning—a core that transcends though it does not obliterate the many diversities and transformations of liberal and conservative doctrine. . . . Is there a constellation of policies and attitudes that tend to correspond to and appear concomitantly with the one or the other label? If there is a recurring convergence of such policies and attitudes, then these labels have a viable and abiding significance, and it is possible to speak of them in terms of a tradition or a unity.

I believe that such a unity does exist, even though it is not always described in precisely the same way. Sometimes it is presented as a cleavage between parties or classes. Here liberalism, or the Left, is identified with that party associated with and representative of the interests of the lower classes, while conservatism, or the Right, is the party associated with and representative of the interests of the upper or dominant class. Sometimes this unity is found at the intellectual or philosophical level. Here liberalism is tied to the principle of experimentalism, to the open-ended negotiation of differences, whether of ideas or of policies, while conservatism bespeaks the cause of absolute truth, of a belief in an objective moral order, of a relatively closed rather than an open society. Both these conceptions of liberalism and conservatism, I think, are broadly correct, but because they do not readily distinguish between or adequately encompass the different spheres of thought and action—the political, the economic, the intellectual or cultural—they need to be incorporated into a larger and multidimensional framework.

*Source:* Excerpt from *The Real World of Liberalism* by David Spitz, pp. 30, 34–40. Copyright © 1982. Reprinted by permission of The University of Chicago Press.

In the political sphere, the unity or tradition of liberalism is unambiguous. Its preeminent principle is political equality. Whatever the form of state, whatever the historical situation or national character, the liberal has associated himself with the battle against entrenched privilege. Always the liberal has denied that power and station are the appropriate perquisites of lineage, or of the exercise of force, or of something called History or God. Always the liberal has looked to that which is common to men, not to that which divides them. This does not mean that the liberal is oblivious to the fact that men are not identical, that there are indeed differences of religion and race, wealth and power, talent and intelligence. What it does mean is that for the liberal such differences, important though they may be for certain purposes, are politically irrelevant. Each man has a life to live, the poorest as well as the richest man. Each man requires freedom—to exercise his reason, to discover and develop his talents, to achieve his full growth and stature as an individual. And each man suffers the consequences of deprivation and injustice, the oppressor no less than the oppressed. Hence each man has a common stake in the conditions, and in the determination of the conditions, under which he lives.

Liberals have no faith in human infallibility, or in the capacity of an allegedly superior few to respect the principle of equality or to withstand the corrupting temptations of power. Hence, while liberals recognize that political decisions taken by the people may be wrong, decisions taken by a self-proclaimed aristocracy are not necessarily right. Indeed, their wrongs have been far more numerous! What is crucial, then, is a political arrangement that makes possible the peaceful and effective correction of error. This dictates democracy, for only democracy provides a constitutional mechanism for the removal of the rulers by the ruled. Whatever its limitations or defects, democracy commends itself to liberals by this one overriding virtue—the principle of responsibility, by which the governed can protect themselves from misgovernment. This is why liberalism has consistently opposed authoritarianism in politics, why it has fought against all forms of oligarchical rule.

Conservatism, in contrast, has traditionally been identified with the impulse to hierarchy, a hierarchy based on the inequality of men. What is impressive to the conservative is that societies are made up of men, not Man, and that men are different. Some men (it is held) are wiser, more intelligent, more talented, better informed, than others. And if some men are superior and others average or inferior, it is the height of folly, conservatives argue, to let the unwise, through their numerical superiority, govern the wise or even themselves. For if they are unwise, they will make wrong decisions and thus defeat the very purposes they seek to accomplish. Indeed, because they are unwise, they cannot, save by accident, know what the right purposes are. It is true that conservatives are not always in agreement as to the character of the superior few. Some believe this superiority derives from race or blood; others, that it is an attribute of wealth or strength; still others, that it is associated with intelligence or virtue. But that there are a superior few, whether determined by nature or nurture, conservatives do not doubt. Hence the right political order is in the conservative view that which in one way or another institutionalizes this crucial fact.

Moreover, when the conservative speaks of order, he has in mind an order that is given, not contrived. Its laws are to be discovered, not created, to be adhered to, not defied. Just as the heavenly bodies have their accustomed place, just as the waters fall and the trees rise, so there is pattern and degree in human communities. Each man, said the ancient philosopher, must be given his due; but no man must seek more than his due. Hence those who are qualified to rule must rule; those who are fit but to obey must obey. And if, at a particular moment, the few who actually occupy the seats of power are not those fitted by reason and nature to rule, if, as Santayana and others of this persuasion sometimes admit, past aristocracies have been artificial rather than natural and just aristocracies, still it is better to have order than disorder. This is why conservatives, despite internal disagreements, have throughout history defended the prevailing aristocratic order, resisted the encroachments of egalitarianism, and associated themselves with the upper or dominant class.

In the economic sphere, this distinction between liberalism as representative of the interests of the lower classes and conservatism as spokesman for the interests of the upper classes is even more clear. There is, however, one crucial exception that must be noted. This is the disjunction among conservatives on the indentification of wealth and virtue. When Socrates asked why it is that philosophers are to be found at the doors of the rich but the rich do not wait at the doors of the philosophers, he expressed in rhetorical form a contempt—shared by liberals and some conservatives alike—for the notion that money means wisdom. For the philosophers attend the rich only because philosophers know what they need; the rich do not. Consequently wealth, far from constituting proof of one's virtue or superiority—unless perhaps we speak here of superiority in chicanery and greed—establishes the reverse. With respect to the things that matter, the wealthy, precisely because they have spent their lives and their thoughts on the acqustion of money and material goods, are essentially philistines.

Yet it is a peculiar fact that even conservatives of this sort, who like to denote themselves "philosophical" conservatives, or even drop the term conservatism completely, tend in their practical conduct to unite with other conservatives who esteem wealth and account it a mark of virtue. When the lines are drawn, conservatives of all persuasions come together, in greater rather than in lesser degree, to defend the interests of the upper classes. In part, this may be because all conservatives revere "order," not any system of order, to be sure, but that order which reflects the tastes and values of men of quality, men who embody the aristocratic spirit, who understand the dictates of nature or of nature's God. In part, therefore, this joint conservative defense of the upper classes is the product of their conviction that, however we conceive the relation between wealth and virtue, the lower classes are the classes of the common man, who is in this view the vulgar, the mass, the inferior man. As such, he is disrespectful of law and order, he lacks knowledge and understanding of the "right" order, he does not—because he cannot—appreciate the need for standards and quality. In part, however, it is also to be explained by the fact that, whatever the grounds on which conservatives arrive at their position, all tend to share the view, even if only the suspicion, that the men at the top of the economic ladder are there because they really are men of superior ability. They are, on the whole, educated men. They have nice manners. They exhibit some at least of the outward trappings of "culture." They are, therefore, in certain visible ways superior to the men at the bottom. Above all, they think to themselves as superior men, they act like superior men. By comparison, the poor, the uneducated, the hewers of wood and the drawers of water, are a sad and visibly inferior lot. Economic policies, consequently, should not only be made by those who are competent, who "know" what is right; they should be geared, in the first instance, to the advantage of those superior men, for only that state which uses its political power to secure and further the interests of those who have economic power can hope to achieve that abundance and stability necessary to survival in our troubled world.

The argument, in fact, can be pushed further. As a conservative like Alexander Hamilton fully understood, economic power divorced from and antagonistic to political power makes for an unhealthy, perhaps an impossible, situation. For economic power will not stand idly by and permit itself to be destroyed. On the contrary, because it perceives its interests, because it has the knowledge and skills appropriate to the promotion of those interests, and because, above all, it possesses the means and the will to act in defense of those interests, it will destroy the forces antagonistic to it. If, then, order is to be maintained, it must be an order which unites economic power with political power. And this, in the conservative view, inexorably means an attachment of political power to the interests of the dominant economic class. This is why conservatives defend not simply wealth, but inherited wealth. This is why conservatives oppose tax policies and measures that seek to regulate the conduct of businessmen, that is, to reduce their power and position. This is why conservatives speak little of human or civil rights, but much of property and vested rights.

Liberalism, on the other hand, has always been identified with the interests of the lower classes—not because the lower classes have by some mystery of incarnation been blessed with a monopoly of virtue but because wealth, especially inherited wealth, is not a sufficient test of function or capacity. In the liberal view, all men are equal. Insofar as distinctions of place and power must be admitted, they properly derive only from the freely recorded and continuing consent of the people, not from such arbitrary factors as ancestry or ruthless force. It is hoped, and by some believed, that the people will choose wisely, that they will recognize men on the basis of merit, of demonstrated competence. To discover merit, equality of opportunity is essential. This requires the elimination of hereditary privilege and of unwarranted discriminatory practices, such as those based on race or religion or sex. It requires, even more, reduction of great inequalities of wealth which make equality of opportunity impossible. It requires, from a positive standpoint, the creation of those conditions which assure access to all positions to those who, whatever their origins, demonstrate by their individual qualities and achievements that they merit them. It is thoroughly false and misleading to assert, as some critics of liberalism do, that liberals seek absolute equality of condition, that liberals recognize and respect no differences. On the contrary, what liberals contend is that equality of opportunity is the necessary condition for the rational determination of those qualities in which men are different and truly unequal, and hence in what respects power and position may properly be apportioned. Anything other than this is a defense of artificial and false inequalities.

Liberalism is concerned not only with equality of this sort in the economic sphere; it is concerned also with liberty. Now what is crucial about private ownership of property in the real world is that such ownership confers power without responsibility; those who own property have the legal right to use it to promote their own interests, whatever the consequences of their decisions on the welfare of others. Such ownership divides men into independent and dependent men; by denying some men equal access to the use of the earth—though we have not, curiously, sought to deny them equal access to air and to water, perhaps because this presents certain practical difficulties—such ownership forces some men to become the slaves or servants of others. This enables those who possess property to use, to exploit, other men for their advantage. And it is this fact, that some men can use other men, can treat them as a means to their purposes rather than as ends in themselves, that constitutes in the liberal view a debasement of man.

For this reason, liberals have traditionally supported the efforts of the lower classes, through legislation by government and through the countervailing pressures of economic organizations, e.g., the labor unions, to curb the great economic powers of the owners and managers and to give workers a voice in determining the conditions under which they labor. They have sought to restrain and curtail the growth of corporate monopoly, which destroys individual enterprise and penalizes the consumer. They have sought to introduce into the operation of the giant large-scale enterprises that today constitute the economic-technological system a pattern of controls that mitigate the depersonalizing and dehumanizing effects of a master-servant relationship. They have even urged government to move directly into the economic sphere through the public ownership and operation of certain services and industries, where private ownership either has served the public interest inadequately or has diverted natural and social resources away from this public interest to the promotion of private gain. In diverse ways, including schemes that look to the transformation of the entire system of economic power, liberals have sought to lessen the harsh impact of oligarchical rule in economic life, to introduce a measure of democracy within or democratic controls over the industrial-technological process, to assure freedom from arbitrary command within the economic no less than within the political sphere. For how can a man be equal and free when he is a dependent and servile man? Not the rights of property, then, however these may be defined, but the rights of man are for liberalism the guiding principle of economic organization and action.

We come, finally, to the distinction between liberalism and conservatism in the intellectual or cultural sphere. Here the issue that divides these camps, while not unrelated to social classes, turns primarily on their respective attitudes toward freedom of inquiry and expression.

Conservatism, it is claimed, seeks to conserve not everything but only the Good. But the Good is not self-evident; hence conservatism requires a standard or body of principles by which we can distinguish the good from the bad. It requires, even more, a demonstration that this standard or set of principles is both applicable and right. Conservatives agree that there is, indeed there must be, such a standard or body of principles. It exists because it is inherent in the very nature of things. It needs, then, only to be discovered and, when discovered, to be obeyed. What defines and accounts for the present malaise, the malpractices and discontents of our time, is from this standpoint the fact that men no longer seek or abide by these true principles. They look to opinion rather than to knowledge, and opinion, precisely because it is not knowledge, is an uncertain and puny guide. More than that, opinion in democratic states is formed by average, which means inferior, men. Hence policies based upon public opinion are likely to be wrong. Only if we recapture and adhere to the true principles of political life, conservatives argue, can we hope to achieve right and good government.

It is true that conservatives are in no sense agreed as to what these true principles are, or why they are warranted. Some conservatives believe that these principles are revealed by God, or, in some constructions; by His teachings as these are mediated by and through His One True Church, whichever it might be—for not all conservatives agree as to which God is God and what it is that God says. Others derive these correct principles from history or tradition, but since there are, alas, conflicting traditions or at least diverse readings of the same tradition, this leads to multiple and not always consistent principles. Still others look to nature, to the doctrines of natural law or natural right, but here again there seems to be considerable disagreement as to what it is that nature teaches. And some, finally, appeal to intuition, to a subjective but nonetheless (it is said) correct apprehension of what is right as distinct from what is wrong; though here again, since men do not all palpitate in the same way, intuitive judgments do not always coincide. Despite these differences and conflicts, which often divide conservatives into congeries of warring sects, they are all, in one crucial respect at least, still conservatives; for they all believe in the existence of an absolute truth, of an objective moral order, and hence of a political system and body of policies deriving from and corresponding to the principles of this true morality.

This is why Walter Lippmann, for example, seeking to transcend internecine conflicts and to unite conservatives behind a cohesive, if general, body of principles, invokes the Public Philosophy, or the Traditions of Civility, as an appropriate substitute for otherwise diverse conservative labels. This is why, too, he seeks their warrant not in logical or historical demonstration but in need. We must, he says, "repair the capacity to believe"; we must accept as valid those principles on which sincerely and lucidly rational men, when fully informed and motivated by good will, tend to agree. This is why, finally, conservatives are so partial to religion, though it is curious to note that their defense of religion is often couched not in terms of its truth but in terms of its utility. For conservatives generally, as even for men otherwise so diverse in their outlooks as Hobbes and Rousseau, concerned as they are with stability, it is far more important to have a single religion than to have the "right" religion. A universal or general commitment to the same religion—in contemporary America, according to some conservatives, *any* religion—not only precludes religious, i.e., civil, wars; it also makes for piety, which makes for obedience, which makes for stability and peace.

Whatever the specific formulation of the conservative creed, the fact that it does build throughout on a claimed objective truth produces the same practical consequences. Above all, these include the disparagement of freedom of inquiry and a readiness to limit and control freedom of expression. Since the truth is already known, freedom of inquiry rests in the conservative view on a false premise: that it is proper seriously to entertain error. In fact, because error may appear in attractive and plausible guise, unsophisticated minds may well mistake it for truth. To permit the unrestrained expression of such falsehoods may lead to their widespread acceptance. Then error, not truth, will govern mankind. Since it is the business of government, according to conservatives, to apply justice and achieve virtue, not speech but "good" speech, not conflicting ideas but "right" ideas, should alone be tolerated. The idea of an open society, in which men are free to utter and debate diverse opinions, including the wrong opinions, is from this standpoint both evil and absurd. What is vital is the inculcation of right attitudes, right habits, right conduct; and this can only be achieved if men who know what is right teach and control those who would not otherwise understand or do what is right. Thus conservatism moves toward an authoritarian, conformist society, based upon the rule of allegedly aristocratic minds. This has been its traditional pattern. This is, on the whole, its present practice.

Liberalism differs from conservatism most sharply in its insistence on the value of individual liberty, and concomitantly on the value of freedom of inquiry and of expression.

It may, though it need not, deny that absolute truths, at least with respect to the "right" political principles, are known; but whether these truths are known or not, liberalism insists nonetheless on the freedom to examine them, to subject them to empirical and logical criticism, and to expose them to the challenge of conflicting ideas. Skepticism about ultimate values, that is to say, is often associated with the liberal creed; but while it is appropriate to that creed it is not necessary to it. Individual liberty, however, with all that this implies in the way of cultural diversity or nonconformity in cultural and intellectual life, is indispensable to the liberal idea.

Insofar as liberalism repudiates the conservative claim to absolute and infallible truth, it rests on the assumption that man is born not stupid but infinitely ignorant, and that however much he may learn in his very short span of life, the things he learns amount to but a small portion of what there is to be known. Always the things he does not know are greater than the things he does know. Consequently, the beliefs he holds to be true may prove, on the basis of later knowledge, to be erroneous or only partially true. Awareness of this fact makes for a certain measure of humility; it also leads to a commitment to the methods of rational inquiry, rather than to the specific results that may at any one time emerge from such inquiry. The basic value of the liberal is, from this standpoint, the value of free inquiry; his basic attitude, the skeptical, or at least the inquiring, mind.

It follows that when two rational and relatively well-informed men disagree, it is less likely that one has complete possession of the truth and the other error, than that each has a partially valid insight. This is why liberals find so persuasive John Stuart Mill's argument for the toleration of dissenting ideas: The heretical view, Mill pointed out, where right, enables us to abandon error and embrace the more valid doctrine; where wrong, it helps us perceive the wholeness of our truth, indeed, it prevents us by its very challenge from clinging to our accepted truth in the manner of a prejudice or a superstition, without an adequate comprehension of its meaning; and where partly right, it reinforces our own partial truth and helps us correct our partial error. This is why a political liberal (but economic conservative) like Mr. Justice Holmes insisted that "To have doubted one's own first principles is the mark of a civilized man." And why a liberal philosopher like Morris Cohen added: "To refuse to do so is the essence of fanaticism."

Liberalism need not, however, be identified only with this skeptical approach to knowledge. It is altogether possible for one to believe that the truth is known and still hold to a liberal defense of toleration. In part, this rests on the very arguments advanced by Mill. One's confidence in the validity of his position, along with a conviction that opinion should be countered only by opinion, not by force, is alone sufficient to sustain his readiness to entertain dissent. In part, however, it rests on the recognition that in a society constituted of diverse men and groups many may claim to know the truth. Though all cannot be right, the political problem is to deal with a situation in which all believe they are right. Authoritarians provide a simple method of resolving this difficulty: The "right," that is, the most powerful, group suppresses the others. But since force is irrelevant to truth, the most powerful group may not in fact be the group that is right. Hence reason dictates a solution other than force. This solution, for the liberal, is twofold. On the one hand, he would have the state leave these different groups alone. Where it is possible for each group to pursue its own truths, its own values, without infringing upon or denying the values of the other, there is a prima facie case for freedom. To this extent, at least, the state is a limited state. On the other hand, where such differences produce conflicts, the liberal would seek to negotiate these conflicts through free debate and free criticism in the marketplace of opinion. This does not, of course, assure the victory of the "right" view, but it gives the "right" view its maximum opportunity to prevail. And unless one is prepared to maintain that evidence and logic generally lead men to the wrong conclusions, it is difficult for the liberal to understand why so rational and peaceful a method of resolving differences is inappropriate, why it is better, say, to resort to mutual slaughter. Even if the "wrong" view should carry the day, there remains, through this method, full opportunity to continue to criticize and to show, with the added knowledge of experience, that it requires correction.

The ultimate argument of the liberal in this context, however, is his belief that individual liberty is a good in itself. What defines a man, according to an ancient teaching, is his reason. Now for reason to be exercised, a choice must exist. There can be no choices without alternatives, and there can be no alternatives without liberty. To deny individual liberty, either in the presentation of alternatives or the making of choices, is to deny an individual that which constitutes his humanity. Instead of his right to exercise his reason, someone else's reason is exercised for him. He is then not a man but a child. If he is to be a man, he must be free—to inquire, to consider diverse possibilities, to choose among them, and to pursue, so far as he can, his own way or style of life. From these conflicting ideas and practices, liberalism believes, men can learn and mutually aid one another to grow. Without these, there can be only a deadening uniformity. Individual liberty, and its consequent diversities, becomes then a cardinal principle of liberalism.

It is not to be denied that equality and liberty, both central tenets of liberalism, stand at times in a state of tension. Equality of opportunity, for example, may well run into conflict with the liberty of a parent to raise his child with the benefit of whatever advantages he may be able to give him. Then men must choose between equally ultimate values, and this is admittedly not an easy choice. But this is not a problem unique to liberals, and what liberals can well argue is that through freedom of inquiry and expression men can more rationally and peacefully negotiate these conflicts.

In sum, then, what distinguishes liberalism from conservatism is that, politically, liberalism stands for democracy and the equality of men, while conservatism inclines toward oligarchy based on certain alleged inequalities of men; economically, liberalism represents the interests of the lower classes and argues for equality of opportunity and the protection of human rights, while conservatism is associated with the interests of the upper classes and defends vested property rights; intellectually, liberalism is committed to individual liberty and the freedoms of inquiry and expression, while conservatism is far more concerned with the applications of an already existing objective Truth and the consequent curbing of erroneous and pernicious doctrines. It would be misleading to imply that all liberals, much less all so-called liberal states, affirm and consistently practice all these aspects of the liberal creed, or that conservatives do so with respect to their doctrines. But as categories of analysis rather than as descriptions of actual men or groups, the elements that make up this multidimensional understanding of liberalism and conservatism may enable us more easily to comprehend and to identify what it is that men and groups actually do.

# 2

# What Unites Progressives

*GEORGE LAKOFF*

*For over twenty years George Lakoff has been applying cognitive linguistics to the study of politics. In this reading, he provides a detailed explanation of the unifying ideas of progressives. Based on those unifying ideas, he enumerates policy directions progressives can agree on, and concludes by contrasting a ten-word progressive philosophy with a ten-word conservative philosophy.*

Most Americans want to know what you stand for, whether your values are their values, what your principles are, what direction you want to take the country in. In public discourse, values trump programs, principles trump programs, policy directions trump programs. I believe that values, principles, and policy directions are exactly the things that can unite progressives, if they are crafted properly. The reason that they can unite us is that they stand conceptually above all the things that divide us.

## IDEAS THAT MAKE US PROGRESSIVES

What follows is a detailed explication of each of those unifying ideas:

- First, *values* coming out of a basic progressive vision
- Second, *principles* that realize progressive values
- Third, *policy directions* that fit the values and principles
- And fourth, a *brief ten-word philosophy* that encapsulates all the above

### The Basic Progressive Vision

The basic progressive vision is of community—of America as family, a caring, responsible family. We envision an America where people care about each other, not just themselves, and act responsibly with strength and effectiveness for each other.

*Source:* Excerpt from *Don't Think Like an Elephant: Know Your Values and Frame the Debate* by George Lakoff, pp. 88–95. Copyright © 2004 by George Lakoff. Used by permission of Chelsea Green Publishing Company.

We are all in the same boat. Red states and blue states, progressives and conservatives, Republicans and Democrats. United, as we were for a brief moment just after September 11, not divided by a despicable culture war.

## The Logic of Progressive Values

The progressive core values are family values—those of the responsible, caring family.

**Caring and responsibility, carried out with strength.** These core values imply the full range of progressive values. Here are those progressive values, together with the logic that links them to the core values.

**Protection, fulfillment in life, fairness.** When you *care about* someone, you want them to *be protected from harm,* you want their *dreams to come true,* and you want them to be *treated fairly.*

**Freedom, opportunity, prosperity.** There is no *fulfillment* without *freedom,* no *freedom* without *opportunity,* and no *opportunity* without *prosperity.*

**Community, service, cooperation.** Children are shaped by their *communities.* Responsibility requires *serving* and helping to shape your community. That requires *cooperation.*

**Trust, honesty, open communication.** There is no *cooperation* without *trust,* no *trust* without *honesty,* and no *cooperation* without *open communication.*

Just as these values follow from caring and responsibility, so every other progressive value follows from these. Equality follows from fairness, empathy is part of caring, diversity is from empathy and equality.

Progressives not only share these values, but also share political principles that arise from these values.

## Progressive Principles

**Equity.** What citizens and the nation owe each other. If you work hard; play by the rules; and serve your family, community, and nation, then the nation should provide a decent standard of living, as well as freedom, security, and opportunity.

**Equality.** Do everything possible to guarantee political equality and avoid imbalances of political power.

**Democracy.** Maximize citizen participation; minimize concentrations of political, corporate, and media power. Maximize journalistic standards. Establish publicly financed elections. Invest in public education. Bring corporations under stakeholder control, not just stockholder control.

**Government for a better future.** Government does what America's future requires and what the private sector cannot do—or is not doing—effectively, ethically, or at all. It is the job of government to promote and, if possible, provide sufficient protection, greater democracy, more freedom, a better environment, broader prosperity, better health, greater fulfillment in life, less violence, and the building and maintaining of public infrastructure.

**Ethical business.** Our values apply to business. In the course of making money by providing products and services, businesses should not adversely affect the public good, as defined by the above values.

**Values-based foreign policy.** The same values governing domestic policy should apply to foreign policy whenever possible.

Here are a few examples where progressive domestic policy translates into foreign policy:

- Protection translates into an effective military for defense and peacekeeping.
- Building and maintaining a strong community translates into building and maintaining strong alliances and engaging in effective diplomacy.
- Caring and responsibility translate into caring about and acting responsibly for the world's people; world health, hunger, poverty, and ecology; population control (and the best method, women's education); and rights for women, children, prisoners, refugees, and ethnic minorities.

All of these would be concerns of a values-based foreign policy.


## Policy Directions

Given progressive values and principles, progressives can agree on basic policy directions. Policy directions are at a higher level than specific policies. Progressives divide on specific policy details while agreeing on directions. Here are some of the many policy directions they agree on.

**The economy.** An economy centered on innovation that creates millions of good-paying jobs and provides every American a fair opportunity to prosper.

**Security.** Through military strength, strong diplomatic alliances, and wise foreign and domestic policy, every American will be safeguarded at home, and America's role in the world will be strengthened by helping people around the world live better lives.

**Health.** Every American should have access to a state-of-the-art, affordable health care system.

**Education.** A vibrant, well-funded, and expanding public education system, with the highest standards for every child and school, where teachers nurture children's minds and often the children themselves, and where children are taught the truth about their nation— its wonders and its blemishes.

**Early childhood.** Every child's brain is shaped crucially by early experiences. We support high-quality early childhood education.

**Environment.** A clean, healthy, and safe environment for ourselves and our children: water you can drink and air you can breathe. Polluters pay for the damage they cause.

**Nature.** The natural wonders of our country are to be preserved for future generations.

**Energy.** We need to make a major investment in renewable energy, for the sake of millions of jobs that pay well, independence from Middle Eastern oil, improvements in public health, preservation of our environment, and the effort to halt global warming.

**Openness.** An open, efficient, and fair government that tells the truth to our citizens and earns the trust of every American.

**Equal rights.** We support equal rights in every area involving race, ethnicity, gender, and sexual orientation.

**Protections.** We support keeping and extending protections for consumers, workers, retirees, and investors.

These and many other policy directions follow from our values and our principles.

### Ten-Word Philosophies

The conservatives have figured out their own values, principles, and directions, and have gotten them out in the public mind so effectively over the past thirty years that they can evoke them all in a ten-word philosophy: Strong Defense, Free Markets, Lower Taxes, Smaller Government, Family Values. We progressives have a different ten-word philosophy, but it won't be as meaningful yet because it will take us a while to get our values, principles, and directions out there. My nomination for our ten-word philosophy versus theirs is the following:

| Progressives | Conservatives |
|---|---|
| Stronger America | Strong Defense |
| Broad Prosperity | Free Markets |
| Better Future | Lower Taxes |
| Effective Government | Smaller Government |
| Mutual Responsibility | Family Values |

A **stronger America** is not just about defense, but about every dimension of strength: our effectiveness in the world, our economy, our educational system, our health care system, our families, our communities, our environment, and so forth.

**Broad prosperity** is the effect that markets are supposed to bring about. But all markets are constructed for someone's benefit; no markets are completely free. Markets should be constructed for the broadest possible prosperity, and they haven't been.

Americans want and deserve a **better future**—economically, educationally, environmentally, and in all other areas of life—for themselves and their children. Lowering taxes, primarily for the super-rich elite, has had the effect of defending programs that would make a better future possible in all these areas. The proper goal is a better future for all Americans.

Smaller government is, in conservative propaganda, supposed to eliminate waste. It is really about eliminating social programs. **Effective government** is what we need our government to accomplish to create a better future.

Conservative family values are those of a strict father family—authoritarian, hierarchical, every man for himself, based around discipline and punishment. Progressives live by the best values of both families and communities: **mutual responsibility,** which is authoritative, equal, two-way, and based around caring, responsibility (both individual and social), and strength.

The remarkable thing is just how much progressives do agree on. These are just the things that voters tend to care about most: our values, our principles, and the direction in which we want to take the nation.

I believe that progressive values *are* traditional American values, that progressive principles are fundamental American principles, and that progressive policy directions point the way to where most Americans really want our country to go. The job of unifying progressives is really the job of bringing our country together around its finest traditional values.

# 3

# What Was Really Great
# about the Great Society?

*JOSEPH A. CALIFANO, JR.*

*Lyndon Johnson inherited the presidency after John F. Kennedy's death in Dallas in November 1963. Shortly thereafter, in one of the boldest affirmations on behalf of progressive legislation and policies, President Johnson challenged citizens to join him in building the "Great Society." Joseph A. Califano Jr. served as President Johnson's Assistant for Domestic Affairs from 1965 to 1969, and he served as the United States Secretary of Health, Education, and Welfare from 1977 to 1979. As one closely associated with the policies and outcomes of the Great Society, Califano describes the extraordinary social influence the Great Society has had on U.S. society over the past forty years.*

If there is a prize for the political scam of the 20th century, it should go to the conservatives for propagating as conventional wisdom that the Great Society programs of the 1960s were a misguided and failed social experiment that wasted taxpayers' money.

Nothing could be further from the truth. In fact, from 1963 when Lyndon Johnson took office until 1970 as the impact of his Great Society programs were felt, the portion of Americans living below the poverty line dropped from 22.2 percent to 12.6 percent, the most dramatic decline over such a brief period in this century. Since then, the poverty rate has hovered at about the 13 percent level and sits at 13.3 percent today, still a disgraceful level in the context of the greatest economic boom in our history. But if the Great Society had not achieved that dramatic reduction in poverty, and the nation had not maintained it, 24 million more Americans would today be living below the poverty level.

This reduction in poverty did not just happen. It was the result of a focused, tenacious effort to revolutionize the role of the federal government with a series of interventions that enriched the lives of millions of Americans. In those tumultuous Great Society years, the President submitted, and Congress enacted, more than 100 major proposals in each of the

*Source:* "What Was Really Great about the Great Society?" by Joseph A. Califano, Jr. from *The Washington Monthly*, vol. 31, No. 10, October 1999, pp. 13–19. Copyright by Washington Monthly Publishing, LLC, 733 15th St. NW, Suite 520, Washington, DC 20005. (202) 393-5155. Web site: www.washingtonmonthly.com. Reprinted by permission.

89th and 90th Congresses. In that era of do-it-now optimism, government was neither a bad man to be tarred and feathered nor a bag man to collect campaign contributions, but an instrument to help the most vulnerable in our society.

What has the verdict been? Did the programs we put into place in the 1960s vindicate our belief in the responsibility and capacity of the national government to achieve such ambitious goals—or do they stand as proof of the government's inability to effect dramatic change that helps our people?

### A FAIR START

The Great Society saw government as providing a hand up, not a handout. The cornerstone was a thriving economy (which the 1964 tax cut sparked); in such circumstances, most Americans would be able to enjoy the material blessings of society. Others would need the kind of help most of us got from our parents—health care, education and training, and housing, as well as a nondiscriminatory shot at employment—to share in our nation's wealth.

Education and health were central to opening up the promise of American life to all. With the 1965 Elementary and Secondary Education Act, the Great Society for the first time committed the federal government to helping local school districts. Its higher education legislation, with scholarships, grants, and work-study programs, opened college to any American with the necessary brains and ambition, however thin daddy's wallet or empty mommy's purse. Bilingual education, which today serves one million individuals, was designed to teach Hispanic youngsters subjects like math and history in their own language for a couple of years while they learned English, so they would not fall behind. Special education legislation has helped millions of children with learning disabilities.

Since 1965 the federal government has provided more than a quarter of a trillion dollars in 86 million college loans to 29 million students, and more than $14 billion in work-study awards to 6 million students. Today nearly 60 percent of full-time undergraduate students receive federal financial aid under Great Society programs and their progeny.

These programs assure a steady supply of educated individuals who provide the human resources for our economic prosperity. When these programs were enacted, only 41 percent of Americans had completed high school; only 8 percent held college degrees. This past year, more than 81 percent had finished high school and 24 percent had completed college. By establishing the federal government's responsibility to finance this educational surge—and the concept that access to higher education should be determined by ability and ambition, not dollars and cents—we have amassed the trained talent to be the world's leading industrial, technological, communications and military power today.

Head Start, which has served more than 16 million preschoolers in just about every city and county in the nation and today serves 800,000 children a year, is as American as motherhood and apple pie. Like so many successes, this preschool program has a thousand parents. But how many people remember the battles over Head Start? Conservatives opposed such early childhood education as an attempt by government to interfere with parental control of their children. In the '60s those were code words to conjure up images of Soviet Russia wrenching children from their homes to convert them to atheistic communism. But Lyndon Johnson knew that the rich had kindergartens and nursery schools; and he asked, why not the same benefits for the poor?

The impact of the Great Society's health programs has been stunning. In 1963, most elderly Americans had no health insurance. Few retirement plans provided any such coverage. The poor had little access to medical treatment until they were in critical condition. Only wealthier Americans could get the finest care, and only by traveling to a few big cities like Boston or New York.

Is revolution too strong a word? Since 1965, 79 million Americans have signed up for Medicare. In 1966, 19 million were enrolled; in 1998, 39 million. Since 1966, Medicaid has served more than 200 million needy Americans. In 1967, it served 10 million poor citizens; in 1997, 39 million. The 1968 Heart, Cancer and Stroke legislation has provided funds to create centers of medical excellence in just about every major city—from Seattle to Houston, Miami to Cleveland, New Orleans to St. Louis. To staff these centers, the 1965 Health Professions Educational Assistance Act provided resources to double the number of doctors graduating from medical schools, from 8,000 to 16,000. That Act also increased the pool of specialists and researchers, nurses, and paramedics. Community health centers, also part of the Great Society health care agenda, today serve almost eight million Americans annually. The Great Society's commitment to fund basic medical research lifted the National Institutes of Health to unprecedented financial heights, seeding a harvest of medical miracles.

Closely related to these health programs were efforts to reduce malnutrition and hunger. Today, the Great Society's food stamp program helps feed more than 20 million men, women, and children in more than 8 million households. Since it was launched in 1967, the school breakfast program has provided a daily breakfast to nearly 100 million schoolchildren.

Taken together, these programs have played a pivotal role in recasting America's demographic profile. In 1964, life expectancy was 66.6 years for men and 73.1 years for women (69.7 years overall). In a single generation, by 1997, life expectancy jumped 10 percent: for men, to 73.6 years; for women, to 79.2 years (76.5 years overall). The jump was highest among the less advantaged, suggesting that better nutrition and access to health care have played an even larger role than medical miracles. Infant mortality stood at 26 deaths for each 1,000 live births when LBJ took office; today it stands at only 7.3 deaths per 1,000 live births, a reduction of almost 75 percent.

These enormous investments in training medical and scientific experts and funding the National Institutes of Health have played a key part in establishing our nation as the world's leader in basic research, pharmaceutical invention, and the creation of surgical procedures and medical machinery to diagnose our diseases, breathe for us, clean our blood, and transplant our organs.

Those of us who worked with Lyndon Johnson would hardly characterize him as a patron of the arts. Yet think about what cultural life in America would be like without the National Endowments for the Arts and Humanities, which were designed to "create conditions under which the arts can flourish," and make fine theater and music available throughout the nation, not just at Broadway playhouses and the Metropolitan Opera in New York. The Endowment for the Arts has spawned art councils in all 50 states and more than 420 playhouses, 120 opera companies, 400 dance companies and 230 professional orchestras. Johnson also oversaw the creation of the Kennedy Center for the Performing Arts, whose programs entertain three million people each year and are televised to millions more, and the Hirshhorn Museum and Sculpture Garden, which attracts more than 700,000 visitors annually.

Another creature of the Great Society is the Corporation for Public Broadcasting, which today supports 350 public television and 699 public radio stations. These stations have given the nation countless hours of fine arts, superb in-depth news coverage, and educational programs such as Sesame Street that teach as they entertain generations of children. Now many conservatives say there is no need for public radio and television, since there are so many cable channels and radio stations. But as often as we surf with our TV remotes and twist our radio dials, we are not likely to find the kind of quality broadcasting that marks public television and public radio stations.

The Great Society's main contribution to the environment was not just passage of laws, but the establishment of a principle that to this day guides the environmental movement. The old principle was simply to conserve resources that had not been touched. Lyndon Johnson was the first president to put forth a larger idea:

> *"The air we breathe, our water, our soil and wildlife, are being blighted by poisons and chemicals which are the by-products of technology and industry. The society that receives the rewards of technology, must, as a cooperating whole, take responsibility for [their] control. To deal with these new problems will require a new conservation. We must not only protect the countryside and save it from destruction, we must restore what has been destroyed and salvage the beauty and charm of our cities. Our conservation must be not just the classic conservation of protection and development, but a creative conservation of restoration and innovation."*

Those new environmental commandments inspired a legion of Great Society laws: the Clear Air, Water Quality and Clean Water Restoration Acts and Amendments, the 1965 Solid Waste Disposal Act, the 1965 Motor Vehicle Air Pollution Control Act, and the 1968 Aircraft Noise Abatement Act. They also provided the rationale for later laws creating the Environmental Protection Agency and the Superfund that exacts financial payments from past polluters.

Of the 35 national parks established during the Great Society years, 32 are within easy driving distance of large cities. The 1968 Wild and Scenic Rivers Act today protects 155 river segments in 37 states. The 1968 National Trail System Act has established more than 800 recreational, scenic, and historic trails covering 40,000 miles.

## EQUAL ACCESS

Above all else, Lyndon Johnson saw the Great Society as an instrument to create racial justice and eliminate poverty. Much of the legislation already cited was aimed at those objectives. But we directly targeted these areas with laser intensity. When LBJ took office, this country had segregated stores, theaters and public accommodations; separate toilets and water fountains for blacks; and restaurants, hotels, and housing restricted to whites only. Job discrimination was rampant. With the 1964 Civil Rights Act, the Great Society tore down all the "whites only" signs. The 1968 Fair Housing Act opened up housing to all Americans regardless of race.

But the measure of the Great Society, particularly in this field, cannot be taken alone in statutes enacted. In one of the most moving speeches of the century, Johnson's 1965 Howard University commencement address, "To Fulfill These Rights," he said: "But freedom is not enough. You do not take a person who, for years, has been hobbled by chains and liberate him, bring him to the starting line of a race and then say, 'You are free to compete with all the others,' and still justly believe that you have been completely fair. This is the next and the more profound stage of the battle for civil rights." Thus was born the concept of affirmative action, Johnson's conviction that it is essential as a matter of social justice to provide the tutoring, the extra help, even the preference if necessary, to those who had suffered generations of discrimination, in order to give them a fair chance to share in the American dream. Perhaps even more controversial today than when then set forth, affirmative action has provided opportunity to millions of blacks and has been a critical element in creating a substantial black middle class and an affluent black society in a single generation.

That speech provided another insight the nation ignored. In cataloguing the long suffering of blacks, Johnson included this passage: "Perhaps most important—its influence radiating to every part of life—is the breakdown of the Negro family structure. It flows from centuries of oppression and persecution of the Negro man. And when the family collapses it is the children that are usually damaged. When it happens on a massive scale the community itself is crippled. So, unless we work to strengthen the family, to create conditions under which most parents will stay together, all the rest—schools, and playgrounds, and public assistance, and private concern—will never be enough to cut completely the circle of despair and deprivation."

Conservatives charge the Great Society with responsibility for the disastrous aspects of the welfare program for mothers and children. But that program was enacted in the '30s and conservatives (and liberals) in Congress rejected Great Society efforts to revamp it. LBJ called the welfare system in America "outmoded and in need of a major change" and pressed Congress to stop conditioning welfare benefits on the man leaving the house and to create "a work incentive program, incentives for earning, day care for children, child and maternal health, and family planning services." In the generation it has taken the nation to heed that warning, millions of children's lives have been savaged.

In the entire treasury of Great Society measures, the jewel Lyndon Johnson believed would have the greatest value was the Voting Rights Act of 1965. That law opened the way for black Americans to strengthen their voice at every level of government. In 1964 there were 79 black elected officials in the South and 300 in the entire nation. By 1998, there were some 9,000 elected black officials across the nation, including 6,000 in the South. In 1965 there were five black members of the House; today there are 39.

Great Society contributions to racial equality were not only civic and political. In 1960, black life expectancy was 63.6 years, not even long enough to benefit from the Social Security taxes that black citizens paid during their working lives. By 1997, black life expectancy was 71.2 years, thanks almost entirely to Medicaid, community health centers, job training, food stamps, and other Great Society programs. In 1960, the infant mortality rate for blacks was 44.3 for each 1,000 live births; in 1997, that rate had plummeted by two-thirds, to 14.7. In 1960, only 20 percent of blacks completed high school and only 3 percent finished college; in 1997, 75 percent completed high school and more than 13 percent earned college degrees.

In waging the war on poverty, congressional opposition was too strong to pass an income maintenance law. So LBJ took advantage of the biggest automatic cash machine around: Social Security. He proposed, and Congress enacted, whopping increases in the minimum benefits that lifted some two million Americans 65 and older above the poverty line. In 1996, thanks to those increased minimum benefits, Social Security lifted 12 million senior citizens above the poverty line.

The combination of that Social Security increase, Medicare and the coverage of nursing home care under Medicaid (which today funds care for 68 percent of nursing home residents) has had a defining impact on American families. Millions of middle-aged Americans, freed from the burden of providing medical and nursing home care for their elderly parents, suddenly were able to buy homes and (often with assistance from Great Society higher education programs) send their children to college.

No Great Society undertaking has been subjected to more withering conservative attacks than the Office of Economic Opportunity. Yet the War on Poverty was founded on the most conservative principle: Put the power in the local community, not in Washington; give people at the grassroots the ability to stand tall on their own two feet.

Conservative claims that the OEO poverty programs were nothing but a waste of money are preposterous—as preposterous as Ronald Reagan's quip that "LBJ declared war on poverty and poverty won." Eleven of the 12 programs that OEO launched in the mid-'60s are alive, well and funded at an annual rate exceeding $10 billion; apparently legislators believe they're still working. Head Start, Job Corps, Community Health Centers, Foster Grandparents, Upward Bound (now part of the Trio Program in the Department of Education), Green Thumb (now Senior Community Service Employment), Indian Opportunities (now in the Labor Department) and Migrant Opportunities (now Seasonal Worker Training and Migrant Education) were all designed to do what they have been doing: empowering individuals to stand on their own two feet.

Community Action, VISTA Volunteers, and Legal Services continue to put power in the hands of individuals down at the grassroots level. The grassroots that these programs fertilize just don't produce the manicured laws that conservatives prefer.

Only the Neighborhood Youth Corps has been abandoned—in 1974, after enrolling more than five million individuals. Despite the political rhetoric, every president, Ronald Reagan included, has urged Congress to fund these OEO programs or has approved substantial appropriations for them.

**A BETTER DEAL**

The Great Society confronted two monumental shifts in America: the urbanization of the population and the nationalization of commercial power. For urban America, it created the Department of Housing and Urban Development. It drove through Congress the Urban Mass Transit Act, which has given San Franciscans BART, Washingtonians Metro, Atlantans MARTA, and cities across America thousands of buses and modernized transit systems. The 1968 Housing Act has provided homes for more than 7 million families. The Great Society also created Ginnie Mae, which has added more than $1 billion to the supply of affordable mortgage funds, and privatized Fannie Mae, which has helped more than 30 million families purchase homes.

The '60s also saw a nationalization of commercial power that had the potential to disadvantage the individual American consumer. Superstores and supercorporations were rapidly shoving aside the corner grocer, local banker, and independent drug store. Automobiles were complex and dangerous, manufactured by giant corporations with deep pockets to protect themselves. Banks had the most sophisticated accountants and lawyers to draft their loan agreements. Sellers of everyday products—soaps, produce, meats, appliances, clothing, cereals, and canned and frozen foods—packaged their products with the help of the shrewdest marketers and designers. The individual was outflanked at every position.

Sensing that mismatch, the Great Society produced a bevy of laws to level the playing field for consumers: auto and highway safety for the motorist; truth in packaging for the consumer; truth in lending for the home-buyer, small businessman and individual borrower; wholesome meat and wholesome poultry laws to enhance food safety. It created the Product Safety Commission to assure that toys and other products would be safe for users and the Flammable Fabrics Act to reduce the incendiary characteristics of clothing and blankets. To keep kids out of the medicine bottle we proposed the Child Safety Act.

The revolution in transportation led to the creation of the National Transportation Safety Board, renowned for its work in improving air safety, and the Department of Transportation.

In numbers of Americans helped, the Great Society exceeds in domestic impact even the New Deal of LBJ's idol, Franklin Roosevelt. But far more profound and enduring are the fundamental tenets of public responsibility it espoused, which influence and shape the nation's public policy and political dialogue to this day.

Until the New Deal, the federal government had been regarded as a regulatory power, protecting the public health and safety with the Food and Drug Administration and enforcing antitrust and commercial fraud laws to rein in concentrations of economic power. With the creation of the Securities and Exchange Commission and the other alphabet agencies, FDR took the government into deeper regulatory waters. He also put the feds into the business of cash payments: welfare benefits, railroad retirement, and Social Security.

Johnson converted the federal government into a far more energetic, proactive force for social justice—striking down discriminatory practices and offering a hand up with education, health care, and job training. These functions had formerly been the preserve of private charities and the states. Before the Johnson administration, for example, the federal government was not training a single worker. He vested the federal government with the responsibility to soften the sharp elbows of capitalism and give it a beating, human heart; to redistribute opportunity as well as wealth.

For the public safety, Johnson took on the National Rifle Association and drove through Congress the laws that closed the loophole of mail order guns, prohibited sales to minors, and ended the import of Saturday night specials. He tried unsuccessfully to convince Congress to pass a law requiring the licensing of every gun owner and the registration of every gun.

Spotting the "for sale" signs of political corruption going up in the nation's capital, Johnson proposed public financing of presidential campaigns, full disclosure of contributions and expenses by all federal candidates, limits on contributions and eliminating lobbying loopholes. He convinced Congress to provide for public financing of Presidential campaigns through the income-tax checkoff. But they ignored his 1967 warning: "More and more, men and women of limited means may refrain from running for public office. Private wealth increasingly becomes an artificial and unrealistic arbiter of qualifications, and the source of public leadership is thus severely narrowed. The necessity of acquiring substantial funds to finance campaigns diverts a candidate's attention from his public obligations and detracts from his energetic exposition of the issues."

**FEAR OF THE L-WORD**

Lyndon Johnson didn't talk the talk of legacy. He walked the walk. He lived the life. He didn't have much of a profile, but he did have the courage of his convictions, and the achievements of his Great Society were monumental.

Why then do Democratic politicians who battle to preserve Great Society programs ignore those achievements? For the same reason Bill Clinton came to the LBJ library on Johnson's birthday during the 1992 campaign and never spoke the name of Lyndon Johnson or recognized Ladybird Johnson, who was sitting on the stage from which he spoke.

The answer lies in their fear of being called "liberal" and in their opposition to the Vietnam War. In contemporary America politicians are paralyzed by fear of the label that comes with the heritage of Lyndon Johnson's Great Society. Democrats rest their hopes of a return to Congressional power on promises to preserve and expand Great Society programs like Medicare and aid to education, but they tremble at the thought of linking those programs to the liberal Lyndon. The irony is that they seek to distance themselves from the president who once said that the difference between liberals and cannibals is that cannibals eat only their enemies.

Democratic officeholders also assign Johnson the role of stealth president because of the Vietnam War. Most contemporary observers put the war down as a monumental blunder. Only a handful—most of them Republicans—defend Vietnam as part of a half-century bipartisan commitment to contain communism with American blood and money. Seen in that context, Vietnam was a tragic losing battle in a long, winning war—a war that began with Truman's ordeal in Korea, the Marshall Plan, and the 1948 Berlin airlift, and ended with the collapse of communism at the end of the Reagan Administration.

Whatever anyone thinks about Vietnam and however much politicians shrink from the liberal label, it is time to recognize—as historians are beginning to do—the reality of the remarkable and enduring achievements of the Great Society programs. Without such programs as Head Start, higher-education loans and scholarships, Medicare, Medicaid, clear air and water, and civil rights, life would be nastier, more brutish, and shorter for millions of Americans.

# 4

# The Price of a Free Society

*PAUL STARR*

*The author of this reading has written extensively on U.S. society, politics, and public policy. In this reading he asserts that currently there is an intensive conservative assault on the fundamental liberal idea that we can use progressive governmental policies and practices to enable Americans to achieve their goal of living in a free and democratic society that provides for the common good of all citizens. He then suggests ways to counter this trend.*

These are times that try liberal spirits. . . .

Under assault is the core liberal idea that we can use government to provide for the common good and protect our safety, security, and well-being even as we prohibit government from controlling our private lives and compromising our liberties. Lately, however, in the face of the right-wing crusade against liberal government, moderates and even some liberals have too often conceded political and philosophical ground that ought to be defended.

How to change these dynamics? Resist the moves toward privatization—yes. Contest the underlying assumptions—even better. Use every opportunity to champion the things government does well. But any defense of public solutions to America's problems has to begin with realism about the obstacles, and not just from special interests.

The majority of Americans are ambivalent about government, and they have been even at the peak moments of liberal reform. It was during the 1960s that the public-opinion analysts Lloyd Free and Hadley Cantril famously pointed out that Americans tend to be ideologically conservative and operationally liberal. They are hostile to government in the abstract yet like the particular services that government provides. When asked about those services one by one—national security, education, health care, public safety, transportation, the environment, and so on—the majority typically want more done and more money spent.

The conventional view of American politics as being divided between two camps, conservative and liberal, is incomplete. Americans are also divided within themselves. Their conservative side comes out especially when government is the issue; their liberal side

*Source:* Reprinted with permission from Paul Starr, "The Price of a Free Society," *The American Prospect,* Volume 16, Number 5: May 6, 2005. The American Prospect, 11 Beacon Street, Suite 1120, Boston, MA 02108. All rights reserved.

comes out more when the issues are the issue. So conservatives like to make government the focus of debate, and some liberals respond apologetically. We should forget the apologies—and the mutual recriminations. The obstacles to liberal innovation are formidable. But, if we take them into account, we can make a strong and confident case for government where public remedy, and only public remedy, can do the job of protecting and extending a free society.

Three developments have made it extremely hard to advance liberal reform beyond the achievements of the New Deal and Great Society. The crises of the mid-20th century, from the Depression through World War II and the Cold War, resulted in a great enlargement of federal powers and programs. War has always been an engine of state expansion, especially so in the century of "total war," when governments needed to mobilize their entire societies. Crisis conditions made it both necessary and easier to raise taxes and justify intervention in the economy. Moreover, the mid-20th-century crises hit the United States during the long ascendancy of the Democratic Party, which built major new public programs, as well as confidence in government itself, during that period.

Since September 11, we have had a new kind of crisis and new wars—but without the total mobilization of the big 20th-century conflicts and under a Republican government that has used national security to justify its own hybrid policy: expanded surveillance powers combined with tax cuts, deregulation, and privatization. As president, Al Gore might have used the same crisis for wholly different public purposes. But for the first time since 1898, Republicans have had the opportunity to use war to entrench themselves in power.

A second historical barrier stems from the aftereffects of the '60s. The great challenge of the Depression had been mass unemployment and destitution, and a program responding to those problems commanded a wide majority. By the 1960s, the focus became minority poverty and minority rights, and the politics became inherently more difficult. Even though the '60s brought a few programs with broad appeal, such as Medicare, many white male workers had no sense that liberal policies were benefiting them. Some of the '60s reforms also attempted to do things on behalf of the poor that no one knew how to do well, and the limits and frustrations of those programs left a bitter residue, including resistance to taxes.

The third historical problem has been that the growth of established programs has crowded out new initiatives. A key factor here has been public policy, particularly in health care, that was far too accommodating of private interests and therefore failed from the beginning to impose effective cost controls. The United States has developed the world's most expensive health system, driving up costs for private and public payers alike. As a result, total government health expenditures per capita (mainly for Medicare and Medicaid) are now almost as high as in many countries with universal coverage. With the aging of the population, spending on existing health programs threatens to soak up new tax revenues in coming decades. Furthermore, Social Security, with or without any privatization, will also have higher costs. The very nature of a postindustrial society is that the total share of the economy devoted to education and other services tends to grow.

In health care, more effective cost containment can partially alleviate these pressures; as Jacob S. Hacker argues elsewhere in this section, public programs of social insurance are typically more efficient than their private counterparts. And as the debate over Social Security privatization has helped to clarify, the federal government provides retirement benefits at lower administrative costs and more dependably than a privatized system would. Nonetheless, in all the advanced societies, the rising cost of older programs has posed an obstacle to new ones and a test of political values.

Over the doors to the Internal Revenue Service are inscribed the words of Justice Oliver Wendell Holmes: "Taxes are the price we pay for a civilized society." The United States continues to expand economically; we are not becoming poorer. But some of the goods that we buy through taxes are inevitably becoming more expensive because of underlying demographic and economic trends. We can simply refuse to pay the costs and blind ourselves to the human consequences. Or, controlling costs as best we can, we can meet the challenge of paying the price of running a civilized society in our time.

And not just a civilized society—a productive one, too. Much of what we do via government contributes vitally to economic growth and efficiency. Conservative views of public spending typically portray it entirely as a drain on wealth. But public expenditures on education, science and technology, health, and many programs for children are critical forms of investment, with a demonstrable history of long-term payoffs.

Government also contributes to our wealth in other ways. Environmental regulation, for example, helps to preserve our "natural capital," elevating long-term interests in a sustainable future over short-term gains. Financial regulation reduces the likelihood of old-fashioned panics, raises confidence in the markets, and increases the efficiency of capital allocation. Overall government spending plays a countercyclical role, helping to prevent downturns from becoming depressions.

Beyond these economic payoffs, government enables the public to purchase some goods unavailable in any market. As consumers, we are concerned with no one's benefit but our own. That's a kind of freedom, but a society with only that freedom wouldn't be free—nor would it survive. A free people, acting together, must have some means of placing decisions outside the market to provide public goods and to avoid making all the conditions of life depend on individual economic capacities.

Liberals share with many conservatives a belief in individual freedom that implies limits on the powers of the state (and lately liberals have been freedom's more reliable allies). We don't want government prescribing our religion or how we run our private lives. But we are not convinced that government always need compromise liberty, so when we call for it to intervene, we want the government's powers carefully circumscribed so that individuals enjoy greater liberty than they would have otherwise had. We use Social Security, for example, to help ensure that we can continue to live independently in old age, and we use law to prevent any Social Security official from gaining arbitrary power over us. Unlike conservatives, we believe that the people can enlarge their freedom through the only power that they share in common, which is their government. Taxes are the price we pay for that expanded vision of freedom.

# PART TWO

# Progressive Social Policies

# Social Welfare: The Safety Net

*The test of progress is not whether we add more to the abundance of those who have much; it is whether we provide enough for those who have too little.*

—President Franklin D. Roosevelt, Second Inaugural Address

Social welfare is a method by which a society takes care of those members of its population who are unable to work and cannot provide for their basic needs of food, shelter, clothing, and health. In every society there are people in this condition, so various kinds of social welfare for children, the poor, the elderly, and the physically and mentally disabled have been maintained since the earliest human societies. During the Middle Ages secular organizations were established to provide charity to the needy, and churches and royalty often maintained orphanages for children and hospitals for the ill.

By the eighteenth century the British government had set up a system of laws, called the English Poor Laws, that established a public responsibility for protecting and caring for the poor. These laws divided the poor into the "deserving poor" and the "undeserving poor." The former were those who were unable to work because they were too old or disabled, so they were given money or other types of assistance in the form of food, lodging, and medical care to help them get by. The latter group, the "undeserving poor," was made up of able-bodied men who could not find work, so they were given jobs in public workhouses or on private farms and businesses; public funds paid for work that they did. As nation-states were formed, all of the governments created forms of social welfare that provided fundamental assistance for needy citizens (Brundage, 2001; Day, 1999).

Presently, social welfare programs are found in all of the developed countries of the world, and even in many of the developing countries as well. Modern nations have created systems of welfare as a safety net to assist their citizens for the same reasons earlier societies had established them—to help the poor, disabled, young, and the vulnerable who for a variety of reasons are unable to sustain themselves without such aid. Many nations have developed social insurance systems that supply universal coverage for the unemployed, universal health care, free public education from elementary school through university study, low-cost or free housing, and other forms of assistance to all citizens.

## THE SAFETY NET LEGACY IN EARLY AMERICA

The basic elements of the English Poor Laws were imported into the American colonies and became a part of most of the original colonies' statutes (Brundage, 2001). After the founding of the United States, and continuing throughout the nineteenth century, local and state governments created a variety of methods to provide for the poor and needy. In the aftermath of the Civil War, the federal government implemented the Civil War Pension Program, making veterans of the Civil War and their families eligible for economic, disability, and old-age benefits.

During the latter part of the nineteenth century, "scientific" welfare reformers employed counseling to improve the social functioning of the poor. Caseworkers regularly met with poor clients and tutored them on the importance of self-discipline, personal initiative, morality, and the work ethic. The expectation for this counseling was that the poor would be "rehabilitated," seek work, and keep the jobs they secured. Cash relief would, therefore, become entirely unnecessary (Axinn and Stern, 2004; Trattner, 1998).

The Industrial Revolution, which began in the late eighteenth century, had matured by the beginning of the twentieth century, creating a major social transformation in the United States. Industrialization attracted millions of immigrants from all over the world to the United States in the latter nineteenth century, and a veritable population explosion occurred, more than doubling the population from 31 million in 1860 to 76 million in 1900. Equally dramatic was the growth of cities, as rural folk and newly arrived immigrants took up residence in urban areas to secure work—increasing the urban population from 20 percent to 40 percent of the total population by 1900. The United States grew into a land of big business in the form of corporations that dominated the economy.

The changing demographics brought about other significant social changes as well. With industrialization and urbanization, a smaller and smaller percentage of the country's population was engaged in farming. As the nation shifted from a farm economy to primarily an industrial economy and from rural to urban living, the family as the primary social support system weakened, increasing the need for formal social welfare programs (Katz, 2003).

Industrial development inaugurated and then accentuated the end of agricultural production as the primary source of work, income, and social lifestyle. Indeed, it created a new class structure made up primarily of urban wage workers employed by a wealthy cadre of capitalist owners and managers. Boom periods and depressions became a reality of the U.S. economy, so a certain percentage of available workers was always unemployed or underemployed. Unemployment rates have varied dramatically, to a high of 25 percent at the depth of the Great Depression in the early 1930s to 2.9 percent in 1953. Wherever there is unemployment in a capitalist society, there is a segment of the population living in poverty, which means people do not have the means to meet their basic needs for food, clothing, shelter, and health care.

Under these conditions a society has three choices: (1) let the poor deal with their situation; this is the "rugged individualism" or "pull yourself up by your bootstraps" option. (2) Provide no government help but encourage charity; this option expects churches and philanthropy to take care of the needy. (3) Provide social welfare for those in need; this is the option committed to government stepping up and providing a safety net for those in need. It is on these options that progressives and conservatives most fundamentally disagree. The first two options are preferred by conservatives, whereas progressives opt for the third option. As we noted in Section 1, conservatives advocate powerful restraints on government while endorsing economic individualism. Progressives, on the other hand, believe that government should play an active role in assisting its less fortunate citizens who are in need of help.

## AN EMERGING PROGRESSIVE SPIRIT:
## THE PROGRESSIVE ERA AND THE NEW DEAL

The abuses and corruption of government, the excesses of corporations, and the exploitation of workers, all of which were systemic to U.S. society by the end of the nineteenth century, called for a new set of political and government responses to these economic and social problems. Fortunately, a spirit of progressive reform became a dominant feature of consciousness as the twentieth century began and continued through the first two decades of that century, a period known as the Progressive Era.

However, in spite of the variety of important progressive initiatives that were created by U.S. presidents and Congresses and enacted into laws during the Progressive Era, federal government–supported social welfare was virtually absent in this period. Two-thirds of the state legislatures did pass what were called mothers' pensions (also known as "widow's pensions") to provide for the needs of mothers and children whose husbands were dead, absent, or incapacitated, thus supporting the view that mothers should be honored and cared for (Gould, 2001).

The expansion of federal and state power during the Progressive Era became the foundation for further expansion of a government commitment to a safety net with President Franklin D. Roosevelt. The current U.S. welfare system owes its major formulation to what Roosevelt called the New Deal in his bid for the presidency in 1932. The New Deal was a collection of economic and social reform laws and policies that Roosevelt and Congress enacted as a response to the Great Depression that began near the end of the 1920s and was at its worst in 1933, when Roosevelt became president (McJimsey, 2000). These legislative initiatives and policies were a clear pronouncement that the welfare of U.S. citizens was viewed as a legitimate concern of the government. Furthermore, social policy analyst John B. Judis (2000) claims that "As a result of the New Deal, American politics shifted decisively away from the underlying assumptions about limits of government" (58; see also Axinn and Stern, 2004; Edsforth, 2000).

## THE PAST 70 YEARS: PROGRESSIVE STRUGGLES
## ON BEHALF OF A SAFETY NET

Over the past 70 years, many of the social welfare programs begun during the presidency of Franklin Roosevelt have been modified and expanded. Many new safety net programs have been created, and they too have experienced modification. The current welfare system is highly complex, with some seventy-five programs administered by dozens of departments, agencies, and administrations. Of the numerous federal welfare programs, there are two general categories. One is called non-means-tested and the other is called means-tested. In the first, eligibility for benefits is not affected by one's income or wealth. Social Security benefits to qualified retired persons and Medicare are two examples of this form of welfare. Most welfare programs, however, are means-tested, meaning benefits are targeted to people with low income and assets that are below a certain level. Food stamps to purchase food and vouchers to subsidize rent for housing are examples of this form of welfare (Mink and Solinger, 2003).

As adjuncts to the federal welfare programs, many state governments contribute to federal welfare programs, and some have their own independent welfare programs. According to Robert Rector, "the combined federal and state welfare system now includes cash aid, food, medical aid, housing aid, energy aid, jobs and training, targeted and means-tested education, social services, and urban and community development programs" (Rector, 2001:2).

With the numerous social welfare programs currently in existence at the federal, state, and local municipality level, it would be impossible to identify, describe, and discuss all of them in this chapter. Therefore, we have decided to focus only on a select number of federal programs that seem to have the most profound nationwide impact. Although the safety net programs that we address in this chapter are considered federal programs, most of them have financial and administrative links to welfare agencies at the state and municipal levels.

## SOCIAL SECURITY: THE RETIREMENT PROGRAM

In Section 1 we described several parts of the New Deal, one of which was the Social Security Act of 1935. This legislation and its subsequent amendments created several programs to support different sectors of the population. Furthermore, there are different funding sources and different accounts. There are four components to Social Security:

1. OASI (Federal Old-Age and Survivorship Insurance)
2. DI (Federal Disability Insurance)
3. HI (Federal Hospital Insurance)
4. SMI (Supplementary Medical Insurance)

The HI and SMI programs make up what is known as Medicare.

The most well-known component, in fact the one that most people believe to be the total Social Security system, is the Old-Age and Survivors' Insurance (OASI) which is Social Security's retirement plan. When signed in 1935, the Social Security Act created a non-means-tested social insurance program paying eligible persons over sixty-five years of age and their families a continuing income after retirement. Currently, OASI covers over 95 percent of the work force, and currently about nineteen out of twenty of those who reach age sixty-five are eligible for some OASI benefits.

Employers and workers are required to fund Social Security through automatic deductions from workers' paychecks, and employers have to match the amount paid by the employee. Self-employed persons pay one sum that is equal to wage-earner plus employer compensation. Currently, employers and workers each pay 6.2 percent of an employee's wage or salary. Social Security taxes are not paid on earnings above $90,000 (in 2005). Automatic annual Cost-of-Living Adjustments (COLAs) for retirees on Social Security, based on the annual increase in the Consumer Price Index, were added in 1950, thus preventing inflation from reducing the value of Social Security benefits.

The Social Security Act is also aimed at mitigating economic hardship, including assistance for the destitute elderly, aid to the blind, and aid to dependent children. Amendments to the original Act have been added throughout Social Security's history, and the scope of the welfare safety net has expanded. A disability insurance program was added in 1954, providing benefits to disabled workers and their dependents. On the death of an insured worker, benefits of that worker are paid to surviving dependent widows or widowers, children under 18 years of age, and dependent parents. Payments to the spouse and minor children of a retired worker, which came to be called "dependent benefits," were added. Also added were survivors benefits for the family, when a premature death occurred to the "breadwinner." These changes made Social Security a family-based economic security program. Other amendments increased benefits and made this program one of virtually universal coverage (Social Security online, 2005).

Social Security is considered the most successful government program in the nation's history. Today, more than 47 million people, about one out of every six citizens, collect some kind of Social Security benefit. Without Social Security, nearly one-half of the U.S. population age sixty-five and older would live in poverty; with Social Security 11 percent of that age group live below the poverty line, and more than 60 percent of those lifted from poverty are women. Thus, Social Security lifts some 12 million older people out of poverty (NCPSSM, 2004).

At the sixty-fifth anniversary of the Social Security Act, the Commissioner of Social Security, Kenneth Apfel, said:

> *In the 1930s, being old all too often meant being poor. Many men and women at that time faced what was termed "the stark terror of penniless, helpless old age." The Social Security Act of 1935 helped to change all of that. When President Franklin Delano Roosevelt signed the original Act, he said, "The civilization of the past hundred years, with its startling industrial changes, has tended more and more to make life insecure. Young people have come to wonder what would be their lot when they came to old age." Today, thanks largely to Social Security, people know that they will have a dependable foundation of income when they retire; only about 11 percent of older Americans now fall below the poverty line. (Apfel, 2000:3)*

Currently, considerable political concern is being expressed about the future of the Social Security system. There is a major national debate on a key question: Can the current Social Security system manage the retirement of nearly 77 million baby boomers born between 1946 and 1964 and the generations that will follow? There is widespread agreement that the Social Security system does need changes to meet future demands on it. But there are wide differences on how to make those changes. Conservative interests propose modifying the secure features of the system and allowing workers to create private accounts using part of their Social Security payroll taxes, thus making at least part of their Social Security subject to stock market risk. Progressive interests propose a variety of reforms that preserve and protect the guaranteed social insurance safety net features of Social Security ("Bush moves," 2004; Feldstein, 1997; Goozner, 2005; Orr, 2004).

## CONSERVATIVE OPPOSITION TO SOCIAL SECURITY

From the beginning, there has been persistent conservative opposition to the Social Security retirement plan, but it has been muted because this program has been enormously popular with most Americans. Conservatives object to the federal government serving as a broker for a social insurance program, which is what Social Security is. For conservatives, the government has no business in what they consider to be a private matter. Conservatives also adamantly dislike the deduction taken from workers' paychecks and the required contribution employers must make to the government to fund Social Security. This, conservatives believe, is a violation of both workers' and employers' individual rights to conduct their private business affairs unfettered by government interference. These are the ideological bases that underlie conservatives' desire to privatize Social Security.

Politicians' attacks on Social Security were immediate. In the 1936 presidential campaign, the Republican platform criticized Social Security, declaring that Republicans looked "to the energy, self-reliance and character" of the American people, and to the system of free enterprise rather than to government aid (quoted in Skidmore, 1999:39).

Conservative business interests were also quick to denounce the Social Security Act. The National Association of Manufacturers called Social Security the "ultimate socialistic control of life and industry" (quoted in Judis, 2000:55). The United States Chamber of Commerce formulated a "Statement of Principles" about Social Security that stated, in part, that "interference by government in attempts to reduce the whole complex problem" of economic security for retired workers "to one of legislative formulae can only postpone the final solution by making it more difficult for business to assume its own obligations" to workers ("Issues Principles," 1936). The chairman of the board of directors of the Chase National Bank called Social Security a "grave menace to the future security of the country as a whole and therefore to the security of the very people it was designed to protect" ("Chamber Assails," 1936). In the end, most employers were strongly opposed to the Social Security Administration, and conservatives were able to block most major social legislation from the late 1930s until the early 1960s.

Conservative opposition to Social Security has persisted. Skidmore (1999) recounts statements by conservative spokesman Ronald Reagan, then governor of California and soon to be president, saying "Reagan said flatly that 'social security reduces your chances of ever being able to enjoy a comfortable retirement income.' He described Social Security as 'a sure loser' and said that 'Social Security taxes should be eliminated'" (90).

## UNEMPLOYMENT INSURANCE (UI) PROGRAM

The Social Security Act of 1935 also created the Unemployment Insurance (UI) program, which provides cash assistance for workers who have lost work temporarily. Nearly all wage and salary workers are covered under the UI provisions of the Social Security Act or one of several other separate federal programs for the unemployed: veterans, railroad workers, and federal employees.

The UI law imposes a payroll tax on employers, which is a percentage of an employee's annual earnings. Over 85 percent of this federal money is then returned to the states to help fund state UI benefits. State programs are subjected to few federal regulations for the UI coverage of eligible industries and workers, so it is the states that determine the amount of benefits, their duration, and the eligibility of unemployed workers.

Weekly UI benefits vary widely among states. The duration of benefits has typically been around twenty-six weeks, but that has varied among states and has been extended in some states during periods of rising unemployment. Thus, even though the federal tax on employers has been maintained, state programs vary widely in their coverage for unemployment insurance.

The UI was not created to be an antipoverty program; it was designed to help workers during periods of unemployment. Actually, few of the nation's poor receive UI because many state eligibility rules deny or restrict benefits for the poor; indeed, only about one-third of the nation's unemployed at any particular time actually receive benefits and only about 12 percent of poor families with children receive UI benefits. Nevertheless, the program has served a preventive antipoverty function. Many low-wage workers who become unemployed and are eligible for UI and apply for it would become impoverished without the protection of UI (Center on Budget and Policy Priorities, 2003; DeMarco, 2003).

## MEDICARE PROGRAM

In 1965 President Lyndon Johnson declared a War on Poverty in his domestic reform agenda called the Great Society. One of the most significant parts of the Great Society legislation involved changes to the Social Security system through the creation of Medicare and Medicaid. With these two programs, the federal government assumed the major responsibility for the health care for the elderly and the poor.

Medicare is a non-means-tested federal health insurance program that extends health coverage to Social Security beneficiaries sixty-five years of age and over without regard to their income or medical history; it also covers younger adults with permanent disabilities. It provides beneficiaries with access to doctors, hospitals, and other health care providers. It is financed mainly by a payroll tax paid by both employees and employers. Presently, both employers and employees pay 1.45 percent, and Medicare taxes are paid on all earnings; there is no limit where payment into the program ends.

Prior to the passage of Medicare less than one-half of U.S. citizens sixty-five and older had health insurance; by 1970, 97 percent of that age group was enrolled in Medicare. That percentage has stayed about the same for the past 35 years. In 2005 Medicare served 42 million beneficiaries. Currently, retirees are the adult population group least likely to be living in poverty and most likely to have health insurance coverage. Medicare has been one of the nation's most popular safety net programs, and it is regularly evaluated more highly than most private health insurance programs that cover younger adults (Gornick et al., 1996).

## MEDICAID PROGRAM

Medicaid is the nation's major public health care safety net for low-income citizens. Launched in 1965 as part of President Lyndon Johnson's Great Society initiatives, it is a means-tested safety net program that provides health services to low-income children and their parents. It is also a source of acute and long-term care coverage for elderly and disabled individuals, including Medicare beneficiaries. In providing these services, Medicaid is a cornerstone in the nation's health care system.

In 2005 Medicaid provided coverage to 53 million enrollees at a cost of $300 billion. Low-income children and their parents account for only 30 percent of Medicaid expenditures, while the elderly and people with disabilities account for 70 percent of Medicaid spending for services. Unlike Medicare, Medicaid is administered by each state, although funded in part by a federal agency within the U.S. Department of Health and Human Services. About half of Medicaid expenditures is paid for by the federal government, and the rest is covered by state funding (Kaiser Commission on Medicaid and the Uninsured, 2004).

## CONSERVATIVE OPPOSITION TO MEDICARE AND MEDICAID

From its beginnings, many conservatives were critical of the Medicare program because they saw it as the first step toward creating the national health care system, which they opposed because, for them, health care goods and services are best produced and efficiently distributed by the forces of capitalism and competition. But because Medicare provided federal funding of medical costs for everyone over sixty-five, regardless of need, and payments were linked to the existing private insurance system, conservative cries of "socialized medicine" were subdued.

Congress and the states are currently wrestling with the high costs of Medicare and Medicaid. The spiraling costs of health care have left these programs as targets for persistent calls for wide-ranging cost-control changes. Although there is no doubt that health care costs are out of control, progressives contend that problems with Medicare and Medicaid are less serious than conservatives allege and that health care is a social good. So the immediate challenge is to preserve these successful safety net programs by appropriate reform measures rather than weakening them to the point of putting millions of vulnerable people at risk of not having affordable medical care (Marmor, 2000; Oberlander, 2003).

## AID TO FAMILIES WITH DEPENDENT CHILDREN (AFDC)

When Congress passed the 1935 Social Security Act, Title IV of the Act contained provisions to help states provide financial assistance to needy dependent children. The original title of the program was Aid to Dependent Children (ADC) but was later changed to Aid to Families with Dependent Children (AFDC). AFDC was originally designed to help children whose fathers had died, but it evolved into the main source of regular income for millions of poor families.

AFDC is a means-tested program that provides cash assistance to parents and dependent children in need of help, and assistance to the aged, blind, and disabled through the Supplemental Security Income (SSI) program. Because state governments were required to play such an important role in the AFDC program, this program remained relatively small-scale until well into the 1960s. In 1960 less than 4 percent of children received AFDC benefits. But over the years, AFDC grew so large and became so expensive that the word *welfare* became identified with the AFDC program in the minds of many—even though there are over seventy means-tested welfare programs—because it has accounted for much of the increase in means-tested welfare income support. Throughout most of its history, no state has paid benefits sufficient to keep AFDC recipients out of poverty, unless they had other income or in-kind assistance ("A Brief History," n.d.).

AFDC families receive more than just cash assistance. They are also eligible for Medicaid, around 85 percent receive food stamps, over 20 percent receive housing assistance or live in public housing projects, and some receive assistance in finding jobs. By the early 1990s this led to a great deal of criticism of AFDC, and a national uproar that the program needed to be reformed. In 1996 Congress passed, and President Clinton signed, the Personal Responsibility and Work Opportunity Reconciliation Act (PRWORA), which abolished AFDC and replaced it with a set of block grants to states called Temporary Assistance to Needy Families (TANF). This transferred welfare responsibility for poor women and their children to the state level and accomplished what President Clinton declared in 1994 he wanted to do—"end welfare as we know it."

In exchange for the block grants, the TANF programs tightened requirements for benefits and imposed a five-year lifetime limit on recipients of federal cash assistance (though hardship exemptions are included in the law). Also, states are required to meet certain targets in moving portions of their welfare caseloads into work activities. States are also required to set shorter time limits and add other requirements for recipients.

By 2005, unprecedented changes had occurred in what was once AFDC (now TANF). The combination of the 1996 welfare reform act and the new welfare program it instituted, along with time limits and work requirements, pushed one-time (and would-be) welfare claimants toward work. The result: reduced benefits and reduced caseloads by as much as 80 percent in some states.

Hailed as a great success, TANF welfare reform resulted in a dramatic decline in the welfare rolls, from 4.4 million families in 1996 to 2.1 million in 2001. These changes in welfare caseloads mirror changes in employment rates of single women, which rose to 76.5 percent in 1998–1999, from 67.5 percent in 1989–1990 (Ventry, 2001). So job-holding rates among indigent single parents rose dramatically after reform, but poverty in these families remained high. By 2005 only about one-half of the nation's poor children were living in families that received public assistance payments, and in families that did receive the maximum monthly benefit, it was well below the U.S. poverty threshold. Thus, welfare reform has not produced a rosy picture for those who have been subjected to it (Blank and Haskins, 2001; DeParle, 2004; Hays, 2003).

## SUPPLEMENTAL SECURITY INCOME (SSI) PROGRAM

Low-income families with children are not the only persons eligible for cash assistance. A program called the Supplemental Security Income (SSI) program provides assistance for poor people who are aged sixty-five or older, blind, or disabled. It provides cash to meet basic needs for food, clothing, and shelter. The Social Security Administration administers the SSI program.

State and local governments largely establish eligibility and benefit levels and carry out the programs, but the federal government contributes a share of the expense. SSI benefits and state supplemental payments vary based on income, living arrangements, and other factors. In most states SSI beneficiaries obtain Medicaid to pay for doctors, prescription drugs, hospital stays, and other health expenses. They may be eligible to receive food stamps as well. Benefits vary from state to state, but they are generally more generous than under AFDC.

## THE FOOD STAMP PROGRAM

Along with TANF, which provides cash assistance to parents and children in need of help, federal, state, and local governments provide programs designed to help meet nutritional needs of low-income people and their families. It is the first line of defense against hunger. The federal government first began supplying food to the poor during the Great Depression. In addition to helping needy persons, it also relieved farmers of surplus agricultural products, and helped many farmers avoid poverty. Then in 1939 the federal Food Stamp Plan was initiated to assist needy families. It ended in the midst of World War II, and it was not until 1964 that Congress passed the Food Stamp Act of 1964 authorizing the establishment of a permanent food stamp program to help provide nutritionally adequate diets to needy individuals and low-income families. At the federal level the Food Stamp Program is financed through the Social Security Administration and administered by the U.S. Department of Agriculture. Various agencies administer the program at state and local levels.

Food stamps are coupons that recipients can use like cash to purchase only food items. The Food Stamp Program is by far the largest of the federal food assistance programs providing support to the needy. Low-income families with dependent children and households without children are the targeted groups for this program. The program is not considered a "welfare" program; instead, it is viewed as a nutrition program designed to help low-income families afford a nutritious diet.

According to the Agricultural Department, eligible households are given a monthly allowance of food stamps based on the Thrifty Food Plan, which is a low-cost model diet plan based on National Academy of Sciences' Recommended Dietary Allowances, and on food choices of low-income households. In 2003 it put food on the table each day for over 21 million persons. The average monthly benefit was about $80 per person and close to $185 per household; 79 percent of all benefits went to households with children, 17 percent to households with disabled persons, and 7 percent to households with elderly persons. Throughout its history, participation in FSP has risen in periods of high unemployment, inflation, and recession.

## FEDERAL HOUSING ADMINISTRATION (FHA) PROGRAM

Since the creation of the New Deal in the 1930s, an assortment of federal programs has mitigated the housing problem for low-income households. The most prominent of those programs, the Federal Housing Administration (FHA), was established by the National Housing Act of 1934. As part of the New Deal economic recovery efforts, the FHA's purpose was to restore mortgage lending, protect lending institutions, fill the gap created by the failure of private mortgage insurance, and stimulate home construction. In 1965 the FHA became a part of the Department of Housing and Urban Development's (HUD) Office of Housing, and FHA mortgage insurance has increasingly combined with other housing programs as HUD has sought to achieve visible results.

The FHA is now the largest component of HUD; it issues more than $100 billion to mortgage insurance annually, not by lending money directly but by insuring private loans made by FHA-approved lenders. According to the National Low Income Housing Coalition, FHA's current core mission is to "contribute to the building and maintenance of healthy, prosperous neighborhoods and expand opportunities of affordable homeownership, rental housing and healthcare" (National Low Income Housing Coalition, 2004:1).

The FHA insures mortgages on single-family and multifamily homes, including manufactured homes. It is the largest insurer of mortgages in the world. There is no entitlement for this kind of assistance, unlike other forms of welfare. An entitlement is assistance the government provides if an individual or family qualifies as eligible based on income, assets, and categorical eligibility criteria.

Proceeds from the mortgage insurance paid by the homeowners enables the FHA to operate entirely from its self-generated income; the FHA is the only government agency that costs taxpayers nothing. It actually provides a huge economic stimulus to the nation in the form of home and community development, which trickles down to local communities in the form of jobs, building supplies, tax bases, schools, and other forms of revenue.

A notable characteristic of the FHA has been its resilience and flexibility. FHA programs helped finance military housing and homes for returning veterans and their families during the 1940s. It assisted in helping spark the building of millions of privately owned apartments for elderly, handicapped, and lower-income people during the 1950s, 1960s, and 1970s. In the 1980s the FHA made it possible for potential homebuyers to get the financing they needed when the oil boom and bust–induced recession prompted private mortgage insurers to pull out of oil-producing states. Since 1934 the FHA and HUD have insured 30 million home mortgages and 38,000 multifamily project mortgages. U.S. citizens are now arguably the best housed people in the world, due largely to FHA and HUD programs.

Section 8 of the United States Housing Act of 1937, which was added to by the Housing and Community Development Act of 1974, is a federal housing voucher program administered by HUD that assists very low-income families, the elderly, and the disabled to afford decent, safe, and sanitary rental housing of their choice. Federal funds from HUD for this program are channeled to states, which then disburse them to local public housing agencies (PDAs) to administer the program. This program currently services about two million low-income families with children, senior citizens, and people with disabilities.

The Section 8 rental voucher program works this way: Eligible tenants are issued a voucher and are responsible for locating a rental unit that meets certain standards prescribed by the housing authority. A landlord who agrees to participate in the Section 8 program and rent to a tenant enters into a contract with the local housing authority. A one-year lease is then signed, with the housing authority agreeing to pay a portion of the tenants' rent directly to the landlord while the tenant pays the remaining portion. The principal advantages of this program are that low-income tenants have a choice of location and housing type in publicly or privately owned units, and landlords have the assurance that the majority of the rent will be paid on time by the housing authority. Since the tenants' portion of the rent is relatively modest, tenants are usually able to pay their share of the rent on time (U.S. Department of Housing and Urban Development Homes and Communities, 2001).

In 2000 HUD expanded the rental housing voucher program to permit the use of Section 8 voucher assistance for homeownership purposes. The new Section 8 homeownership option allows PHAs to permit Section 8 voucher holders to convert their voucher rental assistance to homeownership assistance in order to purchase a single-family home, manufactured home, condominium, or interest in a cooperative. This program is expected to provide relief for tenants who cannot afford high rents but can still afford a mortgage payment. It can also provide help for tenants faced with a lack of landlord participation in the Section 8 rental voucher program. Further, the homeownership option can create a broader choice of housing units from which to choose. Finally, the program offers lower-income families with an opportunity to achieve their homeownership dream (U.S. Department of Housing and Urban Development, 2004).

Participation in the homeownership program requires that families be eligible under HUD regulations as well as meet any discretionary requirements a PHA may adopt in its local program. The family must also be either an existing recipient of the Section 8 rental housing voucher program or be newly admitted to the program. The family must also qualify as a first-time homebuyer.

## OTHER SAFETY NET PROGRAMS

In addition to the social welfare programs that we have identified and described in this chapter, the federal government sponsors a number of others. These include Women, Infants, and Children (WIC), a nutrition information and food support program; Jobs Training Partnership program, Job Opportunities and Basic Skills Training program (JOBS), and other job-training and job-seeking assistance programs; Head Start, which is an early education program for disadvantaged children; and the Low Income Home Energy Assistance Program (LIHEAP), which aids former war veterans. There are other programs too numerous to identify here.

## CONSERVATIVE RESPONSES TO WELFARE PROGRAMS

Social welfare is antithetical to the conservative mindset. Individual striving, the creed of personal responsibility, and personal achievement are exalted in the ideal conservative social order. For many conservatives, combining those individual virtues with a fundamental faith in maintaining a small unobtrusive government leads them to believe the federal government simply should not administer a welfare system. Several years ago, in one of the most candid pronouncements by a conservative spokesman about social welfare, Charles Murray (1994) proposed "scrapping the entire federal welfare and income-support structure for working-aged persons, including AFDC, Medicaid, Food Stamps, Unemployment Insurance, Worker's Compensation, subsidized housing, disability insurance, and the rest. It would leave the working-aged person with no recourse whatsoever except the job market, family members, friends, and public or private locally funded services" (227–228). For less reactionary conservatives, if social welfare is adopted by a society, it is believed that government assistance programs should be small and narrowly tailored.

Specific conservative complaints about the AFDC program have centered on what they perceive as government allowing able-bodied adults to avoid work and becoming dependent on government handouts. Criticism has been further fueled by what is called "welfare dependence," which refers to children growing up in families where no one has ever had a paying job and who themselves became dependent on welfare as adults.

Conservatives have also been critical of the vast bureaucracy generated by overlapping services and endless regulations of AFDC/TANF. They contend that this has placed an increasing and unnecessary burden on the nation's taxpayers.

Conservative responses to the Food Stamp Program have fluctuated with the whims of presidents, Congress, and the mood of citizens. During the 1970s and 1980s food stamp reforms swung from enacting cutbacks to incremental improvements. In 1996, with the passage of PRWORA, congressional conservatives were able to enact major cutbacks and restrictions in food stamp benefits, even though the Food Stamp Program was reauthorized in the 1996 Farm Bill.

Based on the PRWORA legislation and falling unemployment, participation in the Food Stamp Program declined more than expected in the late 1990s. Indeed, in the first six years after the passage of PRWORA, some $28 million was cut from the Food Stamp Program, with 70 percent of the cuts impacting families with children. However, the Food Security and Rural Investment Act of 2002 restored eligibility for many of the benefits and made several other adjustments that had been lost with the passage of PRWORA (Food Stamp Program, n.d.; Greenstein and Guyer, 2001; Levitan, Mangum, and Mangum, 1998).

As with most safety net programs, the trend for the past twenty years has been to try to rein in the cost. This has been the case of the Section 8 housing voucher program. In fact for the fiscal year 2005, the Bush administration has requested an appropriation for this program that is $1 billion less than Congress appropriated in fiscal year 2004 and over $1.6 billion less than would be needed to maintain the current level of services. The cutbacks rise to about $4.6 billion by fiscal year 2009 (Center on Budget and Policy Priorities, 2004a, 2004b). This action by the Bush administration comes despite a report in 2001 by the Millennial Housing Commission calling the Section 8 rental voucher program the "linchpin" of federal housing policy, and describing it as "flexible, cost-effective, and successful in its mission."

**CONCLUSION**

Aid, comfort, and support for the vulnerable and needy members of society are deeply embedded in human history, and today social welfare programs are found in most countries of the world. In the United States philanthropic organizations, churches, and local governments were the first to assist less fortunate citizens in need of help. The expansion of the federal government into the social lives of U.S. citizens during the Progressive Era became the foundation for a collection of economic and social reform laws and policies enacted under the New Deal.

The current U.S. welfare system owes its major formulation to President Franklin D. Roosevelt and his New Deal legislative initiatives and policies. Many of the social welfare initiatives begun during President Roosevelt's presidency have been modified and expanded. In addition, the various progressive social initiatives and policies that were part of President Lyndon Johnson's Great Society and War on Poverty reforms advanced efforts for providing a safety net for the elderly, poor, unemployed, and disabled. Presently, federal, state, and local government spending on safety net programs accounts for approximately one-fifth or our nation's gross domestic product (GDP). Still, the U.S. welfare is limited in scope and ambition. After almost one hundred years of welfare-state building, U.S. citizens remain more vulnerable than do the people of nearly every other rich capitalist nation.

## REFERENCES

Apfel, Kenneth S. (2000). Quoted in Social Security Administration, *A Brief History of Social Security.* Social Security Publication No. 21-059 (ICN 44000):3.

Axinn, June, and Stern, Mark J. (2004). *Social Welfare: A History of the American Response to Need,* 6th ed. Boston: Allyn & Bacon.

Blank, Rebecca, and Haskins, Ron (eds.). (2001). *The New World of Welfare.* Washington, DC: Brookings Institution.

"A Brief History of the AFDC program" (n.d.): http://aspe.hhs.gov/hsp/AFDC/baseline/1history.pdf.

Brundage, Anthony. (2001). *The English Poor Laws, 1700–1930.* London: Palgrave Macmillan.

"Bush Moves to Privatize Social Security." (2004, November 10). *USA Today:* www.usatoday.com/news/washington/2004-11-10-social-security_x.htm.

Center on Budget and Policy Priorities. (2003, November 10). "Introduction to Unemployment Insurance": www.cbpp.org/12-19-02ui.pdg.

Center on Budget and Policy Priorities. (2004a). "HUD'S Reliance on Rent Trends for High-End Apartments to Criticize the Housing Voucher Program Is Mistaken": http://cbpp.org/3-16-04hous2.htm, March 16.

Center on Budget and Policy Priorities. (2004b). "Administration Seeks Deep Cuts in Housing Vouchers and Conversion of Program to a Block Grant": www.cbpp.org/2-12-04hous.pdf.

"Chamber Assails Profits Tax Bill." (1936, May 8). *New York Times,* p. 4.

Day, Phyllis J. (1999). *A New History of Social Welfare,* 3rd ed. Boston: Allyn & Bacon.

DeMarco, Edward J. (2003). "Unemployment Insurance." *Social Security Bulletin.* Annual Issue.

DeParle, Jason. (2004). *American Dream: Three Women, Ten Kids, and a Nation's Drive to End Welfare.* New York: Viking.

Edsforth, Ronald. (2000). *The New Deal: America's Response to the Great Depression.* Malden, MA: Blackwell.

Feldstein, Martin. (1997, January 31). "Privatizing Social Security: The $10 Trillion Opportunity": www.cato.org/pubs/ssps/ssp7.html.

Food Stamp Program (n.d.). "A Short History of the Food Stamp Program: www.fns.usda.gov/fsp/rules/Legislation/history.htm.

Goozner, Merrill. (2005). "Don't Mess with Success." *AARP Bulletin* (January):12–15.

Gornick, Marian E., et al. (1996). "Thirty Years of Medicare: Impact on the Covered Population." *Health Care Financing Review* 18 (2):179–237.

Gould, Lewis. (2001). *America in the Progressive Era, 1890–1914.* Harlow, Essex, England: Pearson Education.

Greenstein, Robert, and Guyer, Jocelyn. (2001). "Supporting Work through Medicaid and Food Stamps." In Rebecca M. Blank & Ron Haskins (eds.), *The New World of Welfare* (pp. 335–368). Washington, DC: Brookings Institution Press.

Hays, Sharon. (2003). *Flat Broke with Children: Women in the Age of Welfare Reform.* New York: Oxford University Press.

"Issues Principles to Guide Business." (1936). *New York Times* (August 30):2.

Judis, John B. (2000). *The Paradox of American Democracy: Elites, Special Interests, and the Betrayal of Public Trust.* New York: Pantheon Books.

Kaiser Commission on Medicaid and the Uninsured, (2004, January). "The Medicaid Program at a Glance": www.kff.org/medicaid/loader.cfm?url=commonspot/security/getfile.cfm&PageID=30463.

Katz, Michael. (2003). "In the Shadow of the Poorhouse: A Social History of Welfare in America." In Dalton Conley (ed.), *Wealth and Poverty in America: A Reader* (pp. 225–253). Malden, MA: Blackwell.

Levitan, Sar A., Mangum, Garth L., and Mangum, Stephen, L. (1998). *Programs in Aid of the Poor,* 7th ed. Baltimore: Johns Hopkins University Press.

McJimsey, George. (2000). *The Presidency of Franklin Delano Roosevelt.* Lawrence: University of Kansas Press.

Marmor, Theodore R. (2000). *The Politics of Medicare,* 2nd ed. New York: A. deGruyter.

Mink, Gwendolyn, and Solinger, Rickie. (2003). *Welfare: A Documentary History of U.S. Policy and Politics.* New York: New York University Press.

Murray, Charles. (1994). *Losing Ground: American Social Policy 1950–1980.* New York: Basic Books.

National Low Income Housing Coalition. (2004). "Federal Housing Administration": http://nlihc. org/advocates/fha.htm.

NCPSSM. (2004). "Social Security Fast Facts": www.ncpssm.org/socialsecurity/fastfacts.

Oberlander, Jonathan. (2003). *The Political Life of Medicare.* Chicago: University of Chicago Press.

Orr, Doug. (2004). "Social Security Isn't Broken," *Dollars and Sense* (November/December):14–16, 33.

Rector, Robert E. (2001, March 7). "Means-Tested Welfare Spending: Past and Future Growth," *The Heritage Foundation:* www.heritage.org/Research/Welfare/Test030701b.cfm.

Skidmore, Max J. (1999). *Social Security and Its Enemies: The Case for America's Most Efficient Insurance Program.* Boulder, CO: Westview Press.

Social Security online. (2005). "The History of Social Security": www.ssa.gov/history/history.html.

Trattner, Walter I. (1998). *From Poor Law to Welfare State: A History of Social Welfare in America,* 6th ed. New York: Free Press.

U.S. Department of Housing and Urban Development Homes and Communities. (2001, April 13). "Housing Choice Voucher Program Fact Sheet (Section 8)": www.hud.gov/utilities/print/print2. cfm?page=80$^@http%3A%2F%2Fwww%2Eh.

U.S. Department of Housing and Urban Development. (2004, October 1). "Homeownership Vouchers": www.hud.gov/utilities/testonly.cfm?address=http://www.hud.gov/offices/pih/prog.

Ventry, Dennis J., Jr. (2001). "The Collision of Tax and Welfare Politics: The Political History of the Earned Income Tax Credit." In Bruce D. Meyer and Douglas Holtz-Eakin (eds.), *Making Work Pay: The Earned Income Tax Credit and Its Impact on America's Families* (pp. 15–66). New York: Russell Sage.

# 5

# The Faces of Social Security

*HEATHER GAIN AND LISA BENNETT*

*When the Social Security Act was passed in 1935, no one could have guessed that it would become the centerpiece of security and comfort for virtually all older citizens. But Social Security is not only social insurance for retirees. It addresses the needs of different sectors of the population, thus expanding the scope of our safety net. This reading reveals how lives benefit by describing how three women's lives have been affected by Social Security programs. Many other stories could be told because about 17 percent of U.S. citizens collect some kind of Social Security benefit.*

Social Security reform is an issue of special importance to women. And not just retired women—but also young women, disabled women, lesbians, household workers and others. NOW offers here the real stories of three women whose lives have been affected by the program. These are only three of the many faces of Social Security, and the *National NOW Times* will continue to bring you more women's stories in upcoming issues.

## TOBI HALE

Tobi Hale's story is an eye-opener. Early in January, the Social Security Administration informed Hale that she was going to lose her Medicaid coverage at the end of that month. As a woman with a disability—she is legally blind and uses a wheelchair—Hale depends on Social Security for her income, a meager $581 a month. Because she is currently ill, she also depends on Medicaid to help pay her $4,000 a month medication bills.

Although she was working fewer than 10 hours a week, that income plus her Social Security check made Hale ineligible for Medicaid. But as a part-time employee, she had no access to health insurance through work.

Fortunately, Hale is a longtime activist (and a member of NOW's National Board), so she knew just what to do. In addition to contacting a Social Security caseworker to lobby on her behalf, Hale called her governor, her state senator and her state representative.

*Source:* "The Faces of Social Security" by Heather Gain and Lisa Bennett (2002) from *National NOW Times*, Spring, p. 16. Washington, DC: NOW.

"Without my medication, I will die," Hale told them. Colorado State Sen. Stan Matsu-naka immediately urged her to apply for the Home Based Community Services program, which will allow her to get back on Medicaid. As we went to print, a relieved Hale had just learned that she qualified for the program.

"I don't know how anyone works their way through this system without help," said Hale. But she does credit Social Security with making it possible for her to go back to school and get her graduate degree in Social Work, focusing on Gerontology.

Hale points out that if Social Security is privatized, people with disabilities will suffer greatly, as they have the highest unemployment rate of any group—somewhere between 72 and 90 percent. "You have to work in order to put money into a privatized system," she says. Although privatization is not the answer, Hale stresses that the system does need fixing—as illustrated by her recent crisis.

### GERALDINE MILLER

As a woman who worked for decades as a domestic worker, 81-year-old Geraldine Miller understands the necessity of Social Security. Since she was a teenager, Miller has worked in hotels, restaurants and kitchens, but primarily in private homes. She was young when she began working and the Social Security program was still in its infancy. Miller was not aware that she could put away for retirement until years later and so today her Social Security check isn't as large as it should be. Despite its size, this Bronx, N.Y., resident relies on the check's arrival each month. It helps her with necessities like medical costs and prescriptions.

"It's not a lot," says Miller, "but it pays the rent."

The discrepancy in check amounts between those who registered immediately and those who did not propelled Miller to found the Household Technicians Union, which works to ensure equal rights for women who work mainly in "under-the-table" jobs, such as maids, nannies, and cooks. The union also pressures employers to comply with the Federal Minimum Wage Act of 1972.

Miller strongly urges household workers, especially immigrants, to know their rights. She ran a workshop for Project Open Doors that brought to light the similarities and shared concerns of homemakers and household workers. By breaking down the barriers of class and race, Miller sought to show participants that all of them needed to have access to the same benefits in old age. Similarly, information and education must be more readily available, proclaims Miller, to avoid the tragedy of elderly women in poverty.

As past president of the National Congress of Neighborhood Women and also the first chair of NOW's Women of Color Task Force, Miller is no stranger to activism. One of her many concerns is the enforcement of Social Security laws for all employees, in and out of the home. Miller has recently been appointed Chair of NOW's national committee on Eliminating Racism.

### TYRA BROWN

Tyra Brown's life was deeply touched by Social Security, although she is nowhere near retirement. Many people think of Social Security as providing benefits only to those 65 years of age and older, but benefits are also paid to the families of deceased workers. Since the death of a primary breadwinner can devastate the surviving family, Social Security offers Survivor's Insurance.

When Brown was fifteen, her mother and sole provider died of heart failure. This tragic loss put her in her grandmother's care and money became tight. Brown's mother, who had earned a middle-class income, had paid into Social Security for her retirement. However, she died before she became eligible to enjoy those benefits. The money she paid in, however, did not go to waste. Instead, her Social Security became her daughter's security.

Brown and her grandmother received Social Security Survivor's Insurance checks each month, as well as her grandmother's retirement benefit checks.

"We could count on that income every month, and without it, we wouldn't have made it," said Brown. These two incomes also enabled her to attend college.

Brown graduated from Howard University in Washington, D.C. and now spends much of her time organizing to protect the future of Social Security. The Oklahoma native has spoken before the President as well as the Social Security Subcommittee of the House Committee on Ways and Means. She is aware that her story is one of a million similar stories of young people across the nation, and she struggles to secure and strengthen social security for generations to come.

# 6

# Social Security, the Nation's Most Effective Safety Net Program

## *FISCAL POLICY INSTITUTE*

*Nearly one-half of all U.S. citizens over sixty-five years of age have income below the poverty line before receipt of Social Security benefits. With Social Security benefits, only about 11 percent remain in poverty. Social Security's effects in shrinking poverty are most striking among elderly women. This reading illustrates the effects of Social Security in New York. It paints a rather impressive record of the benefits of Social Security for hundreds of thousands of New Yorkers.*

As the nation debates the future of Social Security, the phenomenal impact of Social Security on the economic well-being of the elderly should be at the forefront of all discussions. A new analysis of Census Bureau data measures the impact of Social Security on the elderly population in New York. Pooling the three most recent years of data from the Census Bureau's Current Population Survey, this report estimates poverty rates with and without Social Security benefits for the elderly in New York.

Without Social Security, over one million elderly New Yorkers would have incomes below the official poverty line. With Social Security benefits added to income, the number of elderly poor is reduced by 818,500 to just over 373,000. When other governmental cash programs (e.g., Supplemental Security Income, unemployment compensation, worker's compensation) are taken into account, the number of poor elderly New Yorkers falls even further to about 304,000.

## NEW YORK'S ELDERLY POVERTY RATE IS CUT SIGNIFICANTLY BY SOCIAL SECURITY

Almost one half of New York's elderly population would be poor if it were not for Social Security and other government programs. When Social Security benefits are taken into consideration, New York's elderly poverty rate (for the 2001–2003 period) falls to 15.4%.

*Source:* "Social Security, the Nation's Most Effective Safety Net Program, Keeps More than 800,000 Elderly New Yorkers out of Poverty" from *Fiscal Policy Notes,* November 2004, pp. 1–3. New York: Fiscal Policy Institute. Reprinted by permission.

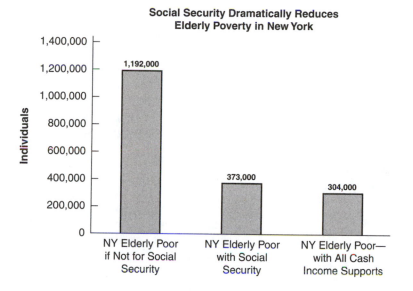

**Social Security Dramatically Reduces Elderly Poverty in New York**

When other government cash assistance programs are considered, the elderly poverty rate is reduced further to 12.6% which is the poverty rate reported in official Census Bureau publications.

While Social Security benefits are not sufficient to bring the incomes of all elderly persons above the poverty line, Social Security is still extremely important for the elderly whose incomes remain below that level. If it were not for Social Security, the poorest of the elderly would fall even further below the poverty line. In fact, Social Security makes up a very substantial proportion of the income of the low income elderly. Nationwide, Social

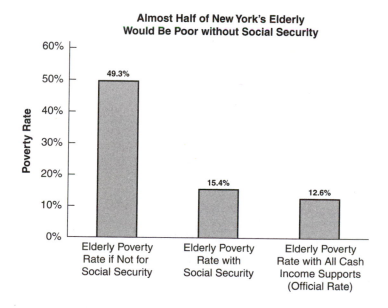

**Almost Half of New York's Elderly Would Be Poor without Social Security**

**Social Security Is More Important Than Other Government Programs in Reducing Elderly Poverty in New York**

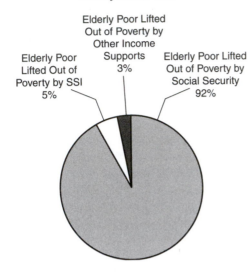

Elderly Poor Lifted Out of Poverty by Other Income Supports 3%

Elderly Poor Lifted Out of Poverty by SSI 5%

Elderly Poor Lifted Out of Poverty by Social Security 92%

Security constitutes 80% of the income of the elderly in both the lowest and the next lowest quintiles.

## SOCIAL SECURITY IS THE MOST IMPORTANT SAFETY NET PROGRAM FOR ELDERLY NEW YORKERS

Various federal, state and local programs supplement the incomes of New York's elderly population. Although the other government programs are significant, Social Security is clearly the most important anti-poverty program for the elderly. More than 92% of the elderly lifted from poverty by government cash assistance programs in New York, are kept from poverty by Social Security benefits. SSI benefits keep another 5% of elderly New Yorkers out of poverty.

### IMPORTANCE FOR ELDERLY WOMEN

The majority of elderly people lifted from poverty by Social Security are women. More than half a million elderly New York women are pulled out of poverty by Social Security

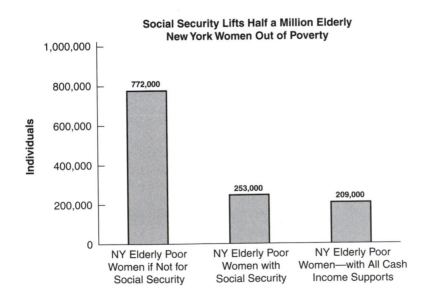

**Social Security Lifts Half a Million Elderly New York Women Out of Poverty**

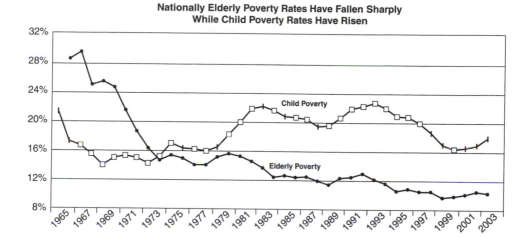

**Nationally Elderly Poverty Rates Have Fallen Sharply
While Child Poverty Rates Have Risen**

benefits. The poverty rate of elderly women in New York falls from 54.5% to 17.8% when Social Security benefits are counted. Two-thirds of elderly women who otherwise would be poor—67%—are removed from poverty by Social Security. Another 44,000 elderly women's incomes are increased above the poverty level by other government cash assistance programs, reducing the official poverty rate for elderly women in New York to 14.8%.

## ELDERLY POVERTY RATES HAVE FALLEN WHILE CHILD POVERTY RATES HAVE RISEN

The power of Social Security in lifting the elderly out of poverty is underscored by comparing the long term trends in the elderly and child poverty rates. Prior to the enactment of Social Security, poverty was widespread among the nation's elderly. Even 30 years ago, the elderly were more likely to live in poverty than the population as a whole. In 1966, 28.5% of the elderly in the United States had incomes below the poverty line, compared with 14.7% of the general population and 17.6% of children. By 2003 the national poverty rate for the elderly had fallen to 10.5% while the child poverty rate was 17.6%.

# 7

# Faces of Medicaid

## *THE KAISER COMMISSION ON MEDICAID AND THE UNINSURED*

*Medicaid was launched in 1965 as part of President Lyndon Johnson's Great Society. In the four decades since then, it has evolved from a basic federal–state health care program for people on welfare into a broad and highly efficient safety net providing health care for more than 53 million poor, older, and disabled people. This reading is from a report conducted by the Kaiser Commission on Medicaid and the Uninsured. The focus of this reading is on ten families who are beneficiaries of Medicaid's wide variety of services to low-income families, individuals with disabilities, and elderly individuals.*

## OVERVIEW

Medicaid is often the only source of health insurance coverage for more than 50 million low-income people, including 40 million children and parents, and 12 million people with chronic, disabilities, who fall outside the private health insurance market. A principal building block in efforts to extend coverage to the low-income uninsured and the only source of long-term services and supports, Medicaid is a linchpin in our nation's health care system. Designed to address the more complex health needs of people with disabilities and the limited financial resources of low-income people, Medicaid covers a broad range of health and supportive services.

Medicaid is a cornerstone in the nation's health care system, paying for nearly one in five health care dollars overall and nearly one in two long-term care dollars. Federal funds match state spending making Medicaid a program that can respond to emerging population needs including rising unemployment and loss of health coverage, emergencies or disasters, increasing disability rates and an aging society.

Over the last three years, state fiscal situations deteriorated with the decline in state tax revenues, leading to pressure to reduce Medicaid spending as officials struggled to balance state budgets. Because most of Medicaid spending goes toward services for seniors and people with disabilities, painless reductions are not possible. Actions that cut eligibility, limit benefits, and increase cost-sharing obligations are likely to lead to greater numbers of

*Source:* "Faces of Medicaid" (#4116), The Henry J. Kaiser Family Foundation, April 2004. This information was reprinted with the permission of the Henry J. Kaiser Family Foundation. The Kaiser Family Foundation, based in Menlo Park, California, is a nonprofit, independent national health care philanthropy and is not associated with Kaiser Permanente or Kaiser Industries.

uninsured, unmet need for people with disabilities, and loss of help for people with significant medical and long-term care expenses.

This report profiles Medicaid's role for the low-income population in providing basic health insurance, particularly for children; in supporting services that enable people with disabilities to function and be independent; and in filling gaps in Medicare for seniors, including prescription drugs and long-term care. The ten families highlighted here provide a snapshot of Medicaid beneficiaries and illustrate the integral role that Medicaid plays in keeping children, adults, and seniors healthy, active, and engaged in family and community life.

### Low-Income Families
Natalia and Fernando Diaz, Washington, DC
Missy Martinez, Espanola, New Mexico
The Prisk Family, East Hartford, Connecticut

### Individuals with Disabilities
Patrick Quinn, East Greenwich, Rhode Island
Jenna Johnson, St. Paul, Minnesota
Elsie Carter, Washington, DC
Vincent Miranda, Naples, Florida

### Elderly Individuals
Mildred Benham, Bloomington, Illinois
Naomi Stufflebeam, Ottumwa, Iowa
Margaret Stetler, Rockville, Maryland

## MEDICAID PROVIDES ESSENTIAL PRENATAL CARE AND WELL-CHILD SERVICES

> "Before Medicaid I was just you know, biting my nails off and biting my lips just cause I couldn't pay anything."
>
> —Natalia Diaz

Before becoming enrolled in Medicaid, Natalia was uninsured and relied on neighborhood clinics to get health care. She did not have a regular doctor and was worried she would not be able to pay for her delivery. After learning about Medicaid through an outreach worker, Natalia, eligible because of her low-income, was able to obtain regular check-ups for her pregnancy. When Natalia went into premature labor, Medicaid provided her the care and medicine needed to carry her baby to full term. Natalia attributes Fernando being born a healthy baby to her excellent prenatal care. Today, Fernando is a healthy and active two-year-old, and Natalia is working full-time and pursuing a degree in nursing.

## MEDICAID PROVIDES ROUTINE AND SPECIALIZED CARE FOR HEALTHY CHILDHOOD DEVELOPMENT

> "I'm very grateful to Medicaid that they did step in because there was no way my wife and I could have even touched the expenses."
>
> —Jeremiah Martinez

Jeremiah and Nadine Martinez have legal custody of their grandchild, Missy. They both work hard at their jobs—Jeremiah works in construction and Nadine works at a fast-food restaurant. Missy was born premature, weighing 3 pounds, 5 ounces and required a three-month hospital stay. The Martinezes were very worried that their granddaughter would not survive if she did not get the health care she needed. They were relieved to learn that she qualified for Medicaid; and that Medicaid would provide all the health services that Missy needed at very low or no cost. Medicaid provides Missy with access to physical and speech therapy to help her in development. Medicaid also provides routine care for Missy such as immunizations. Because of the care she receives, Missy is growing up happy and healthy.

## MEDICAID PROVIDES AFFORDABLE COVERAGE AND COVERS THE UNEXPECTED

*". . . A lot of families don't take their kids because they don't have the money. That's why this insurance is really good. Cause you just don't have that worry anymore."*

—Sandy Prisk

Sandy Prisk is a certified nurse assistant and her husband Rob Prisk is a self-employed carpet layer in East Hartford, Connecticut. They have three children all under ten years old—Matthew 5, Jessica 8, Katie 10. Sandy and Rob know the importance of health coverage, but neither of them receives health insurance through work. Their children qualify for Medicaid because of the family's low income. Medicaid covers sudden expenses such as emergency dental work or antibiotics for a throat infection. Living on a tight family budget, the Prisk's find Medicaid very affordable and say that it provides them with peace of mind.

## MEDICAID PROVIDES AN AUTISTIC CHILD ESSENTIAL IN-HOME THERAPY

*"The Katie Beckett program is one of the many good things about Medicaid."*

—Joanne Quinn

Joanne Quinn says that she was relieved when her son Patrick, now age 8, was diagnosed with autism, because before his diagnosis Patrick's unexplained behavior caused the whole household stress. Autism prevents individuals from properly understanding what they see, hear, and otherwise sense, resulting in severe problems with social relationships, communication, and behavior.

After his diagnosis, Patrick started to receive Medicaid through a home and community-based service waiver called the "Katie Beckett option." The most critical services he receives are speech therapy, occupational therapy, and home-based therapeutic services for 20 hours a week. Occupational therapy teaches Patrick a broad range of life skills, such as how to dress, how to make his bed, and how to respond to other children.

The Quinn's value the Katie Beckett program because it allows Patrick to stay with his family in the community. They feel fortunate to live in a state (Rhode Island) that has enacted the optional program.

## MEDICAID HELPS A YOUNG ADULT WITH CEREBRAL PALSY GAIN INDEPENDENCE

*"Medicaid is my lifeline, my hope, and my future."*

—Jenna Johnson

Jenna is an out-going 21-year-old with cerebral palsy and other serious health conditions, such as seizure disorder, learning disabilities, and impaired vision. Due to her disabilities, she is essentially confined to a wheel chair. Medicaid has helped Jenna become more independent. Without the help she receives from Medicaid, she would be unable to remain at home and would have to be institutionalized. Instead, because of the help she receives from her personal care attendants, she is able to work part-time at Target, volunteer at a local veterinarian clinic, and take classes at the community college.

## MEDICAID HELPS A WOMAN FIGHT THE HIV/AIDS BATTLE

*"If I didn't have Medicaid, I don't think I would be here. . . . I really don't. . . . I think I would have passed away a long time ago. I really do."*

—Elsie Carter

Elsie is 51-years-old and has been enrolled in Medicaid since 1987. Elsie was diagnosed with HIV in the early 1980s and was uninsured for 7 years before she got Medicaid coverage due to her chronic condition. During that time Elsie relied on emergency rooms to get health care; however, she remained very sick with her disease, contracting pneumonia more than 6 times. Since enrolling in Medicaid, Elsie's health has dramatically improved. She relies on Medicaid for her twice-daily dose of medications that include 10 prescription drugs. Without Medicaid, Elsie would be unable to afford the high cost prescription drugs that she needs to fight her disease. Elsie also uses physician, mental health, dental and vision services through Medicaid. Elsie relies on Medicaid to keep her disease in check so that she can live a healthy life and take care of her 17-month-old nephew, who is in her custody. Her hopes for the future are to take some computer courses and return to work once her nephew gets older.

## MEDICAID HELPS AN ADULT WITH MENTAL ILLNESS

*"Medicaid covers everything I need. I am so grateful because the medication is very expensive—about $400 a month without Medicaid."*

—Vincent Miranda

When Vincent was 21-years-old, he was first diagnosed with schizophrenia and began receiving treatment for his illness. In 2001, he moved in with his mother and stepfather, his main caretakers, because he was unable to take care of himself. Vincent applied for SSI and Medicaid because he could not afford the prescription drugs he had been taking for his schizophrenia. After receiving Medicaid, he was able to afford the several medications he needed to treat his serious mental illness.

Vincent's diagnosis has been changed from schizophrenia to bipolar disorder. This diagnosis means that he takes fewer and less potent prescription drugs; however, he still needs medications and therapy visits. Vincent's health has improved and he is presently enrolled in computer classes at a local vocational institute. Vincent, now 37, looks forward to the day when he can pay his own way, live independently, and enjoy life to its fullest.

## SENIOR WOMAN REMAINS INDEPENDENT DUE TO MEDICAID

*"If I didn't have Medicaid to pay for my drugs, I would cease to exist, it's what keeps me going."*

—Mildred Benham

Mildred is 68-years-old and relies on Medicaid for help with her Medicare premiums, home health services, and prescription drugs. Mildred has fibrosis of the lungs, rheumatoid arthritis, high blood pressure, and cataracts—conditions that she takes up to 12 prescription drugs each day for. Before qualifying for Medicaid and Medicare, Mildred was uninsured and relied on free clinics for health care. Each time she went to the clinic, she saw a different doctor and admittedly put off seeking care for chronic conditions. Now, with Medicaid, she has a regular physician who knows her medical history and prescribes the appropriate medications that she receives at nominal costs. Mildred also uses a home health aide that helps her 5–6 hours a week. The aide helps her with activities she would not be able to do on her own, such as taking Mildred to doctor's appointments and picking up her prescription drugs. Mildred believes having Medicaid coverage helps her maintain her independence. Her hopes for the future include staying healthy and watching her grandchildren grow up.

## MEDICAID WAIVER HELPS ELDERLY MEDICARE BENEFICIARY REMAIN AT HOME WITH HER FAMILY

*"It's treated me great, I appreciate every bit of it without question."*

—Naomi Stufflebeam

Naomi is 90-years-old and became enrolled in Medicaid after being hospitalized for pneumonia one year ago. She qualifies for Medicaid because of her low-income. After her hospital stay, Naomi had to move in with her daughter and son-in-law because she needed full-time care. She qualified for Medicaid personal care services but instead chose to be cared for by her family members. Naomi relies on Medicaid for low-cost prescription drugs and for her walker and other medical equipment to help her remain mobile. She also wears a lifeline necklace, an assisted device covered by Medicaid that signals an ambulance in the case of an emergency. Medicaid also helped her family make the bathroom handicap accessible for Naomi's special needs. Without the Medicaid waiver, Naomi would not be able to afford her Medicare premiums and her prescription drugs she needs for her asthma, diabetes, and high blood pressure.

Naomi enjoys spending time each day at a local child day-care center. She also likes to get out and shop on the weekends. Overall, Naomi is in good health and plans to continue enjoying her life surrounded by her family, grandchildren and great-grandchildren.

## MEDICAID HELPS AN ELDERLY WOMAN PAY FOR NURSING HOME CARE

*"I'm very grateful for Medicaid."*

—Margaret Stetler

Margaret has been living in a nursing home for almost 2 years. When she entered the nursing home, she had over $40,000 in assets; however, the high cost of nursing home care quickly depleted her funds and her nursing home care is not covered by Medicare. Because she was able to "spend-down" to become eligible for Medicaid, Margaret has been able to remain in the nursing home. Although Margaret is in fair health for a woman in her early 80's, she has multiple chronic conditions including diabetes and chronic heart failure. She relies on multiple prescriptions. The nurses at the nursing home help her monitor her diabetes and make sure she takes her medicines at the appropriate times. Margaret enjoys spending time with friends and family.

## ACKNOWLEDGEMENTS

Interviews were conducted in 2003 by Kaiser Commission staff members: Julie Hudman, Molly O'Malley, and Risa Elias. This project would not have been possible without the generous participation and generosity of the families we interviewed. The Commission would also like to thank the following people for their assistance with identifying individuals to be interviewed for this report: Dan Burke, Jeff Crowley, Michael Cover, Lisa Carr, Donna Cohen Ross, Hyacinth Daniel, Shawn McDermott, Mason Essif, and the Connecticut's Children's Health Council.

# 8

# Bigger and Better

## JACOB S. HACKER

*Yale political scientist and New American Foundation fellow Jacob Hacker argues that the belief that the federal government is inept and inefficient in conducting broad-based health care, retirement pensions, and disability coverage in comparison to the provision of these services by the private sector is inaccurate. Hacker persuasively maintains that government social insurance programs are vastly superior to private plans in regard to efficiency, cost containment, and distributive justice.*

Remember those bumper stickers during the early-1990s fight over the Clinton health plan? "National Health Care? The Compassion of the IRS! The Efficiency of the Post Office! All at Pentagon Prices!" In American policy debates, it's a fixed article of faith that the federal government is woefully bumbling and expensive in comparison with the well-oiled efficiency of the private sector. Former Congressman Dick Armey even elevated this skepticism into a pithy maxim: "The market is rational; government is dumb."

But when it comes to providing broad-based insurance—health care, retirement pensions, disability coverage—Armey's maxim has it pretty much backward. The federal government isn't less efficient than the private sector. In fact, in these critical areas, it's almost certainly much more efficient.

To grasp this surprising point, it helps to understand how economists think about efficiency. Although politicians throw the word around as if it were a blanket label for everything good and right, economists mean something more specific. Or rather, they usually mean one of two specific things: *allocational* (or Pareto) efficiency, a distribution that cannot be changed without making somebody worse off; or *technical* efficiency, the most productive use of available resources. (There's a third possibility, *dynamic* efficiency, but we'll take that up in a moment.)

When the issue is health insurance or retirement security, *allocational* efficiency is really not what's under discussion. Nearly everyone agrees that the private market won't distribute vital social goods of this sort in a way that citizens need. Before we had Social

*Source:* Reprinted with permission from Jacob S. Hacker, "Bigger and Better," *The American Prospect*, Volume 16, Number 5: May 6, 2005. *The American Prospect*, 11 Beacon Street, Suite 1120, MA 02108. All rights reserved.

Security, a large percentage of the elderly were destitute. Before we had Medicare, millions of the aged (usually the sickest and the poorest) lacked insurance. If we didn't subsidize medical care—through tax breaks, public insurance, and support for charity care—some people would literally die for lack of treatment. Market mechanisms alone simply can't solve this problem, because private income is inadequate to pay for social needs. This is one of the chief reasons why government intervenes so dramatically in these areas by organizing social insurance to pay for basic retirement and disability, medical, and unemployment coverage, and by extensively subsidizing the cost of these benefits, especially for the most vulnerable.

What's usually at issue, instead, is *technical* efficiency: Are we getting the best bang for our necessarily limited bucks in these areas? The notion that the private market is, by definition, better at delivering such bang for the buck is the main rationale offered for increasing the already extensive role of the private sector in U.S. social policy. Thus, Medicare vouchers or partly privatized Social Security would supposedly engage the discipline of competition and lead to more efficient use of resources.

Liberals usually retort that social policies have other goals besides efficiency, most notably distributive justice. That's true enough, and it's another major reason why we should be profoundly skeptical of unqualified paeans to the private sector. In theory, it might be possible to design social-insurance programs that rely on the private sector but do everything that current programs do. In practice, however, privatized approaches almost invariably change the distribution of who gets the benefits, because they tend to erode common pools and subsidies (indeed, that's what their advocates often want). Yet there's no reason for advocates of social programs to cede the ground on efficiency while raising broader concerns of this sort, because in health and social policy, what is most just is also, in a great many cases, most efficient as well.

Broad-based insurance, after all, is not like widgets. In the fiercely competitive market of economics textbooks, multiple sellers appeal to multiple buyers who have good information about the comparative merits of relatively similar products. Competition squeezes out inefficiencies and yields optimal outcomes. But "markets" for social insurance don't work like this. In particular, information in these markets is both scarce and unequally distributed. This leads, in turn, to all sorts of familiar distortions on both sides of the transaction. Consumers, for example, can saddle private insurers with "adverse selection," which occurs when only high-risk folks buy insurance. The "moral hazard" problem crops up when people are insured against costs that are partially under their control, and then engage in risky behavior. On the producer side, health-insurance companies can take steps to avoid costly patients, and purveyors of retirement products can gull unwary retirees in order to enrich insiders. All of this is why insurance aimed at achieving broad and necessarily social objectives has never worked well, or indeed at all, without some government support and regulation. And it's also why it often makes sense for that support to take the form of public insurance.

Notice I say "insurance." The real issue in the big-ticket areas of U.S. social policy isn't public versus private services. It's public versus private insurance. Medicare buys essentially all its services from the private sector, and no one wants that to change. What some want to change is the degree to which Medicare is in the insurance business, and it's here that all the efficiency advantages of the public sector become clear.

Perhaps the most obvious is the advantage that neither side wants to talk about: compulsion. In the realms of public policy under discussion, however, compulsion is often necessary to make the market work. Think about what would happen if younger and healthier senior citizens were allowed to opt out of Medicare for private coverage: The broad risk-pool of the program would collapse.

Broad programs also have another big advantage: They are ridiculously inexpensive to administer. The typical private health insurer spends about 10 percent of its outlays on administrative costs, including lavish salaries, extensive marketing budgets, and the expense of weeding out sick people. Medicare spends about 2 percent to 3 percent. And Social Security spends just 1 percent. Even low-cost mutual funds have operating costs greater than that.

Here is where critics of social insurance usually pull out their trump card—the claim that social insurance is not just inefficient but unaffordable. Maybe social insurance is, in some sense, efficient; but, these critics argue, its inexorable growth will lead the United States to financial ruin. And it is true that the growth of social insurance isn't slowed by the usual market brake of consumer willingness to pay. (If it were, as just emphasized, it wouldn't work.) But that doesn't mean that there are no brakes at all. If it did, the federal government would now be a leviathan, rather than—as is the case—about as large as it was in the early 1970s. Americans don't decide individually how much of their income to devote to social insurance. But, through their elected representatives, they do decide—in a rough way, of course—how much of the *nation's* income to devote. Spending has trade-offs, in the form of higher taxes and forgone priorities, and those trade-offs are visible in people's tax bills and everyday lives, and in public debate. Anyone who has followed recent political fights knows that politicians are not evading the rising costs of social programs.

What's more, the government has another advantage when it comes to holding down costs: It is a powerful negotiator. Medicare pays doctors and hospitals less per service than does the private sector, and its costs have grown more slowly than private health plans over the last 30 years, despite huge technological advances in care for the aged. Medicaid is even more austere (some might say too austere): Its payments are well below private levels, and it negotiates bargain-basement prices on prescription drugs—something Medicare has been barred from doing. The main reason that Medicaid's costs are rising so rapidly is not that it pays exorbitantly for services but that it covers a lot more children and families than it used to, a good thing in an era in which private coverage has plummeted. Lest government's use of its countervailing power to hold down prices seems illegitimate, it's worth remembering that this is exactly what HMOs and other big health plans were supposed to do—but Medicare and Medicaid do it better.

To be sure, public insurance could still dampen what economists call *dynamic* efficiency, that is, innovation and improvements in quality. But in some areas, like sending out retirement checks, it's not clear where the innovation will come from, while in others, like micromanaging providers, it's not clear that the private sector's "innovations" are really worth emulating. Many of the innovations have to do with discriminating against people at risk of getting sick, micromanaging doctors, and shifting out-of-pocket costs onto patients. Profit-motivated entrepreneurs quickly realize that the most effective way to minimize costs is to get rid of the people most likely to need care. This may be efficient from their perspective, but it's obviously not efficient for society.

Plus, when it comes to the most basic and important form of dynamic efficiency—namely, quality control and improvement—the public sector is arguably as capable as the private sector, and probably more so. As Phillip Longman has argued in an important *Washington Monthly* article on veterans' health care, the Department of Veterans Affairs (VA) has used its central power to create a model evidence-based quality-improvement program. Although the Medicare program still has a long way to go to match the VA, no one disputes that it conducts more rigorous reviews of technology and treatments than private health plans do. Indeed, private plans use Medicare's criteria for covering treatments as their standard of medical necessity. Information about quality is a classic public good—everyone benefits from it, but few have strong incentives to supply it. A large insurer with extensive data on its patients and considerable power to reshape market practice is arguably best positioned to provide such a good.

And this is simply to focus on efficiency. As noted already, the public sector runs circles around the private sector in terms of equity, the other major rationale for social insurance. If the current functions of social insurance were just turned over to the private market, vast numbers of people simply wouldn't be able to afford anything as good as Social Security and Medicare. Conservatives like to argue that everything provided in the Social Security package—the annuity, disability, and life-insurance coverage—could just be purchased in the private market. It could, but at far greater cost for most Americans, and many applicants would be deemed "uninsurable." All of which suggests that the claim that social programs are "inefficient" is often just a politically correct way of saying that they don't follow the usual market logic of giving the most to those with the greatest means.

Liberals frequently stress the equity argument but buy into the efficiency critique because they recognize, correctly, that the market is usually tremendously efficient. But they shouldn't accept that premise when it comes to social insurance. Well-functioning markets are indeed efficient for ordinary commerce, but well-designed social insurance is almost always more efficient than its market counterparts when it comes to dealing with the basic social risks that capitalism invariably produces. It's high time for liberals to say what logic, evidence, and the lived experience of citizens all show: The efficiency attack on social insurance, far from a self-evident truth, is usually an attack on the ideal of social insurance itself—the notion that everyone, regardless of income or likelihood of need, should be covered by a common umbrella of protection. And, ultimately, social insurance is good for the efficiency of society as a whole, not just because it provides much-needed protections at a reasonable cost, but also because it allows people to deal with what FDR once called the "hazards or vicissitudes" of modern capitalism without draconian restraints on the free play of the competitive market.

So the next time someone complains to you about the compassion of the IRS, the efficiency of the post office, all at Pentagon prices, tell them you'd be happy with the efficiency of Social Security, the compassion of Medicare, all at Medicaid prices.

# Income and Wealth Redistribution

*In the nature of things, government might choose to enhance the economic prospects for the many or to safeguard the accumulated wealth held by the few, but frequently the two purposes [are] in irreconcilable conflict.*

—Kevin Phillips

The politicoeconomic system of a society does not simply evolve from random events and aimless choices. The powerful in societies craft policies to accomplish certain ends within the context of historical events, budgetary constraints, and the like. Addressing the issue of inequality, Claude S. Fischer and his colleagues say:

> *The answer to the question of why societies vary in their structure of rewards is . . . political. . . . By loosening markets or regulating them, by providing services to all citizens or rationing them according to income, by subsidizing some groups more than others, societies, through their politics, build their ladders [the height and breadth of the rungs of the stratification system]. To be sure, historical and external constraints deny full freedom of action, but a substantial freedom of action remains. (Fischer et al., 1996:8)*

The United States has the most unfair distribution of wealth and income in the industrialized world, and the gap is growing. Fischer and his colleagues argue that the inequality in the United States is, in significant measure, the historical result of policy choices U.S. citizens—or at least their representatives—have made. In the United States, the result is a society that is distinctly unequal (Fischer et. al., 1996:8). In other words, the United States' level of inequality is *by design* (Fischer et al., 1996:125). This design begins with policies regarding taxation. To tax the wealthy at a higher rate than the less affluent lessens inequality, as do policies that provide a floor on the wages of the working poor. These efforts occurred during the first two decades of the 1900s and during the Great Depression. Generally, though, policies have favored the wealthy and increased the inequality gap.

## INCOME AND WEALTH MALDISTRIBUTION
## AT THE BEGINNING OF THE TWENTY-FIRST CENTURY

Let's begin by looking at some representative facts about the current maldistribution of wealth and income in the United States.

- The total net worth of the four hundred richest people in 2003 was $955 billion. At the other extreme 34 million were living below the poverty line.
- The median Chief Executive Office (CEO) pay at a large company in 2002 was $1,017 per hour (Strauss and Hansen, 2003), whereas the minimum wage was $5.15 an hour for millions of workers. The average CEO annual compensation of *Fortune 500* companies was $37.5 million in 2002, whereas the average worker's annual salary for all companies was $38,000, or a ratio of 1,000 to 1 (Americans for Democratic Action, 2004).
- Comparing 1998 to 2001, the net worth of families in the top 10 percent of income jumped 69 percent to $833,600, whereas the net worth of families in the lowest fifth rose by 24 percent to $7,900 (Andrews, 2003).
- The top 1 percent of the wealthiest people has more financial wealth than the bottom 90 percent of Americans combined (Nader, 2000). Put another way, the richest 13,000 families possess a net worth equivalent to the combined assets owned by the country's 20 million poorest families (Lapham, 2003).
- "In 1992 it took the combined wages of 287,400 retail clerks at, say, Wal-Mart, to equal the pay of the top 400 [individuals with the highest income]. By 2000 it required the combined pay of 504,600 retail clerks to match the pay of the top 400" (Barlett and Steele, 2004:42).
- In 2001 the median net worth for families of color was $17,100, whereas it was $120,400 for white families (United for a Fair Economy, 2004). In terms of income, black per capita income in 2003 was 62 percent of that of whites, "mirroring the 1787 Constitutional formula that counted slaves as three-fifths of a free person in determining each State's apportionment of taxes and Congressional representatives" (Sklar, 2003).

One measure of the magnitude of income concentration (inequality) is the Gini index. In 2003 the Gini index was 0.464 for the United States, which was the highest (indicating the greatest degree of inequality) of all rich countries. The Gini index has been rising—in 1970 it was 0.394 for households, in 1980 it was 0.403, in 1990 it was 0.428, and in 2000 it was 0.462 (U.S. Census Bureau, 2004).

The inequality gap has grown dramatically for a number of reasons. The gain at the top reflects the increased tax benefits received by the affluent from changing tax laws such as gradual repeal of the inheritance tax, reducing tax rates on unearned income such as dividends and capital gains, and reducing tax rates on people with high incomes. The plight of workers has worsened because of the exporting of jobs and subsequent downsizing of domestic workforces, which resulted in a decline in union membership. Organized labor, which acted as a counterweight to the power of corporations for nearly thirty years following World War II lost its ability to negotiate from strength (*Dollars and Sense* and United for a Fair Economy, 2004:2).

The plight of the poor and the near-poor has declined because since the mid-1970s there has been a gradual dismantling of parts of the New Deal and Great Society legacies (e.g., elimination of Aid to Families with Dependent Children; reduced monies for food stamps, Pell grants, and housing vouchers; and inadequate funding for Head Start). These declining social services ensure that those at the bottom of the socioeconomic ladder stay there. The efforts to starve or eliminate social programs by conservatives have accelerated during President George W. Bush's administration.

Chuck Collins adds two other government actions that have worsened inequality (Collins, 2004). First, there is the plummeting (in purchasing power) minimum wage, which we will consider shortly. Second, the federal government's emphasis has been on taxing wages, not wealth. Over the past thirty years, the federal tax burden has shifted from wealth to wages. Since 1980 the payroll tax rate has risen 25 percent while the top tax rates on investment income have fallen by 31 percent and taxes on large inheritances have been cut by 79 percent.

## PROGRESSIVE PROGRAMS TO REDUCE INEQUALITY IN THE PAST

Forms of socioeconomic inequality have been present in all human societies. In some societies the gap between the poorest and wealthiest has been enormous. Other societies have found ways of narrowing the gap, either by deliberate social policies and practices that help the less fortunate or by methods of restraining the accumulation of great wealth. Economic inequality in the United States has not always been as pronounced as it is now thanks to occasional federal policies to help the less fortunate gain the possibility of upward mobility. For example, Abraham Lincoln signed the Homestead Act in 1862. This act turned over 270 million acres to settlers, each of whom was given ownership to 160 acres if they were at least twenty-one years of age, paid a filing fee of $18, lived on the land for five years, and built a house on it, dug a well, and plowed ten acres. Similarly, after World War II, the government expanded opportunities for advancement with the G.I. Bill, low-interest loans, and subsidies for small-business development. Our focus in this section, however, will be on three federal programs: the progressive income tax, the estate tax, and various attempts to assist low-wage workers.

### The Progressive Federal Income Tax

Taxes can be divided roughly into two types: progressive and regressive. A progressive tax structure is one in which one's tax liability as a fraction of income rises with income. In other words, the higher the income, the greater the tax rate. This type of taxation redistributes income by taking more from the affluent and therefore is favored by progressives. A regressive tax, by using the same rate for everyone, regardless of income level, takes a larger proportion of the income from the less affluent than from the affluent, thus increasing the inequality gap. Income taxes at the federal and state levels are progressive; states and municipalities tend to raise income through regressive taxes such as a sales tax or user fees.

Congress enacted the nation's first income tax to finance the Civil War. It was a progressive income tax ranging from 3 to 5 percent. It was phased out by 1872. In 1908 Theodore Roosevelt endorsed both an income tax and an inheritance tax, thus becoming the first president to openly propose that the political power of government be used to redistribute wealth. President William Howard Taft in 1909 proposed amending the Constitution to impose a federal income tax. In 1913 the 16th Amendment had the approval of the required three-fourths of the states. Support for the amendment came from a coalition of progressives alarmed by the rapid concentration of industrial wealth, from the West and South where incomes of $5,000 or more were comparatively few, and from some conservatives who believed that the government needed a reliable system of revenue to cope with national emergencies. After the passage of the amendment, a special session of Congress quickly passed an income tax with a rate of 1 percent on taxable net income above $3,000 ($4,000 for married couples), less deductions and exemptions. The rate rose to 7 percent on incomes above $500,000.

The United States has had a progressive income tax continuously since 1913. The highest tax rate rose from the original 7 percent to as high as 92 percent in 1952 and 1953. Since then, it has declined to around 34 percent. In actuality, however, it is not as progressive as it appears. For example, the tax base—the income that is taxed—is reduced by an array of adjustments, deductions, and exclusions (e.g., federal tax exemption from interest on state and local bonds, partial exclusion of long-term capital gains) (Siemrod, 2002).

### The Inheritance (Estate) Tax

As noted earlier, the income and wealth disparities in U.S. society make it the most unequal among the industrialized nations of the world (the following data are from Gates and Collins, 2002:15). In 1870, the top 1 percent of households had an estimated 27 percent of the wealth. By 1912, the year before the progressive income tax became law, the share owned by the top 1 percent had jumped to 56 percent. From the Great Depression through the two decades after World War II the inequality gap lessened with federal policies that favored shared prosperity and equality of opportunity. That trend reversed under President Reagan and subsequent presidents, resulting in today's inequality gap showing the wealthiest 1 percent owning over 38 percent of all private wealth.

The question is: Should the wealthy be able to pass all of their wealth to their heirs, or should a portion be paid to the government through an estate tax? If the goal is the redistribution of wealth, as progressives favor, then an estate tax is the answer. Conservatives argue, to the contrary, that the wealthy deserve their wealth, have already paid taxes on it, and on death, it remains, rightfully, to their heirs. This argument contradicts the fundamental values that conservatives claim to admire such as individual initiative, individual achievement, and equality of opportunity.

The federal government has enacted estate taxes sporadically to pay for various wars, nullifying them after each crisis. But in 1916 an estate tax was inaugurated in response to the vast fortunes amassed by a handful of robber barons and industrialists. Gates and Collins state:

> When the estate tax was established in 1916, our nation was deep in struggle over the values of equality of opportunity versus heredity privilege. The accumulation of great wealth and the power of the great trusts lead to questions about the direction of our society. One of the expressed intentions of the tax, as articulated by Theodore Roosevelt, was to break up "those fortunes swollen beyond all healthy limits." (2002:13)

The estate tax has been in effect continuously since 1916, although the rates have changed. In 2002, a conservative Congress and president raised the estate level when the tax begins from $675,000 (affecting fewer than 2 percent of estates) to $1 million in 2003 and up to $3.5 million in 2009, and then abolishing it altogether in 2010 (a loss in government revenue of an estimated $400 billion) and reinstating it in 2011. President George W. Bush, conservative members of Congress, and wealthy private citizens seek to make the elimination of the estate tax permanent. But as esteemed economist Paul Volcker has argued: "What strikes me as insupportable—insupportable as a matter of fiscal and economic analysis and insupportable in terms of a simple fairness and traditional American values—is to abolish the estate tax altogether" (Volcker, Foreword in Gates and Collins, 2002:xiii).

## Assistance to Low-Wage Workers: Minimum Wage, the Living Wage, and the Earned Income Tax Credit

The government instituted a minimum wage in the Fair Labor Standards Act of 1938 at $0.25 an hour. At first, the minimum wage applied only to employees engaged in inter-state commerce or in the production of goods for interstate commerce. Over time it has been extended to include retail and service employees, and workers in construction, transit, health, schools, hotels, and restaurants. As the name implies, the minimum wage sets the wage floor. The assumption behind it is that everyone should have the opportunity to earn a decent wage. "Furthermore, no employer should be allowed to unreasonably profit by exploiting the lack of negotiating power of low-wage workers. The free market fails to set a fair price when one side holds all the bargaining chips" (Chapman and Ettlinger, 2004:3).

Over 2.1 million workers earn today's federal minimum wage of $5.15 per hour, an amount that has not been raised by Congress since 1997. Since the minimum wage does not have a cost-of-living adjustment, its value declines. The 1968 minimum wage of $1.60 ($8.68 in 2004 dollars) was 86 percent of the amount needed to raise a family of four above the poverty line. Today's minimum wage is only 61 percent of the amount needed to raise a family of four above the poverty line. As a result, the plight of poor workers and their families becomes more and more grim as Congress refuses to raise the minimum wage. For example, in 2004, in only four of the nation's 3,066 counties could someone working full-time at the federal minimum wage afford to pay rent and utilities on a one-bedroom apartment (National Low Income Housing Coalition study, reported in Armas, 2004).

Progressives in Congress have tried to raise the minimum wage many times, but con-servatives have prevailed. The latest attempt by Democrats (March 2005) to raise the mini-mum wage to $7.25 over two years was defeated by the Republican majority. Minimum wage opponents (and some of them do not want a minimum wage at all) argue that a rise in the minimum wage would result in two negative outcomes. First, it will hurt the economy by increasing the costs to consumers. Second, it will harm the employment prospects of low-wage workers. But, as economists Chapman and Ettlinger state, "there is mounting economic evidence [that] refutes those claims" (2004:1).

Although the federal government has balked at raising the minimum, some states have raised the minimum wage. In 2003 some thirteen states had minimum wages higher than the federal level (with two states, Alaska and Washington, over $7). Also, a number of counties and municipalities have opted for what is called a "living wage." A living wage is what a full-time worker would need to support a family above the poverty line, or about $9.10 an hour in today's dollars, well above the federal minimum wage of $5.15. Balti-more, in 1994, was the first municipality to set a living wage.

ACORN (the Association of Community Organizations for Reform Now) is the nation's largest grassroots organization working on behalf of low and moderate income people in sixty-five cities (ACORN, 2004). Among it projects, ACORN has taken the lead nationally in campaigns for a living wage, winning such ordinances in cities such as St.

Louis, St. Paul, Minneapolis, Boston, Oakland, Denver, Chicago, New Orleans, Baltimore, San Francisco, and New York City. Currently, some 115 cities and counties have passed living wage laws.

Living wage requirements serve several important societal goals. First, they place an importance on the value of work by making work pay. Second, they remove people from the physical misery and social stigma of poverty. Third, they reduce the need and cost of subsidizing those below the poverty line. Fourth, they put more purchasing power in the hands of more consumers, which benefits the business community and the community tax base.

The main objection to living wage ordinances is that they will result in job losses because it is too costly to employers. However, a study by the nonpartisan Public Policy Institute examined the consequences in thirty-six cities with such laws. It found that slight job losses caused by the law were more than compensated by the decrease in family poverty (reported in AFL-CIO, 2000).

Another strategy to help the working poor is the Earned Income Tax Credit (EITC), which reduces the tax burden on the working poor. It was created by Congress in 1975 to offset the Social Security payroll tax and to make work more attractive than welfare. The credit provides a dollar-for-dollar reduction in one's federal taxes. In 2005, for example, to qualify one's 2004 adjusted gross income had to be less than $34,458 ($35,458 if married) with two or more children down to $11,490 if no children. If qualified, the maximum credit was $4,300 with two or more children, $2,604 with one child, and $390 with no children (Block, 2005). For minimum wage workers who do not owe any taxes, it provides additional income.

In sum, social policy is about design, setting goals, and determining the means to achieve them. Should we create and invest in policies and programs to insulate citizens from poverty, or should the market economy sort people into winners and losers based on their abilities, efforts, and the luck or misfortune of the families into which they were born and raised? During the Progressive Era in the first two decades of the twentieth century and Franklin D. Roosevelt's New Deal policies in the 1930s and 1940s, when progressive policies held national favor, the federal government favored a redistribution of wealth. At other times when conservatives were in power, the government has resisted efforts to reduce inequality. In fact, inequality was exacerbated during those periods. Since the middle 1970s the trend, accelerating recently, has been to minimize help to the less fortunate, opting rather for Adam Smith's "invisible hand" of market forces to equitably allocate economic rewards as each individual acts in his or her own interest. The result is an ever more unequal society—more people living in desperate poverty while a privileged few enjoy unbelievable extremes of wealth.

## REFERENCES

ACORN. (2004). "Introduction to ACORN's Living Wage Web Site": www.livingwagecampaign.org.
AFL-CIO Department of Public Policy. (2000). "Living Wage Laws: Answers to Frequently Asked Questions." Washington, DC: AFL-CIO.
Americans for Democratic Action. (2004). *Income and Inequality: Millions Left Behind,* 3rd ed. Washington, DC: Author.
Andrews, Edmund L. (2003). "Gap for Haves, Have-Nots Grew as '90s Economic Bubble Burst." *Denver Post* (February 2):36A.

Armas, Genaro C. (2004). "Minimum Wage Can't Cover Rent Cost." Associated Press. (December 21).

Barlett, Donald L., and Steele, James B. (2004). "Has Your Life Become a Game of Chance?" *Time* (February 2):42–44.

Block, Sandra. (2005). "Complicated Tax Credit's Worth Hassle." *USA Today* (February 1):3B.

Chapman, Jeff. (2003). "States Move on Minimum Wage." *EPI Issue Brief* 195 (June 11). Washington, DC: Economic Policy Institute.

Chapman, Jeff, and Ettlinger, Michael. (2004). "The Who and Why of the Minimum Wage." *EPI Issue Brief* 201 (August 6):1–7. Washington, DC: Economic Policy Institute.

Collins, Chuck. (2004). "The Visible Hand: Seven Government Actions That Have Worsened Inequality." In *Dollars and Sense* and United for a Fair Economy (eds.) *The Wealth Inequality Reader* (pp. 24–31). Cambridge, MA: Economic Affairs Bureau.

*Dollars and Sense* and United for a Fair Economy (eds.). (2004). *The Wealth Inequality Reader.* Cambridge, MA: Economic Affairs Bureau.

Fischer, Claude S., Hout, Michael, Jankowski, Martin Sanchez, Lucas, Samuel R., Swidler, Ann, and Voss, Kim. (1996). *Inequality by Design: Cracking the Bell Curve Myth.* Princeton, NJ: Princeton University Press.

Gates, William H., Sr., and Collins, Chuck. (2002). *Wealth and Our Commonwealth: Why America Should Tax Accumulated Fortunes.* Boston: Beacon Press.

Lapham, Lewis H. (2003). "Notebook." *Harper's* 306 (January):9–11.

Nader, Ralph. (2000). "Closing the Democracy Gap." *Progressive Populist* (April 15):13–14.

Siemrod, Joel B. (2002). "Progressive Taxes." *The Concise Encyclopedia of Economics:* www.econlib.org/library/Enc/ProgressiveTaxes.html.

Sklar, Holly. (2003). "Racial Gaps Still Wide This King Holiday." Knight Ridder/Tribune News Service (January 15).

Strauss, Gary, and Hansen, Barbara. (2003, March 31). "Bubble Hasn't Burst Yet on CEO Salaries Despite the Times." *USA Today,* p. 1B.

United for a Fair Economy. (2004). "Wealth Inequality by the Numbers." *Dollars and Sense* 251 (January/February):20–21.

U.S. Census Bureau. (2004). "Historical Income Tables: Income Inequality": http:www.census.gov/hhes/income/histinc/ie6.html.

# 9

# The Death of Horatio Alger

*PAUL KRUGMAN*

*Economist Paul Krugman argues that U.S. society has less upward social mobility than is commonly believed. Actually, he contends, the stratification system is becoming more rigid because of government policies that benefit the wealthy and make it more difficult for people with low incomes to get ahead.*

The other day I found myself reading a leftist rag that made outrageous claims about America. It said that we are becoming a society in which the poor tend to stay poor, no matter how hard they work; in which sons are much more likely to inherit the socio-economic status of their father than they were a generation ago.

The name of the leftist rag? *Business Week,* which published an article titled "Waking Up From the American Dream." The article summarizes recent research showing that social mobility in the United States (which was never as high as legend had it) has declined considerably over the past few decades. If you put that research together with other research that shows a drastic increase in income and wealth inequality, you reach an uncomfortable conclusion: America looks more and more like a class-ridden society.

And guess what? Our political leaders are doing everything they can to fortify class inequality, while denouncing anyone who complains—or even points out what is happening—as a practitioner of "class warfare."

Let's talk first about the facts on income distribution. Thirty years ago we were a relatively middle-class nation. It had not always been thus: Gilded Age America was a highly unequal society, and it stayed that way through the 1920s. During the 1930s and '40s, however, America experienced what the economic historians Claudia Goldin and Robert Margo have dubbed the Great Compression: a drastic narrowing of income gaps, probably as a result of New Deal policies. And the new economic order persisted for more than a generation: Strong unions; taxes on inherited wealth, corporate profits and high incomes; close public scrutiny of corporate management—all helped to keep income gaps relatively small. The economy was hardly egalitarian, but a generation ago the gross inequalities of the 1920s seemed very distant.

*Source:* "The Death of Horatio Alger" by Paul Krugman, reprinted with permission from the January 5, 2004, issue of *The Nation.* For subscription information, call 1-800-333-8536. Portions of each week's *Nation* magazine can be accessed at http://www.thenation.com.

Now they're back. According to estimates by the economists Thomas Piketty and Emmanuel Saez—confirmed by data from the Congressional Budget Office—between 1973 and 2000 the average real income of the bottom 90 percent of American taxpayers actually fell by 7 percent. Meanwhile, the income of the top 1 percent rose by 148 percent, the income of the top 0.1 percent rose by 343 percent and the income of the top 0.01 percent rose 599 percent. (Those numbers exclude capital gains, so they're not an artifact of the stock-market bubble.) The distribution of income in the United States has gone right back to Gilded Age levels of inequality.

Never mind, say the apologists, who churn out papers with titles like that of a 2001 Heritage Foundation piece, "Income Mobility and the Fallacy of Class-Warfare Arguments." America, they say, isn't a caste society—people with high incomes this year may have low incomes next year and vice versa, and the route to wealth is open to all. That's where those commies at *Business Week* come in: As they point out (and as economists and sociologists have been pointing out for some time), America actually is more of a caste society than we like to think. And the caste lines have lately become a lot more rigid.

The myth of income mobility has always exceeded the reality: As a general rule, once they've reached their 30s, people don't move up and down the income ladder very much. Conservatives often cite studies like a 1992 report by Glenn Hubbard, a Treasury official under the elder Bush who later became chief economic adviser to the younger Bush, that purport to show large numbers of Americans moving from low-wage to high-wage jobs during their working lives. But what these studies measure, as the economist Kevin Murphy put it, is mainly "the guy who works in the college bookstore and has a real job by his early 30s." Serious studies that exclude this sort of pseudo-mobility show that inequality in average incomes over long periods isn't much smaller than inequality in annual incomes.

It is true, however, that America was once a place of substantial intergenerational mobility: Sons often did much better than their fathers. A classic 1978 survey found that among adult men whose fathers were in the bottom 25 percent of the population as ranked by social and economic status, 23 percent had made it into the top 25 percent. In other words, during the first thirty years or so after World War II, the American dream of upward mobility was a real experience for many people.

Now for the shocker: The *Business Week* piece cites a new survey of today's adult men, which finds that this number has dropped to only 10 percent. That is, over the past generation upward mobility has fallen drastically. Very few children of the lower class are making their way to even moderate affluence. This goes along with other studies indicating that rags-to-riches stories have become vanishingly rare, and that the correlation between fathers' and sons' incomes has risen in recent decades. In modern America, it seems, you're quite likely to stay in the social and economic class into which you were born.

*Business Week* attributes this to the "Wal-Martization" of the economy, the proliferation of dead-end, low-wage jobs and the disappearance of jobs that provide entry to the middle class. That's surely part of the explanation. But public policy plays a role—and will, if present trends continue, play an even bigger role in the future.

Put it this way: Suppose that you actually liked a caste society, and you were seeking ways to use your control of the government to further entrench the advantages of the haves against the have-nots. What would you do?

One thing you would definitely do is get rid of the estate tax, so that large fortunes can be passed on to the next generation. More broadly, you would seek to reduce tax rates both on corporate profits and on unearned income such as dividends and capital gains, so that those with large accumulated or inherited wealth could more easily accumulate even more. You'd also try to create tax shelters mainly useful for the rich. And more broadly still, you'd try to reduce tax rates on people with high incomes, shifting the burden to the payroll tax and other revenue sources that bear most heavily on people with lower incomes.

Meanwhile, on the spending side, you'd cut back on healthcare for the poor, on the quality of public education and on state aid for higher education. This would make it more difficult for people with low incomes to climb out of their difficulties and acquire the education essential to upward mobility in the modern economy.

And just to close off as many routes to upward mobility as possible, you'd do everything possible to break the power of unions, and you'd privatize government functions so that well-paid civil servants could be replaced with poorly paid private employees.

It all sounds sort of familiar, doesn't it?

Where is this taking us? Thomas Piketty, whose work with Saez has transformed our understanding of income distribution, warns that current policies will eventually create "a class of rentiers in the U.S., whereby a small group of wealthy but untalented children controls vast segments of the US economy and penniless, talented children simply can't compete." If he's right—and I fear that he is—we will end up suffering not only from injustice, but from a vast waste of human potential.

Goodbye, Horatio Alger. And goodbye, American Dream.

## 10

# Tax the Plutocrats!

### GAR ALPEROVITZ

*Gar Alperovitz, professor of political economy at the University of Mary-*
*land, points out that there has been an extraordinary upward redistribu-*
*tion of income in recent decades. Since the affluent have more than their*
*share, the solution is to repeal the tax cuts given to them since 2001,*
*increase the progressivity of the income tax, and, most significant, institute*
*a tax on wealth.*

It's is time to confront the central obstacle blocking a new progressive politics: the Democratic Party's abject fear of the truth that new taxes are going to be needed if the party is
ever to offer—and finance—a dramatic program capable of mobilizing large numbers of
working Americans, white, black and brown. The way forward is to go on the offensive by
sharply delineating a strategy targeting America's plutocratic top 1–2 percent elite, plus
the corporations they largely own. Changes in income and wealth patterns in recent years
make it possible to do this without simultaneously alienating middle-income and middle-
class suburban voters.

A progressive program worth fighting for would begin with fixing—improving, not
reducing—Social Security; it would move on to prescription drugs, major reform of the
healthcare system, support for broad-based college tuition assistance, serious day-care provision, an expansion of the earned-income tax credit. Public transportation, environmental
and other infrastructure needs are also huge, between $60 billion and $100 billion a year
in recent estimates. A serious effort might also add some tax relief for middle- and low-
income families.

The first step is to stop compromising at the outset, thus eliminating any hope of offering something powerful that we can mobilize around over the long haul. Progressives must
challenge the idea that the United States, the richest nation in the world, must always be the
poor sister among the advanced nations—that our nonmilitary public sector, at 29.7 percent
of GDP, must always lag behind Britain's (35.8 percent), Germany's (43 percent), France's
(44.8 percent) and, of course, that of countries like Sweden, at 50 percent.

*Source:* "Tax the Plutocrats!" by Gar Alperovitz, reprinted with permission from the January 27, 2003, issue of
*The Nation.* For subscription information, call 1-800-333-8536. Portions of each week's *Nation* magazine can be
accessed at http://www.thenation.com.

Most Democrats have been afraid to demand such a program—and for good reason: They have been unable or unwilling to answer the obvious question of where the money will come from. In the near term, deficit spending is a reasonable, indeed, inevitable option—both to move the economy out of the recession and to solve pressing public problems (beginning with the $67 billion state revenue shortfall). Ultimately, however, progressives must confront the tax issue.

Until recently, the Democratic Party, as a party, has been almost totally silent on taxes—cravenly so: Twenty-eight House Democrats and twelve Democratic senators voted for the Bush tax cuts. For the most part, the party has been on the defensive—reacting, after the fact, to each new Bush tax-cutting initiative. Even as Democrats fussed over how to respond to the last Bush offensive, the Administration has revved up its new campaign for greater elite and corporate tax cuts—and, amazingly, is now arguing that the poor are undertaxed. (Just ignore Social Security taxes, the most regressive part of the system, ignore the huge redistribution of income in favor of the rich in recent years, scrap all thought of capacity to pay as an element in tax policy, etc.)

If Democrats are unable to redefine the long-term politics of taxation, they will always be on the defensive, trying to play catch-up in response to each new right-wing initiative. To be sure, some members of Congress have put together a short-term stimulus package involving tax rebates, and some liberals have urged rescinding the Bush top income and estate reductions. But even if this were done, it would only take us back to where we were when Bush took office—which, in turn, would provide little capacity for Democrats to go on the offensive with a positive, longer-term program capable of exciting the basic Democratic constituencies.

New Democrats are probably right that it is politically impossible to tax the white suburban middle class much further. They are wrong, however, to suggest that this is the end of the story. The place where the money can—and must—be found is where it is concentrated: at the very top and with the corporations. This also defines a sharp and very clear political target—one that ultimately puts the other side on the defensive.

There has been an extraordinary upward redistribution of income in recent decades, especially at the very top: The top 1 percent garnered almost 15 percent of the nation's income for itself in 1998—up from just over 8 percent in 1980. This is more income than was received by the more than 100 million people in the bottom 40 percent of the population taken together!

Currently, the top marginal tax rate is 38.6 percent, scheduled to drop to 35 percent by 2006. The dramatic capacity of elites to take care of themselves is etched in the changes they have secured over the past half-century. The top marginal rate was 91 percent to and through the Eisenhower years, indeed continuing up to 1964; 70 percent from 1965 to 1981; 50 percent from 1982 through 1986 (for the first Reagan Administration). If those earning $1 million or more in 1999 (a recent year for which data are available) were to face the same effective rate as top elites faced in the mid-1950s, tax revenues could increase by $130 billion (this would involve raising taxes on only slightly more than one-tenth of 1 percent of all households).

In the Eisenhower era, corporations paid an average 25 percent of the federal tax bill; they paid only 10 percent in 2000 and 7 percent in 2001. The effective tax rate on corporate income amounted to 47 percent in 1960; it is only 35 percent today (before tax credits).

Closing the most egregious shelters and returning to the 1960 tax rate could increase annual revenues by $110 billion.

A progressive political strategy that sharply defined the difference between the very top of the income and wealth distribution and the vast majority could benefit the bottom 98 percent of society—i.e., those with incomes of less than roughly $200,000.

The conventional wisdom is that you can't tax the rich. However, something profound has happened to America in recent years. The super-elite—the people Kevin Phillips and Paul Krugman now term the new "plutocracy"—live in a very, very different world from most Americans, and in a radically different culture. It is a world where homes cost $5–10 million and where $5,000 grills, $3,000 alligator-skin shoes, $17,500 Patek Philippe wrist-watches, $63,000 Lexus LX470 sport-utility vehicles and $14,000 Hermès Kelly handbags are commonplace. At the height of the 1998–99 stock market, Phillips observes, "vanity and consumption moved toward a new post-Veblen fulfillment. . . . Behind an increasingly Latin American array of gates, guards, walls, and distance, the scarcely visible displays included helicopter delivery of meals from one's favorite Manhattan, Los Angeles, or Florida restaurant. . . ." A tour guide he cites notes: "Some trees now gracing Hamptons estates have been driven down from the Pacific Northwest in refrigerated tractor-trailers, and some have been planted with the aid of military-size Sikorsky helicopters to obviate the necessity of rutting the lawns with wheel tracks."

Most people have not caught up with what Krugman terms "the tectonic shifts" that have taken place: "The rich have always been different from you and me, but they are far more different now than they were not long ago—indeed, they are as different now as they were when F. Scott Fitzgerald made his famous remark." In the past, he observes, we were "a middle-class society. But that was another country."

The world of the new plutocracy is also a world of routine corruption and side deals in which millions of dollars are casually shifted into the pockets of the elites as part of "business as usual" corporate practice. The retirement package that GE's Jack Welch negotiated included an $86,000-a-year retainer for consulting services, use of GE corporate aircraft, a Manhattan apartment (including wine, laundry services, newspapers, flowers, condominium fees, cook, wait and housekeeping staff, postage and restaurant charges in the building)—plus tickets to sporting and cultural events.

Polls strongly suggest that the plutocracy is vulnerable to challenge. In 1998 Gallup found that 63 percent agreed with the statement that "money and wealth in this country should be more evenly distributed." Roughly seven in ten also complained that "the rich just get richer while the poor get poorer." Even in the period shortly after 9/11, when patriotism obscured many other concerns, the number who held this view fell only one percent, to 69 percent. Recent Harris polls have regularly found that an extraordinary 80–87 percent of the public believe big companies have "too much power and influence in Washington." The Enron and related accounting scandals only added to longstanding and deeply rooted public distrust. As Century Foundation senior fellow Ruy Teixeira has shown, we have reached a nadir in public opinion of large corporations: One 2002 poll found that only 15 percent felt a "great deal" or "quite a lot" of confidence in big business—the lowest number since pollsters started asking the question in 1986. Another showed that 38 percent saw big business as the "biggest threat to America's future," up from 22 percent as recently as October 2000 and again the highest level ever recorded for this question (asked since 1965).

Jeffrey Garten, dean of the Yale School of Management and a former Under Secretary of Commerce, follows the data closely. Hardly a populist, Garten believes citizen anger is ultimately likely to produce a backlash "as radical and as prolonged as the backlash against unbridled corporate power that took place during the first forty years of this century."

Two issues need to be sharpened over time: The first is "public need versus private greed." The second is simple fairness. A comprehensive, long-term tax program focused on the plutocracy and corporations and that aimed to go on the offensive might include:

- Repeal of the Bush tax cuts at the top.
- A return, ultimately, to the 50 percent top marginal tax rates of the first Reagan Administration.
- Corporate taxes equivalent to those in force during the Nixon Administration.
- A wealth tax of at least 1 percent.

Note especially the tax on wealth. Wealth is far, far more concentrated than income. A mere 1 percent of Americans owns just under 50 percent of financial wealth; a mere 5 percent owns almost 70 percent of financial wealth. Americans with incomes of more than $1 million (roughly 0.1 percent of all taxpayers) made more money from stock sales than the rest of the nation combined in recent years.

Most Western European nations tax wealth—in Sweden, the highest annual rate is 3 percent; at the low end of the scale is Switzerland, with a tax of only one third of a percent. The United States, however, for the most part only taxes the kind of wealth most people own—their home. Moreover, we tax the total value of the home even though most people actually own only a part of the house—i.e., their net property value after subtracting the mortgage amount they owe. We simply do not directly tax ownership of the kind of wealth which is concentrated in the hands of the plutocracy: stocks and bonds.

Repealing the Bush tax cuts would return $86.5 billion from the top 5 percent annually when fully phased in—or close to $800 billion over ten years if, as is likely, the tax cut is made permanent. Estimates by Brendan Leary of the University of Maryland suggest that returning to a tax structure similar to that of the first Reagan Administration could potentially capture an additional $90 billion from the top 2 percent. If corporate tax rates were returned to Eisenhower levels, tax revenues could increase by roughly $110 billion. A 1 percent tax on wealth (with a $1 million exemption) could bring in $90 billion a year. (A 3 percent wealth tax with a $500,000 exemption could generate up to $290 billion.)

A long-term progressive strategy would also aim to build new ways to structure the ownership of wealth—for example, by offering Individual Development Accounts, through which the government would directly match the savings of the poor; and by introducing government-funded $5,000 capital grants at birth that, with additional annual federal contributions, could build a capital fund of roughly $50,000 for every individual by age 18. Wealth-holding to benefit "small publics" is also important: For example, federal legislation has helped create 11,000 Employee Stock Ownership Plans and related efforts, many of which are moving toward substantial, indeed, often majority-worker ownership of significant assets in their firms.

The key to winning acceptance of a bold program is to build support—rather than simply react to polls that register "something" about public attitudes before and in the absence of a serious effort to dramatize an alternative. Conservatives have understood this all along:

Ten years ago few would have believed privatization of Social Security was an idea that could ever be taken seriously—or, for that matter, more recently Bush's deficit-producing tax cuts for the rich. Conservatives created what support such ideas have by taking a clear stand and then arguing forcefully for it.

A progressive strategy that went on the offensive to mobilize broad support would put those who attempt to protect the plutocracy and the corporations on the defensive. It would also help redefine the political spectrum as a whole: So long as the Democratic Party fails to take a clear economic stand, "faux-populist" conservatives will exploit cultural and racial issues to divide and conquer the majority. The bottom-line question to confront, however, is: Over the long haul is there any other way to achieve the policies most progressives in their hearts know are right?

# 11

# The Consequences of Concentrated Wealth

*WILLIAM H. GATES, SR. AND CHUCK COLLINS*

*The inequality gap—the economic distance between the rich and the poor—has negative consequences for society especially by endangering democracy, limiting equality of opportunity, undermining economic prosperity, and eroding society's social solidarity. To reduce the inequality gap, the authors argue for an estate tax. Ironically, the senior author of this excerpt is the father of Bill Gates, the richest person on the planet.*

Why does inequality matter? Some commentators have made the case that we should focus our efforts on alleviating poverty, not inequality. For this reason, a tremendous amount of public and charitable resources go toward lifting the floor, building pathways out of poverty for individuals and communities. But inequality does matter, because concentrations of wealth and power distort our democratic institutions and economic system and undermine social cohesion.

## CONCENTRATED WEALTH AND DEMOCRACY

If concentrations of wealth did not translate into political power and influence in our democracy, they might be less troubling. But unfortunately they go hand in hand. As Supreme Court Justice Louis Brandeis observed a century ago, "We can have concentrated wealth in the hands of a few or we can have democracy. But we cannot have both."[1]

Once a household accumulates wealth above a certain threshold, say $15 million, it has moved beyond the point of meeting its needs and aspirations of itself and its heirs. Such households are now in the nation's top quarter of the richest 1 percent of households and stand atop a global pinnacle of wealth almost too enormous to contemplate. By the late 1990s, there were an estimated forty thousand households with more than $25 million and five thousand with over $100 million.[2] They may be asking themselves, as Bud Fox queried speculator Gordon Gekko in the 1987 film *Wall Street*, "How many yachts can you water-ski behind?"

The amassing of great wealth, above a certain point, becomes an accumulation of social and political power. This is not inherently evil power, as the legacy of Carnegie's

*Source:* Excerpt from *Wealth and Our Commonwealth: Why America Should Tax Accumulated Fortunes* by William H. Gates, Sr. and Chuck Collins, pp. 17–25. Boston: Beacon Press.

libraries and Rockefeller's contributions to medical research attest. But in a democratic, self-governing society, we should be concerned with the potential threat that concentrated wealth poses to our democratic institutions. Political scientist Samuel Huntington observed that in the United States "money becomes evil not when it is used to buy goods but when it is used to buy power. . . . Economic inequalities became evil when they are translated into political inequalities."[3]

Our democracy is now at risk because of the enormous power of accumulated wealth. The practices of government, administration, and law writing have been molded by the money power of the few, against the interests of the many. For example, the concentration of media ownership narrows and cheapens public discourse. When Ben Bagdikian wrote *The Media Monopoly* in 1983, about fifty media conglomerates controlled more than half of all broadcast media, newspapers, magazines, video, radio, music, publishing and film in the country. Today, fewer than ten multinational media conglomerates dominate the American mass media landscape.[4]

A more publicized example of the influence of money and power is how we finance our elections and write our laws. Both the high cost of running for elected office and the enormous amount of resources devoted to lobbying underscore the quantum leap in financial influence that has changed our national politics. In 2000, the average winner of a Senate election spent $7.7 million; the average winner of a House election spent $842,000.[5] Less than 1 percent of the population make contributions of two hundred dollars or more to candidates; half the donors have incomes over $250,000 per year.[6] These contributions clearly have an influence on public policy, particularly on roll call votes on issues that do not attract significant publicity, like special interest tax legislation.[7] And this skewed influence also explains why most senators, while needing to raise over seven thousand dollars a day to run for reelection, don't spend more time at neighborhood diners or soup kitchens. Similarly, the number of paid lobbyists and the scale of contributions to political action committees has spiraled upward for two decades.

Even with campaign finance reform aimed at plugging up some of the avenues of influence, big money will continue to dominate our elections and governing institutions. The result is a government primarily concerned with writing rules and administering regulations to serve the interests of its paying patrons. The power of the political contribution will continue to diminish the power of the ballot. And in the policy contests over the great issues of our day, concentrated wealth will emerge victorious almost all the time.

In this context, the estate tax is a very important issue. The estate tax does make a dent in the dynasties of wealth.[8] If the organized money that is now working to eliminate the tax succeeds, the distribution of wealth and power in our society will become more skewed. The result will be societal rules that are even more beneficial only to those who can pay.

## CONCENTRATED WEALTH AND EQUALITY OF OPPORTUNITY

This concentration of political power directly and indirectly undermines equality of opportunity. The wealthy and powerful generally "privatize" their personal and family needs through private education, private ownership of books and learning tools, private clubs and recreation, private transportation, and so on. For those who are not born wealthy, however, opportunities depend on the existence of strong community and public institutions. The ladder of opportunity for America's middle class depends on strong and accessible public educational institutions, libraries, state parks, and municipal pools. And for America's poor, the ladder of opportunity also includes access to affordable health care, quality public transportation, and child care assistance.

During decades when the concentration of wealth is great, our society puts a greater priority on tax cuts and spending priorities that benefit the wealthy rather than on building the institutions of opportunity.[9] In the 1920s, after several decades of Progressive Era reforms aimed at improving the conditions of ordinary people, there was a widespread rollback of social reforms and public investment. In a similar way, the 1980s and 1990s have witnessed the erosion of investment in equality of opportunity in education, home ownership, and small enterprise development, compared with that of the 1950s and 1960s.

During periods of less wealth inequality, our country has strengthened equality of opportunity, particularly for access to education for people of modest means. This is not only beneficial to the economy but a precondition for electoral democracy. Although our education system has many strong points, we are losing ground in ensuring affordable access for all. In 1965, the Pell grant, the largest federal program for lower-income students, covered 85 percent of the cost of four years at a public university. By 2000, it covered just 39 percent of the cost.

The current political and economic situation, shaped by the priorities of organized wealth, will not improve this picture. College costs have dramatically risen since the late 1970s and will continue to rise. State governments are raising tuition at community colleges and public universities. All of these will be additional obstacles for lower-income students seeking higher education. Those who enroll will endure distracting financial stresses, working long hours while in school and graduating with enormous personal and school debt burdens.

A society with widening disparities of wealth and power chooses other priorities over access to education for all. Historian of U.S. inequality Sam Pizzigati writes that "if we allow great wealth to accumulate in the pockets of a few, then great wealth can set our political agenda and shape our political culture—and the agenda and the culture that emerge will not welcome efforts to make America work for all Americans."[10]

The policy priorities of organized big money are not the same as the priorities of those who are unable to privatize their needs.

## GROWING INEQUALITY IS BAD ECONOMIC POLICY

Too much concentrated wealth and power is bad for the economy because it undermines prosperity. Economists have tended to look narrowly at the impact of wealth inequality on economic efficiency—and they have left it to the worldly philosophers to speculate on the social dangers of concentrated wealth. But a number of economic studies show how too much inequality of income and wealth can be a drag on economic growth. In a survey of academic research on the topic, Philippe Aghion summarizes: "Several studies have examined the impact of inequality upon economic growth. The picture they draw is impressively unambiguous, since they all suggest that greater inequality reduces the rate of growth."[11]

There are several reasons for this pattern. First, as discussed above, countries with high levels of inequality fail to invest adequately in education. Second, as discussed below, inequality leads to a breakdown of social cohesion, and in its most extreme form, to widespread social unrest and political instability.[12] Finally, too much concentrated wealth distorts the investment priorities and market decisions of the country at large, leaving lower- and moderate-income people without the incomes needed to stimulate the economy with widespread consumer spending.

For instance, inequalities of wealth and income backfire in the commercial marketplace. In the last two decades we've seen the emergence of a "Tiffany/ Kmart" dichotomy, a two-tier consumer market. One consumer market is shaped to suit the particular tastes and dollars of the top 5 percent of wealth holders. The mass market appeals to the rest. But as the buying power of the middle class erodes, the whole economy is put at risk. The purchasing power of the super wealthy alone is not enough to propel our economy.

After the terrorist attacks and economic downturn of September 2001, several troubling economic trends were unmasked. Commentators expressed concern that the long-term impact of rising consumer debt and stagnant wages might slow our economic recovery. Lower- and middle-income Americans couldn't afford to continue to prime the pump of the U.S. economy with additional consumer borrowing, especially in the face of rising job layoffs. They were maxed out.

Historians have seen this before. In his history of the Depression and Second World War, *Freedom from Fear*, David Kennedy notes how the Hoover administration conducted an extensive survey of social trends on the eve of the Great Depression:

> As Hoover's investigators discovered, the increasing wealth of the 1920s flowed disproportionately to the owners of capital. Worker incomes were rising, but not at a rate that kept pace with the nation's growing industrial output. Without broadly distributed purchasing power, the engines of mass production would have no outlet and would eventually fall idle.[13]

Too much economic inequality undermines economic stability and growth, threatening prosperity for all.

## INEQUALITY AND OUR CIVIC AND PUBLIC HEALTH

If too much inequality is bad for our democracy and economy, it is also harmful to the social fabric of a society that aspires toward fairness. British historian Arnold Toynbee analyzed the collapse of twenty-one past civilizations and determined that there were two common factors that led to their demise. The first was a concentration of wealth, and the second was inflexibility in the face of changing conditions.[14] Jeff Gates notes that concentrated wealth and societal rigidity are "two sides of the same coin." Concentrated ownership leads to inflexibility when what societies need is greater cooperation and adaptability.[15]

As our society pulls apart, there is a greater distance between haves and have nots, eroding society's social solidarity and reinforcing a sense that we are in very different realms. Our culture becomes more like an apartheid society, where haves and have nots no longer simply occupy opposite sides of the tracks but inhabit wholly different worlds. And the distance between these worlds has become so wide that it erodes any social sense that we are in this together.

Apartheid societies are unhealthy places to live, for the rich and everyone else. Public health researchers have shown how societies with wide disparities of wealth have poor health. Although it is unhealthy to live in an impoverished community, it is even worse to live in communities with high levels of income and wealth disparities. Within the United States, counties and states with greater inequality, not absolute poverty, have the highest incidences of infant mortality, heart disease, cancer, and homicide. Regions with greater equality enjoy the opposite, longer life expectancies and less violent trauma.[16]

Why is it healthier to live in a community with less inequality? Inequality leads to a breakdown in the social solidarity that is necessary for public health. British medical researcher Richard Wilkerson argues that communities with less inequality have stronger "social cohesion," more cultural limits on unrestrained individual actions, and greater networks of mutual aid and caring. "The individualism and values of the market are restrained by a social morality." The existence of more social capital "lubricates the workings of the whole society and economy. There are fewer signs of antisocial aggressiveness, and society appears more caring."[17]

Nothing demonstrates the fragmentation of community in the United States more vividly than the rise in gated residential communities for the affluent and the simultaneous record numbers of people in prison. Some 9 million households now voluntarily live in gated residential communities and another 2 million people are involuntarily incarcerated.[18] More people than ever are living behind gates and walls with entrances patrolled by armed guards. This polarization disturbs the equilibrium of a democratic society. It is in no one's interest for the United States to become more like some of our South American neighbors, such as Brazil, with such extreme levels of inequality. What kind of nation do we want to become?

The "American experiment" has attempted to balance two competing values: economic liberty versus democracy and equality of opportunity. We want to create a prosperous society, a goal we have achieved for a significant percentage of the population. We also aspire to create a society in which there is equity, where the playing field is level and the runners all start at the same starting line.

As you look over the Forbes 400 list, contemplate what the inevitable multiplication of these large estates will mean for this country in the decades to come. If they are not interrupted by a significant transfer tax, these will become the political dynasties of tomorrow.

There is no possible way for the children, grandchildren, and great-grandchildren of the Forbes 400 to spend the income from these huge estates. Their dynastic wealth will grow and grow, and the accumulation of excessive power in the hands of a limited number poses a significant risk for our society.

## DOES THE ESTATE TAX HAVE AN IMPACT?

Some might argue that if one of the goals of the estate tax is to reduce the concentration of wealth, it is not doing a very good job. After all, the growth in wealth concentration has been enormous and seemingly unchecked by the tax over time. Bruce Bartlett of the libertarian National Center for Policy Analysis observed that "wealth is probably more unequally distributed in the United States than in countries with no estate tax." He compared the maldistribution of wealth in the United States to four countries—Canada, New Zealand, Australia, and Israel—that don't have an estate tax and have lower levels of wealth inequality. He concludes that since the estate tax is ineffective, it should be scrapped.[19]

Wealth researcher Lisa Keister, however, points out that the wealth distribution in the United States would be much worse without the estate tax. In one simulation, she shows how the distribution of wealth would be different if the estate tax had remained as progressive as it was in the mid-1970s, when the top estate tax rate was 77 percent and exemptions were lower. Had this rate and exemption structure remained in place during the stock market explosion of the 1990s, it would have greatly reduced wealth inequality. Keister finds that the richest 1 percent would have held just 30 percent of the wealth in 1983, rather than the actual 34 percent of wealth they did possess. And, according to her model, the top 1 percent would have had 32 percent in 1998, rather than the actual 38 percent. The middle class, defined as households between the twentieth and sixtieth percentiles in the distribution, would have had a 10 percent greater share of the wealth pie, rather than losing ground.[20]

In another scenario, Keister demonstrates that the concentration of wealth would have been much greater if the progressivity of the estate tax had been reduced. Under this scenario, the top 1 percent would have owned 37 percent of the nation's wealth in 1983 and 43 percent in 1998. Remember, the actual figures are that the top 1 percent owned 34 percent of the nation's wealth in 1983 and 38 percent in 1998.[21]

It is clear that the 2001 reforms of the estate tax will increase wealth inequality—and that complete repeal will further fuel greater concentrations of wealth. Indeed, the estate tax could be more effective in deterring wealth imbalances. We should strengthen the tax, not eliminate it.

## NOTES

1. Jeff Gates, *Democracy at Risk: Rescuing Main Street from Wall Street* (Cambridge, Mass.: Perseus Press, 2000), p. xii.
2. Kevin Phillips, *Wealth and Democracy: A Political History of the American Rich* (New York: Broadway Books, 2002), p. 118.
3. Samuel Huntington as quoted in Phillips, *Wealth and Democracy*, p. xv.
4. John Nichols and Robert W. McChesney, *It's the Media, Stupid* (New York: Seven Stories Press, 2000). The big nine are AOL–Time Warner, Disney, Rupert Murdoch's NewsCorp, Viacom, Sony, Seagram (Universal), AT&T/Liberty Media, Bertelsmann, and General Electric. They have revenues between $6 billion and $30 billion a year, and each controls a wide variety of media holdings that include film, radio, television, and newspapers. Another twelve to fifteen firms, which do between $2 billion and $8 billion a year in business, are less diversified and control only two or three different news mediums. These include Washington Post, Cox, New York Times, Hearst, Advance, Tribune Company, and Gannett (Nichols and McChesney, *It's the Media*, pp. 16 and 28). This concentration, compared with that of two generations ago, should give us pause. But will we hear about it on television?
5. Center for Responsive Politics, "Election Overview, 2000 Cycle," www.opensecrets.org.
6. John Green, Paul Hermson, Lynda Powell, Clyde Wilcox, and the Center for Responsive Politics, "Individual Congressional Campaign Contributors: Wealthy, Conservative and Reform-Minded," www.opensecrets.org/pubs/donors/donors.asp, June 9, 1998.
7. For survey of research see James R. Repetti, "Democracy, Taxes and Wealth," *New York University Law Review*, June 2001.
8. Lisa A. Keister, *Wealth in America: Trends in Wealth Inequality* (Cambridge: Cambridge University Press, 2000), pp. 196–98. Updated data for 1998 discussed in Lisa A. Keister, "The Estate Tax as Robin Hood?" *American Prospect*, May 21, 2001.

9. See Kevin Phillips's discussion of financialization, politics, and "capitalist heydays" in *Wealth and Democracy,* pp. 293–316.

10. Sam Pizzigati, "America Needs More Than a Raise," *Working USA,* September/October 1997, p. 76.

11. Philippe Aghion, Eve Caroli, and Cecilia Garcia-Peñalosa, "Inequality and Economic Growth: The Perspective of the New Growth Theories," *Journal of Economic Literature 1615–1617* 37, no. 4 (December 1999). Also Alberto Alesina and Dani Rodrik, "Distribution, Political Conflict, and Economic Growth: A Simple Theory and Some Empirical Evidence," in Alex Cukierman, Zvi Hercowitz, and Leonardo Leiderman, eds., *Political Economy, Growth, and Business Cycles* (Cambridge: MIT Press, 1992), pp. 23–24. For a good survey of these arguments see Repetti, "Democracy, Taxes, and Wealth."

12. See Roberto Perotti, "Growth, Income Distribution, and Democracy: What the Data Say," *Journal of Economic Growth* 1, no. 2 (1996): 149–87. Also see Jess Benhabib and Aldo Rustichini, "Social Conflict and Growth," *Journal of Economic Growth* 1, no. 1 (1996):125–42.

13. David Kennedy, *Freedom from Fear: The American People in Depression and War, 1929–1945* (New York: Oxford University Press, 1999), p. 21.

14. Jeff Gates, *The Ownership Solution: Toward a Shared Capitalism for the Twenty-first Century* (Reading, Mass.: Addison Wesley, 1998), pp. 207–8.

15. Gates, *Ownership Solution.* Also see Gates, *Democracy at Risk.*

16. Ichiro Kawachi, Bruce Kennedy, and Richard Wilkinson, eds., *Income Inequality and Health: A Reader* (New York: New Press, 1999). Thanks to Stephen Bezruchka at the University of Washington for his assistance with this section. His research, teaching, and writing on this topic are prolific.

17. Richard Wilkinson, *Unhealthy Societies: The Afflictions of Inequality* (London: Routledge, 1996), p. 102.

18. Edward J. Blakely and Mary Gail Snyder, *Fortress America: Gated Communities in the United States* (Washington, D.C.: Brookings Institution Press, 1997). Justice Policy Institute Study, as reported in Jesse Katy, "A Nation of Too Many Prisoners?" *Los Angeles Times,* February 15, 2000.

19. Keister, "Estate Tax as Robin Hood?"

20. Keister, *Wealth in America,* pp. 196–98. Updated data for 1998 discussed in Keister, "Estate Tax as Robin Hood?"

21. Edward N. Wolff, *Top Heavy: The Increasing Inequality of Wealth in America and What Can Be Done about It* (New York: New Press, 2002), p. 12.

# Overcoming Institutional Racism, Sexism, and Ableism

*I have a dream that one day on the red hills of Georgia, the sons of former slaves and the sons of former slave-owners will be able to sit together at the table of brotherhood . . . that one day even the State of Mississippi, a state sweltering with the heat of injustice, sweltering with the heat of oppression, will be transformed into an oasis of freedom and justice.*

—Martin Luther King, Jr.

*Resolved, that the women of this nation in 1876, have greater cause for discontent, rebellion, and revolution than the men of 1776.*

—Susan B. Anthony

*The nature of society . . . disables physically impaired people.*

—Victor Finkelstein

Americans have always placed high value on the equality of all people. This is seen in the Declaration of Independence, which averred without qualification: "We hold these truths to be self-evident, that all men are created equal." That statement, however, was signed by slave holders, and the Constitution that was to follow allowed only white males to vote. The discrepancy between this core American value and behavior is shown in racist, sexist, and ableist behaviors and laws found throughout U.S. history. Although this fundamental contradiction remains, over time it has been muted by laws and policies aimed at overcoming discrimination.

## RACIAL EQUITY

There is a long history of racial and ethnic bigotry and discrimination codified in state and federal laws.[1] The buying, selling, and owning of slaves were legal activities in many states until the Emancipation Proclamation in 1863. The laws and the customs permitted the oppression of the slaves:

*Beginning in Virginia at the end of the 1630s, laws establishing lifelong African slavery were instituted. They were followed by laws prohibiting black-white intermarriage, laws against the*

*ownership of property by Africans, laws denying blacks all basic political rights. . . . In addition,*
*there were laws against the education of Africans, laws against the assembling of Africans, laws*
*against the ownership of weapons by Africans, laws perpetuating the slavery of their parents*
*to African children, laws forbidding Africans to raise their hands against whites even in self*
*defense. (Harding, 1981:27)*

## Voting Rights before 1960

Blacks were not conferred citizenship until the 14th Amendment was ratified in 1868. Until
1870, with the passage of the 15th Amendment, blacks were prohibited from voting. In the
1890s southern states began to amend their constitutions to enact a series of laws intended
to entrench white political supremacy by suppressing the black vote (U.S. Department of
Justice, n.d.). Such disenfranchising laws included poll taxes, literacy tests, vouchers of
"good character," and disqualification for "crimes of moral turpitude." These laws, seemingly color-blind, were designed to exclude blacks from voting by allowing white election
officials to apply the procedures selectively. As a consequence, by 1910 nearly all black
citizens were disenfranchised in the former Confederate states.

The process of restoring the voting rights taken from blacks by these devices began
in 1915, when the Supreme Court held that voter registration requirements containing
"grandfather clauses," which made registration dependent on whether the applicant was
descended from men enfranchised before the enactment of the 15th Amendment, violated
that amendment. Similarly, in 1944, the Supreme Court held that the Texas "white primary," which meant that blacks could only vote for candidates selected by whites in the
primary, violated the 15th Amendment.

## Segregation Prior to 1960

In the aftermath of the Civil War, southern states passed what were called "Black Codes"
in order to control the newly freed black population. Although varying from state to state,
the patterns were essentially the same. There were restrictions against land ownership
or rental to blacks. There were vagrancy laws insisting that blacks have lawful employment. Punishments for vagrancy included fines, forced labor, and whipping. Other laws
restricted blacks to only certain kinds of work. In addition to efforts to disenfranchise
blacks in the South, blacks were oppressed by economic slavery through low-wage jobs
and sharecropping arrangements with landowners and by legal efforts to keep blacks "in
their place."

By the early twentieth century, the South had a rigid system of segregation in place,
severely denying interaction between the races as equals. These Jim Crow laws (supported
by an 1896 U.S. Supreme Court decision, *Plessy v. Ferguson,* which justified the principle
of "separate but equal") meant that all public facilities in the South such as restaurants,
restrooms, schools, and public transportation could be legally segregated.

World War II was the beginning of the end for racial segregation in the South. President Franklin D. Roosevelt by executive order prohibited discrimination based on race in
defense industries. After the war, this was followed by President Harry Truman's appointment of a Committee on Civil Rights, which recommended (1) a permanent Commission
on Civil Rights, (2) that Congress pass laws against lynching and voting discrimination,

and (3) new laws to end racial discrimination in jobs (Zinn, 1980:440). In 1948, President Truman, by executive order began the desegregation of the armed forces.

In 1954, in a momentous Supreme Court decision, the "separate but equal" doctrine was struck down in *Brown v. Board of Education.* The Court said "the separation of school-children generates a feeling of inferiority . . . that may affect their hearts and minds in a way unlikely ever to be undone."

Late in 1955 a black seamstress, Rosa Parks, refused to give her seat on a Montgomery, Alabama, public bus to a white man. Following her arrest for violating a city ordinance, blacks in Montgomery organized a boycott of public transportation and chose as their leader a young black minister, Martin Luther King, Jr. During the boycott, white segregationists bombed four black churches and King's home, and black leaders were arrested and jailed. But the blacks of Montgomery persisted, and in November 1956, the U.S. Supreme Court declared that Alabama's state and local laws requiring segregation on buses was unconstitutional (Branch, 1989:143–205).

## The Landmark Civil Rights Laws of the 1960s

In 1963 President John F. Kennedy sent a civil rights bill to Congress. In his speech proposing the bill, Kennedy said:

> The Negro baby born in America today, regardless of the section of the nation in which he is born, has about one-half as much chance of completing high school as a white baby born in the same place on the same day; one third as much chance of completing college; one third as much chance of becoming a professional man; twice as much chance of becoming unemployed; about one-seventh as much chance of earning $10,000 a year; a life expectancy which is seven years shorter; and the prospects of earning only half as much. (Quoted in Spartacus, n.d.)

Kennedy's civil rights bill was still being debated by Congress when he was assassinated in November 1963. His successor, Lyndon B. Johnson, a Southerner whose legislative record was tepid on civil rights, nevertheless took up the cause with zeal. Fierce opposition to the bill in the Senate was led by Georgia Senator Richard B. Russell, who said: "We will resist to the bitter end any measure or any movement which would have a tendency to bring about social equality and intermingling and amalgamation of the races in our [southern] states" (quoted in Spartacus, n.d.). The law was passed after a seventy-five-day filibuster by eighteen southern Democratic senators. The Civil Rights Act of 1964 banned discrimination because of a person's color, race, national origin, religion, or sex. The rights protected by the act included a person's freedom to seek employment, vote, use hotels, parks, restaurants, and other public places. It forbid discrimination by any program that received money from the federal government, and it established the Equal Employment Opportunity Commission (EEOC), which would take a case to court when an individual complained of discrimination by an employer.

President Johnson then successfully pushed for the Voting Rights Act of 1965. This Act codified the 15th Amendment's permanent guarantee that, throughout the nation, no person shall be denied the right to vote on account of race or color. This ended the use of literacy requirements for voting in seven southern states. Impressive gains in voter registration occurred immediately. For example, only 6 percent of the black citizens of Mississippi were registered to vote in 1965; by 1967, more than 33 percent were registered. Martin Luther King, Jr. called the first two laws passed (1964 and 1965) "a Second Emancipation."

Congress passed the Civil Rights Act of 1968, which banned discrimination in housing transactions on the basis of race, color, religion, national origin, and sex. Also in that year, the Supreme Court banned racial discrimination by private, as well as governmental, housing providers.

These three transformative legislative acts were successful in large part because of President Johnson's commitment to a just society and his skill at moving legislation through Congress. After his signing of the Civil Rights Act of 1968, he said:

> *The proudest moments of my Presidency have been times such as this when I have signed into law the promises of a century. . . . With this bill, the voice of justice speaks again. . . . We all know that the roots of injustice run deep. . . . I think we can take some heart that Democracy's work is being done. In the Civil Rights Act of 1968, America does move forward and the bell of freedom rings a little louder. We have come some of the way, not near all of it. There is much yet to do. (Quoted in Kotz, 2005:421)*

## Civil Rights Progress from 1968 to the Present

The year 1968 marked the high point of progressive civil rights legislation. The push for civil rights lost momentum under Presidents Nixon and Reagan and an increasingly conservative Congress and Supreme Court. There was some progress, however, as a 1982 law strengthened the Voting Rights Act; a 1988 law increased enforcement of the Fair Housing Act; and in 1991 Congress reinforced the 1964 law against employment discrimination. In 1995 the Supreme Court placed limits on the use of race (affirmative action) in awarding government contracts. In the late 1990s, California banned the use of race- and sex-based preferences.

In short, blacks still face discrimination in an unequal society. Today, the poverty rate for blacks is almost three times that for whites, the unemployment rate is consistently at least twice that for whites, residential and school segregation by race continue, and lending agencies continue to discriminate against blacks, to name a few ongoing problems. As President Johnson said in 1968, "We have come a long way, not near all of it. There is much yet to do."

## GENDER EQUITY

### Early U.S. History and Patriarchy

U.S. laws from colonial times are derived in large measure from English common law. This heritage has perpetuated male dominance. Included in the customs and codes of English common law was the doctrine of coverture (the legal subordination of a married woman to her husband). Among the elements of the doctrine of coverture were the following (Coltrane, 1998:144–148):

- A married man assumed legal rights over his wife's property on marrying.
- A married woman could not sign contracts unless her husband joined her.
- A married woman could not execute a valid will unless her husband consented to its provisions.
- Because a woman after marriage is unable to act as an individual, her husband could spend her money, sell her stocks, and even appropriate her possessions.

- When a woman became a wife, she lost any freedom of movement because she was required by law to live in her husband's home.
- Because a husband was legally accountable for his wife's behavior, he was entrusted with the power to physically chastise his wife. In this regard a North Carolina court held in 1862 that "the law gives the husband power to such a degree of force as is necessary to make the wife behave herself and know her place."
- Husbands maintained rights to have sex with their wives, referred to by the courts as husbands' right to "consortium." This right also applied to the right of masters to have sex with slaves and indentured servants. In short, the courts considered women's sexuality to be the property of their masters.

Clearly, in the early years of the United States women were second-class citizens. They had no power in the courts. If unmarried they were social outcasts, with few, poorly compensated jobs available to them. They were excluded from roles that yielded power and privilege. So unmarried women tended to be economically dependent on their fathers and brothers. If married, they were the property of their husbands with no rights and no power.

## Married Women's Property Acts

Coverture prevailed until the middle of the nineteenth century. Structurally, the economic realities of the times demanded greater flexibility for women. Since men were often away from home for extended periods, married women needed to be able to execute contracts, buy and sell property, and execute wills. As a result, the states, beginning with Mississippi in 1839, passed legislation that changed various aspects of coverture. These acts, known collectively as the "Married Women's Property Acts," were made in all states, in one form or another, by the end of the century.

## Women's Suffrage

The women's suffrage movement began with a women's convention in 1848 in Seneca Falls, New York. Although that convention called for women to have equal rights in education and property rights, the conference centered on the women's suffrage—the right to vote. They believed that with the vote, women could gain other rights. Several generations of woman suffrage supporters lectured, wrote, petitioned, marched, lobbied, and practiced civil disobedience to achieve what many considered a radical change in the Constitution (U.S. National Archives and Records Administration, n.d.).

> *Public opinion varied widely on women's suffrage. Most people who opposed woman suffrage believed that women were less intelligent and less able to make political decisions than men. Opponents argued that men could represent their wives better than the wives could represent themselves. Some people feared that women's participation in politics would lead to the end of family life.* (World Book, 2004)

In 1838, Kentucky authorized women to vote in school elections. Later Kansas granted women the right to vote in municipal elections. In 1869 the Wyoming Territory gave women voting rights on an equal basis with men and continued this practice following admission to statehood. By 1914 ten other states joined Wyoming in granting women full voting rights.

In 1918 President Woodrow Wilson argued for women's suffrage. The House of Representatives passed a suffrage amendment bill, but it was defeated in the Senate. Another attempt in February 1919 also ended in failure but later that spring, the Senate finally passed the bill. Three-fourths of the states were needed to add the Amendment to the Constitution. This occurred in 1920 when the legislature in the last state needed, Tennessee, passed the 19th Amendment by one vote.

## Gender Equity in Sports

Title IX of the Educational Amendments of 1972 states: "No person in the United States shall, on the basis of sex be excluded from participation in, or denied the benefits of, or be subjected to discrimination under any educational program or activity receiving federal aid." Although this pertains to educational opportunities in general, it has had the most pronounced effect on high school and college sports for women. Prior to Title IX few schools had competitive sports for girls and women. The physical education equipment for men was far superior to that for women. No collegiate athletic scholarships were available for women. With the new legislation, athletic participation for girls and women soared, budgets for them improved, and athletic scholarships became readily available.

Although the intent of this legislation was to provide equal educational opportunities for all, Title IX has not brought about the goal of gender equity in sports (Eitzen and Sage, 2003: 320–324). Conservative high school and collegiate athletic administrators (men) were slow to implement changes. Delay in enforcement by federal agencies, especially during President Reagan's administration, hampered efforts toward equality.

There was a setback in 1984 with a U.S. Supreme Court decision (*Grove City v. Bell*) that ruled that Title IX did not apply to school athletic programs because they did not receive federal monies directly (even though the schools did). Within a year of that Supreme Court decision, the Office of Civil Rights suspended sixty-four investigations, more than half involving college athletics. In response, various women's groups lobbied Congress and in 1988 both houses of Congress overrode President Reagan's veto, and the Civil Rights Restoration Act became law. This act was designed to restore the original intent of Title IX.

Another obstacle that continues to block gender equity in schools and colleges is the accepted practice that the high-budget program of football is not included in establishing fairness. Thus, because football is excluded, overall participation by women at the collegiate level is 42 percent; however, only 33 percent of the athletic budget goes to women; and women athletes receive 41 percent of the athletic scholarship money that is distributed (Eitzen, 2006). In short, although progress has been made toward gender equity, comparing data from 1971 to now, it has leveled out short of equality for women.

## Equal Rights Amendment

In 1967 the National Organization for Women (NOW) sought an Equal Rights Amendment to the Constitution, which was a statement of principle about a national moral commitment to gender equality and justice. The proposed amendment was approved overwhelmingly by the House and Senate in 1971. Within a year, twenty-two of the thirty-eight states needed for ratification had approved it. The momentum slowed, and by 1977 it still lacked the approval of legislatures in three states needed for ratification. Congress voted to set a deadline of June 30, 1982, for its ratification. The ERA became an important issue in the presidential election of 1980. The Democratic Party strongly supported it, but the Republican Party took no official position. However, the Republican candidate for president, Ronald Reagan, who was elected, openly and actively opposed the amendment. The ERA was never ratified (Hodgson, 2004:143–145).

### Reproductive Rights

Issues of birth control and abortion are core issues for feminists, who see women's rights to control their own bodies as essential to the realization of other rights and opportunities in society (Andersen, 1997:203). This is at odds with state and federal governments, which have a long history of involvement in reproductive matters (Baca Zinn and Eitzen, 2005:283–285). For example, some states with Catholic majorities outlawed the use of contraceptives. That prohibition was lifted by the U.S. Supreme Court in 1968 (*Griswold v. Connecticut*), which ruled that state laws making the use of contraceptives by married couples a criminal offense was unconstitutional. In 1972 (*Eisenstadt v. Baird*) the Court ruled that laws prohibiting the dispensing of contraceptives to unmarried persons were unconstitutional.

In 1973, the U.S. Supreme Court, in *Roe v. Wade,* invalidated all state laws against abortion. "This ruling raises one of the most highly charged emotional and political issues in the United States. Pro-choice and antiabortion forces clash over whose rights are to be protected—those of the woman or those of the fetus. Abortions are interpreted by one side as a viable option for a woman to control her life and by the other side as murder" (Baca Zinn and Eitzen, 2005:485).

Anti-abortion forces have directed their efforts to weakening or changing *Roe v. Wade.* They have taken cases to the Supreme Court, where in 1989, the Court in *Webster v. Reproductive Health Services,* gave states the right to impose restrictions on abortion. They have worked to elect officials opposed to abortion and lobbied Congress for rules that would make abortion more and more difficult for women to choose abortions. For example, in 1976 Congress passed the Hyde Amendment, which cut off federal funds for all abortions except for pregnancies resulting from rape, incest, or that endangered a woman's life. The Supreme Court supported this by ruling that a woman, although possessing the right to have an abortion, did not have a constitutional right to have the federal government pay for it. Similarly, more than half of the states now have laws prohibiting the use of tax monies to pay for abortions. "As a result, a woman in America today has far less freedom to have an abortion than a woman in America after *Roe v. Wade* was handed down in 1973. And for poor women, who are disproportionately of color, that freedom is hanging by a thread" ("A Woman's Right Is in Peril," 2005:8).

In sum, comparing the rights of contemporary women with those of the eighteenth and nineteenth centuries, there have been huge strides toward equality with men. That goal, however, remains elusive. Women are found disproportionately in secondary roles. Their pay for equal work remains about 20 percent lower than what men receive. In politics and the professions, despite having gained some status, women are still underrepresented in positions of power and privilege.

The greatest improvements in gender equity (just as was the case with efforts at racial equity) occurred during the 1960s and early 1970s. These were times of triumph for progressives. This was followed, however, by times of disappointment. "By the mid-1980s, a substantial, well-organized political movement was actively attempting to turn back the tide of feminism and present an alternative, conservative vision of the role of women in society" (Hodgson, 2004:149). The larger political climate, once open to change and equity, turned hostile to feminist goals. That climate, with the control of Congress and the executive branch by conservatives at the beginning of the twenty-first century, has stopped the advance toward gender equity and may signal its retreat.

## EQUITY FOR PEOPLE WITH DISABILITIES

The largest minority group in the United States is composed of people with physical, sensory, or cognitive impairments. About 55 million people (20 percent) have some form of impairment. About 15 percent were born with a disability, and 85 percent experienced a disabling condition in the course of their lives (from accidents, disease, environmental hazards, criminal victimization, or aging). People with disabilities experience discrimination in housing, education, and work. They are defined by negative stereotypes. Moreover, they have to accommodate to environments and social settings that were designed for the able-bodied. Equal access is frequently denied because of transportation and architectural barriers in streets and buildings (Eitzen and Baca Zinn, 2006).

Throughout most of U.S. history people with disabilities were ignored by government and were forced to rely on family and charity for their needs. The original Social Security Act of 1935 was amended in 1956 to include benefits for the disabled, and in 1958 for benefits to dependents of disabled workers. In 1972 Social Security was again amended to provide Medicare eligibility to the disabled.

There are two major elements of Social Security benefits to people with disabilities. The first is Social Security Disability Insurance (SSDI), which provides monthly benefits to disabled workers. For purposes of eligibility disability is defined as "the inability to engage in any substantial gainful activity by reason of any medically determinable physical or mental impairment . . . which has lasted or can be expected to last for a continuous period of not less than 12 months or results in death." The amount of benefit payment is determined by several factors, the most important being the average earnings up until the time of disability. In 2002 some 7.2 million people received these benefits (including 5.5 million disabled workers, 1.5 million dependent children, and 150,000 spouses) (Freedman, Martin, and Schoeni, 2004:25).

The second Social Security program for people with disabilities is Supplemental Security Income (SSI). This benefit is for low-income disabled adults and disabled children. In 2002, 4.8 million people under age 65 received assistance under this program (Freedman, Martin, and Schoeni, 2004:25).

The major legislation to benefit people with disabilities was the Americans with Disabilities Act of 1990 (ADA). This legislation is especially important because it addresses the problems of discrimination and the structural barriers that inhibit mobility and access. Specifically, the ADA prohibits discrimination against people with disabilities in employment and access to services. Public accommodations must comply with basic nondiscrimination requirements that prohibit exclusion, segregation, and unequal treatment. In effect, the ADA provides civil rights protection to people with disabilities that is similar to those given to citizens on the basis of race, sex, national origin, age, and religion. The ADA also insists that people with disabilities be allowed access. Telecommunications companies (telephone and television) must provide access for people with hearing and speech disabilities (U.S. Department of Justice, 2002). Finally, all private businesses open to the public must make sure that all buildings, new and existing, are accessible to individuals with disabilities.

Put more simply, because of this landmark legislation, access is now commonplace with parking lots having reserved spaces for people with disabilities, bathrooms are equipped for wheelchair access, ramps and elevators provide access to public buildings, and elevators that feature Braille floor numbers or audio assistance.

It is crucial to remember that these major changes did not occur because it was the right thing to do. The battle was won, despite the opposition of the National Association of Manufacturers, the U.S. Chamber of Commerce, and the National Federation of Businesses, because of fears about the costs to meet ADA's provisions and the specter of increased government regulations. Despite the resistance of big business, the progressive legislation was passed because people with disabilities and their compatriots had organized rallies to publicize their grievances and used tactics of civil disobedience. Some policymakers were persuaded by the message and logic of the protestors, others by the potential political power of people, realizing that about one-fifth of U.S. citizens have disabilities (Eitzen and Baca Zinn, 2006).

Despite significant victories, the battle for full rights for the disabled is far from over. The provisions of ADA have been altered to narrow and weaken some of the provisions. For example, only newly purchased buses are required to have lifts. Similarly, only new buildings or those undergoing renovation must be accessible, and the original act exempted small business employers from compliance and provided a loophole allowing exemption from "undue hardship." Moreover, the government has been lax in enforcing compliance with ADA provisions because the monitoring effort is underfunded (Russell, 1998:108–124).

## CONCLUSION

A fundamental progressive goal for society is social justice (Eitzen and Baca Zinn, 2006). With regard to race, gender, and disability, U.S. society has moved toward social justice but remains far from that elusive goal. In the words of Gail Schoettler, former lieutenant governor and treasurer of Colorado:

> *The Civil Rights Movement made great strides. Yet as long as any person in America is denied a job or housing or simple courtesy because of her or his personal characteristics, whether they be disabilities or skin color or beliefs or sexuality, we have not affirmed the basic equal opportunity promised by our Constitution. (Schoettler, 2000:2L)*

## NOTE

1. The discussion here is limited to policies and actions in the civil rights struggles between blacks and whites. This by no means minimizes the wars against Native Americans, the taking of their land, and their forced relocation, the long-standing oppression of Mexican Americans in the Southwest, or the discrimination against various ethnic groups at different times and places. Prime examples of legal actions against certain racial and ethnic groups were the immigration

laws. For example, during the 1920s Congress passed laws setting immigration quotas, which favored immigrants from England, Ireland, and Germany but severely limited the coming of Latinos, Slavs, Bulgarians, Lithuanians, Jews, Africans, and Asians. In short, whites from Europe were invited whereas Latinos, Asians, and Eastern Europeans were not welcome. During World War II President Roosevelt signed an executive order giving the army the power, without warrants or indictments or hearings, to arrest every Japanese American on the West Coast and transport them to camps and keep them there under prison conditions. As a final example, after the September 11, 2001, attacks on the World Trade Center and the Pentagon, the Patriot Act permitted, under the rubric of "homeland security," to subject Arab Americans (and other possible suspects) to surveillance, searches, and sometimes imprisonment without legal counsel.

## REFERENCES

Andersen, Margaret L. (1997). *Thinking about Women: Sociological Perspectives on Sex and Gender,* 4th ed. Boston: Allyn and Bacon.

Baca Zinn, Maxine, and Eitzen, D. Stanley. (2005). *Diversity in Families,* 7th ed. Boston: Allyn and Bacon.

Branch, Taylor. (1989). *Parting the Waters: America in the King Years, 1954–1963.* New York: Simon and Schuster Touchstone.

Coltrane, Scott. (1998). *Gender and Families.* Thousand Oaks, CA: Pine Forge Press.

Eitzen, D. Stanley. (2006). *Fair and Foul: Beyond the Myths and Paradoxes of Sport,* 3rd ed. Lanham, MD: Rowman and Littlefield.

Eitzen, D. Stanley, and Baca Zinn, Maxine. (2006). *Social Problems,* 10th ed. Boston: Allyn and Bacon.

Eitzen, D. Stanley, and Sage, George H. (2003). *Sociology of North American Sport,* 7th ed. New York: McGraw-Hill.

Freedman, Vicki A., Martin, Linda G., and Schoeni, Robert F. (2004, September). "Disability in America." *Population Bulletin* 59.

Harding, Vincent. (1981). *There Is a River: The Black Struggle for Freedom in America.* New York: Harcourt Brace Jovanovich.

Hodgson, Godfrey. (2004). *More Equal than Others: America from Nixon to the New Century.* Princeton, NJ: Princeton University Press.

Kotz, Nick. (2005). *Judgment Days: Lyndon Baines Johnson, Martin Luther King Jr., and the Laws That Changed America.* New York: Houghton Mifflin.

Russell, Marta. (1998). *Beyond Ramps: Disability at the End of the Social Contract.* Monroe, ME: Common Courage Press.

Russell, Marta. (2005). "Targeting Disability." *Monthly Review* 56 (April):45–53.

Schoettler, Gail. (2000). "You Can't Buy Human Decency." *Denver Post* (October 1):2L.

Spartacus (n.d.). "Civil Rights Act (1964)": www.spartacus.schoolnet.co.uk/USAcivil64.htm.

U.S. Department of Justice. (2002). "A Guide to Disability Rights Laws": www.usdoj.gov/crt/ada/guide.htm.

U.S. Department of Justice, Civil Rights Division (n.d.). "Before the Voting Rights Act": www.usdoj.gov/crt/voting/intro/intro_a.htm.

U.S. National Archives and Records Administration (n.d.). "Women's Suffrage and the 19th Amendment": www.archives.gov/digital_classroom/lessons/woman_suffrage.

"A Woman's Right Is in Peril" [Comment]. (2005). *The Progressive* 69 (April):8–9.

*World Book.* (2004). "The History of Women's Suffrage": www2.worldbook.com/features/whm/html/whm010.html.

Zinn, Howard. (1980). *A People's History of the United States.* New York: Harper & Row.

# 12

# Testimony before the Credentials Committee of the Democratic National Convention, August 22, 1964

*FANNIE LOU HAMER*

*The Democratic party faced a crisis at its national convention to nominate a presidential candidate in 1964. At that convention the state of Mississippi had a delegation selected by the state's all-white Democratic establishment. This slate was challenged by delegates selected from the Mississippi Freedom Democratic Party (MFDP), a delegation bent on opening the vote to blacks in Mississippi. The MFDP's challenge was epitomized in the testimony of Fannie Lou Hamer to the Credentials Committee. Fannie Lou Hamer, the youngest of twenty children born to Mississippi sharecropper parents and with only six years of schooling, was active in the effort to win the right to vote for blacks. Her moving testimony provides the context of the civil rights struggle for the right to vote.*

*The MFDP was not seated as the official delegation for Mississippi. President Lyndon B. Johnson refused to support the Mississippi Freedom Democratic Party because he was afraid of losing his white southern support. There was a compromise, which gave voting and speaking rights to two delegates from the MFDP and seated the others as honored guests. The Democrats agreed that in the future no delegation would be seated from a state where anyone was illegally denied the vote. A year later, President Johnson signed the Voting Rights Act.*

Mr. Chairman, and the Credentials Committee, my name is Mrs. Fanny Lou Hamer, and I live at 626 East Lafayette Street, Ruleville, Mississippi, Sunflower County, the home of Senator James O. Eastland, and Senator Stennis.

It was the 31st of August in 1962 that 18 of us traveled 26 miles to the county courthouse in Indianola to try to register to try to become first-class citizens. We was met in Indianola by Mississippi men, Highway Patrolmens and they only allowed two of us in to

*Source:* Fannie Lou Hamer testimony before Democratic National Committee Credentials Committee, August 22, 1964. Atlantic City, New Jersey.

take the literacy test at the time. After we had taken this test and started back to Ruleville, we was held up by the City Police and the State Highway Patrolmen and carried back to Indianola where the bus driver was charged that day with driving a bus the wrong color.

After we paid the fine among us, we continued on to Ruleville, and Reverend Jeff Sunny carried me four miles in the rural area where I had worked as a time-keeper and sharecropper for 18 years. I was met there by my children, who told me that the plantation owner was angry because I had gone down to try to register. After they told me, my husband came, and said that the plantation owner was raising cain because I had tried to register, and before he quit talking the plantation owner came, and said, "Fanny Lou, do you know—did Pap tell you what I said?"

And I said, "yes, sir."

He said, "I mean that," he said, "If you don't go down and withdraw your registration, you will have to leave," said, "Then if you go down and withdraw," he said, "You will—you [still] might have to go because we are not ready for that in Mississippi."

And I addressed him and told him and said, "I didn't try to register for you. I tried to register for myself." I had to leave that same night.

On the 10th of September 1962, 16 bullets was fired into the home of Mr. and Mrs. Robert Tucker for me. That same night two girls were shot in Ruleville, Mississippi. Also Mr. Joe McDonald's house was shot in.

And in June the 9th, 1963, I had attended a voter registration workshop, was returning back to Mississippi. Ten of us was traveling by the Continental Trailway bus. When we got to Winona, Mississippi, which is in Montgomery County, four of the people got off to use the washroom, and two of the people—to use the restaurant—two of the people wanted to use the washroom. The four people that had gone in to use the restaurant was ordered out. During this time I was on the bus. But when I looked through the window and saw they had rushed out I got off of the bus to see what had happened, and one of the ladies said, "It was a State Highway Patrolman and a Chief of Police ordered us out."

I got back on the bus and one of the persons had used the washroom got back on the bus, too. As soon as I was seated on the bus, I saw when they began to get the four people in a highway patrolman's car, I stepped off of the bus to see what was happening and somebody screamed from the car that the four workers was in and said, "Get that one there," and when I went to get in the car, when the man told me I was under arrest, he kicked me.

I was carried to the county jail, and put in the booking room. They left some of the people in the booking room and began to place us in cells. I was placed in a cell with a young woman called Miss Ivesta Simpson. After I was placed in the cell I began to hear the sound of kicks and horrible screams, and I could hear somebody say, "Can you say, yes, sir, nigger? Can you say yes, sir?"

And they would say other horrible names. She would say, "Yes, I can say yes, sir."

"So say it."

She says, "I don't know you well enough."

They beat her, I don't know how long, and after a while she began to pray, and asked God to have mercy on those people.

And it wasn't too long before three white men came to my cell. One of these men was a State Highway Patrolman and he asked me where I was from, and I told him Ruleville, he said, "We are going to check this." And they left my cell and it wasn't too long before they came back. He said, "You are from Ruleville all right," and he used a curse word, and he said, "We are going to make you wish you was dead."

I was carried out of that cell into another cell where they had two Negro prisoners. The State Highway Patrolmen ordered the first Negro to take the blackjack. The first Negro prisoner ordered me, by orders from the State Highway Patrolman for me, to lay down on a bunk bed on my face, and I laid on my face. The first Negro began to beat, and I was beat by the first Negro until he was exhausted, and I was holding my hands behind me at that time on my left side because I suffered from polio when I was six years old. After the first Negro had beat until he was exhausted the State Highway Patrolman ordered the second Negro to take the blackjack.

The second Negro began to beat and I began to work my feet, and the State Highway Patrolman ordered the first Negro who had beat me to sit upon my feet to keep me from working my feet. I began to scream and one white man got up and began to beat me my head and told me to hush. One white man—since my dress had worked up high, walked over and pulled my dress down and he pulled my dress back, back up. . . .

All of this is on account of us wanting to register, to become first-class citizens, and if the freedom Democratic Party is not seated now, I question America, is this America, the land of the free and the home of the brave where we have to sleep with our telephones off of the hooks because our lives be threatened daily because we want to live as decent human beings, in America?

# 13

# Roe v. Wade

## BRITISH BROADCASTING COMPANY

*In 1973 the U.S. Supreme Court in a landmark decision made abortion legal in the United States. This decision recognized for the first time that the constitutional right to privacy included a woman's right to terminate her pregnancy. Controversy over a woman's "right to choose" has increased in the ensuing years. Anti-abortion has become a cornerstone for social conservatives who have unified their support behind Republicans and thus are at least partially responsible for Republicans controlling the presidency and both houses of Congress during the first decade of the twenty-first century.*

By a vote of seven to two, the court justices ruled that governments lacked the power to prohibit abortions.

The court's judgement was based on the decision that a woman's right to terminate her pregnancy came under the freedom of personal choice in family matters as protected by the 14th Amendment of the US Constitution.

The decision—on 22 January 1973—remains one of the most controversial ever made by the Supreme Court.

### APPEAL

The ruling came after a 25-year-old single woman, Norma McCorvey under the pseudonym "Jane Roe," challenged the criminal abortion laws in Texas that forbade abortion as unconstitutional except in cases where the mother's life was in danger.

Henry Wade was the Texas attorney general who defended the anti-abortion law.

Ms McCorvey first filed the case in 1969. She was pregnant with her third child and claimed that she had been raped. But the case was rejected and she was forced to give birth.

However, in 1973 her appeal made it to the U.S. Supreme Court where she was represented by Sarah Weddington, a Dallas attorney.

Her case was heard on the same day as that of a 20-year-old Georgia woman, Sandra Bensing. They argued that the abortion laws in Texas and Georgia ran counter to the U.S. Constitution by infringing women's right to privacy. They won their case.

*Source:* "Roe v. Wade: Key U.S. Abortion Ruling" from BBC News at bbcnews.com, December 10, 2004. Reprinted by permission.

## TRIMESTER SYSTEM

The case created the "trimester" system that:

- gives American women an absolute right to an abortion in the first three months of pregnancy
- allows some government regulation in the second trimester of pregnancy
- declares that states may restrict or ban abortions in the last trimester as the foetus nears the point where it could live outside the womb; in this trimester a woman can obtain an abortion despite any legal ban only if doctors certify it is necessary to save her life or health.

But in the following decades anti-abortion campaigners regained some lost ground. More than 30 states have adopted laws limiting abortion rights.

In 1980 the US Supreme Court upheld a law that banned the use of federal funds for abortion except when necessary to save a woman's life.

Then in 1989 it approved more restrictions, including allowing states to prohibit abortions at state clinics or by state employees.

In 2003, Congress introduced the first major limits on abortion in the US for 30 years when it passed a law banning a particular form of late-term abortion labelled "partial birth" by its opponents.

Legal challenges to the ban, signed into law by President Bush, continue.

The result of these restrictions is that many women have to travel further to get an abortion, often across state borders, and pay more for them. According to the pro-choice movement, poor women are penalised most by these restrictions.

## CHANGING SIDES

Norma McCorvey announced in 1987 that her rape testimony in 1969 had been false.

Now a born-again Christian, she converted to the pro-life lobby, and two years later Sandra Bensing followed suit.

But Ms McCorvey's attorney, Sarah Weddington, insists that the rape testimony was not a factor in the *Roe* verdict, and that her decision to change sides has no bearing on the ruling.

The greatest court triumph of the pro-life lobby was the Supreme Court's ruling in *Planned Parenthood v. Casey* in 1992.

While upholding the *Roe v. Wade* ruling, it also established that states can restrict abortions even in the first trimester for non-medical reasons.

The new laws must not place an "undue burden" on women seeking abortion services. However, it is the woman and not the authorities who have to prove that the regulations are damaging.

As a result many states now have restrictions in place such as requirements that young pregnant women involve their parents or a judge in their abortion decision.

Others have introduced waiting periods between the time a woman first visits an abortion clinic and the actual procedure.

Some states also provide information that has to be presented to women having abortions that could discourage them from going ahead.

# 14

# Federal Programs to Ameliorate the Consequences of Disability

*VICKI A. FREEDMAN, LINDA G. MARTIN, AND ROBERT F. SCHOENI*

*What follows is a description of the major federal programs to help people with disabilities. It is taken from a publication of the Population Reference Bureau entitled "Disability in America."*

A variety of government programs in the United States are charged with ameliorating the consequences of disability, particularly as they relate to earnings, capacity and economic well-being.[1] Historically, these programs have been dominated by transfer programs that primarily offer cash assistance. Less often, the programs involve rehabilitation and vocational services, medical care, employment protection, and increasing access to technology.

## MAJOR DISABILITY COMPENSATION PROGRAMS[2]

There are disability compensation programs targeted to Americans with disabilities at each stage of life: children, working-age men and women, and the elderly. Most programs are funded and managed by the federal government, but state governments also provide important assistance.

### Black Lung Disease

The Black Lung program was established in 1969 and provides monthly benefit payments to coal miners who were totally disabled because of pneumoconiosis, or black lung disease. Pneumoconiosis is a chronic dust disease of the lung resulting from employment in or around coal mines.[3] Payments are paid not only to surviving coal miners, but to their widows and surviving dependents as well. The number of beneficiaries has been falling steadily from its peak in 1974 of almost 500,000. In 2002, there were 71,584 beneficiaries, and only 8,394 were miners; the remaining 63,190 were widows or surviving dependents (see Table 14.1). In 2001, the benefit for a miner with no dependents was $518 per month.[4]

*Source:* Excerpt from "Disability in America" by Vicki A. Freedman, Linda G. Martin, and Robert F. Schoeni from *Population Bulletin* 59 (September 2004). Reprinted by permission of Population Reference Bureau.

**TABLE 14.1**   Leading U.S. Disability Programs by Number of Beneficiaries and Amount of Benefit Payments, 2002

| PROGRAM | NUMBER OF BENEFICIARIES (MILLIONS) | TOTAL BENEFIT PAYMENTS ($ BILLIONS) |
|---|---|---|
| Black Lung benefits | 0.1 | $0.4 |
| Social Security Disability Insurance (DI) | 7.2 | 60.4 |
| Supplemental Security Income (SSI) for blind or disabled | | |
| Under age 18 | 0.9 | 0.5 |
| Ages 18–64 | 3.9 | 1.8 |
| Veterans disability benefits[a] | 2.4 | 17.6 |
| Workers' Compensation[b] | 127.0 | 49.4 |

Notes: For Social Security Disability Insurance, the dollar benefit for 2002 was estimated based on total monthly benefit payments of $5.03 billion.

[a]The dollar benefit for 2002 was estimated based on total monthly benefit payments of $1.5 billion. Column 1 reports the number of recipients with military service.

[b]2001 figures. Column 1 reports the number of individuals covered by the program.

Sources: Social Security Administration, "Social Security (Bulletin Annual Statistical Supplement, 2003"; and Department of Veteran's Affairs, Program. Statistics 2002 Annual Accountability Report Statistical Appendix: table 12.

### Social Security Disability Insurance

The Old-Age, Survivors, and Disability Insurance (OASDI) Programs, typically referred to as "Social Security," provide monthly benefits to retired and disabled workers, their dependents, and their survivors. Benefits for retired workers were established as part of the original 1935 Social Security Act, but benefits to disabled workers were enacted only in 1956. The disability insurance (DI) component of OASDI is funded by a payroll tax paid by workers covered by the program and their employers. Currently almost all workers—96 percent—are covered by DI.

Unlike Supplemental Security Income (SSI, see below), DI is not a means-tested program. To be eligible for DI, workers must have worked a minimum number of quarters with earnings above a specific threshold. In 2002, the quarterly earnings eligibility threshold was $810. The number of quarters required for a person to become fully insured is based on the number of years the person lived after age 21 before becoming disabled. Someone who becomes disabled at age 33 would need to have accumulated 12 quarters of covered employment by that time to become eligible for DI.

For DI, disability is defined as the inability to engage in "substantial gainful activity" because of physical or mental impairment. The impairment must be verifiable medically and last at least 12 months, or it must result in death. The amount of benefit payment that a disabled worker receives is determined by a variety of factors—most important, the average earnings in covered employment up until the time of disability. During the 2000–2001 period, the average monthly benefit for disabled workers was $919.

The number of DI beneficiaries was fairly constant between the early 1980s and early 1990s, with 45 million recipients in 1991. In 1996, 6.1 million people were receiving DI benefits, up 36 percent in just 5 years. By 2002, the number had reached 7.2 million (including 5.5 trillion disabled workers, 1.5 million dependent children, and 150,000 spouses).

People become eligible for DI because of a variety of conditions. Mental disorders other than mental retardation accounted for 28 percent of the cases in 2001, double the 1982 percentage. Musculoskeletal disorders accounted for 24 percent of cases.

## Supplemental Security Income (SSI)

SSI provides income support to people age 65 or older, blind or disabled adults, and blind or disabled children. Only people with low income are eligible for assistance. Among the elderly, the program is available to all low-income individuals—but among the nonelderly, recipients must be both low-income and blind or disabled.

For SSI benefit determination purposes, disability is defined as being "unable to engage in any substantial gainful activity by reason of any medically determinable physical or mental impairment expected to result in death or that has lasted or can be expected to last for at least 12 months." The definition means applicants must be unable to work in any job in the national economy for which they are qualified based on age, education, and work experience. Permanent benefits do not begin until after a five-month waiting period.

In 2002, the maximum federal benefit for single people living in their own homes was $545 per month. Some fraction of income from earnings and other sources is subtracted from the maximum benefit to determine the actual benefit amount awarded. Therefore, for example, a person with earnings of $500 in a given month would receive a benefit of $338. In addition, some states have higher benefits than the federal amount, raising the benefit payment. In 2002, 4.8 million people under age 65 received assistance under this program; total federal payments to these beneficiaries was $2.3 billion.

## Temporary Disability Insurance

Five states, Puerto Rico, and the railroad industry have social insurance programs that partially compensate for the loss of wages caused by non-work-related disability or maternity. These programs are called temporary disability insurance to denote that benefit payments are paid for only a limited duration. To qualify, workers must have worked a certain number of quarters, made a certain amount in earnings, and be disabled.

## Veterans Disability Benefits

Veterans of military service are eligible for assistance to compensate them for both service- and nonservice-connected disability. The assistance includes disability payments, educational assistance, health care, vocational rehabilitation, survivor and dependent benefits, and special loan programs.

In 2002, roughly 2.7 million individuals received benefit payments, with 2.4 million having disabilities connected to military service. For these people, benefits are not determined at all by the amount of their income, and benefits are paid to widows and dependents upon death. Veterans who qualify because of a nonservice-related disability must have low income to qualify for assistance.

### Workers' Compensation

Workers' compensation was one of the first forms of disability insurance that was widely available in the United States. The goal is to provide cash benefits, vocational rehabilitation benefits, and medical benefits when employees suffer work-related injuries, accidents, and illnesses. The benefits are supported by payments made by employers. The program is run at the state level, with a great variety in systems across the 50 states and the District of Columbia. Federal workers are covered by their own system.

In 2001, 127 million workers were covered by workers' compensation programs throughout the nation. Roughly 5 percent of the workforce is not covered by this program—for example, employees in nonprofit, charitable, or religious organizations in some states.

More than $49 billion was paid out in workers' compensation benefits to injured workers (or their survivors) in 2001, making it one of the largest assistance programs to people with disabilities. The cash benefits are often monthly payments made over a specified duration that typically depend on the severity of the worker's injury. In other cases, benefits are made in one lump sum payment. Benefits are designed to compensate workers for the reduction in their abilities to make a living resulting from the workplace injury; therefore, workers with more severe injuries receive higher benefits.

### OTHER FEDERAL PROGRAMS AND POLICIES

In addition to the income support programs listed above, the federal government also has a number of health, housing, and rehabilitation programs that provide benefits to certain groups of individuals (often those with low income) and that make special eligibility allowances for people with disabilities.[5] Antidiscrimination policies have also emerged as a tool to enable Americans with disabilities to participate in social, economic, and political activities. Below is a brief description of some of the most salient programs:

- Two health care programs—Medicare and Medicaid—provide the bulk of publicly funded health care to people with disabilities. Medicaid, for example, which is administered by the states, provides nursing-home care, home health care, personal care services, and adult day care to children and adults who are blind, disabled, and/or age 65 and older who meet income and asset tests. So-called Medicaid-waiver programs provide a range of nonmedical support services excluding room and board to individuals who meet eligibility requirements and who would otherwise be in an institution. Medicare provides short-term skilled nursing facility care, home health care, and durable medical equipment to adults age 65 or older and certain younger people with disabilities.
- Supportive housing options are provided to adults with disabilities through the Congregate Housing Services Act of 1978. The Older Americans Act of 1965 provides nutrition, home care, adult day services, respite, transportation, and preventive health services to certain adults ages 60 and older, many of whom have a disability. Home and community-based services are provided through the Social Services Block Grant, as determined by individual states.
- The Rehabilitation Act of 1973 provides services to adults who have a physical or mental limitation that results in a substantial impediment to employment, but who

## Box 14.1: The Americans With Disabilities Act

The Americans with Disabilities Act (ADA) was signed into law on July 26th, 1990, by President George H. W. Bush. The ADA prohibits discrimination against people with disabilities in a variety of domains including employment, transportation, and public accommodation.

**Definition of disability.** The ADA defines disability as a physical or mental impairment substantially limiting one or more major life activities; an individual must have a record of such impairment or be regarded as having such an impairment. In terms of employment, the law defines a "qualified individual with a disability" as a person with a disability who can perform the essential functions of the job with or without reasonable accommodation.

**Employment.** Under the ADA, employers, employment agencies, labor organizations, and joint labor-management committees must have nondiscriminatory application procedures, qualification standards, and selection criteria, and they must make reasonable accommodation to the known limitations of a qualified applicant or employee unless to do so would cause an undue hardship.

**Transportation.** In the domain of transportation services, all publicly and privately purchased or leased orders for new buses and rail cars must be for accessible vehicles. Para-transit services must be accessible to, and usable by, people with disabilities, and they must provide a level of service equivalent to that provided nondisabled persons. All demand-response service provided to the general public and privately funded fixed roots services must purchase accessible vehicles only. Newly purchased over-the-road coaches purchased after July 26, 1996 must be accessible. New bus and rail terminals must be accessible. Key rail stations must be accessible within three years with extensions available up to 20 years (30 years for some rapid or light rail stations). Amtrak stations must be accessible in 20 years. Within five years, one rail car per train must be accessible.

**Public accommodation.** All entities licensed to do business with or serve the public, such as hotels, theaters, restaurants, shopping malls, stores, office buildings, and private social service agencies, must assure that criteria for eligibility of services do not discriminate. Auxiliary aids and services are required unless they result in an undue burden or fundamentally alter the nature of the goods or services. Entities must remove barriers from existing facilities when such removal is readily achievable. If not, alternative methods of making goods and services available must be provided. Facilities accessible to the maximum extent feasible must be established. In major structural renovations, a path of travel to the altered area, including restrooms and other services, must be accessible. New facilities must be accessible. Generally, other than for health-care facilities and multilevel shopping malls, elevators need not be provided in buildings with fewer than three floors, or fewer than 3,000 square feet per floor.

### Reference

More information about the Americans with Disabilities Act can be obtained at www.ADA.gov.

---

also could benefit from vocational rehabilitative services. Services include vocational rehabilitation, employment training, education, and independent living services.

- The landmark Americans with Disabilities Act, enacted in 1990, prohibits discrimination against people with disabilities in a variety of domains, including employment, transportation, and public accommodation (see Box 14.1). Since the passage of the act, the federal government has launched several additional programs to remove barriers to participation.

- Most recently, the 1998 Assistive Technology Act and the 2001 New Freedom Initiative specifically target the removal of environmental barriers and increased access to assistive and universally designed technologies.

## NOTES

1. Richard V Burkhauser and Mary C. Daly, "U.S. Disability Policy in a Changing Environment," *Journal of Economic Perspectives* 16, no. 1 (2002): 213–24.

2. Unless otherwise noted, information in this section is drawn from Social Security Administration, "Social Security Bulletin Annual Statistical Supplement, 2003," accessed online at www.ssa.gov/policy/docs/statcomps/supplement/2003/index.html, on July 24, 2003.

3. Social Security Administration, "Social Security Handbook," accessed online at www.ssa.gov/OP_Home/handbook/handbook.html, on May 28, 2003.

4. Social Security Administration, "Social Security Bulletin Annual Statistical Supplement, 2002," accessed online at: http://www.ssa.gov/policy/docs/statcomps/supplement/2002/index.html, on July 24, 2003.

5. Jane Tilly and Susan M. Goldenson, *Long-Term Care: Consumers, Providers, and Financing* (Washington, DC: The Urban Institute, 2001).

# American Education

## The Struggle for Progressive Policies

*If a nation expects to be ignorant and free . . . it expects what never was and never will be.*

—Thomas Jefferson

In the first decade of the twenty-first century people take the public educational system for granted. Beginning at five years of age, children can enroll in publicly supported kindergarten, by six years of age they can enter first grade and then proceed through the elementary and secondary levels of public education. For those who are capable, public colleges and universities are readily available in every one of the United States. In 2005, 37.4 million children were enrolled in public K–8 schools, and 14.7 million adolescents were attending public high schools. Public colleges and universities had enrollments of some 12.2 million students.

Public education is an enormous enterprise, and one that is considered to be a vital cultural institution. In this chapter we first describe the development of the American system of public education. We then identify some of the most significant progressive events in this development. Finally, we use several readings to illustrate the effects of these progressive events on U.S. education and on its citizens.

### EARLY EDUCATIONAL INITIATIVES

The current public education system is the culmination of over two hundred years of struggle to fulfill the expectations of generations of U.S. citizens to have a democracy based on a free and educated electorate and an educational system that prepares citizens to achieve their potential in their careers and in their leisure. Even before the establishment of the United States, a commitment to education was evident beginning with the first generation of colonists who came to North America. Within the first twenty-five years of founding the Massachusetts Bay colony, the settlers had passed what became known as "the old deluder Satan" law, which required all towns of fifty families to maintain an elementary school. Towns of one hundred families were to provide a secondary school, and the first American college, Harvard, was established (Spring, 2000).

The first major commitment to broad public support for education came when independence was declared in 1776 and the thirteen former British colonies became states under the Articles of Confederation. Provisions for education were included in eight of the

**111**

thirteen state constitutions. Control of the land west of the Appalachian Mountains—the so-called Northwest Territory, which is now made up mostly of states of the Midwest—was included in the Land Ordinance of 1785. This land was divided into townships, and the land of each township was further divided into sections. One section in every township was set aside for the support of public schools.

A subsequent ordinance formulated in 1787 provided for the governing of the Northwest Territory. One provision of the ordinance encouraged public education because the Confederation leadership believed public education was necessary for the successful working of representative government (Pulliam and Van Patten, 2002).

### STRUGGLES FOR PUBLIC EDUCATION IN THE NEW NATION

The framers of the U.S. Constitution omitted all mention of education. This was not because they believed education was unimportant. Rather, they believed education should be reserved for local communities and the various states. That suited citizens in all of the states because they had an inherent fear of federal government control of education.

This meant that with local control communities had to financially support education. From the beginning of the United States until well into the twentieth century, the property tax was the major source of support for most local and state government programs. Gradually state government support for public education has increased in the past seventy-five years. Federal support has been episodic.

It was not until well into the first half of the nineteenth century when public education with tax control and support began to take shape because the struggle for free, tax-supported elementary schools was met with strong resistance. Many church denominations had already established religious schools, or they planned to do so; consequently they objected vigorously to taxation for public schools. Leaders of secular private schools voiced their opposition as well. Conservatives across political parties, as well as many taxpayers, objected to federal government funding to pay for schools. For them, education was an individual matter and not a service needing government support (Rury, 2002).

In spite of persistent opposition to public education, by the outbreak of the Civil War in 1861, public school systems were firmly established but not fully developed in the northern states. In most southern states they existed only on paper, if at all. This was the case primarily because conservative southern political and economic leaders opposed the expenditure of money on public education, and they had a firm hold on political action within each state (Pulliam and Van Patten, 2002; Spring, 2000).

Meanwhile, state legislatures were beginning to create state universities. The first American colleges were established during the colonial period. They were small, widely scattered, religiously oriented, and most were less than thirty years old when the colonial period ended. But within thirty years of the founding of the United States, nine of the present state universities had opened and were operating (Thelin, 2004).

### THE MORRILL ACTS: THE FIRST MAJOR
### PROGRESSIVE FEDERAL AID TO EDUCATION

A significant breakthrough in the funding for public higher education came at the most unlikely time—in the midst of the Civil War. It was also one of the most influential and progressive Congressional actions on behalf of education during the nineteenth century. In 1862 Congress passed the Morrill Act, which provided federal support to the states in the form of grants of land. The income from the sale or rental of this land by each state was to be used for the "endowment, support, and maintenance of, at least, one college, where the leading object shall be, without excluding other scientific and classical studies, and including military tactics, to teach such branches of learning as are related to agriculture and the mechanic arts, in such manner as the legislatures of the States may respectively prescribe, in order to promote the liberal and practical education of the industrial classes in the several pursuits and professions in life" (the First Morrill Act, 1862:2; see also Cross and Cross, 1999). These colleges came to be known as *land-grant colleges.*

As land grant colleges were established throughout the nation they all suffered from underfunding, so in an effort to provide cash support for the land-grant colleges that had been founded by the first Morrill Act, a second Morrill Act was passed in 1890 that provided a substantial annual appropriation from the federal Treasury to each land-grant college. In addition to the appropriation of money to each state, this legislation had a very significant provision requiring that the annual appropriation would be withheld from states that required the segregation of the races unless they provided agricultural and mechanical colleges for African Americans. The law, in effect, required the establishment of seventeen so-called Negro Colleges in the southern states (Land Grants, 1890; see also Christy and Williamson, 1992).

## PROGRESSIVE EFFORTS TOWARD A NATIONAL SYSTEM OF PUBLIC EDUCATION

During the final three decades of the nineteenth century the scope of elementary education was broadened, schools were graded, kindergarten and high school were added, and real systems of curriculum were formed. In the southern states, the post–Civil War congressional program for reconstruction required that public schools be established not only for whites but also for blacks. It seems that one of the reasons for the readiness of southern states to accept the requirement of public schools for African Americans was fear that Congress would require the establishment of integrated schools. But there was no real attempt to make schools for blacks "equal" to the schools for whites. Still, the actions taken by local and state governments pointed to a public that was committed to creating a complete system of public elementary school and high school education.

Great strides toward a national system of public education from elementary school through college were made during the late nineteenth century, but it was a constant struggle of winning over a variety of conservative constituents who opposed any public support for formal education. Churches that conducted schools saw pubic schools as competition; they also knew that religious education would be absent in public schools. Local communities and state legislatures often refused to appropriate money for public schools. Congresses throughout the nineteenth century refused to involve the federal government in public education because conservative members of both political parties feared that federal support of education would lead to federal control of education.

By the beginning of the twentieth century, the U.S. model of public education from kindergarten through twelfth grade was firmly in place. About 52 percent of five- to nineteen-year-old white children and 30 percent of African American children were enrolled in schools, most of them in the lower grades. With the exception of the land-grant colleges, public support for state universities had languished for decades, but movement began to stir in the late nineteenth century when the state legislatures began to provide regular appropriations to them (Pulliam and Van Patten, 2002; Spring, 2000).

During the first two decades of the twentieth century a massive influx of immigrants from Europe contributed to the rapid increase in public school enrollment rates. Overall, enrollment rates for five- to nineteen-year-olds rose from 52 percent in 1900 to 75 percent in 1940. By the early 1990s, enrollment rates had risen to about 94 percent, and these rates have since remained relatively stable.

The pattern of local control of education began with the omission of education from the U.S. Constitution, thus absolving the federal government from any responsibility for education, and it remained largely in place through the mid-twentieth century. State governments gradually assumed some funding, attendance, and curriculum responsibilities during the late nineteenth and early twentieth centuries. Congress periodically declared that a system of public education was in the national interest and occasionally provided some resources to improve public education, namely, through vocational education programs administered by the states, legislation supporting education for Native Americans, and by land grants for colleges. But the federal government's role in education was minimal. Certainly, there were advocates for a more significant role for the federal government in elementary and secondary public education, but they were consistently routed by conservative members of Congress and conservative presidents (Spring, 2000).

## FEDERAL GOVERNMENT'S PROGRESSIVE ROLE IN EDUCATION EXPANDS

In spite of the advances in industrialization during the nineteenth century, the United States was still largely rural in the first two decades of the twentieth century, and farming was the major occupation. As the Progressive Era initiatives swirled around them, farmers sought public educational assistance. It came with a significant change in the federal government's role in education. The Morrill Acts had provided for the advancement of higher education through the land-grant colleges, but problems remained in getting useful research knowledge that was being acquired at these colleges directly to farmers. Several congressional efforts were made to seek regular and permanent government support for extension teaching to farmers during President Woodrow Wilson's first term, and he was persuaded to approve two of the most progressive farm and agricultural education bills in the nation's history. The first was the Smith-Lever Act (1914), which authorized the land-grant colleges "to aid in diffusing among the people of the United States useful and practical information on subjects relating to agriculture and home economics, . . . and to encourage the application [of the] same" (Smith-Lever Act, 1914:1). Although President Wilson had little understanding of rural life, he called the Smith-Lever Act "one of the most significant and far-reaching measures for the education of adults ever adopted by Government" (*The Corporate Economy,* n.d.:6)

The second piece of progressive education legislation approved by President Wilson was the Smith-Hughes Act of 1917. The purpose of this Act was to foster the vocational education of youth aged fourteen or over, chiefly in high schools. The Smith-Hughes Act committed federal funds for vocational education, and it required each state to provide matching funds for the same purpose. The funds were to pay the salaries of teachers of agricultural, building trades, home economics, and industrial subjects; prepare teachers for all these subjects; study problems associated with the teaching of these subjects; and pay for the administration of the law itself. Because the teaching of these subjects was intended to prepare youth for agricultural, industrial, and home occupations of an immediately productive nature, the act was a vocational education law.

The Progressive Era ended with Warren G. Harding's defeat of Woodrow Wilson in the 1920 election, and the nation was plunged into a decade of conservative politics that found little interest in aiding education from any of the branches of the federal government. It was not until the election of Franklin D. Roosevelt in 1932 that the mood of progressivism was renewed. However, Roosevelt had to first contend with a nation in the depths of a major economic depression, so Roosevelt's New Deal, which was described in Sections 1 and 2, was a progressive set of social and economic policies, but it had little in the way of educational initiatives. Second, Roosevelt was confronted with the exigencies of leading the United States through World War II, which left little time or effort for domestic educational concerns (Edsforth, 2000; McJimsey, 2000).

## THE G.I. BILL: FEDERAL AID TO WORLD WAR II VETERANS

As World War II drew to a close there was the urgent job of relocating the millions of men and women in the military services back into the civilian economy. Numerous options were considered by Roosevelt's postwar planning committees and taskforces to address this looming transition of millions of soon-to-be civilians. A most remarkable and progressive legislative solution was found for this problem in the Servicemen's Readjustment Act, passed in 1944. This "G.I. Bill of Rights," as it came to be called, was enacted partly to reward military service to the country and partly to ameliorate the impending negative effects that massive unemployment would have on the nation's economy.

The G.I. Bill provided unemployment compensation, grants for education and training, and loans for the purchase of homes. *New York Times* writer Greg Winter recently noted that "about half of eligible World War II veterans, or 7.8 million, took advantage of the education benefits under the first G.I. Bill of Rights. It was this bill that helped make higher education such an integral part of society" (2005:1; see also Nam, 1964; Olson, 1974). By opening access to higher education to many young men and women who otherwise would never have been able to attend college, the G.I. Bill had a major effect of upward mobility for millions of people. It also assisted the economy by increasing the number of employable persons.

## 1950s THROUGH THE 1970s: A PLETHORA OF PROGRESSIVE EDUCATION INITIATIVES

The Great Depression, Roosevelt's New Deal, and World War II all contributed to modifying U.S. attitudes toward federalism. During his four terms as president, Roosevelt expanded the federal government into welfare and the economy to an extent never before undertaken. Federal involvement in construction projects, welfare programs, and the creation of Social Security raised the national consciousness about what the federal government could do for people. Progressive policies of the New Deal withstood assaults in the 1950s and 1960s, and steady progress was made in both Democratic and Republican administrations toward a growing acceptance of governmental activism.

Public school enrollments had increased throughout the first half of the twentieth century, but many African Americans, Native Americans, and Hispanics found that even an adequate education was impossible to obtain in the segregated school system. Because of prejudice and neglect, the doors of equal education opportunity all too often remained closed to them. But in the period following World War II through the 1960s, the struggle by African Americans and other minorities for freedom and justice became increasingly intense. All three branches of the federal government took significant steps to address racist practices and policies, and they began to assume a new obligation to ensure equality in educational opportunity. But little did anyone expect that one of the most progressive federal actions in the history of the United States would come from the U.S. Supreme Court, and it involved equal opportunity in education (Klarman, 2004).

### Brown v. Board of Education of Topeka

In 1954, in a groundbreaking decision titled *Brown v. Board of Education of Topeka,* the U.S. Supreme Court reversed over fifty years of the Supreme Court *Plessy v. Ferguson* ruling that "separate but equal" public facilities were constitutional. In a rare unanimous decision, the Court ruled that state or local laws requiring African American citizens to send their children to separate schools violated the 14th Amendment. Furthermore, it followed up by requiring local school authorities to work out plans for gradually ending segregation in public school systems (Bell, 2005; Cottrol et al., 2003).

The *Brown* decision was an example of judicial mode of federal influence. But did it eliminate racism? No. Did it end segregated schools? No. Historians have advanced widely differing interpretations of the progressive effects of *Brown* on race relations over the past fifty years. Derrick Bell (2005), the first tenured African American professor at Harvard, argued that *Brown* did have significant social impact as a symbol more than as a legal precedent. While shattering the fifty-eight-year-old "separate but equal" doctrine, it positioned the law on the side of racial equality and thus facilitated later civil rights and integration strategies that followed. Michael J. Klarman, in an interview after his book about the Supreme Court and the struggle for racial equality won the 2005 Bancroft Prize in history, stated: "I think *Brown* mattered in a variety of ways: it gave much greater salience to the school segregation issue; it gave blacks reason to be hopeful about the future; it motivated blacks in the South to litigate against school segregation; and it mobilized southern whites to resist progressive racial change" (quoted in Goodman, 2005:5; see also Klarman, 2004).

On the heels of the *Brown* decision, government legislation for education escalated as national interest in education expanded into campaigns for higher standards of excellence and more equal opportunities. At the state level, legislatures began supplying extensive aid to local school districts. In return, many states regulated curriculum content, teacher certification, and the length of the school year.

### The National Defense Education Act (NDEA)

The launch of the Soviet Union's *Sputnik* satellite in 1957 provided a significant boost for federal aid to U.S. education because the nation's leaders believed that the reason the

Soviet Union won the race into space was that U.S. schools were turning out students deficient in math and sciences. Consequently, Congress and President Dwight D. Eisenhower perceived an urgent Cold War crisis and quickly passed the National Defense Education Act (NDEA) of 1958. This legislation provided funds for summer institutes for teacher training in math, science and foreign languages, as well as providing fellowships to graduate students preparing to become college professors.

## President Lyndon Johnson and His Great Society Initiatives

On ascending to the presidency after President John F. Kennedy's assassination in the fall of 1963, President Lyndon Johnson's administration was faced with an emergency with some of the same characteristics as the *Sputnik* crisis. Only this time it revolved around a crisis of poverty and racial disharmony that many believed could be met through improved educational opportunity. The federal government began to play a more active role in education at lower levels. President Johnson urged the federal government to create a Great Society, and the programs of the Great Society ultimately comprised the most significant expansion of the federal government since the New Deal. Great Society initiatives developed new educational programs to support poor children and to compensate for social and economic disadvantages. Federal funding was funneled through educational agencies to establish programs to provide early childhood education to disadvantaged children. The programs were grounded in a belief that government was obligated to help disadvantaged groups in order to compensate for the inequalities in social or economic conditions (Kotz, 2005).

## Elementary and Secondary Education Act of 1965 (ESEA)

One of President Johnson's most satisfying accomplishments was securing passage of the Elementary and Secondary Education Act of 1965 (ESEA), as one component of his War on Poverty. At the signing of this act into law, President Johnson said, "By passing this bill, we bridge the gap between helplessness and hope for more than 5 million educationally deprived children. . . . As President of the United States, I believe deeply no law I have signed or will ever sign means more to the future of America" (Johnson, 1964–1970:407). This legislation demolished the traditional taboo against providing significant federal aid to public education.

ESEA was a merger of civil rights and public school concerns, and it provided federal aid to underfunded public school districts for the education of children in poor school districts who needed assistance with basic skills. Other ESEA features provided for school improvement, libraries, research, and resources to improve state departments of education. This legislation drew on expanding expectations of what it meant to be a U.S. citizen and what role the federal government should play in providing educational opportunities (Jeffrey, 1978).

## Project Head Start

In May 1965 President Johnson announced the initiation of Project Head Start as another component of his War on Poverty. Its creation was inspired by the civil rights movement and President Johnson's thinking about the nature of poverty and the uses of education to overcome it. Head Start was based on a fundamental belief in education as the solution to poverty, and it was designed as one instrument for breaking the cycle of poverty by giving preschool age children from low-income families a comprehensive educational experience—a "head start"—that would meet their social, psychological, health, and nutritional needs in preparation for attending kindergarten.

Head Start's original goal was to provide preschool children from low-income families with rewarding learning experiences while increasing the social competence of those children; that is a goal that it continues to pursue. Educators, child development experts, community leaders, and parents throughout the nation enthusiastically endorsed Head Start from its beginnings (Fleck, 1995; Kotz, 2005).

In 1969 Head Start was transferred from the Office of Economic Opportunity to the Office of Child Development in the U.S. Department of Health, Education, and Welfare. Currently it is one of the programs within the Administration for Children and Families in the U.S. Department of Health and Human Services. Head Start has expanded from an eight-week demonstration project to include full day and year services for children from birth to age three. For forty years no other early childhood educational program has been more extensive and successful in meeting the needs of targeted children, families, and communities. In 2005 the Head Start program had served more than 23 million children in all fifty states, the District of Columbia, Puerto Rico, the Virgin Islands, and Pacific Insular Areas (Thompson, 1995).

In spite of this impressive record, only three out of every five eligible children in the nation participate in the Head Start program, leaving 2.6 million eligible children and their families without a chance to reduce the harsh impact of poverty on their future. Research has convincingly shown that Head Start makes a positive difference in the lives of children, families, and communities (Zigler and Valentine, 1997).

Head Start is not the only preschool program. States across the country have begun to recognize the necessity for significant investments in early childhood education. Forty-six states operate prekindergarten programs, and state funding for these programs has increased dramatically, from $700 million in the early 1990s to more than $2 billion in 2004. Several states have enacted initiatives that call for universal preschool education. The most recent trend in early education is for children from birth to age three. In 1994 the Early Head Start program began filling a void in formal education during the first three years of life. Parent-focused services such as Parents as Teachers, the Home Instruction Program for Preschool Youth, and the Parent-Child Home Program are attracting states throughout the country and funding by local governments and charities for learning projects for children three years old and younger (Mendel, 2004).

### The Higher Education Act

The third significant federal legislative action on behalf of education during 1965 was the the Higher Education Act (HEA). This legislation provides federal aid to needy college and university students. It has multiple components (or "Titles") relating to specific areas of higher education. The portion of the HEA that deals specifically with student aid programs is Title IV. Most of the federal student aid programs fall under this title. These programs are in place specifically to strengthen the educational resources of our colleges and universities and to assist students and families with meeting the costs associated with pursuing a post-secondary and higher education. Title IV federal financial aid programs were established to provide financial assistance to low-income students who could not otherwise afford a college education. It is reauthorized every other year. During reauthorization, Congress often makes changes and improvements in the legislation, such as adding new programs, streamlining existing programs, and increasing authorized funding levels. The most recent reauthorization of the Higher Education Act was in 2005.

### Conservative Responses to Progressive Federal Assistance to Education from the 1950s to 1970s

By the late 1960s James Sundquist of the Brookings Institution declared, "Some measure of federal leadership, influence, and control is now with us. Federal money is now being used, and will continue to be used, as a lever to alter . . . the American educational scene" (1968:219). Although Sundquist's statement was accurate, some conservative political leaders and business interests were not supporters of what was taking place. A variety of conservative groups and individuals were opposed to the federal government's increased presence in education. Opponents of federal prerogatives in education preferred to see authority in the hands of states, or at the district or school level. For them, federal initiatives into education contradicted the long tradition of state-sponsored public schooling, which they believed should be maintained. Their arguments against federal aid to education, which they considered a menace, ranged from the long-standing positions of the U.S. Chamber of Commerce to the more extreme views of the radical conservative ideologues.

## PROGRESSIVE EDUCATION POLICIES STRUGGLE IN RECENT DECADES

The direction of federal government involvement in education has been generally upward from 1970 to 2005, but it has always been contested terrain and thus has not kept up with the inflation index over the same period. From the 1970s to the present, each Congress and each president has had to reinvent the federal role in education. As Bluestone and Harrison (2001) noted, "Federal expenditures on education and training, over the century's last quarter, actually dropped, as a share of gross domestic product, by 50 percent" (223).

### Education of All Handicapped Children Act

In 1975, Congress passed the Education of All Handicapped Children Act (Public Law 94-142), now called the Individuals with Disabilities Education Act (IDEA), to ensure that all students with disabilities receive a free and appropriate education. According to the law, states are required to develop and implement policies that ensure a free appropriate public education to all children with disabilities, in order to receive the federal funds for this Act (Public Law 94-142, 1975).

This act was passed in spite of President Gerald Ford's objection to it. A committed conservative, Ford said, when he signed the papers for Public Law 94-142, "Unfortunately, this bill promises more than the Federal Government can deliver, and its good intentions could be thwarted by the many unwise provisions it contains. . . . Even the strongest supporters of this measure know as well as I that they are falsely raising the expectations of the groups affected by claiming authorization levels which are excessive and unrealistic. . . . [The] funding levels proposed in this bill will simply not be possible if Federal expenditures are to be brought under control and a balanced budget achieved over the next few years" (Ford, 1975:10).

In 1980, Ronald Reagan, a renowned spokesman for conservative interests, was elected president. When he took office he made it clear that he was adamantly opposed to expanding the federal role in education, and he even threatened to abolish the U.S. Department of Education. In Reagan's first term federal funding for education declined an astonishing 21 percent. But in spite of President Reagan's aversion to federal assistance to education, throughout his two terms in office many public schools received federal subsidies for textbooks, transportation, and school breakfast and lunch programs, as well as grants for school libraries, science and language labs, metric education, school-based experiments in teaching and learning, and services for students with disabilities. Much of this federal assistance came through legislation and policies that preceded Reagan's administration. These various forms of federal assistance were maintained during the 1990s. The federal expenditures for educational purposes during these two decades enriched the lives of millions of schoolchildren throughout the nation, especially those in inner-city schools.

### No Child Left Behind Act

The most dramatic federal incursion into education in the past twenty-five years is the No Child Left Behind (NCLB) Act of 2001, which was sponsored by President George W. Bush and passed by Congress (P.L.107-110, 2002). The roots of NCLB are found in the Improving America's Schools Act (IASA) of 1994, passed during Bill Clinton's presidency. IASA emphasized that with federal funding the government intended to hold states and schools more accountable for the academic performance of its students. But the NCLB law went far beyond IASA. It greatly expanded the federal role in public education by providing an unprecedented increase in federal resources to state governments, but it also required that each state adopt testing and accountability standards in its public schools.

Accountability is the centerpiece of NCLB. If states want to continue receiving federal funding under NCLB provisions, they must comply with the requirements of NCLB standards. To meet the NCLB expectations, states are required to test students annually for reading and math in grades 3 through 8, and they must also test students in one high school grade. A specific percentage of a school's students must reach "proficiency" in those tests and make "adequate yearly progress" in order for the school to be considered successful. Those that fail are labeled "failing schools" and face penalties. Schools that fail in the same area for two or more consecutive years face progressively harsher penalties.

NCLB requires that schools ensure there are qualified teachers in each classroom, and teachers whose students fail to meet specific federal standards may be replaced. States may even restructure a school that has been classified as a failing school and reopen it as a charter or private school. Students in failing schools are allowed to transfer out of such schools.

At first, both political parties in Congress welcomed NCLB when it was proposed by the Bush administration, and it easily passed both houses of Congress. Progressives envisioned NCLB as having promise for being a progressive federal program with the potential of assisting minority children, children from low-income families, and disabled children. Historically these are the children most disadvantaged by traditional public education. However, with implementation it became clear that NCLB came with an extraordinary increase in federal mandates and harsh sanctions, if performance standards were not met by states and schools, while actually doing little for the disadvantaged students.

Within a short time after passage of this law, congressional members, both conservative and progressive, began to have widespread skepticism about NCLB. There is now nationwide bipartisan disapproval of NCLB and a growing conviction that the law may be doing more harm than good for U.S. public schools and their students. A persistent condemnation, and one that cuts across all constituencies, is that NCLB has never been fully funded; thus funding falls far short of what would be needed to make every student in every public school proficient.

Other objections to NCLB include questioning whether the one-size-fits-all approach is appropriate and whether the law has reduced the role that parents and teachers play with respect to key decisions in local schools. Teachers and administrators complain that the time required for preparing and testing reduces students' learning time for other subjects. At the state level there is resentment because although only about 6 percent of the money for education comes from the federal government, NCLB seems intent on controlling 100 percent of the states' education policies.

The National Center for Fair and Open Testing (NCFOT) articulates why the NCLB misses the mark as a progressive program: "NCLB ignores the real reasons many children are left behind. The failure to address factors outside of school that influence academic achievement guarantees NCLB will not succeed. The best school, the best teachers and the best curriculum can make a huge difference in the lives of disadvantaged children, but basic needs like housing, health care and nutrition must also be addressed to truly close the achievement gap between poor and rich children" (NCFOT, 2004:3).

## Higher Education: Needs-Based Assistance, Loans, and Accessibility to Higher Education

Over the past three decades, financial aid for college students increased in total value but did not keep pace with increases in college tuition and expenses. The proportion of federal aid to college students that is awarded on the basis of need has been declining. Needs-based assistance accounted for about 80 percent of all federal aid at the beginning of the 1990s, but it now accounts for less than 60 percent.

The Federal Pell Grant program is an example of a diminishing federal commitment to low-income students. In 1972, the Basic Grant (now Pell Grant) program was created to provide a means of support for higher education to children from low-income families, and Pell Grants were awarded to students based on financial need. In 1977, the maximum Pell Grant—considered the cornerstone of aid for low-income students—paid for 77 percent of the cost of tuition and room and board at a typical public, four-year university. In 2005 it covered only 40 percent, on average. In the race for college access and affordability, the Pell Grant has lagged badly.

The trend toward non-needs-based financial aid for college students is also found at the state level. Although three quarters of state financial aid remains needs-based, since the early 1990s, most states have turned in the direction of non-needs-based merit scholarships. Non-needs-based state aid has grown 336 percent, whereas needs-based aid has grown only 88 percent. Recently, the American Association of Small Colleges and Universities

criticized the trend of increased student aid programs that emphasize academic achievement and middle-class affordability rather than financial need.

Some 60 percent of all college financial aid is now in the form of loans. Consequently,
the prevailing student practice has been to borrow money for college expenses. The average
student loan debt has nearly doubled to $17,000 over the past decade. As a consequence,
many youth from low-income families abandon plans for college or drop out because the
debt and workload is too much, and this pattern is strongest among minority students.
According to the research of economists Michael McPherson and Morton Owen Schapiro,
"the percentage of high-achieving students who do not enroll in college is five times higher
among those who are poor than those who are rich" (quoted in Steinberg, 2002:A18).

When viewed another way, eighteen- to twenty-four-year-olds from the nation's
wealthiest families are nearly nine times more likely to earn a bachelor's degree than the
same age group from the nation's poorest families (Toppo and DeBarros, 2005; see also
Bowen, Kurzweil, Tobin, and Pichler, 2005). Clearly, if the United States is to uphold its
commitment to democracy through higher education opportunities, public policies must
be pursued that will advance that ideal. Recent trends suggest that policies and ideals are
moving access to higher education in opposite directions.

The trend is not all gloomy. Progressive efforts have been made by some state governments. A few states have recently reversed the trend of non-needs-based scholarships
and student loans. For example, in 2003 the University of North Carolina at Chapel Hill
announced a groundbreaking initiative in college accessibility called the Carolina Covenant. The new financial aid plan covers the full costs of education—tuition, room and
board, and books—for children of low-income families to attend UNC–Chapel Hill without borrowing any money. The purpose of the program is to counter a growing view among
high school graduates from poor families that higher education is out of reach. Furthermore, according to the university chancellor, "College should be possible for everyone who
can make the grade, regardless of family income" (University of North Carolina at Chapel
Hill, 2003:1–2; see also Schemo, 2003).

The Carolina Covenant will enable low-income students to attend UNC–Chapel Hill
and graduate debt free if they work on campus ten to twelve hours weekly. North Carolina
is believed to be the first public university in the nation to pledge to meet the full education costs of poor students. With one in four North Carolina children living in poverty, the
need for an accessibility initiative like the Carolina Covenant will undoubtedly remain in
the foreseeable future.

Georgia is another state that has created a program aimed at making higher education
more accessible. In 1993, Georgia established a college scholarship and grant program
called Helping Outstanding Pupils Educationally (HOPE). The HOPE program is funded
entirely by revenue from the Georgia lottery, administered by the Georgia Lottery Corporation (Georgia Lottery, 2005).

There are two separate components of the HOPE program, a merit-based scholarship and a grant. In degree-granting public institutions, the HOPE scholarship includes
tuition, HOPE-approved mandatory fees, and a book allowance of up to $100 per quarter
for attendance at any of Georgia's public colleges, universities, or technical colleges. To
qualify for the scholarship, entering freshmen must have graduated from an eligible Georgia high school since 1993 with at least a B (3.0 grade-point) average and be a Georgia
resident (Cornwell-Mustard HOPE Scholarship, n.d.). Since 1993, over $1.6 billion has

been distributed to almost 700,000 students through the HOPE scholarship, making it the largest state-financed, merit-based aid program in the United States.

In contrast to the HOPE scholarship program, the HOPE grant program is essentially an entitlement that applies to non-degree programs at two-year and less-than-two-year schools. Qualification for a grant is not contingent on high school grade-point average. There are no restrictions based on when a student graduated from high school. The grant covers tuition and HOPE-approved mandatory fees and a book allowance of up to $100 per quarter. There are no merit requirements for applicants, but continued support under the grant is contingent on a student's satisfactory academic performance (Cornwell-Mustard Hope Scholarship, n.d.).

In spite of these progressive initiatives by various states, the best hope for making higher education more accessible for the children of poor families may be the colleges and universities themselves. In the past decade many colleges and universities have established financial aid programs to make higher education more accessible, especially to those from low-income homes. In fact, according to the president of the American Council on Education, at the present time "colleges and universities spend more on grant aid than the states and the federal government combined, and most of that money goes to students with financial need" (Ward, 2005:1).

## CONCLUSION

The framers of the U.S. Constitution were wary of central government's involvement in citizens' lives, so education was left to local and state jurisdictions. During the nineteenth century a public education system consisting of elementary schools, junior high schools, high schools, and state universities was gradually built throughout the nation. The main educational task of the twentieth century was meeting the demands of an increasingly urbanized and rapidly growing population.

In the early twentieth century two federal education bills were passed to foster vocational education related to agriculture and home economics to prepare youth for agricultural, industrial, and home occupations. But it was the G.I. Bill, which provided unemployment compensation, grants for education and training, and loans for the purchase of homes to World War II veterans, that was the first major significant federal government support for education. The *Brown v. Board of Education of Topeka* decision outlawed the forced segregation of races in public schools, opening educational opportunities for African Americans that had previously been denied them. Federal government involvement in educational initiatives has expanded over the past forty years.

Throughout U.S. history there has been a struggle between progressives, who have favored a more active role for the federal government in education, and conservatives, who have argued that since the U.S. Constitution grants no role to the federal government in education the federal government should leave education to local governments.

## REFERENCES

Bell, Derrick. (2005). *Silent Covenants:* Brown v. Board of Education *and the Unfulfilled Hopes for Racial Reform.* New York: Oxford University Press.
Bluestone, Barry, and Harrison, Bennett. (2001). *Growing Prosperity: The Battle for Growth with Equity in the Twenty-First Century.* Berkeley: University of California Press.

Bowen, William G., Kurzweil, Martin A., Tobin, Eugene M., and Pichler, Susanne C. (2005). *Equity and Excellence in American Higher Education.* Charlottesville: University of Virginia Press.

Christy, Ralph D., and Williamson, Lionel. (1992). *A Century of Service: Land-Grant Colleges and Universities, 1890–1990.* Piscataway, NJ: Transaction.

Cornwell-Mustard HOPE Scholarship, "Georgia's HOPE Scholarship," Terry College of Business, University of Georgia (n.d.): http://terry.uga.edu/hope/gahope.html.

*Corporate Economy and Progressive Politics, 1901–1916* (n.d.): www.angelfire.com/alt/michael-butt/chapter19.htm.

Cottrol, Robert J., Diamond, Raymond T., Ware, Leland B., and Ware, Leland. (2003). Brown v. Board of Education*: Caste, Culture, and the Constitution.* Lawrence: University of Kansas Press.

Cross, Coy F., and Cross II, Coy F. (1999). *Justin Smith Morrill, Father of the Land-Grant Colleges.* East Lansing: Michigan State University Press.

Edsforth, Ronald. (2000). *The New Deal: America's Response to the Great Depression.* Malden, MA: Blackwell.

Fleck, Karen M. (1995). "Easing into Elementary School." *Education Digest* 61(November):42–44.

The First Morrill Act. (1862): www.cals.ncsu.edu/agexed/aee501/morrill.html.

Ford, Gerald R. (1975, November). *Statement on Signing the Education for All Handicapped Children Act of 1975:* www.ford.utexas.edu/library/speeches/750707.htm.

Georgia Lottery Corporation. (2005). "Hope Scholarships": www.galottery.com/gen/education/hopeScholarship.jsp?focus=education.

Goodman, Bonnie. (2005, April 18). "Interview with Michael J. Klarman, Winner of the 2005 Bancroft Prize." *History News Network:* www.hnn.us/articles/11371.html.

Jeffrey, Julie Roy. (1978). *Education of the Children of the Poor: A Study of the Origins and Implementation of the Elementary Education Act of 1965.* Columbus: Ohio State University Press.

Johnson, Lyndon Baines. (1964–1970). *Public Papers of the President of the United States.* Washington, DC: Government Printing Office.

Klarman, Michael J. (2004). *From Jim Crow to Civil Rights: The Supreme Court and the Struggle for Racial Equality.* New York: Oxford University Press.

Kotz, Nick. (2005). *Judgment Days: Lyndon Baines Johnson, Martin Luther King, Jr., and the Laws That Changed America.* Boston: Houghton Mifflin.

Land Grants: Second Morrill Act. (1890): www.higher-ed.org/resources/morrill2.htm.

McJimsey, George. (2000). *The Presidency of Franklin Delano Roosevelt.* Lawrence: University of Kansas Press.

Mendel, Dick. (2004, November). "Leave No Parent Behind." *The American Prospect* (November): A8–A10.

Nam, Charles B. (1964, October). "The Impact of the 'GI Bill' on the Educational Level of the Male Population." *Social Forces* 43(October):26–32.

National Center for Fair and Open Testing. (2004). " 'No Child Left Behind' after Two Years: A Track Record of Failure": www.fairtest.org/nclb%20flaw%20fact%20sheet%201-7-04.html.

No Child Left Behind Act: Public Law 107-110 (2002): www.ed.gov./policy/elsec/leg/esea02/107-110.pdf.

Olson, Keith W. (1974). *The GI Bill, the Veterans, and the Colleges.* Lexington: University of Kentucky Press.

Public Law 94-142. (1975). Education of All Handicapped Children Act: www.scn.org./~bk269/94-142.html.

Pulliam, John D., and Van Patten, James J. (2002). *History of Education in America,* 8th ed. Englewood Cliffs, NJ: Prentice Hall.

Rury, John L. (2002). *Education and Social Change: Themes in the History of American Schools.* Mahwah, NJ: Lawrence Erlbaum.

Schemo, Diana Jean. (2003). "Chapel Hill Campus to Cover All Costs for Needy Students." *New York Times* (October 2):A18.

Smith-Lever Act. (1914): www.higher-ed.org/resources/smith.htm.

Spring, Joel. (2000). *The American School 1642–2000,* 5th ed. New York: McGraw-Hill.

Steinberg, Jacques. (2002). "Greater Share of Income Is Committed to College." *New York Times* (May 2):A18.

Sundquist, James. (1968). *Politics and Policy: The Eisenhower, Kennedy and Johnson Years.* Washington, DC: Brookings Institution.

Thelin, John R. (2004). *A History of American Higher Education.* Baltimore: Johns Hopkins University Press.

Thompson, L. S. (1995). *Head Start Program a "Miracle Solution."* Washington, DC: American, P. G.

Toppo, Greg, and DeBarros, Anthony. (2005). "Reality Weighs Down Dreams of College." *USA Today* (February 2):1A–2A.

University of North Carolina at Chapel Hill. (2003, October 1). "UNC–Chapel Hill Breaks New Ground in College Accessibility" (news release).

Ward, David. (2005). "ACE President David Ward Responds to *USA Today* Story, 'Is College Getting Out of Reach?'" Washington, DC: American Council on Education (February 7):1: www.acenet.edu/hena/readArticle.cfm?articleID=1206.

Winter, Greg. (2005). "College and Money: From Combat to Campus on the G.I. Bill." *New York Times* (January 16):4A, 8.

Zigler, Edward, and Valentime, Jeanette. (1997). *Project Head Start: A Legacy of the War on Poverty,* 2nd ed. Washington, DC: National Head Start Association.

# 15

# Two Cheers for *Brown v. Board of Education*

### CLAYBORNE CARSON

*When* Brown *was announced in 1954, it was hailed as a landmark in U.S. history. Supporters and activists drew inspiration from it. But in recent years, some prominent African America scholars have argued that* Brown *did little to secure the African American struggle for freedom and equality. The author of this article contends that even though racial equality remains unfulfilled, that is no reason to deny the superb contribution* Brown *made to advancing African American civil rights and to the use of the law to advance human equality.*

My gratuitous opinion of *Brown v. Board of Education* (1954) is somewhat ambivalent and certainly arrives too late to alter the racial policies of the past fifty years. But for those of us who practice history, hindsight offers a far more reliable kind of wisdom than does foresight. We see clearly now that while the *Brown* decision informed the attitudes that have shaped contemporary American race relations, it did not resolve persistent disputes about the nation's civil rights policies. The Supreme Court's unanimous opinion in *Brown* broke decisively with the racist interpretations of traditional American values set forth in *Scott v. Sandford* (1857) and *Plessy v. Ferguson* (1896), offering instead the optimistic "American Creed" that Gunnar Myrdal saw as the solution to "the Negro problem."[1] Like the two earlier landmark decisions, *Brown* overestimated the extent of ideological consensus among Americans and soon exacerbated racial and regional conflicts instead of resolving them. The Court's ruling against school segregation encouraged African Americans to believe that the entire structure of white supremacy was illegitimate and legally vulnerable. But the civil rights struggles *Brown* inspired sought broader goals than the decision could deliver, and that gap fostered frustration and resentment among many black Americans. In short, the decision's virtues and limitations reflect both the achievements and the failures of the efforts made in the last half century to solve America's racial dilemma and to realize the nation's egalitarian ideals.

That the *Brown* decision spurred subsequent civil rights progress seems apparent, but its impact and its significance as a source of inspiration are difficult to measure.[2] Although the Court's initial unwillingness to set firm timetables for school desegregation undercut *Brown's* immediate impact, African Americans expanded the limited scope of the decision by individual and collective challenges to the Jim Crow system. Small-scale protests escalated during the decade after 1954, becoming a sustained mass movement against all facets of segregation and discrimination in the North as well as the South. Civil rights protests and litigation prompted Congress to pass the Civil Rights Act of 1964 and the Voting Rights Act of 1965, both of which extended the *Brown* decision's egalitarian principles well beyond education. The historic mass struggle that followed *Brown* ultimately destroyed the legal foundations of the Jim Crow system, and their destruction prepared the way for a still more far-reaching expansion of prevailing American conceptions of civil rights and of the role of government in protecting those rights. During the past forty years, women and many minority groups, including immigrants and people with disabilities, have gained new legal protections modeled on the civil rights gains of African Americans.[3]

But the *Brown* decision also created racial aspirations that remain unrealized. Although the decision may have been predicated on the notion of a shared American creed, most white Americans were unwilling to risk their own racial privileges to bring about racial equality. The decision was neither universally accepted nor consistently enforced. "Instead, it provoked overwhelming resistance in the South and only tepid interest in the North," the historian John Higham insisted. "In the South the decision released a tidal wave of racial hysteria that swept moderates out of office or turned them into demagogues. State and local officials declined to obstruct a revival of the Ku Klux Klan. Instead, they employed every conceivable device to maintain segregation, including harassment and dissolution of NAACP chapters."[4] By the 1970s, resistance to school desegregation had become national. Northern whites in Boston and elsewhere demonstrated their unwillingness to send their children to predominantly black schools or to allow large-scale desegregation that would drastically alter the racial composition of "their" schools in "their" neighborhoods. Voters in the states of Washington and California passed initiatives to restrict the right of school boards (Washington) and state courts (California) to order busing to achieve school desegregation (the Supreme Court later held the Washington initiative unconstitutional). Nationwide, white racial resentments encouraged an enduring shift of white voters from the Democratic to the Republican party. The 1964 election would be the last presidential contest in which the majority of black voters and of white voters backed the same candidate. Since 1974, when the Supreme Court's *Milliken v. Bradley* decision set limits on busing, the legal meaning of desegregation has been scaled back to conform to American racial and political realities.[5]

African Americans generally applauded the *Brown* decision when it was announced, but the Court's failure to realize *Brown's* bold affirmation of egalitarian ideals fueled subsequent black discontent and disillusionment. *Brown* cited studies that demonstrated the harmful psychological impact of enforced segregation on black students, reporting, "To separate them from others of similar age and qualifications solely because of their race generates a feeling of inferiority as to their status in the community that may affect their hearts and minds in a way unlikely ever to be undone." Yet the Court did not offer an effective means to correct the problem it had identified. During the decades after *Brown,* most southern black children continued to suffer the psychological consequences of segregation, while a small minority assumed the often considerable psychological and physical risks of attending newly integrated public schools. Rather than bringing large numbers of black and white students together in public schools, the *Brown* decision—and the subsequent years of litigation and social conflict—enabled a minority of black students to attend predominantly white schools. Ten years after the *Brown* decision, according to data compiled by the U.S. Department of Education, almost 98 percent of southern black students still attended predominantly black schools. Now, at the beginning of the twenty-first century, the Court's ideal of educational opportunity as "a right which must be made available to all on equal terms" is still far from being realized. American schools, both public and private, are still highly segregated. According to a recent study, the typical Latino or black student in the United States still attends a school where members of minority groups are predominant.[6]

Certainly, the *Brown* decision's most significant deficiency is its failure to address the concerns of the majority of African American students who have been unable or unwilling to seek better educational opportunities by leaving predominantly black schools for predominantly white ones. While it opened the door for the Little Rock Nine, who desegregated Central High School in 1957, the *Brown* decision offered little solace to the hundreds of students who remained at Little Rock's all-black Horace Mann High School. When Arkansas officials reacted to desegregation by closing all of Little Rock's high schools, those students were denied even segregated educational opportunities.[7] With the encouragement of the lawyers for the National Association for the Advancement of Colored People's (NAACP) Legal Defense and Education Fund, the Supreme Court largely abandoned previous efforts to enforce the separate but equal mandate in order to adopt a narrowly conceived strategy for achieving equal educational opportunity through desegregation. The pre-*Brown* equalization effort had encouraged social scientists to develop increasingly sophisticated ways of measuring differences in the quality of schools. But during the 1950s, pro–civil rights scholars shifted their focus from the educational environment of black students in black schools to the psychological state of black students experiencing desegregation. The NAACP's initial strategy of forcing southern states to equalize facilities at all-black schools had resulted in tangible improvements, whereas the removal of racial barriers in public schools was advertised as offering intangible psychological gains.

For Thurgood Marshall, who headed the NAACP legal staff, the equalization effort had always been a means of achieving the ultimate goal of desegregation. After the Supreme Court decided in *Sweatt v. Painter* (1950) that a makeshift segregated law school at a black college could not provide educational opportunities equal to those offered by the University of Texas Law School, Marshall exulted, "The complete destruction of all enforced segregation is now in sight." Despite having attended predominantly black schools at every stage of his academic career, he saw segregation as a racial stigma that could not be removed by increased state appropriations for Jim Crow schools. In the early 1950s he noted that social scientists were "almost in universal agreement that segregated education produces inequality." He therefore concluded "that segregated schools, perhaps more than any other single factor, are of major concern to the individual of public school age and contribute greatly to the unwholesomeness and unhappy development of the personality of Negroes which the color caste system in the United States has produced."[8]

Few African Americans would wish to return to the pre-*Brown* world of legally enforced segregation, but in the half century since 1954, only a minority of Americans has experienced the promised land of truly integrated public education. By the mid-1960s, with dual school systems still in place in many areas of the Deep South, and with de facto segregation a recognized reality in urban areas, the limitations of *Brown* had become evident to many of those who had spearheaded previous civil rights struggles. The ideological gulf that appeared in African American politics during the period was largely the result of efforts to draw attention to the predominantly black institutions neglected in the drive for racial integration. The black power movement arose in part as an effort by African Americans to control and improve such institutions. Some black power proponents exaggerated the benefits of racial separatism, but their extremism can be best understood as a reaction against the unbalanced post-*Brown* strategy of seeking racial advancement solely through integration. Although James S. Coleman's landmark 1966 study of equality of educational opportunity found that black children attending integrated schools did better than students attending predominantly black schools, it was by no means clear that the gap was the result of interracial interactions rather than of differences in the socioeconomic backgrounds of the students involved. By the late 1960s, growing numbers of black leaders had concluded that improvement of black schools should take priority over school desegregation. In 1967, shortly before the National Advisory Commission on Civil Disorders warned that the United States was "moving toward two societies, one white, one black—separate and unequal," Martin Luther King Jr. acknowledged the need to refocus attention, at least in the short run, on "schools in ghetto areas." He also insisted that "the drive for immediate improvements in segregated schools should not retard progress toward integrated education later." Even veterans of the NAACP's legal campaign had second thoughts. "*Brown* has little practical relevance to central city blacks," Constance Baker Motley commented in 1974. "Its psychological and legal relevance has already had its effect."[9]

Black power advocates sometimes sought to replace the narrow strategy of achieving racial advancement through integration with the equally narrow strategy of achieving it through racial separatism. In both instances, claims of psychological gains often substituted for measurable racial advancements, but the continued popularity of Afrocentric educational experiments indicates that many African Americans now see voluntary segregation as psychologically uplifting. Having personally experienced the burden of desegregating numerous classrooms and having watched my son move with great success from a predominantly black college to a predominantly white law school, I am skeptical of sweeping claims about the impact of racial environment on learning. While believing that debates among African Americans during the last half century about their destiny have been useful, I regret that those debates have often exacerbated ideological conflict rather than encouraging us toward collective action. Rather than having to choose between overcoming racial barriers and improving black community institutions, we should be able to choose both.

In hindsight, the nation would have been better served if the *Brown* decision had evinced a more realistic understanding of the deep historical roots of America's racial problems—perhaps a little more familiarity with the writings of W. E. B. Du Bois and Carter G. Woodson as well as those of Myrdal and his colleagues. Rather than blandly advising that desegregation of public schools be achieved with "all deliberate speed," the Supreme Court—and the NAACP lawyers who argued before it—should have launched a two-pronged attack, not only against racial segregation but also against inferior schools, whatever their racial composition. Such an attack would have heeded the admonition that Du Bois offered in 1935, soon after his forced resignation as editor of the NAACP's journal, the *Crisis:*

*Theoretically, the Negro needs neither segregated schools nor mixed schools. What he needs is Education. . . . Other things being equal, the mixed school is the broader, more natural basis for the education of all youth. It gives wider contacts; it inspires great self-confidence; and suppresses the inferiority complex. But other things seldom are equal, and in that case, Sympathy, Knowledge, and the Truth, outweigh all that the mixed school can offer.* [10]

Because the *Brown* decision was a decisive departure from *Plessy*'s separate but equal principle, it was an important turning point in African American history. Nevertheless, fifty years later the Court's assumptions about the psychological consequences of legally enforced segregation seem dated. The Jim Crow system no longer exists, but most black American schoolchildren still attend predominantly black public schools that offer fewer opportunities for advancement than typical predominantly white public schools. Moreover, there is no contemporary civil rights movement able to alter that fact. Yet, if *Brown* represents a failed attempt to achieve comprehensive racial advancement, the opinion nonetheless still challenges us by affirming egalitarian ideals that remain relevant: "In these days, it is doubtful that any child may reasonably be expected to succeed in life if he is denied the opportunity of an education. Such an opportunity, where the state has undertaken to provide it, is a right which must be made available to all on equal terms."[11]

## NOTES

1.  *Scott v. Sandford,* 19 How. 393 (1857); *Plessy v. Ferguson,* 163 U.S. 537 (1896); *Brown v. Board of Education,* 347 U.S. 483 (1954); Gunnar Myrdal, *An American Dilemma: The Negro Problem and Modern Democracy* (2 vols., New York, 1944).

2.  On *Brown*'s direct and indirect consequences, see, for example, Michael J. Klarman, "How *Brown* Changed Race Relations: The Backlash Thesis," *Journal of American History,* 81 (June 1994), 81–118. Klarman correctly points out that *Brown* had limited impact on school desegregation, especially in the Deep South, and stimulated southern white resistance to racial reform. He concludes that the contributions of *Brown* to the broader civil rights struggle were mostly indirect.

3.  Cf. Hugh Davis Graham, *The Civil Rights Era: Origins and Development of National Policy, 1960–1972* (New York, 1990); Hugh Davis Graham, *Collision Course: The Strange Convergence of Affirmative Action and Immigration Policy in America* (New York, 2002); and John D. Skrenny, *The Minority Rights Revolution* (Cambridge, Mass., 2002).

4.  John Higham, "Introduction: A Historical Perspective," in *Civil Rights and Civil Wrongs: Black-White Relations since World War II,* ed. John Higham (University Park, 1997), 4. See also Klarman, "How *Brown* Changed Race Relations"; Numan V. Bartley, *The Rise of Massive Resistance: Race and Politics in the South in the 1950s* (Baton Rouge, 1969); and Neil McMillen, *The Citizens' Council: Organized Resistance to the Second Reconstruction, 1954–1964* (Urbana, 1971).

5.  See Ronald P. Formisano, *Boston against Busing: Race, Class, and Ethnicity in the 1960s and 1970s* (Chapel Hill, 1991); and J. Anthony Lukas, *Common Ground: A Turbulent Decade in the Lives of Three American Families* (New York, 1985). *Washington v. Seattle School District,* 458 U.S. 457 (1982); *Crawford v. Los Angeles Board of Education,* 458 U.S. 527 (1982); *Milliken v. Bradley,* 418 U.S. 717 (1974). See Gary Orfield and Susan E. Eaton, *Dismantling Desegregation: The Quiet Reversal of* Brown v. Board of Education (New York, 1996).

6.  *Brown v. Board of Education,* 347 U.S. at 494, 493; Gary Orfield, and Chungmei Lee, *"Brown* at Fifty: King's Dream or Plessy's Nightmare?," Jan. 17, 2004, *The Civil Rights Project, Harvard University* <http://www.civilrightsproject.harvard.edu/research/reseg04/resegregation04.php> (April 4, 2004). In every region of the nation, at least 30% black students still attend schools with less than 10% white enrollment. *Ibid.*

7. Cf. Melba Beals, *Warriors Don't Cry: A Searing Memoir of the Battle to Integrate Little Rock's Central High* (New York, 1995); and Melba Beals, *White Is a State of Mind: A Memoir* (New York, 1995).

8. *Sweatt v. Painter,* 339 U.S. 629 (1950); *Baltimore Afro-American,* June 17, 1950, quoted in Juan Williams, *Thurgood Marshall: American Revolutionary* (New York, 1998), 195; Thurgood Marshall, "An Evaluation of Recent Efforts to Achieve Racial Integration in Education through Resort to the Courts," *Journal of Negro Education,* 21 (Summer 1952), 316–27, esp. 322.

9. J. S. Coleman et al., *Equality of Educational Opportunity* (Washington, 1966), *passim; Report of the National Advisory Commission on Civil Disorders* (New York, 1968), 1; Martin Luther King Jr., *Where Do We Go from Here: Chaos or Community?* (New York, 1967), 228. For Constance Baker Motley's statement (quoted from the *New York Times,* May 13, 1974), see James T. Patterson, Brown v. Board of Education: *A Civil Rights Milestone and Its Troubled Legacy* (New York, 2001), 168.

10. *Brown v. Board of Education,* 349 U.S. 294 (1955); W. E. B. Du Bois, "Does the Negro Need Separate Schools?," *Journal of Negro Education,* 4 (July 1935), in *The Oxford W. E. B. Du Bois Reader,* ed. Eric J. Sundquist (New York, 1996), 431.

11. *"Brown v. Board of Education of Topeka:* Opinion on Segregation Laws," in *Civil Rights and African Americans: A Documentary History,* ed. Albert P. Blaustein and Robert L. Zangrando (Evanston, 1991), 436.

# 16

# The Astonishing Story: Veterans Make Good on the Nation's Promise

*KEITH W. OLSON*

*The G.I. Bill of Rights is considered a progressive watershed in U.S. history. It enabled millions of World War II veterans to obtain a college education or technical training that most would not have been able to afford. This piece of legislation caused a social revolution for veterans and their families because the educational and training opportunities transformed millions of poor working-class veterans into a vast new middle class, thus changing society to a degree unprecedented in its history.*

First came the name. Even before final passage of the bill, the press, the public, and the veterans quickly dropped the cumbersome title, "The Servicemen's Readjustment Act of 1944," and substituted the name "GI Bill." Once in operation, the bill replaced the idea of readjustment with that of reward. Then the GI Bill became synonymous with education—especially higher education. In reality, the Servicemen's Readjustment Act of 1944 contained six parts, or titles, only one of which related to higher education. Titles one and six dealt with procedures and administration. Title three concerned home, farm, and business mortgages. Titles four and five covered employment and unemployment. The veterans and the public gave each title its own distinctiveness. Veterans having difficulty finding jobs joined the "52-20 Club" ($20 unemployment checks for up to 52 weeks). Veterans wanting to buy a house applied for a Veterans Administration (VA) mortgage. Veterans thinking about education thought of the GI Bill. Although the education title covered training and education at all levels and of all types, the GI Bill typically was associated with colleges and universities. In a society honoring veterans and valuing education as a means of self-improvement, veterans on campuses provided films, magazines, and other media with a subject easy to publicize and romanticize. This image of the GI Bill as an education bonus for veterans contrasted sharply with the legislation's origins.

*Source:* "The Astonishing Story: Veterans Make Good on the Nation's Promise" by Keith W. Olson in *Educational Record,* Volume 75, no. 4, Fall 1994, pp. 16–26. Copyright © 1994 American Council on Education. Reprinted by permission of the American Council on Education.

## ORIGINS AND MOTIVES

The individuals and organizations responsible for the program that sent veterans to college drew their guidance and inspiration from their understanding of past events, and they acted more out of fear than confidence. Americans traditionally had granted postwar benefits to able-bodied veterans—except after World War I. Following that war, veterans' organizations—especially the young American Legion—championed a bonus to correct the perceived injustice. For 15 years, the bonus question remained a significant political issue, including vetoes of bonus bills by four presidents, a march by veterans on Washington, DC, and eventual payments. Few people wanted to repeat that page of history. The role that unemployed European veterans had played in the rise of fascism evoked an additional element of fear in the minds of Americans. And ever present was the specter of a return of the economic depression that had permeated the prewar decade. Finally, Americans worried about the sheer numbers of returning veterans.

Concern for veterans first surfaced during the summer of 1940, amidst the debate to enact the nation's first peacetime conscription act. Congressional leaders and President Roosevelt included in the act a provision guaranteeing reemployment to men who donned uniforms to serve a required year and who then returned to civilian life. The provision reflected, among other things, a 1940 unemployment rate of nearly 15 percent.

Seven months after the United States entered World War II, the director of the National Resources Planning Board (NRPB), Frederick A. Delano, asked Roosevelt to approve the establishment of a small planning committee to study the demobilization of men in the armed forces and industry and to propose programs to mitigate projected problems. Delano's request flowed logically from the activities of the NRPB, the agency Roosevelt called "the planning arm of my executive office." Roosevelt approved, but he cautioned Delano to avoid publicity and to keep the committee unofficial. Delano moved quickly.

In mid-July, the committee held its first meeting and called its work the "Conference on Postwar Readjustment of Civilian and Military Personnel," often shortened to "Postwar Manpower Conference" (PMC). Delano selected as chair Floyd W. Reeves, NRPB consultant, member of the American Council on Education (ACE), and professor on leave from the University of Chicago. Among the other members were representatives from the VA, the Department of Labor, and the War Department. By April 1943, the PMC had held 27 half-day sessions, and in June, it submitted its final report, "Demobilization and Readjustment."

In its work, PMC drew from past experience with veterans' programs. The education provisions of its final report bore strong similarities to "The Wisconsin Educational Bonus Law of 1919," under which all state residents with at least three months' war service received a monthly stipend for four academic years to attend any non-profit school or college in the state. PMC also studied a description of the "Canadian Preparation for Veterans' Demobilization and Rehabilitation," which included an education program for veterans. In addition, committee members analyzed the World War I rehabilitation program for disabled veterans, a training and education program aimed at returning veterans to regular employment. The report also included proposals that dealt with training and education and their relationship to employment. (These training and education proposals applied to both civilians and veterans.)

Roosevelt had always regarded PMC as exploratory and unofficial. On November 13, 1942, the day he approved lowering the draft age to 18, he also announced the appointment of "The Armed Forces Committee on Postwar Educational Opportunities for Service Personnel." Called the "Osborn Committee" after its director, Brigadier General Frederick H. Osborn, it included among its members the president of Tulane University, the dean of the Columbia University Law School, and the United States Commissioner of Education. Roosevelt asked Osborn to correlate his committee's work with the ongoing work of PMC. In July 1943, a month after PMC submitted its report, the Osborn Committee submitted its report. The recommendations differed from PMC's only slightly.

Both reports focused on problem solving. PMC concluded that "within the first year of the demobilization process, there will exist the likelihood, if not the certainty, of a large volume of unemployed, involving as many as 8 or 9 million."[1] The Osborn report stated, "We have regarded any benefits which may be extended to individuals in the process as incidental."[2]

On July 28, Roosevelt, in one of his fireside chats, described the progress of the war and his early plans for peace. In this first public comment regarding veterans' benefits, Roosevelt declared that veterans "must not be demobilized into an environment of inflation and unemployment, to a place on a bread line or on a corner selling apples."[3] To prevent such an environment, Roosevelt announced that he would propose legislation and asked Congress to "do its duty."

That fall, Roosevelt sent to Congress the Osborn Committee report, along with its education recommendations. A month later, he asked Congress to enact the PMC proposals regarding unemployment insurance, credit in the Social Security program for military service, and veteran mustering-out pay. ACE, although it had worked closely with both PMC and the Osborn Committee, drafted a separate plan for veterans' benefits. On November 3, Senator Elbert D. Thomas, a former political science professor from Utah, introduced a bill embodying Roosevelt's recommendations. The Senate Committee on Education and Labor held hearings in mid-December and reported the Thomas bill to the Senate on February 7, 1944.

In fall 1943, meanwhile, the American Legion had launched its own campaign to produce a rival, more comprehensive plan. Early in January, John Rankin, Democrat from Mississippi and chair of the House Committee on World War II Veterans' Legislation, introduced the Legion's omnibus bill. Joel Bennett Clark, Democrat from Missouri and the Legion's first national commander, introduced the bill in the Senate.

The Legion combined its motive of rewarding veterans with the nation's broader motive of preserving stability. In a radio speech early in May 1944, Legion National Commander Warren H. Atherton warned that veterans "will be a potent force for good or evil in the years to come. They can make our country or break it. They can restore our democracy or scrap it."[4] The *National Legionnaire* editorialized that "there must be no road hereafter from the battle line to the bread line for our defenders."[5]

Most Americans agreed with the Legion. Republican Congressman Hamilton Fish, known for his opposition to New Deal legislation, admonished his colleagues that World War II veterans would not "come home and sell apples as they did after the last war, because if that is all they were offered, I believe we would have chaotic and revolutionary conditions in America."[6] The Senate bill, unanimously approved, prophesied that "if the trained and disciplined efficiency and valor of the men and women of our armed forces can be directed into proper channels, we shall have a better country to live in than the world has ever seen. If we should fail in that task, disaster and chaos are inevitable."[7] On July 20, a month after he signed the GI Bill into law, Roosevelt accepted his party's nomination for president for an unprecedented fourth time and told his supporters that voters in November would decide about leaving the "task of postwar reconversion to those who offered the veterans of the last war bread lines and apple selling . . . or whether they will leave it to those who . . . have already planned and put through much legislation to help our veterans."[8]

The ghost of past economic hard times led several veterans' groups to oppose the Legion bill. These organizations—the Military Order of the Purple Heart (MOPH), the Disabled American Veterans (DAV), the Veterans of Foreign Wars (VFW), and the Regular Veteran Association (RVA—favored veterans' benefits but considered the Legion bill too generous. When a counter bonus plan failed to gain support, however, the VFW and RVA shifted their support to the Legion bill.

Led by ACE, representatives of higher education overwhelmingly supported the education benefits of the Legion bill (except for those who wanted the U.S. Office of Education, not the VA, to administer the program). At times, however, the educators were cautious. For example, in the plan it submitted to Roosevelt the previous October, ACE called for extending education benefits to more than one year of study for only a limited group of veterans. Roscoe L. West, president of the American Association of Teachers Colleges, and George Zook, president of ACE, opposed federal education loans to veterans because, as West declared, "We think it might be difficult to collect."[9] Nevertheless, the Legion found strong support for its plan from educators.

The GI Bill offered generous benefits for veterans with an interest in college. A veteran with at least 90 days' service was eligible for a year of education plus additional education equal to the time spent on active duty, with a four-year limit. The GI Bill paid for the veteran's tuition, fees, books, and supplies, up to $500 a year, plus a monthly living allowance of $50 for an unmarried veteran and $75 for a married veteran. These benefits enabled the veterans to afford nearly any college in the country.

Veterans applied to the colleges of their choice. The VA determined eligibility and mailed the checks but otherwise exerted no control. In December 1945, Congress raised the monthly allowance to $65 ($90 for married veterans). Nineteen months later, Congress again increased the allowances, to $75 and $105, and added an additional $15 for veterans with one or more children.

**PREDICTIONS VERSUS REALITY**

The individuals who crafted the GI Bill gave little thought to the number of veterans who would take advantage of its generous benefits. Their primary concern, of course, had been the potential unrest of unemployed veterans. Officials who pondered the question of numbers had little basis for projection.

In December 1944, President Roosevelt thought that "hundreds of thousands" of veterans would attend college. The next month, VA administrator Frank T. Hines estimated 700,000 veterans "distributed over several years." In March 1945, Earl J. McGrath, a veteran who had served as education advisor to the Chief of Navy Personnel and who later served as U.S. Commissioner of Education, concluded "that in no academic year will more than 150,000 veterans be full-time students in colleges and universities," with a grand total of 640,000. During summer 1945, the Information and Educational Division of the Armed Service Forces conducted a comprehensive survey, including Navy veterans, and found that "at least a million veterans" would enroll "within six months to a year after demobilization is complete." That August, however, Stanley Frank, a regular contributor on the subject of veterans, published in the *Saturday Evening Post* an article entitled "GIs Reject Education." Frank praised the GI Bill as "a splendid bill, a wonderful bill, with only one conspicuous drawback. The guys aren't buying it."[10] VA administrator Hines and *New York Times* education editor Benjamin Fine both believed enrollments would fluctuate in direct relationship to the unemployment rate.

Educators' meager expectations about the ability, behavior, and maturity of veterans as students proved unfounded and, in retrospect, occasionally comical. Four colleges planned to segregate veterans from other students. One professor, serving as an occupation counselor at an Army discharge center, published "Some Hints to Professors" in the *American Association of University Professors Bulletin*.[11] He advised, for example, that professors assign suggested, rather than required, readings in deference to veterans' resentment of orders. Columbia University sociologist Willard Waller wrote that for a veteran, marriage "is a reason for thinking twice or perhaps thrice before entering college. . . . If there is a baby, college is almost out of the question for any reasonable man," even with "sufficient outside income."[12] A University of Chicago dean worried, "What will we do with married students on the campus? . . . Will we be embarrassed by the prospect of babies and by their arrival?"[13]

Two of the nation's most eminent university presidents publicly expressed their disapproval of what they believed would be the veterans' influence. Harvard University President James B. Conant found the GI Bill "distressing" because "we may find the least capable among the war generation . . . flooding the facilities for advanced education." He preferred, instead, a program to finance the education "of a carefully selected number of returned veterans."[14] University of Chicago President Robert M. Hutchins titled his article in the mass-circulation magazine *Collier's* "The Threat to American Education." He predicted that colleges would admit and retain unqualified veterans in order to obtain their tuition. Hutchins labeled the GI Bill "unworkable." The persons who drafted these "absurd" provisions did so, he reasoned, "because they did not think of them as educational provisions at all, but as a method of keeping the veterans off the bread line."[15]

Despite the inaccurate predictions of the numbers of veterans who would enroll—and of how they would perform and act as students—colleges adjusted logically and with relative ease. The biggest obstacle proved to be the housing shortage, a problem shared by every community in the country. Colleges, with rare exception, were flexible in dealing with veterans. Each campus established a veterans' committee but treated ex-service personnel as students first and as veterans second. Colleges modified admissions policies and granted credit for military training and experience. To assist in the granting of credit, ACE published and distributed, with the cooperation of the Army and Navy, *A Guide to the Evaluation of Educational Experiences in the Armed Services*. A 1948 survey found that 99 percent of colleges granted credit for experience and knowledge gained in the military.

The most pronounced flexibility came in dealing with unprecedented enrollments. By the time the GI Bill subsidized its last check, more than 2.2 million veterans, including 64,728 women, had attended college. Women's colleges, such as Sarah Lawrence, Russell Sage, and Vassar, admitted male veterans, while male colleges, such as Colgate, permitted veterans' wives to enroll. Total college enrollments across the country averaged 50 percent above peacetime records. This statistic, however, is misleading. Forty-one percent of all veterans registered at just 38 colleges. "Why go to Podunk College," *Time* magazine asked, "when the government will send you to Yale?"[16] Stanford University's enrollment jumped from 4,800 to 7,200, and Wisconsin's climbed from 11,400 to 18,700. Teachers colleges, by way of contrast, recorded only a 5 percent increase in enrollments.

The biggest and most pleasant of the many surprises associated with the GI Bill was the academic performance of the veterans. In November 1947, Benjamin Fine reported his findings after a tour of campuses: "[H]ere is the most astonishing fact in the history of American higher education. . . . The GIs are hogging the honor rolls and the dean's lists; they are walking away with the top marks in all of their courses. . . . Far from being an educational problem, the veteran has become an asset to higher education."[19] At Hobart College, four civilians flunked out for every failing veteran. Nonveterans at Stanford called veterans "DARs" for "Damn Average Raisers." During the spring 1947 semester, the Carnegie Foundation for the Advancement of Teaching administered a questionnaire to 10,000 students. This elaborate study confirmed the academic superiority of veterans. In November 1950, University of Wisconsin President E. B. Fred concluded that "Our 30,000 student veterans have been a stabilizing influence on Wisconsin's student life. Their maturity has enabled them to raise scholarship levels."[18]

Concomitant with distinguishing themselves academically, veterans established a collective reputation for maturity. *Fortune* magazine studied the class of 1949, 70 percent of whom were veterans, and learned that the class was "the best . . . the most mature . . . the most responsible . . . and the most self-disciplined group" of college students in history.[19] Benjamin Fine surveyed 60 representative colleges and universities and summarized that "almost everywhere," veterans "have brought to classrooms maturity and an attitude for serious motivation."[20] Veterans' performance at Harvard forced President Conant to reassess his earlier opinion; the veterans won his praise as "the most mature and promising students Harvard has ever had."[21]

Veterans' adjustment to civilian life also dispelled apprehensions. At Stanford, for example, the president observed that "the quickness and ease with which the veteran students adjusted to civilian life was very striking."[22] The director of the University of Pennsylvania's Veterans' Advisory Council concluded that "it was remarkable how quickly" veterans "settled down to a normal peacetime level."[23] The Carnegie study perhaps presented the most remarkable evidence to illustrate veterans' adjustment. Veterans who were older, married, and who had been away from the classroom the longest were the best students.

## THE BILL'S LEGACY

The GI Bill left a list of accomplishments, intended and unintended, that far exceeded designs and expectations. During its operation, and throughout the decades since, the GI Bill has remained the most admired and least criticized federal program of the 20th century. To fund all parts, Congress poured $14.5 billion into the economy, $5.5 billion of it in support of the bill's higher education provisions. This economic stimulus contributed immeasurably to the economic prosperity of the first postwar decade. Compared to other groups in society, as well as to American veterans of previous wars, World War II veterans were models of success and citizenship. As a tool to ward off potential veteran discontent and unemployment, therefore, the GI Bill met its objectives. In an ironic twist, veterans—with their academic success, their maturity, and their numbers—unintentionally caused a modest adjustment problem for nonveterans!

The 2.25 million veterans who attended college helped replenish the country's supply of college graduates. Of the 2 million veteran students, approximately 450,000 would not have attended college without the GI Bill. This opportunity paid tribute to the concept of democracy and documented an untapped potential in society. Harvard economist Seymour E. Harris recognized, though disapproved of, this condition when he concluded that "in education . . . the GI Bill carried the principle of democratization too far."[24]

Veterans also changed traditional policies and attitudes. Half of all veterans were married, and their presence on campus demolished the prejudice—on some campuses even a prohibition—against married students. Twenty-five percent of veterans had children, and they, too, became an accepted part of academic life. Universities, with generous assistance from federal programs that supplied surplus war buildings, provided married veterans with prefabs and trailers. Throughout the 1950s, universities replaced them with modern, permanent apartments, recognizing a new, married student culture. By their example, veterans likewise eradicated the belief that older students, with a time gap in their formal education, constituted high risks for full-time study. During their peak enrollment year of 1947, veterans accounted for 49.2 percent of all college enrollments and 69.3 percent of male students. They dominated higher education.

The World War II GI Bill was unique in a multitude of ways, and especially in its unqualified success. In retrospect, the veterans acted logically. They perceived the relationship between education and employment and took advantage of a generous program that appealed to their self-interest. College served as a convenient transition from military to civilian life. An accepted wardrobe of khakis and flight jackets, along with Quonset huts and prefab buildings, reinforced former associations. Most important, the GI Bill was voluntary. Dissatisfied veterans could drop out at any time. Because the bill had so many positive features and inflicted no real handicap, veterans took full advantage of it. But the most astonishing aspect of the story of the GI Bill and higher education, from beginning to end, is the fact that so few politicians and educators recognized its potential.

## NOTES

1. "Demobilization and Readjustment," file 830.31, R. G. 187, National Archives, p. 23.
2. U.S. Congress. "Post-War Educational Opportunities for Service Personnel," 78th Cong., 1st Sess., 1943, H. Document 344, p. 6.
3. Rosenman, Samuel I. *The Public Papers and Addresses of Franklin D. Roosevelt, 1943,* New York: Harper and Brothers, 1950, p. 333.
4. Atherton. Radio speech, 2 May 1944, folder 6, "Great War-Legion Bill," American Legion Archives.
5. *The National Legionnaire* 10 (March 1944): 4.
6. U.S. Congress. *Congressional Record,* 78th Cong., 2d Sess., 1944, vol. 90, pt. 3: 4327.
7. U.S. Congress. *Providing Federal Government Aid for the Readjustment in Civilian Life of Returning World War II Veterans,* Senate Report 755—To Accompany S. 1767, 78th Cong. 2d Sess., 1944, p. 2.
8. *New York Times,* 21 July 1944: 8.
9. U.S. Congress, Senate Committee on Education and Labor. Hearings on S.1295 and S.1509, 78th Cong., 1st Sess., 15 December 1943, p. 134.

10. Frank, Stanley. "GIs Reject Education" *Saturday Evening Post,* 18 August 1945: 20.
11. McDonagh, Edward C. "Some Hints to Professors," *American Association of University Professors Bulletin* 31 (Winter 1945): 643–47.
12. Waller, Willard. "Which Veterans Should Go to College?" *Ladies' Home Journal,* May 1945: 169.
13. Brumbaugh, A. J. "Planning Education for Returning Members of the Armed Forces," *American Association of Teachers Colleges 23rd Yearbook* (1944), pp. 53–54.
14. Conant, James B. "Annual Report of the President of the University," *Harvard Alumni Bulletin* 47 (3 February 1945): 286.
15. Hutchins, Robert M. "The Threat to American Education," *Collier's,* 30 December 1944: 20–21.
16. "S.R.O." *Time,* 18 March 1946: 75.
17. Fine, Benjamin, "Veterans Raise College Standards," *Educational Outlook* 22 (November 1947): 58.
18. Fred, E. B. *Report of the President,* November 1950, University of Wisconsin Archives.
19. "The Class of 1949," *Fortune,* June 1949: 84.
20. Fine, Benjamin. "Educators Praise Their GI Students," *New York Times,* 11 October 1949: 35.
21. Murphy, Charles J. V. "G.I.'s at Harvard," *Life,* 17 June 1946: 17.
22. Fine, "Veterans Raise College Standards": 58.
23. MacFarland, George Arthur. "Veterans at the University of Pennsylvania," *Educational Outlook* 22 (November 1947): 18.
24. Harris, Seymour. December 1947, quoted in Olson, Keith W. *The GI Bill, the Veterans, and the Colleges.* Lexington: The University Press of Kentucky, 1974, p. 99.

# Head Start/Early Head Start Program

*CITY OF CHATTANOOGA HUMAN SERVICES DEPARTMENT*

*Head Start/Early Head Start is a federally funded child development pro-
gram for very low-income young children and their families. Since its
inception in 1965, over 23 million children and families nationally have
benefited from Head Start's comprehensive services. Despite its success,
in recent years conservative politicians in the federal government have
proposed legislation that would eliminate the federal role in administering Head Start, moving it to the states and essentially doing away with its
comprehensive services. The benefits of one Head Start program, in Chattanooga, Tennessee, are illustrated in this reading. There are thousands
that are similar to it throughout the United States.*

Welcome to Chattanooga Head Start/Early Head Start!!! We have the "Best Little Management Team in the South" We are extremely pleased to have these consummate professionals on our staff. They possess the education, experience, compassion and dedication
necessary to make a significant positive impact on the lives and communities of the children and families served by our program.

The Chattanooga Head Start/Early Head Start serves 557 Head Start children and 50
Early Head Start children in seven (7) centers throughout Hamilton County, TN. All of
our centers are accredited by the Academy of Early Childhood Programs, a division of the
National Associaiton for the Education of Young Children. We are implementeing many
exciting new initiatives this year. . . . We have a wonderful program for children and families we would like to share with you. . . .

### PARENT INVOLVEMENT

The Chattanooga Head Start/Early Head Start Program has unique ways of reaching and
involving parents in every aspect of Head Start. We offer different programs within our
organization such as parents becoming Host and Hostesses for their center, assisting in
planning and presenting workshops to parents and participating in a national research study
called FACES (Family and Child Experience Survey). Several of our parents are involved

*Source:* Excerpt from "Head Start/Early Head Start Program," City of Chattanooga Human Services Department,
pp. 1–6. Reprinted by permission of City of Chattanooga Human Services Department, Head Start/Early Head
Start Program.

in the Family Literacy Program that promotes children and parents learning and spending quality time together.

The Parent Involvement philosophy of the Chattanooga Head Start/Early Head Start Program is predicated upon the Head Start/Early Head Start vision for Parent Involvement. The goals and principles of the Parent Involvement vision statement are based upon a partnership with parents which supports parents as the primary educators of their children, and provides opportunities for meaningful experiences in the Head Start/Early Head Start Program. Parents are ensured the opportunities to participate in policy making and program decision-making. Based on the principles which support the culture of families, the program provides Family Literacy Programs to promote family goal setting, economic self-sufficiency, and independence. The Head Start/Early Head Start Program respectfully supports children with disabilities and their families, and reaches out to include fathers. The program is committed to develop and sustain partnerships between Head Start/Early Head Start staff and parents. It is important to note here that no single ingredient is responsible for the success and effectiveness of our Head Start/Early Head Start Program—IT'S THE COMBINATION OF PARENTS AND STAFF WORKING TOGETHER WITH OUR COMMUNITIES, IT'S THE MIX THAT MAKES IT ALL WORK.

### DISABILITIES

The Disability Services of Chattanooga Head Start/Early Head Start Program provides the full range of Head Start services to all enrolled children with the continuum being completed for children with disabilities through the IEP/IFSP processes in compliance with Head Start Performance Standards and IDEA, Part B & H. The LEA and the LEAD Agency, Tennessee Early Intervention System, (TEIS) work collaboratively, guided by Interagency Agreements, to provide IEP/IFSP meetings, training and information and community based resources and services for a seamless system of service delivery for our children and families. Only diagnosticians who meet the State of Tennessee qualifications and licensures are providers of special education and/or related services.

In an effort to provide services to more severely disabled children, the Chattanooga Head Start/Early Head Start Program has formed partnerships with a private UCP Agency, Signal Centers, where typically developing Head Start children attend classes with severely impaired children. The Signal Centers, Inc. and Early Head Start Program also share three classrooms of toddlers who are children primarily diagnosed as Developmentally Delayed. Another collaboration developed when the LEA made a request to include 17 preschoolers from a Comprehensive Developmental Class CDC in our nearby Head Start Program. This is a growing, thriving inclusive program environment for intense development, learning and certainly a sense of "community" for "all" children and their families.

### HEALTH

The Health Component provides comprehensive services to children and families. Registered Nurses work closely with parents and health providers in the community to ensure children receive continuous, high quality health services, both Medical and dental. Members of the health community serve on Policy Council Health Advisory Committees, and the program's yearly self-assessment.

Community agencies and medical personnel are utilized in providing health education programs for parents.

Well balanced breakfasts and lunches are provided to children at no cost. Parents who volunteer in the classroom also receive meals at no cost. Consumer education, menu planning and preparation and safe food preparation programs are available through a cooperative program with the University of Tennessee Agriculture Extension Agency.

## MENTAL HEALTH

The Mental Health Component provides a full time professional counselor who serves as the coordinator of mental health services. Two full-time Behavior Assistants are part of the mental health team that provides services to children, families and staff. The Mental Health Coordinator provides on-site crisis counseling with immediate referral and follow-up to appropriate agencies. The mental health team also provides observationist consultations with classrooms, children, parents and staff at each site weekly or as needed to address the overall goal of "Promoting Positive Discipline" in the classroom and home setting.

## TRANSPORTATION

The Chattanooga Head Start/Early Head Start transportation system gets the children off to a "rolling" start every morning. The "beep-beep" sound of the bus horn, the flashing amber and red lights on the yellow bus, the "good-mornings" from the drivers and assistants and the "click-click-click" sound from the seat belts being buckled are indicators that school is only a short trip away. Bus riding time generates energy, excitement and plenty of enthusiasm from the children in anticipation of the day's activities.

It is our job to get the children to the Head Start/Early Head Start center safely. We will be providing tips for parents on bus safety and other transportation topics on the web page. Please check us out, we've got lots of good information every parent should know about safe transportation for their family.

## EDUCATION

Chattanooga Head Start/Early Head Start knows that children learn through explorative play. Therefore we provide stimulating environments that encourage the intellectual, physical, social and emotional development of children.

Parents team together with staff to plan developmentally appropriate, challenging activities in order to foster their child's development. Through participation in active learning experiences, children are given choices in activities and materials they can manipulate. Adults support their play and the use of language.

We encourage parents to participate and learn along with their children so that they and their child will leave Head Start excited about learning, continuing their education and succeeding in life.

## TRANSITION

LIFE IS A TRANSITION! Before birth we begin this transition process and continue on this journey throughout our life. Along our life's journey we receive help from others and draw from our past experiences. These experiences for children need to be meaningful and planned. We at Chattanooga Head Start/Early Head Start strive to provide opportunities that will enable and empower children and families to go forth on this journey equipped to deal with the challenges to come. We offer an environment that is enjoyable, educational and is also preparatory for the next stage of life.

## VOLUNTEER SERVICES

The City of Chattanooga Head Start/Early Head Start Program has a full time Volunteer Coordinator. Volunteers for Head Start/Early Head Start are recruited from all social and economical groups across the Chattanooga/Hamilton County community. Local professionals, businesses, social clubs, churches, universities, colleges, high schools and other profit and non-profit community agencies make up our pool of volunteers. These volunteers are assigned to work in the classrooms with teachers and teacher assistants providing one-on-one individualized attention for children with special needs and those certified as having a disability. Volunteers also help with special events. They serve as bus aides and provide assistance to our family services staff, nursery staff, dietary workers, and clerical staff. . . . Our program provides a higher caliber of services because we are fortunate enough to have wonderful volunteers.

## FAMILY SERVICES

The most common statement made by parents of Chattanooga Human Services Department Head Start/Early Head Start is **"I want to do whatever I need to do to make life better for my child than it has been for me."** It is the aim of the Family Services Component to assist parents to translate their **concerns** into measurable, attainable goals.

The following example provides a story that illustrates what can happen as a result of helping parents to believe in themselves:

**A young woman entered Head Start in 1996 and was tested in GED classes on the 6.0 grade level in reading, 5.1 in math and 4.6 in language. Last week she entered our center beaming! She wore the uniform of a security guard and proudly announced "I'm off welfare and everything!!!"**

Family Services Assistants are divided into three areas of concentration in order to facilitate the best use of time and meet the needs of families. The **transportation concentration** consists of a caseload providing the majority of transportation to field trips, dental trips and daily bus runs to the children's homes. The **parent involvement concentration** consists of working with the parents at the parent committee, providing workshops, field trips and involvement in the Family literacy program. The **caseload** concentration allows the Family Services workers to concentrate on the goals of families, make direct or agency referrals and follow up with families to see that they are receiving services.

Our families develop goals that are collaboratively worked on with the assistance of Family Services staff. The Family Services staff regularly provide support, encouragement and help the family to celebration each small step they take. Our staff also assist parents when failure is met.

# Public Spaces

## Their Use for the Common Good

*Public space is the stage upon which the drama of communal life unfolds. . . . Good public space should be supportive, democratic, and meaningful.*

—Stephen Carr

We live in a spatial world, and social organization requires the organization of space. The term *public spaces* is commonly used to describe places where everyone has a right to be. Roads, city squares, hiking trails, fishing streams, and parks are typical examples. In several Scandinavian countries all nature areas are considered, by law, public. Steven Carr and his coauthors of *Public Space* describe public spaces as "open publicly accessible places where people go for group or individual activities. . . . Public spaces generally contain public amenities such as walkways, benches, and water; physical and visual elements, such as paving or lawn, and vegetation that support activities. Whether planned or found, they are usually open and accessible to the public. Some are under public ownership and management, whereas others are privately owned but open to the public" (1992:50). Openness is qualified in that some publicly owned public spaces have user fees and privately owned spaces, like shopping malls and gated communities, allow the public in at the discretion of the property owner.

The opposite of public space is privately owned space, or what is commonly called *private property*. Property rights are integral to the freedom that U.S. citizens have enjoyed throughout the nation's history. The precedent for these rights is found in England. King John's acceptance of the Magna Carta in 1215, and the English property laws that followed, greatly influenced private property laws in the United States. In all of the thirteen original American colonies settlers continued to abide by and generally apply the common law toward private property that was well established in England. Bernard H. Siegan asserts that when the American colonies were first settled "fundamental rights such as (but not confined to) rights of life, liberty, and property were generally considered as secured by [English] common law" (2001:50). A strong commitment to property rights was codified in the U.S. Constitution in the Bill of Rights as well as the 14th Amendment. Throughout U.S. history there has been a strong endorsement of property rights by judges in the state and federal courts (Ely, 1997; Kulikoff, 2000).

**144**

There are so many public spaces in the United States that we could not possibly identify and discuss all of them. So we have selected a few for this chapter that have a unique
story, a unique place among the nation's public spaces, and were obtained or are secured
and maintained through progressive motivation.

## PUBLIC SPACE AND THE U.S. GOVERNMENT

At the beginning of the United States, the federal government did not own property in any
of the states, and the various state and local governments had very little property ownership
either. The blockbuster spatial expansion of the United States, and the federal government's
first major step into ownership of land, was the Louisiana Purchase in 1803. President
Thomas Jefferson, over the objections of his political opponents in the Senate who insisted
that the Constitution did not give the federal government power to buy territory, won
approval to make the purchase from France for a mere $15 million. Thus in one transaction
the territory of the United States was doubled, and all the new space was federally owned.

Westward territorial expansion commenced in earnest, and by the early 1840s the
catchphrase "Manifest Destiny," meaning the United States had a preordained, God-
sanctioned mission to acquire all land from the Atlantic to the Pacific Ocean, fueled the
nation's ambitions to seize all the territories of the Southwest and Northwest, the only
regions that remained to complete our Manifest Destiny. The Southwest was acquired by
the annexation of Texas in 1845 and the Treaty of Guadalupe Hidalgo in 1848 ending the
war with Mexico. A treaty with Great Britain in 1846 ceded the Northwest to the United
States. These events resulted in vast new areas of federally owned land and resources
(Johannsen et al., 1997).

From the time the federal government began accumulating ownership of land, powerful political leaders in the various states and influential business interests sought federal
land for their own use. In the case of the states, there was a belief that each state should own
and control what was not privately owned. The "states rights" position claimed that there
was no Constitutional provision for federal government ownership of land in the states.
Business interests in agriculture, mining, timber, and real estate speculation, to name only
a few, wanted access to the land for private use purposes (Ely, 1997).

Powerful conservative interests have been persuasive about acquiring public land for
private use throughout U.S. history, and presidents and Congress have disposed of huge
amounts of federal land and continue to do so. In 1812 the General Land Office was established, which sold federal land for cash at $1.25 per acre. General Purpose Grants began
in 1841 and gave public land to states for support of state governments. The Homestead
Act of 1862 gave 80 acres to anyone willing to settle on the land. Also in 1862 the Pacific
Railroad Act gave townships land along the railroad right of way to encourage them to
build transportation infrastructure. In the same year, the Morrill Act gave public land for
the establishment of state colleges. The Timber and Stone Act of 1878 sold western timber-
land for $2.50 per acre. Between 1812 and the 1930s the federal government dispersed 72
percent of federally owned land.

In 2004 the federal government owned a total of 671,759,298 acres. In terms of proportion, 29.6 percent of all land in the United States is owned by the federal government.
Of the original thirteen states, the federal government owns less than 5 percent of land
in those states. It is in the western states where the largest percent of government land is

located. For example, in Nevada 91.9 percent of the land is owned by the federal government; in Alaska, 66.7 percent; in Utah, 66.5 percent; and in Idaho, 66.4 percent.

## THE DEVELOPMENT OF PUBLIC SPACES FOR PARKS

Ownership of private property was the prominent feature in all states with the launch of the new nation under the leadership of President George Washington. But throughout the Colonial period, with the founding and development of villages and towns, a common pattern had evolved to create public parks near their centers. The Boston Common is considered to be the first public park in the history of what is now the United States. In 1636, less than five years after Boston was founded, an area was designated as common pasture for locals' cattle. Over the next two hundred years it was used for a variety of public gatherings and activities, including military training and public hangings.

Beginning in 1830 the grazing of cattle was forbidden. Since then, the Boston Common has mainly served as a public park for recreational purposes. It is has an open character and informal layout and is bordered by Beacon Hill, a public garden, and central business district. Today Boston Common is called the anchor of the Emerald Necklace, a system of connected public parks that winds through many of Boston's neighborhoods.

As U.S. territory expanded rapidly in the first half of the nineteenth century, the number of towns and cities grew rapidly. Many of the central parks featured a bandstand and memorial statutes in honor of local leaders or military heroes. It was New York City that built the grandest urban public space and central park of them all—Central Park. This public space has become arguably the most famous urban park in the world. At the beginning of the nineteenth century there were some 60,000 people living in New York City, mostly congregated in lower Manhattan. Waves of immigration caused the city's population to grow to more than 300,000 by 1840 and to over 500,000 by 1850. To escape the congestion and noise of city life, people took refuge in undeveloped spaces in the rural settings that were available. Pleas began in the early 1840s to set aside space for the development of a public park before it would be lost to the fast-developing city. All political interests endorsed the idea of a large public park. Armed with this broad public support, and using the power of eminent domain, the city paid more than $5 million between 1853 and 1856 for undeveloped land from 59th Street to 106th Street, between Fifth and Eighth Avenues (in 1863 Central Park was expanded from 106th Street, its original northern boundary, to 110th Street; making it 2.5 miles long and .5 miles wide).

Once the park was completed, it quickly became clear for whom it was built. It was located too far from the city's working class citizens to be within walking distance. The cost of train transportation was an expense most of the labor force could not afford. So in its first decades New York's Central Park was primarily a leisure destination for the wealthy. Luxurious horse-drawn carriages, the status symbol of that era, crowded the park's lanes during the afternoons. Concerts and other entertainments attracted the social elite as well as some middle-class audiences. But the sixty- to seventy-hour work weeks prohibited attendance for most of the laboring class of the city. Consequently, only a fraction of the visitors to Central Park in its early years were from the working class until the last decade of the nineteenth century, when they were successful at getting concerts and other entertainment scheduled for Sundays. It was not until the early twentieth century that Central Park truly became a park for the masses.

New York's Central Park has evolved from a place of pastoral beauty to a combination of natural grandeur, recreational facilities, and outdoor arenas. Today, it is the major site of most New Yorkers' recreation. It averages over 20 million visitors per year engaging in everything from relaxing and sunbathing to rollerblading, to dining at the Tavern on the Green or watching a free performance of Shakespeare in the Park. It is truly a public space for every interest (Miller, 2003; Rosenzweig and Blackmar, 1992; Savas, 1976; Whyte, 1992).

Many other cities have developed exceptional parks that enrich the lives of their residents and visitors. Of special importance is the public space along Chicago's Lake Shore Drive. The city of Chicago has built and maintained picturesque parks, beaches, walking and biking paths, lagoons, sports fields, and museums, linked by a continuous linear park extending more than fifteen miles. This stretch enables city dwellers and tourists to relax and enjoy the natural beauty of the lakeshore as well as engage in outdoor physical activities. It is one of the world's most user-friendly city public spaces.

## DEVELOPING FEDERAL LAND INTO NATIONAL PUBLIC SPACES

The western expansion that began with the first colonists accelerated once the United States was founded, and in the one hundred years between the entry of Louisiana into the Union in 1812 until Arizona and New Mexico became states, thirty new states were created out of the continent, thus completing the concept of Manifest Destiny. In every new state there were huge areas of public space, most of which was owned by the federal government. Each state had public areas of spectacular natural beauty as well as priceless natural resources that the federal and state governments were selling and giving to private individuals and to corporations—agricultural and grazing lands, forest regions, mineral deposits, oil fields, and water-power sites. It gradually became obvious that some of those areas, and the wildlife that inhabited them, needed to be protected from land speculation, commercial development, and other forms of exploitation of the public spaces. There was also a belief that making these areas available for citizen use would be a common good. By the late 1800s the federal and state governments formulated various ways of protecting the valuable land through the creation of a system of state and federal parks.

In 1872 Congress passed an epochal bill setting aside 2.2 million acres of wilderness as the Yellowstone National Park to be a "public park or pleasuring ground for the benefit and enjoyment of the people" (Congressional Acts Pertaining to Yellowstone, 1872). The nation's first national park was created, and the concept of a national park to preserve and protect national public space was born. Thus began what has been now been 134 years of a worldwide fascination with the natural splendor of Yellowstone National Park.

Like many pubic spaces, in the first few decades Yellowstone Park visitors were from the affluent segment of the population—those who could afford to make the trip and were adventuresome enough to brave the rugged great outdoors. At first there were no permanent facilities for visitors to Yellowstone Park. Travel to and around the park was by horse or mule through horse paths and wildlife trails, and visitors had to sleep on the ground or in tents. The U.S. Army Corps of Engineers began road building in 1883. The Northern Pacific Railroad and the Union Pacific Railroad, which had reached West Yellowstone in 1907, both started passenger service (Haines, 1996; Schullery and Whittlesey, 2003).

At the time that Yellowstone National Park celebrated its one hundredth anniversary in 1972, attention was slowly turning from viewing Yellowstone as a recreational playground to viewing the park as an ecological treasure that needed to be preserved and protected for future generations. In 1976 Yellowstone Park was designated as a Biosphere Reserve, in recognition of its ecological value. Two years later, it was designated as a World Heritage Site, also in recognition of its ecological value.

Currently, Yellowstone has more than 4 million visitors a year, most of whom come in the summer, but the number of winter visitors has grown rapidly in the past twenty years. Although Yellowstone has some four hundred miles of paved roads, even after more than 130 years as a national park, less than 2 percent of the park is developed with roads, concessions, and viewing spots.

Even before establishment of Yellowstone National Park the idea of preserving public lands valuable from a social use standpoint had been given consideration by the federal government. But it was not until 1890 that more national parks were created with the establishment of Yosemite, General Grant, and Sequoia National Parks in California, and nine years later Mount Rainier National Park was created in Washington.

During the first decade of the twentieth century the number of national parks grew, and in 1906 Congress approved the Antiquities Act, giving the president authority "to declare by public proclamation historic landmarks, historic and prehistoric structures, and other objects of scientific interest that are situated upon the lands owned or controlled by the Government of the United States to be national monuments" (American Antiquities Act of 1906:1)

This growing system of national parks and monuments had no particular organization. The Department of the Interior, War Department, and the Agriculture Department each had separate jurisdictions. This chaotic system of organization for the national parks and monuments continued until 1915, when its deficiencies became obviously unsatisfactory and inefficient. A system of administration was clearly needed to provide definite policies and make possible proper and adequate planning, development, protection, and conservation in the public interest. So in 1916 President Woodrow Wilson signed a bill creating a new government agency, the National Park Service, as a separate bureau of the Department of the Interior. The Service was organized in 1917.

Over the next fifteen years the number of historic and archeological sites administered by the National Park Service gradually increased. By 1931 important sites, such as George Washington's Birthplace National Monument and Colonial National Monument (now Colonial National Historical Park), commemorating the establishment of Jamestown, the first permanent English settlement in North America, and the final American victory over the British at Yorktown in 1781, became part of the national park system. Today, 388 park areas are administered by the National Park Service. Since it began in 1916, the National Park Service's annual visitation has increased from 358,000 to more than 276 million in 2004 (Blumhardt, 2005).

## THE CIVILIAN CONSERVATION CORP: A PROGRESSIVE INITIATIVE EXPANDING AND PRESERVING PUBLIC SPACES WHILE AMELIORATING THE EFFECTS OF THE GREAT DEPRESSION

Up to this point, our focus has been on the expansion and development of public spaces. We now turn the focus on a government program whose purpose was twofold: first, ameliorating the disastrous economic effects of the Great Depression by employing young men in federally funded projects; second, preserving, expanding, developing, and reclaiming federal and state public spaces.

The preservation of public spaces (mountains, lakes, canyons, forests, and other great and unusual works of nature) through the National Park Service helped enrich the quality of life for all people, while providing an invaluable national conservation service. Then in the midst of an economic depression in the early 1930s the newly elected President Franklin Roosevelt and the Democratic party, seeking ways to end the rampant unemployment and economic chaos that gripped the country, created a governmental agency through the Emergency Conservation Work (ECW) Act, which became more commonly known as the Civilian Conservation Corps (CCC). Created as part of the New Deal, it provided desperately needed employment for young men, thus bringing immediate work relief to the nation. At the same time, the CCC played an invaluable role in making improvements throughout the publics spaces of the nation, but especially the national park system.

One of the great tragedies of the depression was its effect on millions of young men. Thousands of jobless young men roamed across the nation in search of work. With the creation of the CCC, young men between the ages of eighteen and twenty-five were eligible to enroll in it. Enrollment skyrocketed quickly and at times as many as 500,000 recruits were enrolled, most of whom came from poor homes. Eventually there were over 4,500 camps in all forty-eight states, as well as Hawaii, Alaska, Puerto Rico, and the Virgin Islands.

From 1933 to 1942, CCC enrollees performed more than one hundred kinds of socially useful tasks at public spaces, such as clearing land for public parks, building fire trails, planting trees, clearing swamps, building small dams for flood control, and in other ways helping conserve, improve, and renew millions of acres of federal and state lands, while developing recreational facilities in national, state, county, and metropolitan parks. On the basis of these achievements the CCC became the most popular experiment of the New Deal.

At the same time the CCC was carrying out its work, it was saving hundreds of thousands of young from hunger, idleness, and homelessness. It helped them maintain their self-respect and enabled many to get an education. One Chicago judge speculated that the CCC was primarily responsible for a 55 percent reduction in crime by the young men of that day.

The Japanese attack at Pearl Harbor in December 1941 was a shocking blow to the country, and it quickly became obvious that any federal project not directly connected with the war effort was in trouble. To no one's surprise it was recommended that the CCC be abolished. Although the CCC was never technically abolished, Congress refused any further funding for it (Salmond, 1989).

As a bold, progressive solution to the continuing problem of dissipation of our national resources, the CCC had great public support. At first, both progressives and conservatives of both parties supported it. Individual congressmen and senators realized the importance of the camps to their constituencies and their political futures. But most New Deal relief projects aroused much criticism. By 1939 Congress was cutting appropriations for many New Deal agencies, and conservative criticism of the CCC increased. Much of the opposition to the New Deal came from people who believed that Roosevelt's policies were undermining the nation's economic system.

## THE SMITHSONIAN INSTITUTE: PRIVATE FOREIGN FUNDING ESTABLISHES AN AMERICAN PUBLIC SPACE TREASURE

We now turn to an unusual public space. It is unusual first because it was funded by money provided by a private individual, an individual who was a British scientist who never set foot in the United States, James Smithson. Smithson was born into wealth and he inherited a fortune, but he became a noted scientist through his own achievements. This public space is also unusual because most of the space is located indoors rather than outdoors, as is the case for other public spaces discussed in this section.

James Smithson's ideals were progressive and were reflected in his interest in the Enlightenment principles of democracy and universal education. He disliked the British monarchy and admired early American progressives, such as Thomas Paine and Benjamin Franklin, and this may have led to his bequest for the founding of the Smithsonian Institution. When Smithson died in 1829 his will named his nephew as beneficiary, but it stipulated that if his nephew and sole heir should die childless, most of Smithson's fortune, some half-million dollars, was to go to the United States of America "to found at Washington, under the name of the Smithsonian Institution, an establishment for the increase and diffusion of knowledge among men" (What Is the Smithsonian? n.d.). Six years later his nephew died without an heir.

The U.S. Congress accepted Smithson's bequest in 1836. But the Smithsonian Institution did not become a reality until 1846, when President James K. Polk signed an act of Congress creating the Smithsonian's organizational structure. Although Smithson's bequest became federal government money, the act of creating the Smithsonian Institution in Washington, D.C., between the White House and the capitol building as a public space directed that it would be administered by a board of regents and the secretary of the Smithsonian, independent of the federal government. But it has always remained a public space.

Rather quickly the Smithsonian became known as a prominent scientific research institution. During its first seventy-five years it became a public space and national treasure. In addition to developing museums, the institution expanded both its collections and its scope. The National Zoo, the Smithsonian Astrophysical Observatory, and the National Aeronautics Collection were founded during this time. Asian and American art collections were given to the institution. The National Museum of Natural History was finally housed in an adequate building.

From the 1960s to 2000 the Smithsonian dramatically increased its collections, exhibitions, and educational efforts. During this period, several significant museums were opened: The National Museum of American History, Anacostia Museum, the Hirshhorn Museum and Sculpture Garden, and the National Air and Space Museum. The most recent opening was the National Museum of the American Indian. Research has always been an important function of the Smithsonian, and in the past thirty-five years these facilities have expanded to include the Archives of America and the Smithsonian Astrophysical Observatory, which linked with Harvard University to form the Harvard-Smithsonian Center for Astrophysics (Smithsonian Institution, 1989).

The Smithsonian Institution continues to expand its commitment to all of the varied communities that make up U.S. culture and society, and it has taken important steps to attract, through its exhibitions, artwork, specimens, and programs, racial and ethnic groups that have not traditionally visited Smithsonian museums in large numbers. The collections in museums have been expanded to represent a wide range of cultural, racial, and ethnic minorities.

Federal appropriations and private contributions have grown substantially during the late twentieth century and early years of the twenty-first century, making the Smithsonian an invaluable cultural institution and public space. Today, the Smithsonian Institution is a multifacility complex with eighteen museums, nine research centers, and 120 affiliates around the world. There is no fee for admission to any of the Smithsonian museums. Attendance at its venues reached 20.4 million visitors in 2004.

## THE TENNESSEE VALLEY AUTHORITY: PUBLIC SPACE, DEVELOPMENT OF A REGION'S NATURAL RESOURCES, AND IMPROVEMENT OF SOCIAL AND ECONOMIC CONDITIONS

In Section 1 of this volume we provided an extended discussion of President Franklin D. Roosevelt's New Deal initiatives. We identified the Tennessee Valley Authority (TVA) as one of the New Deal programs. Now we discuss the TVA as a unique public space, unique because it was a cooperative arrangement involving public space and private enterprise.

Within a month after becoming president, Roosevelt sent a bill to Congress authorizing the creation of the Tennessee Valley Authority (TVA). Roosevelt and an ally in the Senate, progressive Republican George W. Norris of Nebraska, were advocates of public ownership and operation of public utilities such as power and water services. Roosevelt saw the TVA as a yardstick for assessing the real costs of private power companies. He also saw the possibilities of the TVA for the conservation of natural and human resources.

Without a doubt, the TVA was one of the boldest and most sweeping progressive reforms of the New Deal; it was an experiment that had no parallel in U.S. history. A government-owned corporation was created to oversee the improvement of conditions in a depressed area of some 40,000 square miles in parts of seven states drained by the Tennessee River and its tributaries: Tennessee, Mississippi, Alabama, Georgia, Kentucky, North Carolina, and Virginia.

The aim of the TVA project was the unified development of all the region's resources and the improvement of economic and social conditions of the people who lived there. This was a region whose forests had been devastated by lumbering companies while oil and natural gas companies had ruined much of the land through drilling and mining operations. In its first ten years the TVA built twenty-one large dams on the Tennessee River and its major tributaries and hundreds of smaller dams on creeks and streams for electric power production, flood control, and improved navigation on the rivers. With the dams, hydroelectric power plants were constructed to convert the water in the rivers into huge quantities of electricity. That electric power was distributed to millions of homes that had never before had electricity. This and the infusion of huge sums of money into the development of the region steadily improved the standard of living of the people living in the Tennessee Valley.

The TVA came under persistent legal assault from private power companies, which viewed it as a direct threat. They argued that the TVA was an illegal intervention of the federal government into the rightful domain of private industry. Conservative interests in both government and business charged that the inexpensive electricity generated by the TVA was an unfair gift to the people of that region by the taxpayers of the entire nation—a form of socialism. The influence of the power corporations and their representatives in Congress was so strong that no project of its kind was initiated elsewhere, although Roosevelt's administration did construct dams and power plants throughout the western states. In fact, the TVA scored many great successes through its dams controlling flooding, improving navigation on the rivers, and generating cheap hydroelectric power. It encouraged industrial development as well as agricultural modernization, thus promoting the social and economic welfare of people throughout the Southeast.

## CURRENT TRENDS AND PUBLIC POLICIES
## TOWARD PUBLIC SPACE

The nation's public spaces have a dismal future, unless current political trends and public policies change dramatically. Many public spaces are in disrepair and deteriorating because funding for them has been inadequate for decades because the trend toward political and social conservatism at all levels of government assigns low priority to the upkeep, maintenance, and repair of public spaces. All levels of government have also been accommodating to private corporate interests in the timber, mining, oil and gas, and property development industries, all of which lobby successfully for private use of vast tracts of land for commercial purposes. To the degree that public space is ceded to narrow private interests, it will be organized to fill only the narrow purpose of profit maximization rather than utilizing the broad potential of public spaces for the common good.

In the vast public spaces of the national, state, and municipal parks and wilderness areas of the nation, lax enforcement of weak environmental laws allows corporations to pollute the air, water, and land for commercial purposes. As Adam Werbach, the executive director of the Common Assets Defense Fund, has argued, recent conservative federal legislation "demonstrates that it views its role as reestablishing the preeminent right of corporations to take from nature what they need with little regard to the long-term health of nature or for the communities that live downwind or can't afford bottled water" (2003:14). This results in the degradation of public spaces in the form of polluted fishing streams, polluted forests, polluted mineral resources, the extinction of many species of wildlife, and the extraction of nonrenewable natural resources. This topic is discussed in more detail in Section 7.

The appropriation of public spaces by urban development corporations is another area in which public spaces are being lost to private interests. Examples of this are found in public sidewalks and streets that limit public access and are often used as commercial venues; luxury shopping malls, which masquerade as great public town centers despite the public's right to free speech and assembly being strictly at the discretion of the mall's owners; and gated communities, where admission to the community is controlled by security gates, making the community off limits as a public space. Appropriation of public space through quasi-privatization results in the control of public space by private corporations that play an escalating role in the management of public space in the United States while limiting space use to the public. Consequently, public space, which traditionally meant that it was owned by and accessible to the general public, is no longer easy to define.

The losers here are the mass of middle- and lower-income citizens without the discretionary money to spend on expensive recreation and entertainment and thus have to depend on public spaces to fulfill their leisure needs. Without a national commitment to invest in and maintain a broad range of public spaces, current trends will only get worse. The nation's rich legacy of public spaces for the common good will be lost to future generations.

## CONCLUSION

Public space is the common area where people engage in a variety of activities that give them mutual pleasure—from rest and relaxation to vigorous physical activity—and a place where community consciousness is often fostered. Throughout history communities have created and developed public spaces that meet their needs. With increasing urbanization and the growth of metropolitan areas, there has been a proliferation of public space types to meet the needs of citizens. Local, state, and federal governments have struggled to keep up with the demands for free or low-cost public spaces. At the same time, state and federal governments have been faced with demands by commercial interests to sell or lease publicly owned space for private use.

The distinction between public and private space has become complicated by a hybridization of space. On the one hand there is privately owned space that is open to the public, such as shopping malls. On the other hand, there is the public owned space that is used by commercial enterprises, such as public sidewalks and streets on which commercial venues are located. In both situations, space utilization is at the discretion of the private owner. The losers here are the general public, whose access and freedom of actions are restricted.

## REFERENCES

American Antiquities Act of 1906. (1906, June 8): www.cr.nps.gov/local-law/anti1906.htm.

Blumhardt, Miles. (2005, April 17). "National Treasuries: Colorado Is Home to 11 NPS Sites." *The Coloradoan* (Fort Collins).

Carr, Stephen, Francis, Mark, Rivlin, Leanne, and Stone, Andrew. (1992). *Public Space.* Cambridge, UK: Cambridge University Press.

Congressional Acts Pertaining to Yellowstone. (1872). *The Act of Dedication*: www.yellowstone-online.com/history/yhfour.html.

Ely, James W., Jr. (ed.). (1997). *Property Rights in the Colonial Era and Early Republic.* New York: Garland.

Haines, Aubrey L. (1996). *The Yellowstone Story: A History of Our First National Park* (Vol. 1, rev. ed.). Boulder: University of Colorado Press.

Johannsen, Robert W., Belohlavek, John B., Hietala, Thomas R., Watson, Samuel J., Haynes, Sam W., and May, Robert E. (1997). *Manifest Destiny and Empire: American Antebellum Expansionism.* College Station: Texas A&M University Press.

Kulikoff, Allan. (2000). *From British Peasants to Colonial American Farmers.* Chapel Hill: University of North Carolina Press.

Miller, Sara Cedar. (2003). *Central Park: An American Masterpiece.* New York: Harry N. Abrams.

Rosenzweig, Roy, and Blackmar, Elizabeth. (1992). *The Park and the People: A History of Central Park.* Ithaca, NY: Cornell University Press.

Salmond, John A. (1989). *The Civilian Conservation Corps, 1933–1942: A New Deal Case Study.* Ann Arbor: University Microfilms International.

Savas, E. S. (1976). *A Study of Central Park.* New York: Central Park.

Schullery, Paul, and Whittlesey, Lee H. (2003). *Myth and History in the Creation of Yellowstone National Park.* Lincoln: University of Nebraska Press.

Siegan, Bernard H. (2001). *Property Rights: From Magna Carta to the Fourteenth Amendment.* New Brunswick, NJ: Transaction.

Smithsonian Institution. (1989). *The Smithsonian Institution: Highlights and History.* Washington, DC: Smithsonian Institution Press.

What Is the Smithsonian? (n.d.): http://newsdesk.si.edu/HistoryandMore/WhatIstheSmithsonian.htm.

Werbach, Adam. (2003, December). "Liquidation of the Commons." *In These Times* 16 (December):14–16.

Whyte, William H. (1992). *The WPA Guide to New York City.* New York: New Press.

# 18

# The Most Democratic Space in America

*ROY ROSENZEIG AND ELIZABETH BLACKMAR*

*New York's Central Park ranks among the world's most renowned public spaces, and it is one of New York City's most popular attractions. Now encompassing 843 acres, Central Park extends from some of the city's wealthiest neighborhoods to some of its poorest. It accommodates people from all social strata, and, as this reading asserts, it is considered by some to be the most democratic space in the United States.*

The fiscal crises of the 1970s and the 1990s have challenged the democratic commitment, built during the previous century and a quarter, to provide public space and public recreation for all. Nevertheless, in the 1980s at least a variety of commentators—using terms reminiscent of the 1860s—continued to celebrate Central Park as "the most popular and democratic space in America" or as "the one truly democratic space in the city." "For years it has been and today continues to be socially and racially integrated, notwithstanding patterns of caste and class stratification and polarization throughout society as a whole," Park Commissioner Gordon Davis wrote in 1981. "Of all its great achievements and features, there is none more profound or dramatically moving than the social democracy of this public space." "One of the geniuses of the park is that, to experience it, people have to desegregate," he told a reporter. "You don't get people coming to you based on sociological groups but on common concerns, about crime or jogging, or what the 110th Street Boathouse should look like. Blacks don't think of themselves as blacks in the park but as, say, bicyclists, and their alliances are with other bicyclists."[1]

But as has been true throughout the park's history, many parkgoers choreograph their use either to avoid unpleasant interactions or because they do not feel welcome in all parts of the park. After the rape of the Central Park jogger, more women hesitated to enter the park after dark. Young people have found it especially difficult to claim full access to such park facilities as ball fields or tennis courts, which require knowledge of the system of permits. Despite increased racial integration within the park, Puerto Rican and black working-class New Yorkers remain concentrated in the northern section, and white upper- and middle-class New Yorkers are overrepresented in the southern section.[2]

*Source: The Park and the People: A History of Central Park* by Roy Rosenzeig, pp. 524–530. Reprinted by permission of the Carol Mann Agency.

Still, Orde Coombs, a *New York Magazine* reporter, agreed with Davis that Central Park was "the single most democratic space in the city." Profiling two Puerto Rican teenagers from East Harlem and the Lower East Side who came to the park on a summer Sunday, Coombs said they had come "to reclaim the only piece of real estate they will ever love. For them, Central Park is a refuge from the slums, the only place in mid-Manhattan where the dispossessed can be at ease without coming under the withering glances of the wealthy." Coombs located the park's democratic character in its openness to the dispossessed; newspaper columnist Sidney Schanberg found it in the provision of "one of the few settings" where New Yorkers come together "not in quest of pluralist perfection but of existing together in respect." For Schanberg the city "at its human best" could be found in a softball game that matched teams of black and white New Yorkers against each other. Although the teams disputed constantly, "they have respect for each other's desire and skills. There may not be love or integration, but there is comprehension."[3]

Openness. Respect. Comprehension. On a warm spring afternoon one can find many such symbols of these basic preconditions of cultural democracy in the park. Almost forty years ago, James Baldwin, in *Go Tell It on the Mountain,* described the visit of the novel's protagonist, John Grimes, from his home in Harlem to Central Park on his fourteenth birthday. He climbed up the Ramble, "his favorite hill," and felt an "exultation and sense of power" as he viewed the park and city around him. "And still, on the summit of that hill he paused. He remembered the people he had seen in that city, whose eyes held no love for him . . . and how he was a stranger there." As he dashed down the hill, John "nearly knocked down an old white man with a white beard, who was walking very slowly and leaning on his cane. They both stopped, astonished, and looked at one another. John struggled to catch his breath and apologize, but the old man smiled. John smiled back. It was as though he and the old man had between them a great secret; and the old man moved on."[4]

The park continues to be a space of acknowledgment for people who have, at times, been "strangers" in the city. On June 24, 1989, a visitor to the Great Lawn could join a Gay Pride rally celebrating the twentieth anniversary of the Stonewall riots or, in the summer of 1988, inspect sections of the AIDS quilt displayed on the lawn. Park rules would have barred such mass gatherings before the mid-1960s. And even as late as the 1970s the police periodically swept through and arrested large numbers of gay men in the park. But now, gay New Yorkers—though still facing the threat of violence in the park as elsewhere—can exuberantly claim a place in this public park.[5]

Moments of mutual respect as well as public celebration and sharing do not, of course, erase the deep and divisive problems of the city. Poverty, crime, and bigotry stalked New York City in the 1980s, and such problems do not stop at the gates of the park. At times the reciprocal tolerance of parkgoers has been badly strained. Black and Puerto Rican teenagers sometimes feel that white parkgoers view them all as potential muggers. And older parkgoers sometimes feel that loud music from boom boxes is a deliberate effort to interfere with their enjoyment of the park. Still, on a warm summer day in Central Park, it is possible to glimpse the city "at its human best" and to think more about the possibilities than the limitations of a democratic public space. The park offers opportunities for preexisting communities (rooted, for example, in ethnic ties) to maintain themselves as well as for people to create new user-based friendships (rooted, for instance, in a passion for running, birds, dogs, chess, model boats, or disco roller skating). At the same time, it provides the chance for people who simply stroll through to place themselves within a much larger "imagined community" of ordinary people equally entitled to enjoy the benefits of public resources.[6] The park is a space to see people of varied backgrounds not as sociological categories (blacks and whites or women and men, for example) but as human beings. The creation of such an "imagined community," in which differences are respected and the equal rights of access affirmed, constitutes one precondition for a more democratic and humane society. Those who share a common space may come to share a common vision of the future.

New Yorkers have forged this conception of "common property" through a struggle older than the park itself, over how to define its public and over what a park should be. The gentlemen who created Central Park in the 1850s had a constricted definition of the public that featured themselves as the "representative" or best public. Generally, they shared Frederick Law Olmsted's view that a "park, properly so-called," needed to be artistically designed and managed as a pastoral landscape set apart from the city. Yet the creation of the park under public and democratic auspices opened up the possibility of alternative notions of the public and the park. Whether or not Calvert Vaux would have celebrated the result, the park was gradually redefined as a "many sided, fluent, thoroughly American high art work."

Over time the idea of the park and its public grew more inclusive, particularly in response to pressure from below. Through formal protests (petitions for Sunday concerts or demonstrations against fees for renting park chairs) and informal use patterns, ordinary New Yorkers transformed the gentlemen's conception of the park and its public. These changes did not proceed evenly or always in a straight line. Moses expanded the recreational facilities but also regulated use more tightly, cracking down on vendors and vagrants. His regime was in turn challenged by a new generation of parkgoers, who transformed Central Park into a place for political dissent and cultural experimentation.

When the park was first created, it represented—at least potentially—a socialization of public resources for the good of all citizens. But over the next 140 years New Yorkers had to struggle to achieve its democratic possibilities. In the 1870s and 1880s, for example, they took control of the park back from the state-appointed board of gentlemen and inserted it into city politics, and park workers demanded working conditions that would permit them to join the public in enjoying the city's preeminent leisure space. New Yorkers have often been reluctant to spend sufficient funds for adequate maintenance or wages. The New Deal, however, brought a dramatic infusion of federal money and an increased sense that citizens had a "right" to recreational facilities and public space. And postwar unionization gave city workers better pay and a greater say over their conditions of employment.

Fiscal crisis, however, shook New Yorkers' confidence in their ability as a public to provide and maintain open spaces. So they pulled back and turned to private corporations and real estate developers to provide new public spaces and to private philanthropy to support Central Park. The Central Park Conservancy helped restore the park, enriched its offerings, and also recommended new regulations. Control of the park is now divided between a self-perpetuating board of private (and wealthy) citizens and the city's park commissioner.

The systems that had governed since the 1870s were far from perfect, and the conservancy (like the boards of the art and the natural history museums in the 1880s) responds to pressure from ordinary citizens and elected officials. Nevertheless, the sovereign public has surrendered its commitment to provide free, well-maintained public spaces and has lost a measure of control over its most important public space. Exactly how much New Yorkers have lost in the bargain that restored Central Park for them remains unclear—and debatable—as the twentieth century draws toward a close.

It is also unclear whether the public access that was achieved over time will be sustained in the future. In the 1860s the park was distant from the homes of most working-class New Yorkers, who, in any case, preferred open spaces better suited to their recreational habits. In the late nineteenth and early twentieth centuries, ordinary New Yorkers often lived within walking distance of the park, and they worked fewer hours. They claimed Central Park as their own. In the late twentieth century, the park remains a refuge for the city's poorest residents, but fewer working-class families can afford to live on its borders.

A more serious threat to equal access is raised, however, by the very success achieved by Central Park. Its magnificent rehabilitation throws into sharp relief the much less adequately maintained public spaces in other parts of the city. Is New York moving toward a system in which private fund raising will support superior public facilities in more affluent (and symbolically central) sections of the city, while allowing the general commitment to a "right" to recreational facilities and public space to lapse elsewhere in the metropolis? In the 1850s the *Staats-Zeitung* had asked for "many smaller parks in different parts of the city," instead of a "mammoth park" that would be used only by "the heirs of the Upper Tendoms." Dispersed and well-maintained public spaces are an essential part of any commitment to social and cultural democracy in the nation's largest city.

At the start of the 1990s the future of our public parks—and indeed of the public sector, in general—looks grim. At both local and national levels politicians talk about the need to "downsize" government, to reverse the historic expansion of public services. In a climate where public hospitals, public schools, and public housing are threatened, the claims of public parks and recreation are particularly difficult to advance. In the fiscal crisis of the early 1990s, the New York City departments of parks and cultural affairs (which supports museums, zoos, and libraries) have faced the largest cuts, losing almost 30 percent of their budgets. To those—like us—who argue that parks *as well as* schools, hospitals, and housing are an essential part of a decent and humane city, many local politicians and civic leaders reply that they simply cannot raise taxes any more or businesses will flee. Such arguments are reminiscent of those of the conservative downtown merchants who in 1851 viewed the creation of a grand public park as "humbug." Their suggestion that "if downtown people wish to rusticate, they can find Elysian Fields [in Hoboken] within half the distance" is echoed today in claims that the "private sector" can adequately provide all needs.

But if history teaches us anything it is the contingency of particular historical moments, the possibility that change can come from new and unexpected directions. After all, New Yorkers began building the nation's greatest public park in the midst of a severe depression in the mid-nineteenth century, and they won a dramatic democratization of recreational resources during the worst depression in the nation's history. There are alternative visions of the urban future that challenge the pessimism of those who argue that cities must do less for their citizens. Like the more expansive coalition that won the day for Central Park in the 1850s and like the coalition that Henry George forged in the mid-1880s, some people would argue that the future greatness of New York lies in a livable environment (rather than a low tax rate) that will attract and maintain a healthy economy and culture. "To give all classes leisure, and comfort, and independence, the decencies of life, the opportunities of mental and moral development," George declared more than a century ago, "would be like turning water into a desert."

The fiscal crisis and recession of the early 1990s has already prompted a rethinking of how to fund, create, and administer adequate and accessible public spaces. New coalitions of park activists, environmentalists, and public officials are proposing regional park districts to overcome the barriers between cities and suburbs, decentralized administration to make parks more responsive to their constituencies, and new strategies of funding—including increased federal and state support as well as private philanthropy. But such initiatives can succeed only with the support of a wider public, with, as Calvert Vaux put it, recognition of the "possibilities that are within all classes" and the "genuine life blood" of public participation.

Thus, the challenge of preserving democratic public space within an inegalitarian society remains. To exclude poor New Yorkers from public spaces, to rely solely on private agencies to support and manage public institutions, to fail to ensure that all New Yorkers have access to adequate public spaces and recreational facilities, to settle for cultural democracy without political and economic democracy—all jeopardize the democratic public possibilities New Yorkers have struggled to realize since the founding of Central Park. The greatness of Central Park has more to do with these democratic possibilities than with the artful arrangement of trees, shrubs, bridges, paths, and lawns. In the early 1990s, as in the early 1980s, Central Park is still "the most democratic space" in New York, if not in the United States. For Central Park to remain genuinely a "public" park—in all the senses of that term—New Yorkers must continue to struggle toward that goal both in the park and in the city in which it is inextricably embedded.

## NOTES

1.  Donald Knowler, *The Falconer of Central Park.* New York: Karz-Cohl, 1984, 6; Orde Coombs, "Cherry Orchard," *NY Magazine, July 5–12, 1982,* 45; Gordon J. Davis, "Report and Determination in the Matter of Christo: The Gates," unpub. report, February 1981, 21–22, copy in possession of authors; Elizabeth Hawes, "Whose Park Is It Anyway?" *NYT Magazine,* September 5, 1982. 38.

2.  On racial and ethnic patterns in the 1970s, see, e.g., E. S. Savas, et al., *Study of Central Park,* 1976. chap. 2:29, 30–31.

3.  Coombs, "Cherry Orchard," 45; *NYT,* June 9, 1981.

4.  James Baldwin, *Go Tell It on the Mountain,* New York: Knopf. (1952, 1953), 35–37.

5.  *NYT,* July 24, 1973, June 14, 1988, June 25, 1989 (rally); Doug Ireland, "Rendezvous in the Ramble," *NY Magazine,* July 24, 1978, 41. Gay Pride rallies took place in Central Park regularly in the 1970s and early 1980s, then moved to the end of Christopher Street, and then back to Central Park. See *NYT,* June 29, 1970, June 29, 1972; George Chauncey, Jr., to authors, August 9, 1990. But for more recent attacks on gay men in the park, see *NYT,* July 24, 1990, July 24, 28, 1991.

6.  We have borrowed the phrase "imagined community" from Benedict Anderson, but our use of it is obviously different. See *Imagined Communities: Reflections on the Origins and Spread of Nationalism* (London: Verso, 1983).

# 19

# Civilian Conservation Corps (CCC)
# 1933–1941

## U-S-HISTORY.COM

*In 1933, with the United States in the depths of the worst depression in its history, the nation turned to Franklin D. Roosevelt hoping for an end to the out-of-control unemployment and economic turmoil that gripped the country. The president wasted no time. In less than one month after his inauguration, the Civilian Conservation Corps had been created to provide jobs for thousands of unemployed young men, assist families across the country, and stimulate the economy of numerous local communities. The program had near universal approval and was one of the most successful New Deal programs.*

### THE CREATION OF THE CCC

In 1932, when the American public voted President Herbert Hoover out of office, they were searching for an end to the economic chaos and unemployment that had gripped the nation for two years. They turned to a man promising a better life than the one they had known since the beginning of the Great Depression—Franklin D. Roosevelt.

When FDR took office, he immediately commenced a massive revitalization of the nation's economy. In response to the depression that hung over the nation in the early 1930s, President Roosevelt created many programs designed to put Americans back to work.

Roosevelt was not interested in the dole. He was determined, rather, to preserve the pride of American workers in their own ability to earn a living, so he concentrated on creating jobs.

In his first 100 days in office, President Roosevelt approved several measures as part of his "New Deal," including the Emergency Conservation Work Act (ECW), better known as the Civilian Conservation Corps (CCC). With that action, he brought together the nation's young men and the land in an effort to save them both. Roosevelt proposed to recruit thousands of unemployed young men, enlist them in a peacetime army, and send them to battle the erosion and destruction of the nation's natural resources. More than any other New Deal agency, the CCC is considered to be an extension of Roosevelt's personal philosophy.

The speed with which the plan moved through proposal, authorization, implementation, and operation was certainly a miracle of cooperation among all the agencies and

*Source:* "Civilian Conservation Corps (CCC) 1933–1941" from U-S-History.com. Reprinted by permission Online Highways LLC.

branches of the federal government. From FDR's inauguration on March 4, 1933, to the induction of the first CCC enrollee, only 37 days had elapsed.

## REVITALIZATION AND REFORESTATION

The CCC, also known as Roosevelt's Tree Army, was credited with renewing the nation's decimated forests by planting an estimated three billion trees from 1933 to 1942. This was crucial, especially in states affected by the Dust Bowl, where reforestation was necessary to break the wind, hold water in the soil, and hold the soil in place. So far reaching was the CCC's reforestation program that it was responsible for more than half the reforestation, public and private, accomplished in the nation's history.

Eligibility requirements for the CCC carried several simple stipulations. Congress required U.S. citizenship only. Other standards were set by the ECW. Sound physical fitness was mandatory because of the hard physical labor required. Men had to be unemployed, unmarried, and between the ages of 18 and 26, although the rules were eventually relaxed for war veterans. Enlistment was for a duration of six months, although many reenlisted after their allotted time was up.

Problems were confronted quickly. The bulk of the nation's young and unemployed youth were concentrated in the East, while most of the work projects were in the western parts of the country. The War Department mobilized the nation's transportation system to move thousands of enrollees from induction centers to work camps. The Agriculture and Interior departments were responsible for planning and organizing work to be performed in every state. The Department of Labor was responsible for the selection and enrollment of applicants. The National Director of the ECW was Robert Fechner, a union vice president chosen personally by President Roosevelt.

Young men flocked to enroll. Many politicians believed that the CCC was largely responsible for a 55 percent reduction in crimes committed by the young men of that day. Men were paid $30 a month, with mandatory $25 allotment checks sent to families of the men, which made life a little easier for people at home.

Camps were set up in all states, as well as in Hawaii, Alaska, Puerto Rico, and the Virgin Islands. Enrollment peaked at the end of 1935, when there were 500,000 men located in 2,600 camps in operation in all states. California alone had more than 150 camps. The greatest concentration of CCC personnel was in the Sixth Civilian Conservation Corps District of the First Corps Area, in the Winooski River Valley of Vermont, in December 1933. Enlisted personnel and supervisors totaled more than 5,300 and occupied four large camps.

The program enjoyed great public support. Once the first camps were established and the CCC became better known, they became accepted and even sought after. The CCC camps stimulated regional economies and provided communities with improvements in forest activity, flood control, fire protection, and overall community safety.

## SEGREGATION AND EDUCATION

Although policy prohibited discrimination, blacks and other minorities encountered numerous difficulties in the CCC. In the early years of the program, some camps were integrated. By 1935, however, there was, in the words of CCC director Fechner, a "complete segregation of colored and white enrollees," but "segregation is not discrimination." At its peak, more than 250,000 African Americans were enrolled in nearly 150 all-black CCC companies.

An important modification became necessary early in 1933. It extended enlistment coverage to about 14,000 American Indians whose economic circumstances were deplorable and had mostly been ignored. Before the CCC was terminated, more than 80,000 Native Americans were paid to help reclaim the land that had once been theirs.

In addition, in May 1933, the president authorized the enrollment of about 25,000 veterans of the Spanish American War and World War I, with no age or marital restrictions. This made it possible for more than 250,000 veterans to rebuild lives disrupted by earlier service to their country.

In June 1933, the ECW decided that men in CCC camps could be given the opportunity of vocational training and additional education. Educational programs were developed that varied considerably from camp to camp, both in efficiency and results. More than 90 percent of all enrollees participated in some facet of the educational program. Throughout the CCC, more than 40,000 illiterate men were taught to read and write.

## LEAVING ITS MARK ON THE LAND

By 1942, there was hardly a state that could not boast of permanent projects left as markers by the CCC. The CCC worked on improving millions of acres of federal and state lands, as well as parks. New roads were built, telephone lines strung, and trees planted.

CCC projects included:

- more than 3,470 fire towers erected;
- 97,000 miles of fire roads built;
- 4,235,000 man-days devoted to fighting fires;
- more than 3 billion trees planted;
- 7,153,000 man days expended on protecting the natural habitats of wildlife; 83 camps in 15 Western states assigned 45 projects of that nature;
- 46 camps assigned to work under the direction of the U.S. Bureau of Agriculture Engineering;
- more than 84,400,000 acres of good agricultural land receive manmade drainage systems; Indian enrollees do much of that work;
- 1,240,000 man-days of emergency work completed during floods of the Ohio and Mississippi valleys;
- disease and insect control;
- forest improvement—timber stand inventories, surveying, and reforestation;
- forest recreation development—campgrounds built, complete with picnic shelters, swimming pools, fireplaces, and restrooms.

In addition, 500 camps were under the control of the Soil Conservation Service. The primary work of those camps was erosion control. The CCC also made outstanding contributions to the development of recreational facilities in national, state, county, and metropolitan parks. By design, the CCC worked on projects that were independent of other public relief programs. Although other federal agencies, such as the National Park Service and Soil Conservation Service contributed, the U.S. Forest Service administered more than 50 percent of all public work projects for the CCC.

Residents of southern Indiana will always remember the extraordinary work of the CCC during the flood of the Ohio River in 1937. The combined strength of the camps in the area saved lives as well as property. The CCC also was involved in other natural disasters, including a hurricane in New England in 1938, floods in Vermont and New York, and blizzards in Utah.

The CCC approached maturity in 1937. Hundreds of enrollees had passed through the system, and returned home to boast of their experiences. Hundreds more demonstrated their satisfaction by extending their enlistments.

### THE END OF THE CCC, THE BEGINNING OF WAR

There were numerous reasons why Congress refused to establish the Civilian Conservation Corps as a permanent agency. However, disenchantment, or failure to recognize the organization's success, were never topics of debate. In fact, Congress extended its life as an independent, funded agency for two years.

The year 1939 brought about a major challenge, because there was a struggle with internal problems brought on by changing conditions in both the United States and Europe. The potential of war in Europe was belatedly recognized. Storm clouds were forming that positively affected the United States economy. The president's Lend-Lease program made jobs more plentiful in the armaments industry, and applications for the CCC declined.

Also in 1939, Congress authorized the Federal Security Agency (FSA) to consolidate several offices under one director. The CCC lost its status as an independent agency. Congress added $50 million to the CCC's 1940–41 appropriation and the Corps remained at its current strength of about 300,000 enrollees. However, by late summer 1941, it was obvious that the Corps was in serious trouble. A lack of applicants, desertion, and a great number of enrollees leaving for jobs had reduced the Corps to fewer than 200,000 men in about 900 camps. Many were beginning to question the necessity of retaining the CCC when unemployment had all but disappeared.

Although there was still work to be done, most agreed that defense had to come first. Following the attack on Pearl Harbor, it became obvious that any federal project not directly related to the war effort was in jeopardy. A joint committee of Congress recommended that the CCC be abolished by July 1, 1942. Technically, however, the corps was never abolished. Congress simply refused it any additional money. Eventually, $8 million was set aside to cover all costs of liquidation, and the War Department, Labor Department, and Civil Aeronautics Administration were given first opportunity to acquire CCC properties. The War Department claimed the majority of the equipment.

The Civilian Conservation Corps was one of the most successful New Deal programs of the Great Depression. It existed for fewer than 10 years, but left a legacy of strong, handsome roads, bridges, and buildings throughout the United States. Between 1933 and 1941, more than 3,000,000 men served in the CCC.

The effects of service in the CCC were felt for years, even decades, afterwards. Following the depression, when the job market picked up, businessmen indicated a preference for hiring a man who had been in the CCC, and the reason was simple. Employers believed that anyone who had been in the CCC would know what a full day's work meant, and how to carry out orders in a disciplined way.

Today, many of the remaining physical features the CCC built have been placed on the National Register of Historic Places.

# 20

# A Salute to the Civilian Conservation Corps at White Rock Lake Park

*STEVEN R. BUTLER*

*The Civilian Conservation Corps provided jobs for thousands of unemployed young men. Created in 1933, by the end of 1935 2,600 CCC camps were located across the United States. One of those camps was established at White Rock Park, Texas. This article describes the projects carried out by the CCC men at White Rock Park from 1935 until 1942. They created a legacy for a public space that is still in use six decades later.*

## FDR AND THE CCC

*I propose to create a civilian conservation corps to be used in simple work, not interfering with normal employment, and confining itself to forestry, the prevention of soil erosion, flood control, and similar projects. I call your attention to the fact that this type of work is of definite practical value, not only through the prevention of great financial loss, but also as a means of creating future national wealth.*

—President Franklin D. Roosevelt, 1933 Message to Congress

While the City of Dallas can be credited with the initial development of White Rock Lake Park, the federal government also left its mark. From 1935 to 1942, several permanent park improvements were made by the Civilian Conservation Corps (CCC), which performed the lion's share of the work, or were funded by the Works Progress Administration (WPA), two of the more visible and noteworthy federal agencies created by Congress as part of Democratic President Franklin D. Roosevelt's plan to combat the Great Depression.

The CCC, which is almost universally held to have been a success, was formed in April 1933, shortly after Roosevelt took office. Authorized by Congress and created by Executive Order, the agency lasted until shortly after the United States entered World War II. Its goal was to provide unemployed young men between the ages of 18 and 25 with both work and the opportunity to learn a useful trade. (The Civilian Conservation Corps Act of June 28, 1937, which formally established the agency, later stipulated that "enrollees . . .

*Source:* "A Salute to the Civilian Conservation Corp at White Rock Lake Park, April 8, 2004" by Steven R. Butler from www.watermelon-kid.com/. Reprinted by permission.

shall be unmarried male citizens between the ages of 17 and 23.") Veterans on relief "with dependents to whom they are willing to make allotments from their salary" were also eligible for the program. Jointly administered by the National Park Service and the United States Army, the CCC established camps all over the United States where youthful recruits labored at a wide variety of public works projects. They were paid $30 per month, $25 of which was sent home to their families. In addition to providing the youths with jobs, the agency also hoped to educate the men and provide them with an opportunity to learn a useful trade.

### DALLAS GETS A CCC CAMP

The Dallas-area camp, designated SP-55-TX, was originally intended for Bachman Lake but in mid-July 1935 the National Park Service decided to place it at White Rock instead, "in order to get sanitary sewage and other facilities more suited to the project." On July 10, 1935, work on the barracks and other buildings began under the supervision of Army construction officer Tom B. Martin, the man who chose the site, a 37½-acre tract located east of Winfrey Point. Second Lt. Sidney H. Weideman, Superintendent Roy E. Lane, and Mr. J. M. Windner assisted him. By August 7 the work was completed. On August 8, with First Lt. James S. England of the 359th Infantry in charge, the camp officially opened. England's second-in-command was First Lt. Donald C. Sandison of the United States Army Cavalry Reserve. Capt. William R. Deatherage was the camp's medical officer.

The White Rock CCC camp consisted of several wooden structures painted yellow. These included barracks, a mess hall and canteen, a dispensary, and several small sheds or outbuildings. Arranged around an open "service yard" were an office, a combination blacksmith shop and storage building, a ten-car garage, and a combination woodworking, repair shop, and storage facility. A road, roughly following the same route as present-day Emerald Isle Drive, led to the camp from State Highway 78 (present-day Garland Road) and encircled it. Another short road connected the camp with East Lawther Drive.

On Wednesday, August 14, 1935, one hundred and twenty recruits from Collin County arrived at the White Rock Camp to form CCC Company 2896. The following day, sixty-nine young men from Dallas County joined them. These were the first of approximately 3,000 youths who, over the course of the next seven years, would spend from six months to two years learning a trade and performing a valuable public service at the same time. Among the early arrivals were "three Negroes" for whom it was reported that Commander England was awaiting "orders regarding where they should be sent." These orders were necessitated due to the fact that like the U.S. Army at that time, CCC companies were not racially integrated. What became of these three young men is unknown. In all likelihood, they soon joined an all-black company in some other part of the country.

The average age of a recruit at the Dallas camp was 20. Although some were city boys, the majority came from rural areas in Dallas and surrounding counties, principally Collin, Denton, and Tarrant. They aspired, according to one report, "to be modern farmers, mechanical engineers, or Civil Service employees." Several were "attending night school in order to complete their education and training in an endeavor to realize their various aspirations."

During the first two weeks of their six-month enlistment, reported the Dallas Morning News, this first wave of recruits performed some "necessary work around the camp" and were given "medical and dental treatment" prior to embarking on a "two year park improvement program" that would include "deepening and widening the lake," as well as "clearing underbrush, building bridle paths, trails, picnic grounds, barbecue pits and shelter houses and terracing work."

After only two weeks on the job, Lieutenant Sandison, England's second-in-command, was transferred to Gatesville, Texas. He was not immediately replaced. In early 1936, First Lieutenant George P. Parker of the 53rd Field Artillery succeeded Lieutenant England as camp commander and Captain Deatherage, the camp's doctor, was also replaced. His successor was Captain A. H. Atlas of the 328th Medical Regiment. Later that year, Second Lieutenant A. S. Jones of the 53rd Field Artillery was appointed second-in-command to Lieutenant Parker.

The first area to receive the company's closest attention was Doran's Point, now called "Flag Pole Hill." The appearance of Doran's Point, "a barren rock hill" overlooking the northern end of the lake, was almost completely transformed between 1936 and 1937. The work included and probably started with the obliteration of a dirt road that previously led to the apex of the mound on its east side. After leveling off the top of this natural vantage point, the youthful workers formed $283 worth of logs, cement and 40 tons of flagstone into a picturesque overlook surmounted by a tall flagpole and accessible by sixteen wide stone steps from a newly-paved parking area. Some local craftsmen assisted them. On the top of an adjacent, more gently rising slope, they constructed an 81-foot long open-air picnic shelter made of Cordova limestone, a small stone latrine, and an all-purpose stone building that was afterward used for many years to house transmitting equipment for city-owned radio station WRR. All these structures are still standing, although the former radio transmitting building is today a designated "athletic building." The transmission towers that stood nearby it are gone, however.

At the bottom of the hill, at the corner of Northwest Highway, Goforth Road, and a newly-built ring road called Doran Circle, the CCC enrollees constructed a cluster of limestone buildings, the largest of which was originally used as a concession stand where park-goers could purchase fish bait, picnic supplies, cold drinks, and similar commodities. A garage and a latrine completed the complex. Today this collection of CCC-built structures forms the East Region headquarters of the Dallas Park and Recreation Department.

During this same period of time, utilizing plans drawn up by local architect named M. A. Burke, the young men of the CCC began constructing a limestone and wood concession building on a slightly elevated tract of land overlooking Sunset Bay, at the mouth of Dixon's Branch creek. Both this building and the park caretaker's cottage, constructed immediately behind it, are still standing today, along with a T-head fishing pier that continues to attract anglers, duck feeders, and people curious to see the large flock of pelicans that often spend the winter in this location. As its name implies, Sunset Bay is also a popular place to view the sun setting over the distant skyscrapers of downtown Dallas. In 2004, a statue honoring the White Rock CCC enrollees was erected here.

When it was built the Sunset Bay concession building featured a dark walnut wooden sign complete with cast iron hardware forged in the CCC camp's blacksmith shop. The sign, which was decorated with carved oak leaves and colorfully embellished 3 inch carved letters, read: "Sun Set Inn, Dinner, Drinks, [and] Sandwiches." A smaller wooden placard, which hung below, advertised the availability of bicycles for rent. This sign has long since disappeared. Similar signs were erected at the Doran's Point concession complex and the Big Thicket concession building. The CCC blacksmith shop was also used, no doubt, to create the whimsical cast iron frogs, birds, fish and other creatures that decorate the windows of a stone latrine built by the CCC, which still stands near the Dixon Branch or "Stone Tables" picnic area. M. A. Burke designed them. A small bridge and spring-fed lily pond, designed by another local man, N. S. McCommas, were also constructed nearby during this same period. All have since fallen into disrepair.

Another noteworthy CCC project designed by M. A. Burke is the park's entrance portal, constructed at the junction of East Lawther Drive and Garland Road. It incorporates a stone bridge in its design. Cast iron letters spelling out the name of the park are attached to the front of the portal.

By chance, the presence of the CCC camp at White Rock coincided with the 1936 Texas Centennial Exposition, which was held at nearby Fair Park. There, throughout the term of the six-month event more than 2,000 "man-days" were expended enlightening exposition visitors about the role of the CCC in combating the Great Depression and in all probability, highlighting the agency's contribution to the improvement of White Rock Park. A one-story stone building, constructed by the CCC, housed the exhibit, which included a tabletop model of a typical CCC camp.

At the conclusion of the its first two years of operation, a report was prepared (probably by Lieutenant Parker) summarizing the White Rock camp's initial accomplishments. In addition to the buildings constructed at Doran's Point, Dixon Branch, and Sunset Bay, the young workers transplanted 1,500 trees to the Doran's Point area, constructed 6,000 feet of "rip-rap" retaining walls at various points around the lake, completed several erosion control projects, and planted 75 acres of pecan seedlings in what is now Norbuck Park, which they took special care to protect from grass fires. Today's park visitors probably take these and other trees planted by the CCC for granted but aerial photos taken prior to 1930 reveal that trees were not as abundant before the arrival of "Roosevelt's Tree Army." Only in the Dixon Branch area and along some of the other creeks that feed the lake was there any sizeable foliage prior to the establishment of the park.

Between 1935 and 1937, the CCC also placed "thirty-five hundred bundles of willows and one hundred yards of gravel . . . in the lake." "The willow bundles," explained CCC officials, were "for the protection of small fish and the gravel beds for spawning beds." For the benefit of park visitors, approximately 90 "table and bench combinations" were "constructed and placed in extensively used picnic areas, adjacent to the eastern shore of the lake" along with "70 camp stoves and fireplaces." The 1937 report concluded with a list of "Proposed Developments." Foremost among them was a plan to use a dredge boat to reclaim the shallow marshlands that had formed at the mouth of Dixon's Branch, owing to the deposit of silt over a period of time. When spanning fish were trapped here during periods of drought, read the report, "rapid evaporation and [the] hot sun soon kill them, resulting in the loss of the fish and causing offensive odors plus unsanitary conditions."

### CCC HELPS WITH FIRST DREDGING

Although dredging was originally scheduled to begin on September 15, 1937, the work did not start until after November 5, when the City of Dallas took possession of a shallow-draft hydraulic boat costing $31,973 that they christened the Joe E. Lawther, in honor of the former mayor "who long urged preservation of the lake." The work had barely begun, however, when problems occurred. About a week after the Joe E. Lawther was put into operation, the boat began leaking. At first, workers used a hand-pump to remove the water but it soon became apparent that a motorized pump was necessary. Then, at about 8:30 p.m. on the evening of Wednesday, November 17, the Joe E. Lawther was at work in Dixon's Branch when Jess Perkins, a crewmember, looked down at the deck and noticed water lapping at his shoes. Within the next minute and a half the boat sank in six feet of water as Perkins and fellow worker F. H. Luttrell scrambled to escape from the sinking vessel.

At first, no one was sure whom to blame for the accident and "rumors began flying that the CCC workers were drunk much of the time." Eventually, these accusations proved to be unfounded. After W. J. Redman, a professional diver from Galveston, re-floated the Lawther, it was discovered that manufacturing defects, including a lack of "hard timbers to overcome vibration of the engines", caused four leaks in the boat's hull.

During the winter of 1937–1938 the Joe E. Lawther was repaired. Dredging resumed in April 1938 and continued until February 1939. Together with some further dredging that was performed intermittently until the beginning of World War II, nearly 90 acres of land was eventually reclaimed; 68 acres at the northern end of the lake and 20 at Dixon's Branch. The removed silt was used to fill marshy areas around the lake or sold for 25 cents per cubic yard to anyone who had the means to take it away.

Bachman Lake, a smaller park located on the northwestern edge of the city, also received attention from the "boys in green" at White Rock. One of most enduring improvements they made was a shelter house or picnic pavilion that was fashioned out of stone and heavy timbers. It is still standing on the Northwest Highway side of the reservoir. Recruits also built a latrine, planted trees and shrubs, and constructed numerous picnic table and bench combinations to complement the many fireplaces they also put in place for the convenience of picnickers. Entrance portals, probably similar to the one they built on East Lawther Drive at White Rock, were proposed but never built.

## COMPANY 2896's LAST PROJECT

In 1941 the CCC began planning what would become one of their final projects at White Rock Lake Park, a large "combination building" atop Winfrey Point, a hill overlooking the lake that was named in honor of former Dallas Police Commissioner R. L. "Dick" Winfrey. Construction of the building began in 1941, but before it could be completed, the United States entered the Second World War. Shortly afterward, on January 15, 1942, the White Rock camp ceased operations and it fell to the City of Dallas Park Board to complete the Winfrey Point building, a task that was accomplished in August of that same year.

## NEW USES FOR THE CCC CAMP

During 1942–43 the abandoned CCC camp was used by the Army Air Corps Fifth Ferrying Command, for use as a temporary induction center. From November 1944 to October 1945, German Prisoners-of-War were incarcerated there. From 1946 to 1947, the barracks were used by Southern Methodist University as overflow housing for students. Finally, between 1947 and 1951 the buildings were either sold, torn down, or put to new uses.

The boards from one were used to build a floor in the Agricultural exhibition building at Fair Park. Another was moved to the Cedar Crest golf course, for use as a maintenance or storage shed. At least three of the old barracks may have become homes in the vicinity of White Rock Lake. In 1951 pranksters, believed to be college students, used dynamite to blow a hole in one of the last remaining structures. Since 1954, two baseball diamonds have marked the site of the camp.

### CCC LEGACY

More than six decades after the CCC camp at White Rock closed, many of the projects constructed by the boys in green are still standing, although most are now in varying states of disrepair. From the combined effects of time, weather, and simple benign neglect, the "rip-rap" retaining walls that were constructed around the lakeshore at various points have suffered the most. In many places, they have collapsed or have been submerged. The lilly pond near the Stone Tables Picnic Area is another casualty of the passage of time. It bears little resemblence to its original appearance, while the bridge that spans it is missing some stones. All the recreation buildings—Big Thicket, Sunset Bay, and Winfrey Point—also have visible signs of neglect such as missing or damaged siding or stones. It is a shame that more effort has not been made to keep these structures in better repair. It is equally unfortunate that unlike the bridges in the park, which bear plaques crediting their construction to the WPA (Works Project Administration), there is nothing attached to any of the CCC projects telling by whom they were built and when. Like the hundreds of pecan trees planted in the park by the now anonymous CCC workers, they stand in silent testimony to an earlier time, when a dynamic President did his best to help an ailing nation get back on its feet and Dallas, like many other communities around the country, became the beneficiaries of his efforts and the hard work of the "boys in green."

### SOURCE

Butler, Steven R. *From Water Supply to Urban Oasis: A History of White Rock Lake Park* (Richardson, Texas: Poor Scholar Publications, 2004).

───────────────────────── 21 ─────────────────────────

# TVA's Arrival Turned Valley Around

*HOWARD MILLER*

*The Tennessee Valley Authority is an independent federal government corporation managed by a board of directors, and its operations spread across seven states. The TVA was created to develop the Tennessee River system for inland navigation, flood control, and to generate and sell surplus electricity produced through water power. The effects of this water- and land-use system on the lives of the people of the Tennessee Valley have been enormous, as this article explains.*

The most significant event to affect Huntsville and the surrounding region during the 1930s played a key role in breaking the strangling grip of the Great Depression: the creation of the Tennessee Valley Authority and the hope it offered people living here.

While October 1929 is generally considered the beginning of the worldwide economic slump so devastating it is often called "the" Depression, its shadow stretched over the entire decade that followed.

Except for persons who lived through those years, it is difficult in 2005 to grasp how much the hard times shaped the lives and attitudes of a generation. For many today, TVA is merely another alphabet agency or letters on a sign near a place you go fishing or boating.

TVA was created on May 18, 1933, when President Franklin D. Roosevelt signed the authorizing legislation into law. It was one of many innovative ideas that made up his New Deal, his plan to get the United States out of the mire.

TVA's primary marching orders were to reduce flood damage, improve navigation on the Tennessee River and generate electric power. An extremely important goal was to promote agricultural and industrial development in a region that desperately needed it.

How bad were things in the Huntsville-Madison County area in 1933? Pretty bad.

## EXHAUSTED FARMLAND

Among the problems facing folks living in the Tennessee Valley was land that had been exhausted from too much farming and erosion. As a result, crop yields were low and farm incomes plunged. Many families barely eked out a living below the poverty level.

*Source:* "TVA's Arrival Turned Valley Around" from *The Huntsville Times,* April 24, 2005, by Howard Miller. Copyright © 2005 The Huntsville Times. All rights reserved. Reprinted with permission of *The Huntsville Times.*

**169**

Timber was another natural resource that had been nearly exhausted. The best of the timber had already been cut.

TVA provided a number of solutions. When the agency got rolling, it developed new fertilizers, taught farmers how to use them, replanted forests, worked to control forest fires and also aided hunting and fishing by improving habitat. In those days, game animals and fish were welcome additions to the family supper table.

And, thanks to TVA, many rural residents literally "saw the light." The dams that the agency built controlled floods, improved navigation on the waterways, created miles of reservoir shoreline for recreational use and generated large amounts of electricity.

Work began on the construction of Guntersville Dam on Dec. 4, 1935, and it was completed in 1939. Its a good example of these structures that meant so much to residents in the area and brought them a better life.


**ATTRACTED INDUSTRIES**

It may be difficult for many to imagine now, but the arrival of electricity throughout rural areas of northern Alabama is within living memory. Electric lights began to replace kerosene lamps, washing machines replaced washtubs and scrub boards and refrigerators replaced smokehouses and canning.

Equally important, this abundance of electricity attracted new industries and jobs to the Tennessee Valley. Nothing was more desperately needed during the 1930s.

A TVA staff member wrote in a letter from the field in Alabama on June 6, 1934, after touring project sites, that about 9,500 men were at work in the Tennessee River Valley at Norris and Wheeler dams, doing a variety of clearing and building projects.

Considering the joblessness of the Depression, that statistic may seem relatively small, but it was a significant turn upward and TVA's effect on Huntsville, Madison County and all of northern Alabama can hardly be overstated.

TVA remains an important contributor to the region's well-being. Eleven coal-burning plants produce most of the agency's electricity. Four of those plants and two freestanding sites have combustion turbines that burn natural gas or fuel oil.

In addition, TVA has three nuclear plants, 29 hydroelectric dams, a pumped-storage plant and for several years has used such things as solar and wind power and methane for energy production.


**WIPE OUT DISEASE**

Another positive side effect of TVA was improved public health. During the 1930s, residents of the Tennessee Valley were still dying of smallpox and typhoid. Through a TVA-sponsored system of vaccinations, the diseases were virtually eradicated in the region.

Despite all the benefits, there was a downside to the dams' construction. TVA had to relocate 9,000 families to make way for the reservoirs.

# Environmental Protections

*We allow the chemical death rain to fall as though there were no alterna-*
*tive, whereas in fact there are many.*

—Rachel Carson

*The individual who pollutes the air with his factory and the ghetto kid who*
*breaks store windows both represent the same thing. They don't care about*
*each other—or what they do to each other.*

—Senator Daniel Patrick Moynihan

The history of government policies to preserve and protect the environment has not always been a battle between progressives and conservatives. Occasionally, usually because of some environmental crisis, the two sides have come together to pass legislation beneficial to society. Often, though, there is a clash between the two ideologies, as progressives seek to establish standards to curb corporations from making cars that pollute and waste energy or from dumping industrial wastes into the air, water, or landfills. Progressives also promote measures that ensure that when the standards are violated, offending corporations will have to pay to clean up their messes. Conservatives, to the contrary, want businesses to flourish unhindered by laws and costly remedial actions. To regulate businesses, conservatives argue, increases the cost of products and services and may cause the businesses to lay off workers. They argue that businesses and industries will regulate themselves.

For the first one hundred years of U.S. history the population was small, cities were modest in size, and there was little or no industrialization. Because there were abundant resources in land, timber, and water, there was little regard for the environment. Even though people were not good stewards of their resources, the collective environmental impact of people on the environment was negligible because the resources were so vast and the people so few. All of this changed in the last 125 years or so with the discovery of oil, the invention of the internal combustion engine, the increased use of coal, and the rapid growth of industry. Add to this mix the rapid growth in population fueled by waves of immigration, and the greater concentration of people in cities as people moved off the farms to work in factories. Soon the air around cities and factories became polluted. Rivers and lakes were endangered by industrial wastes, acid rain, and the runoff of pesticide- and

**171**

herbicide-laden water. Fertile farmland became more and more threatened by wind and water erosion. So in the past century, U.S. society changed from an individual/private property, laissez-faire approach to the environment to one of collective concern and intermittent government intervention to protect it.

## GOVERNMENT ACTIONS TO PROTECT THE ENVIRONMENT

### The Civilian Conservation Corps

During the first part of the twentieth century farmers plowed up too much marginal land in the prairie states. When a major drought occurred in the 1930s this fragile land experienced major wind erosion. Also, indiscriminate cutting of the forests meant declining timber resources and further problems with erosion. To stem this destruction of the nation's natural resources and to provide jobs to the unemployed because of the Great Depression, President Roosevelt and Congress established in 1933 the Emergency Conservation Work (ECW) Act, more commonly known as the Civilian Conservation Corps (CCC). The CCC was "the most popular experiment of the New Deal" (CCC Alumni Organization, n.d.). During its nine-year history it received support from progressives and conservatives alike. Progressives favored it because it was a timely and necessary mechanism to help the unemployed but also to protect the environment. Because it did not constrain businesses and even helped them, it was also embraced by conservatives.

Before it was dismantled in 1942, over three million young men in the CCC erected 3,470 fire towers, built 97,000 miles of fire roads, devoted over four million person-days to fighting fires, and planted more than three billion trees. The CCC also saved twenty million acres from further erosion and protected the natural habitats of wildlife. Also, through education efforts in each of the 2,650 camps, more than 40,000 illiterate workers learned to read and write (CCC Alumni Organization, n.d.).

### Environmental Protection Agency

During the 1960s, public concern about pollution and resource quality increased. This growing awareness was the result of several factors. Among them were environmental warnings from Rachel Carson's worldwide bestseller, *Silent Spring* (1962), which indicted the indiscriminate use of pesticides; a fire on the Cuyahoga River in Ohio that burned for eight days from oily pollutants; and a major oil spill off the coast of Santa Barbara, California, in 1969, which created an ecological disaster. Further evidence of severe environmental problems was the ongoing problem of smog from automobile and industrial pollutants in cities across the country, especially in the Los Angeles basin, where schools were periodically shut down.

One result of this emerging environmental concern was the establishment of Earth Day in 1970, when some 20 million people demonstrated their support for improvements in resource conservation and environmental quality. A lasting consequence of this new environmental fervor was the creation of the Environmental Protection Agency (EPA) by President Richard Nixon's Executive Order in late 1970. Nixon called for the creation of a "strong, independent agency . . . to make a coordinated attack on the pollutants which debase the air we breathe, the water we drink, and the land that grows our food"

(Environmental Protection Agency, 1990). This agency was to coórdinate the government's environmental activities (fifteen programs and seven agencies).

The EPA administered the Clean Water Act of 1972, the Safe Drinking Water Act of 1974, and subsequent laws regarding water pollution. Under these Acts the EPA was authorized to regulate levels of contamination in the nation's drinking water supplies and to establish water pollution control standards for various sources of water pollution such as mines, manufacturing plants, paper mills, electric utility plants, and municipal sewage plants. If an offending entity exceeded the limits set by the EPA, it was required to install pollution control equipment that met the standard.

Similarly, the EPA administered the Clean Air Act (first enacted in 1963 and amended in 1970, 1977, and 1990). The EPA sets the quality standards for various air pollutants (carbon monoxide, nitrogen oxide, sulfur oxide, ozone, lead, and particulates) but the states are responsible for their enforcement. The major sources of air pollution are exhaust from vehicles and smokestack emissions from industrial plants, oil refineries, and public utilities. If the states do not enforce these federal air pollution standards, then the EPA has the right to enforce them, requiring that the offenders install the proper pollution control equipment.

Due to growing environmental concerns, the Clean Air Act of 1990 addressed some new issues: motor vehicle emissions and alternative fuels, toxic air pollutants, acid rain, and stratospheric ozone depletion. This legislation raised automobile emission standards, set a timetable for further reductions for these emissions, and encouraged the use of low-sulfur fuels as a means of reducing sulfur dioxide in the atmosphere, a main component of acid rain.

In 1976 Congress enacted the Toxic Substances Control Act, giving the EPA authority to administer the Act. Primarily, this Act required manufacturers and processors to test new chemicals to determine the effect on human health and environment and to report these results to the EPA. The EPA, in turn, could limit or prohibit the manufacture and sale of toxic substances, or remove them from commerce, if it found that they posed a threat to human health or the environment.

From 1942 to 1953 Hooker Chemical disposed of almost 22,000 tons of toxic chemical waste (over three hundred different chemicals, many of them carcinogenic) in the 3,000-foot-long Love Canal near Niagara Falls, New York. The site was filled, and Hooker donated the land to the local board of education. A school and houses were built on the site. In 1977 it was discovered that toxic waste (dioxin) from that chemical dump had contaminated the homes and people in Love Canal. This episode provided the impetus for the passage of the federal Superfund law in 1980. This law was designed to clean up the worst hazardous sites caused by toxic wastes primarily from industry, military weapons plants, and landfills. The hazardous wastes that were to be cleaned up included acids, dioxins, explosives, heavy metals, solvents, polychlorinated biphenyls (PCBs), pesticides, and radioactive substances.

The federal government estimates that the United States has more than 400,000 hazardous waste sites, not counting many toxic waste sites at military installations (e.g., Rocky Mountain Arsenal outside of Denver, which was the site of the U.S. Army's manufacture and storage of nerve gases, mustard gas, napalm, and rocket fuel). Sites that pose the greatest risk to public health and the environment are placed on the Superfund National Priorities List by the EPA. The cleanup of these sites is urgent because 27 million citizens, including

4 million children, live within four miles of one or more Superfund sites (Raven and Berg, 2004:560–561). Those living near toxic waste and other forms of pollution are commonly poor minorities (this is known as *environmental racism* and *environmental classism*). This occurs because the poor must choose land and housing that are cheap (and polluted neighborhoods are the cheapest) or because corporations locate their polluting activities near poor neighborhoods because the poor do not have the political clout to oppose them. In either case, the poor are disproportionately exposed to the health hazards of the air, water, and land from hazardous waste facilities, landfills, sewage treatment plants, smokestack emissions, and incinerators.

The problem with the Superfund program is that it is underfunded. Congress has not appropriated sufficient funds, and in 1995 it allowed the tax on oil and chemical companies that helped to fund the program expire. Moreover, the offending corporations that are supposed to share in the costs of the cleanup often find ways to keep from doing so, including declaring bankruptcy.

### Protection of National Forests

Eight days before he left office President Clinton, by executive order, banned roads on 58.5 million acres of national forests. This effectively kept these lands pristine, protected wildlife habitat, and preserved their natural beauty. President Bush, however, overturned this ban in 2005. Under the Bush plan, the state governors are allowed to petition the government to keep certain areas in the national forests within their states free of roads to reduce wildfire risks, protect health and safety, or maintain infrastructures such as dams or watercourses. Negotiations will follow these proposals, with the Forest Service making the final decision. It is estimated that probably 60 percent of the 58.5 million acres, however, will be open for ski area development, logging, mining, oil and gas exploration, and other commercial uses. Environmental groups argued that this strips protections of the natural environment, resulting in the destruction of wilderness areas and leading to environmental degradation.

Also in 2005, the Bush administration with the consent of Congress opened 19 million acres in an Alaskan wilderness area, the Arctic National Wildlife Refuge (ANWR), for oil and gas exploration. Proponents argue that opening this area for drilling will create hundreds of thousands of jobs and that it is part of President Bush's plan to reduce the country's dependence on foreign sources of energy. Environmentalists opposed opening ANWR because of its negative impact on an ecologically sensitive area of coastline and its effects on wildlife. Others argued that the amount of recoverable oil from this area is only 3.2 billion barrels (U.S. Geological Survey estimate), which given the U.S. rate of consumption (19.65 million barrels of oil a day) will fuel the demand for less than six months. Moreover, it would be years before the oil would become available.

### THE STATE OF THE ENVIRONMENT AND ENVIRONMENTAL POLICIES AT THE BEGINNING OF A NEW CENTURY

What has happened since the first Earth Day in 1970? Have the efforts of the federal government been successful in curbing or even reversing the damage from the various forms of pollution?

Although getting a late start, the federal government has taken an active role since 1970 in combating the various forms of pollution. Let's evaluate the results. First, the good news (Clarren, 2005; Kelly, 2004; Raven and Berg, 2004:50):

- Between 1970 and 2003, total emissions of the six principal air pollutants decreased by 51 percent.
- Annual hydrocarbon emissions from motor vehicles have declined from 10.3 million tons to 5.5 million tons.
- The amount of clean waterways has jumped from 10 percent in 1972 to about 60 percent today.
- It is safe to drink the water almost everywhere in the United States. In 2002, 94 percent of people served by community water systems got drinking water that met all health-based standards, compared to 79 percent in 1993.
- Lead levels in the air have dropped by 98 percent with the phaseout of leaded gasoline.
- Certain toxic chemicals such as DDT, asbestos, and dioxins have been banned from use in the United States.
- Since the Superfund was created in 1980, some 850 toxic waste sites have been cleaned up.

But for all of the progress, the efforts by the federal government have fallen short. Human activities still endanger the environment. So too, the health of people is threatened.

**Air Quality**

The pollutants emitted into the air have extremely serious consequences for the environment—the greenhouse effect that produces global warming and the loss of ozone protection from radiation. For example, the United States produces one-fourth of the world's greenhouse gas emissions. Emissions from U.S. power plants alone exceed the total emissions of 146 nations combined, representing 75 percent of the world's population (Gergen, 2001). Moreover, the United States uses 25 percent of the world's energy and in doing so produces 25 percent of the global emissions of carbon dioxide (Walter, 2001). The United States, then, is the world's biggest smokestack and contributor to global warming.

In 2005 the Kyoto protocol for controlling greenhouse gases and global warming was signed by 114 nations and went into effect. The agreement, although modest, marked the first time that the world's industrial nations committed to binding limits on emissions of carbon dioxide, methane, and other greenhouse gases, in this case to about 95 percent of 1990 levels. The United States (the Senate and the president) refused to be part of this agreement. President Bush said, "We'll be working with our allies to reduce greenhouse gases. But I will not accept a plan that will harm our economy and hurt American workers."

The two major sources of air pollution are emissions from vehicles and from industrial plants (lesser but nonetheless serious sources are toxic waste dumps, burning trash, wood burning, and aerosols). According to the EPA, more than 133 million people in 2001 lived in areas where air quality was unhealthful at times because of high levels of at least one pollutant (reported in Kelly, 2004).

The United States is the world's greatest consumer of oil products, using 19,650,000 barrels a day (26 percent of the world's daily consumption). The United States, with less than 5 percent of the world's population, has one-third of the world's cars and drives 50 percent of the total world mileage. Under current federal laws, a passenger car must average 27.5 miles per gallon. As a consequence of pressure from automobile manufacturers, there is a loophole, however, in that sport utility vehicles, which produce on average 40 percent more carbon dioxide than ordinary cars, are classified as light trucks and therefore are required to get only 20.7 miles a gallon. Moreover, in 2003 Congress passed legislation tripling the federal business tax credit for SUV purchases, to $75,000 each, compared with a $2,000 deduction for hybrid-electric vehicles (Saivin, 2004).

On the positive side, the EPA in 2004 informed 474 counties (with 160 million people) that they did not comply with federal rules (established in 1997) on the amount of smog allowed in the air and that each county had to reduce smog to comply (Watson, 2004). The EPA set deadlines ranging from 2007 to 2021 for counties to clean up their smog. The worse a county's smog problem, the longer the deadline for cleanup. The areas with the dirtiest air were in California, including Los Angles, Riverside, the San Joaquin Valley, and Sacramento.

Half of the nation's electricity comes from 1,100 coal-burning power plants, a major source of sulfur dioxide and nitrogen oxide, causing 554,000 asthma attacks and 38,200 heart attacks annually, according to Abt Associates, a consulting firm for the EPA (quoted in Clarren, 2005). The burning of coal also produces hydrochloric acid (the source of acid rain), and it is the main source of mercury rain, which passes up the food chain into fish and into people, in whom high levels can cause learning problems or retardation in children (Levine, 2004).

Recent government policies regarding emissions from coal-burning power plants are a mixed bag. In 2003 the Bush administration made it easier for power plants to expand without upgrading their pollution controls. This was done by allowing power plants to buy and sell "emission credits." That is, a power plant in compliance could sell excess credits to a power plant that did not meet the standards. The problem with such a plan is that it legitimizes the status quo, which is a polluting environment. It excuses, in effect, the country's dirtiest power plants from upgrading their pollution controls (Hertsgaard, 2003; for a damning critique of the Bush administration's handling of environmental matters, from the appointment of environmental administrators to changes in the rules to support polluting industries, see Barcott, 2004). On the other hand, environmentalists praised the Bush administration when in 2005 the EPA created stringent new emission limits on air pollution from coal-burning power plants in twenty-eight states in the Midwest and East (Watson, 2005b). By 2015 the offending plants are to cut their emissions of smog-forming gases by 61 percent below 2003 levels and trim their emissions of soot by 73 percent from 2020 to 2025. As a result, the new rule should prevent about 17,000 premature deaths and 700,000 respiratory ailments from bronchitis and asthma each year.

Environmental groups, however, were very critical of the EPA's rule, issued in the same week as the antisoot rule, to limit mercury emissions from coal-burning plants. This rule requires that the amount of mercury pollution will be reduced from 48 tons in 2005 to 31.3 tons by 2010 and 24.3 tons in 2020. This is a substantial reduction but environmentalists argue that, first, the coal-burning plants are not required to do anything for five years to reduce mercury pollution. Second, the rule sets a nationwide cap on allowable pollution and then allocates a specific amount to each state. This means that states in the West will actually be allowed to have an increase in mercury. Colorado, for example, could likely see an increase of 148 percent from 1999 levels by 2010 (McGuire, 2005). Third, as occurred in 2003, the power plants in compliance can sell pollution rights to power plants that exceed the limits (a policy called "cap-and-trade"). Thus, plants in the West, which will have limits much greater than their emissions, will sell "credits" to plants in eastern states. The result will be greater health dangers for some, as noted by Sierra Club executive director Carl Pope: "The cap-and-trade approach sounds great unless you are one of those people who lives near a power plant that chooses to spend money on paper credits instead of making real mercury reductions" (quoted in McGuire, 2005:4B).

## Water Quality

The major sources of water pollution are industries that pour into rivers, lakes, and oceans a vast array of contaminants such as lead, asbestos, detergents, solvents, acid, and ammonia; farmers, whose pesticides, herbicides, fertilizers, and animal wastes drain into streams and lakes; cities, which dispose of their wastes including sewage into rivers or the ocean; and oil spills, caused by tanker accidents and leaks from offshore drilling. These dangers occur because of past pollution and from current activities. Regarding the past, for example, there is a 200-mile stretch of the upper Hudson River in New York, where General Electric had dumped polychlorinated biphenyls (PCBs) into the river over a thirty-year period (Pollack, 2001). PCBs cause cancer in laboratory animals, and they are linked to premature births and developmental disorders in humans. General Electric stopped the practice in 1977 when the federal government banned PCB use. More than two decades later the cancer risk from consuming fish from the upper Hudson is 700 times the EPA protection standard. Or consider Louisiana's "Cancer Alley," a 150-mile stretch of the Mississippi River where 25 percent of the nation's chemical industry is located. More than a hundred heavy industrial facilities there release poison into the air, land, and water at a rate of almost half a billion pounds per year (Witness to the Future, n.d.)

When Congress passed the Clean Water Act in 1972, only 10 percent of lakes and rivers were considered clean. The goal was to make them safe for fishing and swimming by 1983. However, by 2004, twenty-one years after the deadline, only 60 percent of U.S. rivers and lakes are "swimmable and fishable" (Kelly, 2004). The problem is that the law is not always enforced because the enforcement rate varies depending on which political party is in power in Washington. According to a report based on EPA data by the U.S. Public Interest Research Group, more than 60 percent of industrial and municipal plants violated their Clean Water Act permit limits in the first six months of 2002 (reported in Kelly, 2004).

To conclude, the United States has really only awakened to its pollution problems in the last fifty years or so. Much has been accomplished, but the policies put in place have often been weak and sometimes not enforced. The result is that the air, water, and land are still polluted, resulting in serious health dangers. Moreover, the United States is often wasteful of its resources, rarely turning to efforts at conservation and sacrifice (themes to which we will return in the final section). Also, the United States has turned its back on international efforts to halt global environmental crises. This is crucial because the phenomenon of globalization includes the pollution of the planet as emissions into the air and water cross political boundaries. Prevailing winds and ocean currents move pollutants generated in the United States to Canada and to Europe. The United States, in turn, is the recipient of various forms of pollution from Canada, Mexico, Asia, and Africa (Watson, 2005a). Daniel Jaffe, a University of Washington at Bothell scientist studying the global reach of pollution, says, "The recent research really points to the need for global cooperation. It's only one planet, and we've got to learn to live on it" (quoted in Watson, 2005a).

## REFERENCES

Barcott, Bruce. (2004). "Changing the Rules: How the Bush Administration Quietly—and Radically—Transformed the Nation's Clean-Air Policy." *New York Times Magazine* (April 4):38–44, 66, 74, 76–78.

Carson, Rachel. (1962). *Silent Spring.* New York: Houghton-Mifflin.

Civilian Conservation Corps Alumni Organization (n.d.). "Roosevelt's Tree Army: A Brief History of the Civilian Conservation Corps": www.cccalumni.org/history1.html.

Clarren, Rebecca. (2005). "Dirty Politics, Foul Air." *The Nation* (March 14):6–7.

Environmental Protection Agency. (1990). "The Environmental Protection Agency: A Retrospective": www.epa.gov/history/topics/epa/20a.htm.

Gergen, David. (2001). "It's Not Can We, but Will We?" *U.S. News and World Report* (September 24):60.

Hertsgaard, Mark. (2003). "Trashing the Environment: Kyoto Was Just a Start for Bush." *The Nation* (February 3):15–18.

Kelly, Erin. (2004). "Earth Day Has Seen Great Gains, but Earth Can Do Better." *USA Today* (April 20):8D.

Levine, Samantha. (2004). "Who'll Stop the Mercury Rain?" *U.S. News and World Report* (April 5):70–71.

McGuire, Kim. (2005). "EPA's Mercury Rule Attacked." *Denver Post* (March 16):1A, 4B.

Pollak, Richard. (2001). "Is GE Mightier than the Hudson?" *The Nation* (May 28):11–18.

Raven, Peter H., and Berg, Linda R. (2004). *Environment,* 4th ed. New York: John Wiley & Sons.

Saivin, Janet L. (2004). "Making Better Energy Choices." In Linda Stark (ed.), *State of the World 2004* (pp. 24–43). New York: Norton.

Walter, Norbert. (2001). "Gobbling Energy and Wasting It, Too." *New York Times* (June 13): www.nytimes.com/2001/06/13/opinion/13WALT.html.

Watson, Traci. (2004). "EPA Tells 1 in 7 U.S. Counties to Clean Up Smog." *USA Today* (April 16):1A.

Watson, Traci (2005a). "Air Pollution from Other Countries Drifts into USA." *USA Today* (March 14):1A–2A.

Watson, Traci (2005b). "EPA Sets Tighter Clean-Air Rules." *USA Today* (March 11):1A.

Witness to the Future (n.d.): www.witnesstothefuture.com/meet/cancer.html.

# 22

# Learning from Love Canal: A Twentieth Anniversary Retrospective

*LOIS MARIE GIBBS*

*In 1978 Lois Marie Gibbs, a suburban wife and mother, became outraged by the health dangers at Love Canal, New York. Provoked by injustice, she and her neighbors formed the Love Canal Homeowner's Association to find the facts and inform the nation of the environmental dangers posed by a giant corporate polluter. This citizen's movement forced the government to act, creating the Superfund. What follows is Ms. Gibb's account of the Love Canal's dangers to health, the movement by citizens to get government to do something about those dangers, and the continuing environmental crises.*

Twenty years ago the nation was jolted awake when a blue-collar community uncovered a serious public health crisis resulting from the burial of chemical wastes in their small suburban neighborhood. As the events unfolded, network television, radio, and print media covered the David and Goliath struggle in Love Canal, New York. The country watched as mothers with children in their arms and tears in their eyes cried out for help.

The words "Love Canal" are now burned in our country's history and in the memory of the public as being synonymous with chemical exposures and their adverse human health effects. The events at Love Canal brought about a new understanding among the American people of the correlation between low-level chemical exposures and birth defects, miscarriages, and incidences of cancer. The citizens of Love Canal provided an example of how a blue-collar community with few resources can win against great odds (a multi-billion-dollar international corporation and an unresponsive government), using the power of the people in our democratic system.

Now, 20 years later, science has shown that some of the same chemicals found at Love Canal are present in our food, water, and air. As important now as ever, the main lesson to be learned from the Love Canal crisis is that in order to protect public health from chemical contamination, there needs to be a massive outcry—a choir of voices—by the American people demanding change.

The Love Canal crisis began in the spring of 1978 when residents discovered that a dump site containing 20,000 tons of chemical wastes was leaking into their neighborhood.

*Source:* "Learning from Love Canal: A 20th Century Anniversary Retrospective" by Lois Marie Gibbs. This article originally appeared in the Spring 1998 issue of *Orion Afield,* 187 Main Street, Great Barrington, MA 01230, 888-909-6568, www.oriononline.org. For more information about Lois Gibbs and "Love Canal," please visit www.chej.org. Used with permission.

The local newspaper ran an extensive article, explaining that the dump site was once a canal that connected to the Niagara River five miles upstream of Niagara Falls. This canal, 60 feet wide and 3,000 feet long, was built by William T. Love in the 1800s in an attempt to connect the upper and lower Niagara River. Mr. Love ran out of money before completing the project, and the abandoned canal was sold at public auction, after which it was used as a municipal and chemical dump site from 1920 until 1953. Hooker Chemical Corporation, a subsidiary of Occidental Petroleum, was the principal disposer of chemical wastes at the site. Over 200 different chemicals were deposited, including pesticides such as lindane and DDT (both since banned from use in the U.S.), multiple solvents, PCBs, dioxin, and heavy metals.

In 1953, after filling the canal and covering it with dirt, Hooker sold the land to the Niagara Falls Board of Education for one dollar. Included in the deed was a "warning" about the chemical wastes buried on the property and a disclaimer absolving Hooker of any future liability. The board of education, perhaps not understanding the potential risks associated with Hooker's chemical wastes, built an elementary school near the perimeter of the canal in 1954. Home building around the canal also began in the 1950s, and by 1978, there were approximately 800 single-family homes and 240 low-income apartments, with about 400 children attending the 99th Street School next to the dump.

After reading the newspaper article about Love Canal in the spring of 1978, I became concerned about the health of my son, who was in kindergarten at the 99th Street School. Since moving into our house on 101st Street, my son, Michael, had been constantly ill. I came to believe that the school and playground were making him sick. Consequently, I asked the school board to transfer Michael to another public school, and they refused, stating that "such a transfer would set a bad precedent."

Receiving no help from the school board, city, or state representatives, I began going door to door with a petition to shut down the 99th Street School. The petition, I believed, would pressure the school board into investigating the chemical exposure risks to children and possibly even into closing the school. It became apparent, after only a few blocks of door knocking, that the entire neighborhood was sick. Men, women, and children suffered from many conditions—cancer, miscarriages, stillbirths, birth defects, and urinary tract diseases. The petition drive generated news coverage and helped residents come to the realization that a serious problem existed. The media attention and subsequent inquiries by residents prompted the New York State Department of Health (NYSDOH) to undertake environmental testing in homes closest to the canal.

On August 2, 1978, the NYSDOH declared a state of emergency at Love Canal, ordering closure of the 99th Street School, recommending that pregnant women and children under the age of two evacuate, and mandating that a cleanup plan be undertaken immediately. These pronouncements, based on the unsafe level of chemicals found in the air of 239 homes and the soils in yards located closest to the canal, were devastating to pregnant women and families with small children.

Other residents were panicked about the risk of disease to their three, five, and ten year olds—and themselves—pleading, "Our fetuses are our canaries and you are removing the canaries. Why are you leaving the rest of us here to die?" The health department, unable to justify their age-specific decisions scientifically, and Governor Carey, feeling tremendous pressure from the public, agreed on August 7 to evacuate all 239 families, regardless of the number or age of children in the households.

In October cleanup began on the dump site. A drainage trench was installed around the perimeter of the canal to catch waste that was permeating into the surrounding neighborhood. A clay cap was placed on top of the site to reduce water infiltration from rain or melting snow. Sewer lines and the creek to the north of the canal were also cleaned up. However, the waste that had migrated throughout the neighborhood and into the homes remained.

At that time, there were approximately 660 families living in the community who were not given the option to relocate. They continued to pressure the governor and federal authorities, including President Carter, to expand the evacuation area. A health study was conducted by volunteer scientists and community members, revealing that 56 percent of children born between 1974 and 1978 suffered birth defects. The miscarriage rate increased 300 percent among women who had moved to Love Canal. And urinary-tract disease had also increased 300 percent, with a great number of children being affected.

These results prompted the NYSDOH to issue a second evacuation order on February 8, 1979, for pregnant women and children under the age of two from all 660 families. As with the previous order, this too created great panic and fear among the remaining residents. Finally, on October 1, 1980, President Carter visited Niagara Falls to sign a bill authorizing funding to permanently relocate all families who wished to leave. All but 67 families moved out of the Love Canal neighborhood.

President Carter's decision, like Governor Carey's, was due partly to the public pressure generated during an election year. Love Canal Homeowners Association (LCHA) deliberately focused pressure on elected representatives to make the Love Canal crisis a campaign issue, protesting at political conventions and giving hundreds of interviews to the news media, always singling out candidates by name, and always asking for their positions on hazardous-waste issues—Love Canal specifically.

It is unfortunate that every action at Love Canal, from the first health study to the final evacuation, was taken for political reasons. Members of LCHA truly believe that if we hadn't assembled this large, strong citizen organization, we would still be living at Love Canal, with authorities still maintaining that there are no health problems. There are many reasons why the various levels of government did not want to evacuate the people in this community. These reasons include:

- The expense incurred. Together, state and federal governments spent over $60 million on Love Canal, which was later repaid by Occidental Chemical through a government lawsuit.
- The precedent that would be set by evacuating a neighborhood because of chemical exposures. At the time, there were an estimated 30–50,000 similar sites scattered across the nation.
- The lack of peer-reviewed scientific studies. The scientific understanding of human health effects resulting from exposure to low-level chemicals had been based on adult workers exposed over a 40-hour work-week, while at Love Canal the threat was residential, involving pregnant women and children exposed to multiple chemicals 24 hours a day.

Eventually, the 239 homes closest to the canal were demolished and the southern sections of the neighborhood declared unsuitable for residential use. But in September 1988, the 200 homes in the northern section of Love Canal were declared "habitable," which should not be confused with "safe." This decision to move people back into Love Canal is an appalling idea that cannot be justified by legitimate scientific or technical data. These homes are still contaminated, as are the yards around the adjacent evacuated homes. The only separation between them and those still considered uninhabitable is a suburban street. Anyone can freely cross the street and walk through the abandoned sections of the neighborhood. In fact, children ride their bikes and play frequently among the abandoned homes. And 20,000 tons of waste still remain in the dump.

The world is a very different place now for families who lived through the Love Canal crisis. What was once taken for granted is no longer—that if you work hard, pay your taxes, vote on election days, and teach your children right from wrong, you can achieve the American Dream. Eyes were opened to the way our democracy works—and doesn't work. Former residents of this blue-collar community have come to see that corporate power and influence are what dictated the actions at Love Canal, not the health and welfare of citizens.

Each step in the events as they unfolded shocked and stunned the public. It was not conceivable to families that their government would lie or manipulate data and studies to protect corporate interests. It was difficult to grasp the reality—obvious, in retrospect—that corporations have more influence and rights than tax-paying citizens. This realization left us feeling alone, abandoned, and empty inside. Love Canal taught us that government will protect you from such poisoning only when you force it to.

If you think you're safe, think again. And, if you're ever in doubt about what a company is doing, or what government is telling you, talk with your neighbors, seek out the truth beyond the bland reassurances of the authorities, and don't be afraid to dig your heels in to protect your community. The number of children with cancer is increasing, as are the incidences of breast and prostate cancer in adults. Children suffer more today than ever before from birth defects, learning disabilities, attention-deficit disorders, and asthma. These diseases and adverse health problems are no longer located in someone else's backyard; they're in everyone's backyard, and in our food, water, and the air we breathe.

Over the past 20 years, the U.S. has come a long way in identifying buried wastes, cleaning up sites, reducing some air and water pollution, and cutting back on both industrial and household waste. We have cleaned up the rivers that once caught fire and removed the ugly barrels that sat in abandoned industrial sites or fields. We cleaned up what we can see—the obvious, the ugly—but there are deadly poisons invisible to the eye that remain in our everyday environment and food supply. The challenge for the next decade will be to eliminate the poisons we can't see, but that are evidenced in the state of our health, in the growing number of diseases in our society.

As we move forward to correct the pollution mistakes of the past, we are bound to uncover new information and new problems. Waste facilities like the one at Love Canal continue to be discovered—a national phenomenon that has created a flurry of communities organizing themselves to wage their own David and Goliath struggles. These urban and suburban neighborhoods and rural communities now make up the new grassroots movement for environmental justice. Their efforts are critical, but, like Love Canal, they are only first steps.

It will take a massive effort to move society from corporate domination, in which industry's rights to pollute and damage health and the environment supersede the public's right to live, work, and play in safety. This is a political fight. The science is already there, showing that people's health is at risk. To win, we will need to keep building the movement, networking with one another, planning, strategizing, and moving forward. Our children's futures, and those of their unborn children, are at stake.

# 23

# Superfund Update

SIERRA CLUB

*The Superfund was created in 1980 to clean up toxic waste sites. The gov-*
*ernment, however, has been lax in enforcing polluters to pay their share*
*and moving forward with this program. Consequently, many communities*
*remain at risk. The Sierra Club, a strong advocate for a clean environment,*
*provides an update on how the Bush administration has failed to protect*
*the public's health at Superfund sites.*

In 1980, Congress created the Superfund law based on two simple, yet powerful, proposi-tions. First, hazardous waste sites should be quickly and thoroughly cleaned up. Second, polluters, not taxpayers, should pay to clean up the contamination. Parties that pollute are responsible for damages or injuries to natural resources and are liable for the restoration of these resources. Superfund, with the help of tax contributions, gives the EPA the funds it needs to clean up waste sites when no responsible party can be found.

In 1995, however, the taxes waged on industry and used for the cleanup of abandoned toxic waste sites expired. The Superfund Trust Fund, the account used to clean up abandoned toxic waste sites, is now drained of polluter-contributed dollars since October 2003. Today, taxpayers are shouldering the financial burden of cleaning up waste sites, not polluters.[1]

Instead of helping to ensure protection for communities living amongst toxic waste sites, the Bush administration has refused to support reauthorizing the corporate fees on polluting industries as a means to fund the clean up of Superfund toxic waste sites. As a result, the administration has effectively slowed the pace of waste site cleanups, put Ameri-can communities at risk, and let polluting industries off the hook.

Under the Bush administration, completed cleanups[2] have fallen by 50% during the Bush administration compared with the pace of cleanups between 1997 and 2000.[3] Site listings have slowed down as well; the Bush administration has listed an average of 23 Superfund sites a year compared with an average of 30 sites from 1993 to 2000, a drop of 23 percent.[4] Funding in 2002 and 2003 was the lowest for Superfund since 1988. In the early 1990s, the Superfund program averaged $1.6 billion a year—about $2.1 billion n today's dollars. Today's $1.4 billion Superfund budget represents a 30% reduction in spending power from 1992 levels.[5]

Without the polluter pays tax on industries, citizen taxpayers are paying a greater percentage of Superfund cleanup costs.[6] Money collected from the polluter pays tax would go into a trust fund, which would be used to clean up Superfund sites for which no responsible party is found or is viable.

By opposing collection of polluter pays fees, the administration has increased the share of the program's costs carried by regular taxpayers from 18 percent in 1995 to a proposed 79 percent or more in 2004. In 2005, taxpayers will pick up virtually the entire bill for the cleanup of orphaned toxic waste sites.[7] The administration's policies mark a dramatic reversal of the standards that have guided the cleanup of toxic waste sites in this country for more than 20 years.[8] The Bush administration is making taxpayers pay more and requiring polluters to pay less, while cleaning up fewer of the nation's worst toxic waste sites.

How should we pay for thousands of sites[9] still in need of cleanup?

The answer is simple: reauthorize the taxes on corporate polluters. Preliminary estimates show that reinstating the Superfund tax would generate $15 billion to $16 billion over the next 10 years, which is enough to cover the costs of cleanups for the next decade.

### MORE FUNDING IS NEEDED TO CLEAN UP THOUSANDS OF TOXIC WASTE SITES

Superfund toxic waste sites poison our land, water, and air with toxic chemicals that can cause cancer, birth defects, liver, brain and nerve damage, as well as other health problems. With one in every four Americans living within four miles of a toxic waste site, including 10 million children,[10] we need to ensure that funding is readily available to properly clean up the worst of these sites.

Despite studies showing that many toxic sites across the country are in need of massive cleanup action, the EPA has been hard-pressed to follow through because of substantial cutbacks in funding. A 2004 EPA Inspector General's report found that EPA insufficiently funded 29 cleanup projects in FY2003, putting communities' health and safety at risk.[11]

NOTES

1. GAO, Superfund Program: Current Status and Future Fiscal Challenges, GAO/RECD-03-850, July 2003.
2. Katherine Probst and David Konisky, Resources for the Future. Superfund's Future. 2001. (EPA refers to such sites as "construction complete." These sites may not actually be entirely clean of toxins, but the physical construction of all cleanup actions is complete, all immediate threats have been addressed, and all long-term threats are under control.)
3. U.S. EPA, Factsheet, "Superfund Trust Fund and Taxes: Setting the Record Straight," October 7, 2003.
4. U.S. EPA, NPL Site Status Information, "Number of NPL Site Actions and Milestones." Available at http://www.epa.gov/superfund/sites/query/ queryhtm/nplfy.htm.
5. Superfund budget history EPA Factsheet: http://www.epa.gov/superfund/action/process/ budgethistory.htm.

6.  "Superfund Program: Current Status and Future Fiscal Challenges." United States General Accounting Office. Report no. GAO-03-850. Page 3. Available at http://www.gao.gov/new.items/d03850.pdf.

7.  The Budget for Fiscal Year 2004, page 877, The White House, February 2003.

8.  Zeller, Tom. "The Future of Superfund: More Taxing, Less Simple." *The New York Times* 24 Mar. 2002

9.  Katherine Probst and David Konisky, Resources for the Future. Superfund's Future. 2001.

10. "Superfund Program: Current Status and Future Fiscal Challenges." United States General Accounting Office. Report no. GAO-03-850. Page 1.

11. Nikki L. Tinsley, US EPA Inspector General Report, Congressional Request on Funding Needs for Non-Federal Superfund Sites, January 7, 2004.

## 24

# The Power to Change the World: Hydrogen

*JEREMY RIFKIN*

*This selection differs from others we have included in this text. Rather than highlighting a government policy or critiquing it, this one, by social observer Jeremy Rifkin, argues for what the government should do. The United States and the world are dependent on a dirty fuel—oil—which has damaging effects on the environment, most especially, global warming. Thus, the need to conserve energy and to find alternative sources of energy. The government, Rifkin argues, must invest in efforts to replace oil with hydrogen. If that were to occur, there would be positive consequences for the environment and for global security.*

For years, experts have been saying we have only 40 or so years of cheap, available crude oil left. Now some of the world's leading petroleum geologists are suggesting that global oil production could peak and begin a steep decline as early as the end of this decade, sending oil prices through the roof. Increasing tensions between the West and Islamic countries, where most of the world's oil is produced, could further threaten our access to affordable oil.

In desperation, the United States and other nations could turn increasingly to dirtier fossil fuels—coal, tar sand and heavy oil—which would only worsen global warming and imperil the Earth's already beleaguered ecosystems.

There is a better way to go: hydrogen power.

Weaning the world off oil and turning it toward hydrogen, however, will require a concerted effort by industry, government and local communities on a scale comparable to the efforts in the 1980s and 1990s that helped create the World Wide Web.

Hydrogen is the most basic and ubiquitous element in the universe. It is the "forever fuel," producing no harmful carbon dioxide emissions when burned and giving off as byproducts only heat and pure water. All that needs to be done is to extract hydrogen from various elements so that it is useable in fuel cells.

The commercially usable hydrogen currently being produced is extracted mostly from natural gas. However, renewable sources of energy—wind, hydro, photovoltaic, geothermal, biomass—are increasingly being used to generate electricity locally, and in the future that electricity will in turn be used to electrolyze water and separate out hydrogen that can be used to power fuel cells.

Commercial fuel cells powered by hydrogen are just now being introduced into the market for home, office and industrial use. The major auto makers have spent more than $2 billion on development of hydrogen cars, buses and trucks; the first mass-produced vehicles are expected to be on the road in just a few years.

Exactly how soon we will all be driving hydrogen cars will depend on a number of factors, including the price of oil on world markets, the availability of hydrogen refueling stations and numerous other technical questions in the manufacturing process itself.

Even given these stumbling blocks, many energy experts believe that over the next several decades hydrogen fuel cells will become our best source of energy. And the rise of this source of power would open the way for fundamental changes in our markets and political and social institutions, just as coal and steam power did at the beginning of the Industrial Age.

The hydrogen economy would make possible a vast redistribution of power. Today's centralized, top-down flow of energy, controlled by global oil companies and utilities, would become obsolete. In the new era, every human being could become the producer as well as the consumer of his or her own energy—so-called "distributed generation."

When millions of users connect their fuel cells by hooking into existing power grids, using the same design principles and smart technologies that made possible the Web, they can begin to share energy peer-to-peer—creating a new, decentralized form of energy use.

In the hydrogen fuel cell era, even the automobile itself would be a "power station on wheels" with a generating capacity of 20 kilowatts. Since the average car is parked most of the time, it could be plugged in, during nonuse hours, to the home, office or the main interactive electricity network, providing premium electricity back to the grid.

When the end users also become the producers of their energy, the only role remaining for existing power plants is to become "virtual power plants" that can manufacture and market fuel cells, bundle energy services and coordinate the flow of energy over the existing power grids.

Hydrogen would dramatically cut down on carbon dioxide emissions and mitigate the effects of global warming. And because hydrogen is so plentiful and exists everywhere, every human being, once we all become masters of the technology, could be "empowered," resulting in the first truly democratic energy regime in history.

Nowhere would hydrogen energy be more important than in the developing world.

Incredibly, 65% of the human population has never made a single telephone call, and one-third has no access to electricity or any other form of commercial energy.

Lack of access to energy, especially electricity, is a key factor in perpetuating poverty around the world.

Conversely, access to energy means more economic opportunity. In South Africa, for example, for every 100 households electrified, 10 to 20 new businesses are created.

Electricity frees human labor from day-to-day survival tasks. In resource-poor countries, simply finding enough firewood or dung to warm a house or cook meals can take hours out of each day.

Electricity provides power to run farm equipment, operate small factories and craft shops and light homes, schools and businesses.

As the price of hydrogen fuel cells and accompanying appliances plummets with new innovations and economies of scale, cells will become more available, as was the case with transistor radios, computers and cellular phones. The goal ought to be to provide stationary fuel cells for every neighborhood and village in the developing world.

The road to global security lies in lessening our dependence on Middle East oil and making sure that all people on Earth have access to the energy they need to sustain life. The hydrogen economy is a promissory note for a safer world.

# PART THREE

# Historical Trends and Future Prospects

# The Ascent of Conservatism and the Conservative Agenda

*Since the American Revolution the distribution of American wealth has depended significantly on who controlled the federal government, for what policies, and in behalf of which constituencies.*

—Kevin Phillips

## A BRIEF HISTORY

Progressive government involvement in solving social problems has waxed and waned in the last 125 years or so. In response to the excesses of capitalism in the late 1800s, the Progressive Era movement emerged and was reasonably successful in stifling the affluent from unbridled exploitation. The Great Depression in the 1930s triggered massive social programs called the New Deal, instituted by President Franklin D. Roosevelt. Thirty years later President Johnson's Great Society initiatives continued that progressive tradition and also made huge strides in lifting legal barriers that had kept African Americans from achieving equality before the law. Except for the decade of the 1920s, where conservative interests dominated government policies, the period from the last years of the nineteenth century to the mid-1960s could be called the progressive-liberal consensus (Morgan, 2006). Although there were exceptions, this was a time in United States history when government policies favored the common good, eliminating discrimination, and providing a safety net for the less fortunate.

In the late 1960s the political climate began to change and a conservative mood began to grow. The causes of the conservative ascendancy are many (Hodgson, 2004:12–28). President Johnson's success with the civil rights legislation of the mid-1960s prompted a dramatic change in voting practices in the South. The southern states, all of which had historically voted solidly Democratic began voting Republican because they felt that the Democrats had sold them out on racial issues. At first that change was gradual, but by the end of the century this increasingly Republican South shifted both houses of Congress to Republican majorities. This political realignment not only made the Republicans the majority party but it also made the Republican party more ideologically conservative, that is, moderates were replaced by ideologues. Moreover, the Democratic party responded to the triumph of the conservatives by moving to the right. "The whole center of gravity of American politics moved with it" (Hodgson, 2004:30).

A second factor explaining the rise of conservatism was the widespread popular rejection of the changing sexual mores and other behaviors, language, and values of the 1960s counterculture. Many were further shocked, alarmed, and alienated by the upheavals of the 1960s. There was a feeling held by many that the United States government had gone soft (humiliation in Vietnam, renegotiation of the Panama Canal treaty, and doing little about the hostages held in Iran).

Third, the Supreme Court in the 1950s under Chief Justice Earl Warren made a number of decisions that were decidedly progressive, most notably the desegregation of schools. But in the 1970s, under a new chief justice, Warren Burger, and new justices appointed by Republican presidents, the Court moved toward more conservative decisions (e.g., business interests over labor interests, states rights over federalism, and punishment of criminals over the rights of suspects).

The conservative momentum increased dramatically with the election of Ronald Reagan in 1980. Reagan was instrumental in lifting the public mood after the Vietnam debacle and what many considered the three failed presidencies (Nixon, Ford, and Carter) that preceded him (Troy, 2005). However, the conservative policies of his administration consistently favored business interests and market solutions over government solutions, as seen in the deregulation of the airline and banking industries. For Reagan, as he said in his inaugural address in 1981 "government is not the solution to our problem, government is the problem." He instituted tax cuts that favored the already advantaged. Philosophically, he rejected the liberal programs of the New Deal (Troy, 2005). As a result, the Reagan administration cut back on the redistributive functions of the welfare state. According to Reagan's own budget director, David Stockman (1986), Reagan's strategy for cutting social spending was to overspend on the military and to install massive tax cuts, which put the federal government deep into debt. To deal with this deficit, Congress had little choice but to cut social programs.[1] His policies were anti-union (e.g., he dismissed more than 11,000 air traffic controllers, leading to the bankruptcy and collapse of their union), which along with global competition caused over the ensuing years a major decline in the number of members and militancy of labor unions.

During the Reagan years, a major shift occurred in the attitude of many toward taxes. From 1932 until Reagan's term, the great majority of citizens accepted the idea of a welfare state and the necessity of taxes to pay for the services people could not provide for themselves. That assumption was challenged in the middle 1970s with the great tax rebellion, which started in California when voters passed Proposition 13 in 1978. This proposition reduced property taxes significantly (a savings of as much as $200 billion to California property owners over ten years). Of course, that left $200 billion less in the state treasury to pay for services. The result was catastrophic for public services, especially the public education system. This tax rebellion was a political earthquake. According to Peter Schrag, "It set the stage for the Reagan era, and became both fact and symbol of a radical shift in government priorities, public attitudes and social relationships that is as nearly fundamental in American politics as the changes brought by the New Deal" (Schrag, 1998:132).

The tax rebellion, begun in California, had by 1994 spread to all states, as each state had instituted some constitutional restrictions on local or state taxes or imposed spending restrictions. Thus, the mood had changed. Now there was a hatred of taxes and a suspicion, amounting sometimes to loathing, of government (Hodgson, 2004:45).

The political attitudes also shifted in reaction to liberal programs such as busing children to achieve school integration, affirmative action to undo past injustices, and welfare provided for single mothers. According to British historian Godfrey Hodgson, this revealed a major change in the public consciousness: "A shift occurred in the center of gravity of American political opinion from left to right, from those who would use the power of government to right injustice and diminish inequality, to those who cared for none of those things, and saw government as the oppressive state" (Hodgson, 2004:183).

With the election of Bill Clinton as president in 1992, progressives hoped that his administration would rekindle progressive policies, but his eight years as president saw basically moderate to conservative initiatives. Republicans, especially of the conservative variety (as opposed to moderate Republicans) took over the House of Representatives. This led President Clinton to move even further in the conservative direction. To summarize, Hodgson says:

> Between Richard Nixon's departure from the White House in 1974 and the return of the Republican George W. Bush in 2001, a new conservative consensus was forged. Some Democrats felt they had no alternative but to join it. In place of the New Deal philosophy, in which the workings of the free market were to be restrained and controlled by government intervention, the new public philosophy sought to set the market free. Whereas in the middle third of the century the political consensus encouraged modest redistribution of wealth, in its last quarter the free market was set free. If the result was a winner-take-all society, in which the devil took the hindmost, that was acceptable. (Hodgson, 2004:24–25)

## CONSERVATIVE DISCOURSE, LEGISLATION, AND POLICIES DOMINATE THE EARLY TWENTY-FIRST CENTURY

By the time of George W. Bush's election to his second term in 2004, the "great unraveling," to use economist Paul Krugman's phrase (2003), of the progressive-liberal consensus was almost complete. The conservative wing of U.S. politics controlled the executive, legislative, and judicial branches of the federal government. The safety net was in tatters, and the remnants of progressive programs were under attack. Conservatives had the muscle and the will to eliminate or reduce them. Moreover, the huge deficits accrued during Bush's first term because of tax cuts, the wars in Afghanistan and Iraq, and the costs of "homeland security," made it difficult if not impossible to fund existing social programs adequately, let alone add new ones.

Although 35 million people, including 20 percent of all children, lived below the poverty line, 10 million were hungry, and 45 million were without health insurance, President Bush's fiscal 2006 budget proposal revealed his plans to gut social programs for the less advantaged (Broder, 2005; Clark, 2005):

- Elementary and secondary education programs would be cut by $11.5 billion over five years.
- The WIC (Women, Infants, and Children) program, which subsidizes the diets of low-income pregnant women and nursing mothers, would be cut by $658 million.
- Head Start funds would be reduced by $3.3 billion over five years (a 20 percent cut by 2010).
- Community development programs used by cities to build up impoverished neighborhoods would lose $9.2 billion in five years (a 36 percent cut by 2010).

- Pell Grants, aid for college students whose families earn less than $35,000 a year, were proposed to cut back aid for more than one-fourth of the 5.2 million students who now receive money.
- Medicaid cuts of $14 billion over five years.

In short, the Bush administration proposed $212 billion in cuts to domestic discretionary programs over the next five years. At the same time, he proposed making the tax cuts ($1.6 trillion over ten years) passed during his first term permanent. The dividends and capital gains cuts alone amounted to $22.8 billion in a single year, of which $10.4 billion would go to those with incomes over $1 million a year (Dionne, 2005). Moreover, the budget request for the military was for $420 billion, an increase of $19 billion over the previous year and this did not include money to conduct the wars in Iraq and Afghanistan (which will be at least $100 billion more in 2005). The result of combining tax cuts with increased military spending is a huge budget deficit ($427 billion in 2005), about which, a progressive magazine, *The Progressive,* editorialized: "But there's method to his madness. Bush actually likes the deficit. It gives him an excuse to eviscerate any social program he doesn't like. And so, having sunk the deficit to ear-popping lows, Bush now says there's no money left in the cupboard for solving our domestic problems" (*The Progressive,* 2005:8–9). As noted earlier, President Reagan employed the same strategy. Reagan and Bush did not challenge popular liberal programs directly, they just created fiscal conditions that made those programs unsustainable (Starr, 2003).

The cornerstone of Bush's plans during his second term is the implementation of an "ownership society." Included in this ambitious plan are a series of proposals to shrink and privatize government through private health plans for seniors (for prescription drugs under Medicare), vouchers to allow school choice, reduced taxes on accumulated wealth by making the recent tax cuts permanent, moving away from comprehensive government- or employer-provided health insurance to high-deductible "health savings accounts," and personal accounts to supplement Social Security (White House, 2004).

Proponents of the ownership society argue that it encourages self-reliance by letting individuals make choices rather than having one-size-fits-all government programs make choices for them. Citizens thus are engaged rather than passive. As owners, they have a stake in their property, their community, and society. David Boaz, writing for the Cato Institute, a conservative think tank, summarizes the ownership society this way:

> *An ownership society values responsibility, liberty, and property. Individuals are empowered by freeing them from dependence on government handouts and making them owners instead, in control of their own lives and destinies. In the ownership society, patients control their own health care, parents control their own children's education, and workers control their retirement savings. (Boaz, 2003:1)*

Progressives view the ownership society much differently. They see this as a way to destroy the welfare state that began with President Roosevelt's New Deal. They see it as an assault on the idea "that government should work for the common good and that there should be an expansive social contract" (Moberg, 2005:5). Or put another way, "[Bush's] ownership society represents the death of an ideal that we are all members of a community, and that an injury to one is an injury to all" (Bleifuss, 2005:3). Progressives, moreover, see the ownership society as shifting risk (health care, retirement income) from employers, corporations, and the government to individuals. The result, it is argued, is that fewer people than under the present system will have adequate pensions and sufficient health care. Further, in the words of former Labor Secretary, Robert Reich:

> *An Ownership Society based on the stock market would be a casino. The Bush administration wants you to put your Social Security payments into the stock market, but beware. If your timing is bad, you could find yourself retiring in a bear market. It's happened before. That's one of the reasons Social Security—as social insurance—was invented. (Reich, 2004:1)*

Touting the plan as an ownership society, progressives aver, makes little sense in our unequal society where the richest 1 percent of people owns more wealth than the bottom 90 percent combined. And, as "wealth is increasingly sheltered from taxes, inequality will become more entrenched and hereditary in Bush's ownership society" (Sklar, 2005:1).

A final criticism of the ownership society plan is that in an increasingly insecure and unstable economy, the middle- and lower-classes need guarantees of health care, education, a decent retirement and other social protections that President Roosevelt instigated (Moberg, 2005:6). In Roosevelt's State of the Union message to Congress on January 11, 1944, he advocated an economic Bill of Rights:

> *We have come to a clear realization of the fact that true individual freedom cannot exist without economic security and independence. . . . We have accepted, so to speak, a second Bill of Rights under which a new basis of security and prosperity can be established for all—regardless of station, race, or creed.*
>     *Among these are:*
> * *The right to a useful and remunerative job in the industries or shops or farms or mines of the nation;*
> * *The right to earn enough to provide adequate food and clothing and recreation;*
> * *The right of every farmer to raise and sell his products at a return which will give him and his family a decent living;*
> * *The right of every businessman, large and small, to trade in an atmosphere of freedom from unfair competition and domination by monopolies at home or abroad;*
> * *The right of every family to a decent home;*
> * *The right to adequate medical care and the opportunity to achieve and enjoy good health;*
> * *The right to adequate protection from the economic fears of old age, sickness, accident and unemployment;*
> * *The right to a good education.*
>     *All of these rights spell security. After this war is won [World War II] we must be prepared to move forward, in the implementation of these rights, to new goals of human happiness and well-being. (Roosevelt, 1944)*

**NOTES**

1. The same strategy, according to some, has been employed by the Bush administration, a point to which we will return shortly.

**REFERENCES**

Bleifuss, Joel. (2005). "R.I.P. FDR?" *In These Times* (February 28):3.
Boaz, David. (2003). "Ownership Society." The Cato Institute: www.cato.org/special/ownership_society/boaz.html.

Broder, David. (2005). "Recognizing the Cost of Bush's Fiscal Policy." *Washington Post* (February 27):5E.

"Bush's Bitter Deal." (2005). *The Progressive* 69 (March):8–9.

Clark, Jessica. (2005). "Budget Bloodbath." *In These Times* (March 14):3.

Dionne, E. J. (2005). "Some Disturbing Budget Details Are Hiding in Plain Sight." *Denver Post* (March 22):7B.

Hodgson, Godfrey. (2004). *More Equal than Others: America from Nixon to the New Century*. Princeton, NJ: Princeton University Press.

Krugman, Paul. (2003). *The Great Unraveling: Losing Our Way in the New Century*. New York: Norton.

Moberg, David. (2005). "'Ownership' Swindle." *The Nation* (April 4):5–8.

Morgan, William. (2006). *Why Sports Morally Matter*. New York: Routledge.

Reich, Robert B. (2004). "What Ownership Society?" Commentary on National Public Radio show "Marketplace" (September 2): www.tompaine.com/print/what_ownership_society.php.

Roosevelt, Franklin D. (1944). "Economic Bill of Rights." Reprinted in *The Progressive Populist* (2005, March 1):9.

Schrag, Peter. (1998). *Paradise Lost: California's Experience, America's Future*. New York: New Press.

Sklar, Holly. (2005). "Is This Your Ownership Society?" Knight Ridder/Tribune News Service (February 25): www.commondreams.org/views05/0225-28.htm.

Starr, Paul. (2003). "The Bush Bankruptcy Plan." *American Prospect* 14 (June):3.

Stockman, David A. (1986). *The Triumph of Politics*. New York: Harper & Row.

Troy, Gil. (2005). *Morning in America: How Ronald Reagan Invented the 1980s*. Princeton, NJ: Princeton University Press.

The White House (2004). "Fact Sheet: America's Ownership Society: Expanding Opportunities": www.whitehouse.gov/news/releases/2004/08/20040809-9.html.

# 25

# The Breaking of the American Social Compact

*FRANCES FOX PIVEN AND RICHARD A. CLOWARD*

*Esteemed social scientists Frances Fox Piven and Richard A. Cloward provide in this excerpt the reasons for the gradual demise of the welfare state, labor unions, and the Democratic party in the latter part of the twentieth century. Their analysis demonstrates the how and why of the symbiotic relationship between the welfare state and unions.*

The main American welfare state programs were also inaugurated during the party-building era of the New Deal. But the US programs trailed behind those of Western Europe in benefit levels and scope of coverage and, after the Second World War, a number of the limited programs that had been inaugurated in the 1930s were allowed to languish. Meanwhile, new programs proved impossible to win in the Congress, owing to the vigorous resistance of southern Democrats and business-oriented Republicans on the one hand, and the desultory support of northern Democrats who were also influenced by business interests and by the local clientelists parties to which many congressmen remained beholden.

During the crisis months when Roosevelt first took office, elites everywhere, shaken by the depth of the economic crisis and by mounting protest among the unemployed, supported emergency measures, including emergency relief, and so too did southern congressmen, whose impoverished region had been especially hard hit by the economic calamity. Even so, however, objections from the South to national relief programs that overrode local wage scales or interfered with caste arrangements began early. And when the Social Security Act of 1935 replaced emergency relief, southern representatives who dominated the key committees in the Congress carried great weight.[1] So too did business leaders who organized to oppose the Act because they feared income support programs would interfere with low-wage labor markets. Together with southern representatives, they used the political leverage guaranteed them by divided and decentralized government to ensure that the new national welfare state programs would conform with sectionally and sectorally diversified labor markets.[2]

*Source:* From *Labour Parties in Postindustrial Societies,* edited by Frances Fox Piven, Copyright © 1992 by Polity Press. Used by permission of Oxford University Press, Inc.

The intricate provisions of the Social Security Act reflected this confluence of forces. On the one hand, whole categories of low-wage workers were excluded from the old-age and unemployment insurance programs, and in any case eligibility was conditional on a history of steady employment. Moreover, a good deal of authority over the unemployment insurance program, and over the "categorical" or welfare programs, was ceded to the states and even to the counties, where local employers could ensure that conditions of eligibility and benefit levels were calibrated to their requirements.[3]

On the other hand, the inauguration of national welfare state programs under the Social Security Act was primarily a response to the demands of working people who were potential Democratic voters, and it is the bearing of the programs on constituency building that is our primary interest here. Two features of the American welfare state deserve scrutiny in this respect. One is that a complex system of sharply differentiated programs nourished divisions among Democratic constituencies, a feature of the system that became especially pernicious when the programs were enlarged in the 1960s, partly in response to the black movement. White working class taxpayers were especially resentful of categorical programs identified with the minority poor, and perhaps particularly so because they carried the brunt of the steeply regressive state and local taxes which helped fund the categorical programs.

Another feature of the American welfare state was perhaps even more important for its ultimately perverse effects on Democratic party-building efforts. Simply put, there was too little of it. The Social Security Act was not the beginning of a process of welfare state development. For a long time, it was the high point. After the Second World War, the new industrial unions expanded their sights not only to demand higher social security payments, but to demand national health insurance, child care facilities, government housing, and so on. They got none of this from a Congress dominated by southern Democrats and business-oriented Republicans. And so a still-militant and still-strong labor movement used workplace power to bargain with employers for health and old-age protections, and later to bargain for supplementary unemployment benefits as well.[4] The result was that, over time, core working class groups looked less to government for the measures that would guarantee their security, and more to the market place. For example, without a national health program, most Americans relied on employers for health protections. In turn, a government that did less was less likely to generate confidence or affection. And a party that did less was also less likely to hold the allegiance of its constituency over time.

## DEMOCRATIC PARTY POLICIES AND POSTINDUSTRIALISM

All of the rich industrial nations of the West have had to adapt to intensifying international competition, especially in the auto, steel, electronics, and machine tools industries whose workers formed the core base of labor parties. Inevitably, those adaptations have been troubling for labor parties built on constituencies and organizations formed in an earlier industrial era. But labor parties have not only suffered the impact of those adaptations; they have also helped to shape them.

As is becoming increasingly obvious, strong labor parties, high union density, and developed welfare states have imposed political limits on the options of investors responding to the new international economic order. When the large-scale industrial disinvestment and wage and social benefit cuts that are the hallmarks of the American adaptation are politically unfeasible, investors are more likely to turn to competitive strategies emphasizing increased capitalization, technological and production innovations, and active labor market policies.[5] In the United States, however, weak unions and a politically compromised and meager welfare state facilitated rapid and wholesale disinvestment from older industries and a virtual explosion of speculation on the one hand, and campaigns to lower wages, break unions, cut welfare state spending, and roll back government regulatory protections on the other. Partly as a result, average weekly earnings began to fall in the early 1970s, and average household income remained more or less stable only because married women flooded into the labor market to shore up family income by filling the jobs in the enlarging service sector industries. (In the 1980s, a more regressive tax system and cuts in social programs exacerbated these market income trends.) But the conditions which made these large changes in the economy possible were as much political as economic, as we will explain when we turn to the business mobilization that began in the 1970s.

Politics was in command of postindustrial trends in another sense too. While shifts in international markets encouraged the spatial decentralization of industry, the United States led the way among industrial countries in the extent of decentralization.[6] In any case, international markets did not dictate the specific geography of decentralization or its political consequences. A series of national policies, some dating from the New Deal, others inaugurated later, played a major role in this respect. But rather than using their influence on national policy to moderate the impact of postindustrial change on the party, its infrastructure and its constituencies, Democratic Party leaders happily sold their influence to sectional interests in the South, and to local party bosses and business interest groups in the north. As a consequence, the Democrats supported policies that were perhaps rational from the perspective of particularistic sectional and business interests, but which were entirely irrational from the perspective of the longer run interests of the national Democratic Party, and perhaps from the larger perspective of the national economic well-being as well.

Before we make the case for the large role of sectional and interest group politics in shaping the geography of the contemporary American economy, let us summarize the more usual view. In the United States, the industrial centers of the north and midwest were the mainstays, together with the largely rural South, of the New Deal Democratic Party. These centers were overwhelmed and transformed by the shift of industrial production to low cost areas and the rise of a multifaceted service economy, both at least partly the result of global economic developments. Shifts in investment, in turn, changed the kinds of work people do and the conditions under which they do it, the places where they live, and their political identities and allegiances. Not only did the ranks of industrial workers shrink and a new service sector workforce grow, but as the geography of new investment shifted in response to changes in market advantage, people and enterprises moved from the solidly Democratic central cities to the now Republican suburbs, and from the predominantly Democratic northeast and midwest to the increasingly Republican states of the South and West.[7] Together, these trends both reduced the numerical strength of a core constituency of the New Deal Democratic Party and eroded its political cohesion.

All of this happened, of course, and the impact on the old industrial centers was enormous. The city of Detroit, for example, fabled bastion of the United Auto Workers, lost half of its people and most of its businesses in the years since the Second World War,[8]

Chicago lost half of its manufacturing establishments and more than half of its manufacturing employment.[9] But this happened not simply as a result of investor adaptations to new market conditions, but as a result of market conditions that were at least in part the result of government policies promoted by sectional and investor interests. In fact, and as we have already noted, long before the decline of the mass production industries which we associate with post-industrialism, a series of federal policies tilted economic development toward the South. These policies included not only the welfare and labor policies which ratified regional disparities in labor costs, but an array of federal activities which accelerated in the 1960s, including military installations, defense and aerospace contracts directed to the districts of powerful southern congressmen and, to make these and other enterprises possible, an enormously costly federally financed infrastructure, particularly in highways and water projects.[10] In other words, while the shift of mass production industries to low wage areas was a global trend, a pattern of federal—and Democratic—policies created specific additional incentives encouraging the movement of new investment and people away from the urban concentrations of the Northeast and Midwest and into the South and the Southwest.

Much the same point should be made about the shift of economic activity and people to the suburbs which now contain a majority of the nation's voters, and a majority that is turning out to be a major base for the Republican Party.[11] While the prevailing view attributes suburbanization simply to changes in the locational requirements of business investors and to the attractions of home-ownership for the middle class, federal policies were a crucial component of this development as well. Again, federally subsidized highways, and water and sewer grants, enormously enhanced the locational advantages of outlying areas, while federal tax laws created incentives for investment in new facilities rather than the refurbishment of old ones.[12] Meanwhile, federal housing policies which provided low cost mortgages and tax benefits for mainly suburban home-owners vastly overshadowed the modest programs directed to low cost housing in the cities.[13] What the cities did get was urban renewal programs promoted by local "progrowth" coalitions of real estate and downtown business interests and their local political allies, with the result that whole neighborhoods, and often Democratic neighborhoods, were decimated as those who could joined the exodus to the suburbs, those who could not crowded into further impacted slums, and local conflict escalated.[14]

Finally, even the divisive impact of racial conflict on Democratic ranks has something to do with the policies which Democrats themselves promoted. We do not want to overstate this. The race issue is deeply rooted, and in the main the unfortunate Democrats inherited it. White–black conflict was part of the reason the party lost the South, and the Democrats were then torn apart again by racial conflict in the cities. But the several party strategies we have described made race conflict sharper and more telling than would otherwise have been the case. Race conflict was surely worsened by the scale and precipitousness of the displacement of blacks from the South, which in turn had a good deal to do with Democratic agricultural and welfare policies. The failure of the Democrats to shore up unions also mattered, for it deprived the party of an infrastructure that might have worked to moderate racial conflict.[15] And a white working class that felt itself to be getting very little from its party or government was that much more likely to be resentful of programs directed to blacks. Finally, the combination of programs which spurred the great migration to the suburbs of the past three decades may also have worsened race conflict, both by stripping the older cities of employment opportunities and public revenues, and by reifying racial separation in political jurisdictions, so that race polarization came to be seen as a conflict between devastated and pathology-ridden black municipalities and prosperous white suburban jurisdictions.

Not all postindustrial trends necessarily had to work against the Democratic Party. If the ranks of the old working class were reduced and dispersed, new potential constituencies were also being created, among the enlarging numbers of people, many of them young and minorities, who were doing worse, and also among increasingly politicized women. However, the party has done little to recruit either group. Just as this constitutionally fragmented party did not override sectional and interest group influences in order to protect the party's base, neither does it seem capable of strategic action to expand the party's base.

As we noted at the outset, people at the bottom of the income distribution have become increasingly Democratic by preference. Sharply polarizing economic conditions seem to be recreating something of the pattern of political polarization of the New Deal era. Some of the new have-nots are in the industrial sector where the attack on unions and job restructuring had smoothed the way for sharp wage cuts. Many more are in the service sector where the fastest growing occupations—cashiers, nurses, janitors, retail workers—are concentrated.[16] And some are the marginally employed or the never employed who depend on the welfare state. Of course, just how large a Democratic margin this reservoir would actually produce in a given election, and whether it can turn a presidential election, depends on other factors in the contest. For the moment, however, that is beside the point, since the very strata that are turning to the Democrats are also those who are least likely to vote.[17]

The New Deal Democratic majority was made possible by the mobilization of new voters. An unusual concatenation of circumstances and organizations made this possible. On the one hand, economic calamity and rising politicization motivated people to vote; on the other, the new unions, together with big city Democratic organizations temporarily revived by New Deal largesse, helped new voters to hurdle the inherited procedural barriers that had depressed turnout since the turn of the century. In the last two decades, however, this mobilizing infrastructure atrophied, its place taken by media-dominated campaigns associated with particular candidates. But media campaigns do not give people voter registration cards, and the decline of face-to-face recruitment efforts made the procedural barriers inherited from the nineteenth century more telling in their effects. As a result, outside the South where the civil rights revolution had raised registration and turnout, registration levels fell, especially among the low-income strata who were becoming more Democratic in their preferences. Turnout levels fell even faster, from the twentieth century high of 65 percent in 1960 to 51 percent in 1988.[18] As the procedures inherited from the nineteenth century steadily eroded the Democratic base, and the party infrastructure atrophied, a decentered party of loosely connected entrepreneurial politicians exposed to a myriad of special interests remained paralyzed; it could not or would not recruit Democratic voters.

The Democrats have also done little to take advantage of the other large opportunity associated with postindustrial trends, the politicization of women and their shift to the Left. Gender politics is at the core of postindustrial political change. In the Scandinavian countries, as the social democratic parties move vigorously to recruit women, offering them new programs and high levels of representation in the parties, gender is becoming a new axis of party alignment.[19]

That the Democratic Party has taken no comparably large steps is not because women do not constitute a potential target constituency of large importance. To the contrary: women have come to significantly outnumber men in the electorate, both as a result of demographic trends, and because the long-term decline in voter turnout is sharper among men than among women. At the same time as their voting numbers have increased, women have remained more Democratic, while men have veered sharply toward the Republicans. This gap in gender partisanship first became evident in the 1980 election, and since then it has more or less held.[20] Moreover, gender differences in policy preferences are far wider than gender differences in partisan preferences, with women differing from men particularly on issues of war and peace, the environment, and social welfare. These differences in political opinion probably reflect the complex influence of the large-scale entry of women into low-wage and more irregular employment, their increasing involvement with welfare state programs as two-parent family structures weaken and wages fall, and the lingering influence of more traditional "maternal" values.[21] Whatever the reasons, the emergence of a distinct gender politics in the United States has become quite plain. The bungled 1984 nomination of a woman for the vice-presidency aside, the Democrats have not done much to mobilize their gender advantage. They have not championed the issues which incline women toward the Democratic Party, and they have not exerted themselves to represent women prominently in Democratic councils.[22] Perhaps this is why the gender gap broadens between elections, but narrows as each election draws near.

To sum up so far, working class allegiance to the Democratic Party weakened rapidly after the Second World War as a result of the failure of the party to shore up a union infrastructure or to promote welfare state policies oriented to the working class. The economic and demographic trends of the next three decades aggravated the weaknesses that had already developed in the Democratic Party. However, these trends were not simply the result of exogenous market forces. Rather, they were also the result of policies promoted by a centerless Democratic Party. Beholden as it was to sectional and interest group forces, the Democratic Party itself had promoted the dispersal of New Deal Democratic strongholds, and contributed to the growth of the suburban and sunbelt areas that were becoming the base of a revived Republican Party. To be sure, economic transformation was also generating new targets of electoral opportunity for the Democratic Party, both among the enlarging pool of have-nots and among politicized women. But the Democratic Party remained frozen, without a center that could move strategically to mobilize these constituencies in the face of inherited institutional obstacles and the weaknesses in infrastructure that resulted from earlier Democratic Party accommodations to sectional and interest group forces.

## POSTINDUSTRIAL POLITICAL STRATEGIES: REPUBLICAN COUNTERMOBILIZATION AND DEMOCRATIC PARALYSIS

We have so far emphasized the weight of institutional features of the American political system which inhibited Democratic Party building strategies. Those institutional arrangements are a kind of dead politics, the heritage of past political conflicts and the strategies they generated which then come to encumber contemporary actors. But strategic politics continues nevertheless within these constraints, as the Republican-business initiatives of the 1970s and 1980s demonstrate.

The progressive fragmentation of the Democratic Party paved the way for the resurgence of a modernized Republican Party backed by an increasingly politicized and at least temporarily unified business class. There will be disagreements about the turning point. Perhaps it was the election of Richard Nixon in 1968, at the close of a decade of conflict which wracked the Democratic Party. To be sure, the Nixon regime fell in disgrace as a result of the Watergate scandals, but even as it collapsed, business interests and Republican strategists were organizing a new bid for national ascendance.

Indeed, it is not hyperbole to say that, in the 1970s, American business temporarily overcame its usually fractured interest group politics and began to act like a political class. The problems which prompted this transformation were considerable: intensifying competition from Europe and Japan, and later from newly industrializing countries; rising commodity prices demanded by Third World suppliers as dramatized by the oil shocks of the 1970s; and the apparent inability of the administration to stabilize spiralling prices. Prodded by these developments, American business leaders set about developing a political program to shore up profits by slashing taxes and business regulation, lowering wages and welfare state spending, and building up American military power abroad. To that end, they created new organizations to promote the business outlook and revived old ones, poured money into business-oriented think tanks to provide the intellectual foundations for the business program, and set about modernizing and centralizing the Republican Party, using the pooled money of mobilized business contributors to overcome, at least for a time, the usual centrifugal forces of American party politics.

The first results were evident in the toughened stance of employers toward unions in the 1970s. Then, by the end of the decade, business lobbyists succeeded in rolling back regulatory controls, increased military spending, and defeated virtually all of the Carter initiatives on social spending, as well as his modest effort to roll back some of the limits on unions contained in the Taft–Hartley Act. But the real fruits of the business—Republican mobilization were harvested after the election of 1980. The new Republican regime— backed by a now virtually unanimous business community and only weakly resisted by congressional Democrats oriented to sectional and business interests—rapidly slashed taxes on business and the better-off, sharply increased military expenditures, accelerated the deregulation of business, launched a fierce attack on unions with the highly publicized destruction of the air controllers union and a far less publicized series of hostile appointments to the National Labor Relations Board, and, finally, inaugurated a decade-long attack on welfare state programs.

The impact of these several developments was both economic and political, and each reinforced the other. As the decline of the mass production industries proceeded apace, industrial job loss combined with welfare state program cuts to create pervasive economic hardship and insecurity. Under these conditions, new forms of employment spread easily, including "two-tier" arrangements which paid new cohorts of workers sharply less, and increased reliance by business on home-work and temporary employees. Of course, these arrangements undercut the unions, already reeling under the impact of employer anti-union campaigns, and union membership continued to drop. Strike levels fell precipitously, reaching their lowest levels in half a century in the 1980s,[23] and average wages continued their downward slide. By the end of the decade, something like a reordering of the class structure had been effected, as the income share of the top 1 percent rose by 87 percent, while the poor 20 percent lost 5 percent, and most Americans barely stayed even.[24]

These developments did not, however, excite the outrage that might have benefited the Democratic Party. Part of the reason was that while a good many people were doing worse, almost as many were doing better, and these were not only more likely to be voters but were also the more visible participants in a consumer culture. At least as important, however, was the "hegemonic project" which was promulgated along with the new public policies. This was perhaps the most innovative aspect of the Republican-business mobilization, the revival in the 1970s and 1980s of the nineteenth-century doctrine of laissez-faire. The obvious evidence of industrial decline laid the groundwork for a propaganda campaign in which government and business leaders joined with think tank experts to define the policies of the 1980s as the necessary and inevitable response to global economic restructuring. To survive in a competitive international economy, US entrepreneurs had to be stimulated by higher profits and released from government regulation and union constraints. Only then would foreign penetration of the American economy be slowed and domestic economic growth restored, along with the good jobs, high wages, and public programs that economic growth will make possible.

Nineteenth-century laissez-faire naturalized the depredations of nineteenth-century capitalists, defining them as merely the working out of "market laws." Just so does this neo-laissez-faire naturalize the policies that promote US postindustrial strategies, defining these policies as the inevitable adaptation demanded by international markets, no matter that other nations have adopted quite different policies to encourage different postindustrial strategies. Still, this argument is hard to answer. Not only does it resonate with the familiarity of ancient doctrine, but it gains confirmation as people shop for Japanese electronics or Korean clothes, watch foreign investors buy landmarks like Rockefeller Center, and all this while American factories shut their doors.

Still, if some concrete experiences shore up neo-laissez-faire, others contradict it, suggesting that the doctrine is vulnerable. Most important, after a decade with business in command, neo-laissez-faire is not producing its promises of increased prosperity for most people. To the contrary, real wages continue to slide, while public programs become more niggardly, and deficits rage out of control. Meanwhile, the evidence is overwhelming that business-oriented policies have unleashed more greed than entrepreneurialism, with the result that, a long-term boom notwithstanding, American productivity rates have lagged, while income to capital has soared.[25] And, of course, if world capitalist markets collapse, so will the doctrine of neo-laissez-faire.

Our main point, however, is a different one. The exceptional success of neo-laissez-faire and the policies it justifies in the United States itself has to be explained. The explanation obviously has a great deal to do with the political weakness of labor-based political formations, which allowed the business-conservative mobilization of the last two decades to proceed without significant resistance. The historic weakness of American labor, in turn, is traceable to distinctive political structures which allowed sectional and business interests to cripple unionism and the welfare state, and ultimately to prevent the emergence of a labor party.

**NOTES**_____

1. Both the House Ways and Means Committee and the Senate Finance Committee were chaired by Southerners. For discussions of the role of the south in the New Deal, see V. O. Key, *Southern Politics in State and Nation* (New York: Alfred A. Knopf, 1984); G. B. Tindall, *The Disruption of the Solid South* (Athens GA: University of Georgia Press, 1965); F. F. Piven and R. A. Cloward, *Poor Peoples' Movements: Why They Succeed, How They Fail* (New York: Pantheon Books 1977), ch. 5; L. J. Alston and J. P. Ferrie, "Resisting the welfare state: southern opposition to the Farm Security Administration," in *The Emergence of the Modern Political Economy,* ed. R. Higgs (Greenwich, CT: JAI Press, 1985).

2. The key group in formulating the main provisions of the Social Security Act is widely agreed to have been the American Association for Labor Legislation (AALL). While the AALL is often defined as a civic reform organization, G. William Domhoff's analysis makes clear that the organization drew its support from business leaders associated with the National Civic Federation. See *The Power Elite and the State: How Policy is Made in America* (New York: Aldine de Gruyter, 1990), pp. 44–64. On the influence of different factions of business on the Social Security Act, see also J. Quadagno, "Welfare capitalism and the Social Security Act of 1935," *American Sociological Review,* 49 (October 1984), pp. 632–47; and J. C. Jenkins and B. G. Brents, "Social protest, hegemonic competition, and social reform," *American Sociological Review,* 54, 6 (December 1989), pp. 891–909.

3. For a fuller discussion, see F. F. Piven and R. A. Cloward, *Regulating the Poor* (New York: Pantheon Books, 1971).

4. For an analysis, see B. Stevens, "Labor unions, employee benefits, and the privatization of the American welfare state," *Journal of Policy History,* 2, 3 (1990) pp. 233–60.

5. For measures of the impact of social democratic corporatist arrangements on economic growth, see A. Hicks and W. D. Patterson, "On the robustness of the left corporatist model of economic growth," *Journal of Politics,* 51 (1989), pp. 662–75.

6. See S. Lash and J. Urry, *The End of Organized Capitalism* (Cambridge: Polity Press), p. 109.

7. Loïc Wacquant describes the impact of de-industrialization on the Democratic bastion of Chicago. In 1954, over 10,200 manufacturing establishments in the city had provided half a million blue collar jobs. By 1982, the number of establishments had been halved, and blue collar employment had fallen to 172,000. See "The ghetto, the state, and the new capitalist economy," *Dissent* (Fall, 1989), pp. 510–11. See Alan DiGaetano, "The Democratic Party and City Politics in the Postindustrial Era," in *Labor Parties in Postindustrial Societies,* ed. Frances Fox Piven (New York: Oxford University Press, 1992).

8. See I. Wilkerson, "Giving up the jewels to salvage the house," *New York Times,* September 10, 1990.

9. See Wacquant. "The ghetto, the state, and the new capitalist economy."

10. On this point, see A. Watkins, "Good business climates: the second war between the states," *Dissent* (Fall, 1980); and P. Ashton, "The political economy of suburban development," in *Marxism and the Metropolis,* ed. W. Tabb and L. Sawers (New York: Oxford University Press, 1978), pp. 64–89.

11. On this point, see T. Edsall, *Chain Reaction* (New York: Norton, 1991), ch. 1.

12. On the impact of highway subsidies, see J. Mollenkopf, *The Contested City* (Princeton, NJ: Princeton University Press 1983), pp. 14–144.

13. There is an obvious parallel here to the promotion of owner occupied housing by the British Conservatives. See Lash and Urry, *The End of Organized Capitalism,* p. 102.

14. The role of real-estate and banking interests in these several housing and redevelopment policies has been very important. A study of business political action committees in 1990 showed that

political contributions from these interests were by far the largest of any category. See R. Berke, "Study confirms interest groups' pattern of giving," *New York Times,* September 16, 1990, p. 26.

15. While we think a stronger union structure would have worked overall to moderate race conflict, unions were also the focus of conflict, especially in the construction trades. On this point, see J. Quadagno, "How the war on poverty fractured the Democratic Party: organized labor's battle against economic justice for blacks," unpublished paper presented to the Workshop in Political Economy, Florida State University, September 1990.

16. Bennett Harrison and Batty Bluestone cite Bureau of Labor Statistics data showing the ten fastest growing occupations, as well as changes in the distribution of workers by type of employment and wage category. See *The Great U-Turn* (New York: Basic Books, 1990), pp. 70–1, tables A.1 and A.2.

17. According to Harold Meyerson, sales, technical, service, and administrative workers now constitute 28 percent of the voting age population, but only 11 percent of the electorate. Blue collar workers, who are more likely to be unionized, do a little better, constituting 18 percent of the voting age population and 13 percent of the electorate. See "Why the Democrats keep losing," *Dissent* (Summer, 1989), p. 306.

18. On registration and turnout data for this period and a discussion of the biases they contain, see Piven and Cloward, *Why Americans Don't Vote,* appendices A, B and C.

19. On European patterns, see P. Norris, "The gender gap: a cross-national trend?," in *The Politics of the Gender Gap,* ed. C. M. Mueller (Beverly Hills, CA: Sage, 1988), pp. 217–34.

20. Female voting patterns also diverged from male patterns in the 1950s although then women tilted to the Right. See H. C. Kenski, "The gentler factor in a changing electorate," and A. Miller, "Gender and the vote," in *The Politics of the Gender Gap,* pp. 38–60, 258–82.

21. On the institutional changes which underlie gender differences in politics, see F. F. Piven, "Women and the state: ideology, power and the welfare state," in *Gender and the Life Course,* ed. A. Rossi (Hawthorne, NY: Aldine. 1985), pp. 265–87; and S. Erie and M. Rein, "Women and the welfare state," in *The Politics of the Gender Gap,* pp. 173–91.

22. The decentralization of the heated abortion controversy in the United States, however, is prodding some state and local Democratic candidates to headline the right to abortion. In general, women's rights issues appear to have been especially salient as predictors of political preferences among nonvoters, suggesting at least congruence between the potential Democratic constituencies that I am discussing. See J. W. Calvert and J. Gilchrist, "The disappearing American voter," unpublished paper presented at the 1990 Annual Meeting of the American Political Science Association, San Francisco, 1990.

23. In 1978, more than a million workers were involved in stoppages; in 1988, the number of striking workers fell to 118,000. See K. Moody and J. Slaughter, "New directions for labor," *Dollars and Sense,* 158 (July–August 1990), p. 21.

24. The income share of the poorest fifth of the population fell to 4.6 percent, the lowest share since 1954. The next poorest fifth fell to 10.7 percent, and the middle fifth fell to 16.7 percent, both shares the lowest on record. Meanwhile, the share of the top fifth rose to 44 percent, the highest ever. See Center on Budget and Policy Priorities, "Poverty rate and household income stagnate as rich–poor gap hits postwar high," (Washington, DC: Center on Budget and Policy Priorities, October 20, 1989). It is worth noting that a similar polarization of income occurred under Thatcher. See P. Hall, *Governing the Economy* (Cambridge: Polity Press, 1986), pp. 123–6.

25. Again, the parallels with the British pattern are noteworthy. See Hall, *Governing the Economy,* pp. 115, 123.

# 26

# Why Don't They Listen to Us?
# Speaking to the Working Class

*LILLIAN B. RUBIN*

*Lillian Rubin is a sociologist and psychologist with the Institute for the Study of Social Change, University of California, Berkeley. In this essay, written several months before the 2004 election, Professor Rubin ponders why the Republicans have control of the federal government (and, of course, why the Democrats have lost that control). She focuses on why women and men from the working class and the lower-middle class have tended to switch their allegiance to the Republican party.*

While the intensity of political polarization that grips the nation today is relatively new, America has been drifting to the right for decades. Since the assassination of John F. Kennedy in 1963, only three Democrats have occupied the White House, and of those, Bill Clinton alone survived for more than a single term. Although poll data show that most voters think the Democrats are better on such central issues as the economy, jobs, health care, and education, they continue to return Republicans to power. Republicans now occupy the governors' mansions in twenty-eight states and own both the House and Senate, where leadership has been increasingly drawn from the radical right.

With the untimely death of Minnesota senator Paul Wellstone, we lost the most consistently progressive voice in either house of the United States Congress. If our ideas and our politics have been in the service of those less advantaged, as we believe so passionately, why have we had such a hard time making ourselves heard in ways that count? How did our voice—the voice of economic opportunity, the voice that speaks of justice in education, jobs, health care, and taxation—find so little resonance with the very Americans for whom we claim to speak?

In his intriguing book *What's the Matter with Kansas?*, Thomas Frank argues that culture now trumps economics in the political sphere and offers as explanation yet another, if more sophisticated, version of false consciousness. "People getting their fundamental interests wrong is what American political life is all about," he writes on the very first

*Source:* "Why Don't They Listen to Us?" by Lillian B. Rubin from *Dissent* Magazine, Winter 2005, pp. 79–86. Reprinted by permission of *Dissent* Magazine.

page. "This species of derangement is the bedrock of our civic order; it is the foundation on which all else rests." American politics is, he insists,

> *a panorama of madness and delusion worthy of Hieronymous Bosch: of sturdy blue-collar patriots reciting the Pledge while they strangle their own life chances; of small farmers proudly voting themselves off the land; of devoted family men carefully seeing to it that their children will never be able to afford college or proper health care; of working-class guys in Midwestern cities cheering as they deliver up a landslide for a candidate whose policies will end their way of life . . .*

This is heady, angry stuff, words that make me want to cheer and weep at the same time. And in his description of the facts he's right. But there's a kind of contempt underlying the passion of Frank's words, a dismissive shrug, an "it's-hard-to-believe-anyone-could-be-that-blind-and-stupid" dimension that fails to give any credibility or rationality to the behavior he so accurately describes, as if it comes out of some kind of conservative and/or media smoke and mirrors rather than anything in personal experience.

Let me be clear: I don't take a backseat to anyone in my anger at the right, especially the radical religious right and its neocon partners. Their ideological inflexibility, the way they manipulate the facts to fit their preconceptions and sell their falsehoods to the American public, is both outrageous and frightening. But my concern here is to examine the political behavior of the millions of other Americans—those working-class and lower-middle-class women and men who are not driven by ideological rigor, who are not convinced that they speak the word of God, yet who listen appreciatively to the Rush Limbaughs, Sean Hannitys, and Bill O'Reillys as they rail against us as "liberal elites" who have lost touch with the people, and who went to the polls in our recent presidential election and voted accordingly. Why do they subscribe to a politics that in Frank's words, "strangles their own life chances?"

True, the right has had more money and is better organized than we are. True, they spent the last few decades setting up right-wing think tanks whose sole purpose was to turn out millions of words in support of their ideology, while we assumed we would prevail because we stood for the economic interests of the little guy against the rich and privileged. True, they see black and white, while we see a world shaded in grays, which is a much harder sell, especially when people feel a need for certainty in what has become a very uncertain world. True, also, there are larger geopolitical forces that operate without regard to anything we do or don't do.

These are indeed formidable barriers to communicating with those whom progressives think of as their natural constituency. But none of this explains how blue-collar, working-class America, traditionally a Democratic stronghold, transmuted into Richard Nixon's "silent majority" and from there into "Reagan Democrats," setting the stage for the Republican Party and its corporate constituency to dominate the political arena. Why, in the face of exploding deficits, a war that has become increasingly unpopular, a three-year-long recession, millions of jobs lost and not replaced, a public education system that's a national disgrace, prescription drugs made by American manufacturers that cost half or less in neighboring Canada, and a health-care system that's the most expensive in the world yet fails to provide the most elementary care for tens of millions of Americans, why—when we're on the people's side of all these issues—don't they listen to us?

But, one might ask, who is the "we" of whom I speak? It's a legitimate question, one I've asked myself as well, since there is no easily identifiable left, no progressive group that can claim to speak for the variety of people and positions that lay title to the left side of the political spectrum, no "we" that speaks with the kind of authoritative and unified voice we hear from the conservative right. Not since the heyday of the American Communist Party, whose adherents spoke with the kind of on-message discipline we now see among right-wing conservatives, has any group or organization on the left been able to enforce that kind of control. Even the antiwar movement, the closest thing we have to a movement capable of mobilizing tens of thousands of people to action, is an amalgam of individuals and groups whose politics range from liberal Democrats to the various shades of the fractious left.

Nevertheless, there is a more or less unified sensibility among these people and groups who form the "we" I refer to. They are dominantly well-educated urban folk who find common ground on political issues—most important, on the war in Iraq—but also on economic and social policy issues such as Social Security, Medicare, Medicaid, poverty, gun control, civil liberties, and civil rights, as well as on the lifestyle and cultural issues that have roiled American politics so deeply: abortion, gay rights, the role of religion in public life, divorce, family values, stem cell research, the very meaning of life itself, to name a few. And while the academy may not be the hotbed of left politics the right portrays it to be, liberal and progressive social scientists from universities around the country have increasingly sought to become public intellectuals, part of the march of pundits across our television screens and the pages of our daily newspapers, in the service of defending against the right's onslaught in the culture wars.

Yet our voices rarely rise above a whisper in the public consciousness. Why have we had such a hard time making ourselves heard?

The question inevitably takes us back to the history and unfinished business of the last several decades, to the enormous upheavals in the social-cultural makeup of the nation that started with the civil rights movement in the late 1950s, was followed by the various liberation movements of the sixties and seventies—sexual, feminist, gay—and culminated in a cultural revolution that challenged nearly every aspect of established American life, including the way we looked, dressed, and behaved in public. Blacks, who before had been consigned to the back of the bus, were suddenly in contention for white jobs, especially white working-class jobs. Women's traditional roles, whether in the family or in the larger world, gave way before the intense scrutiny and protest of the feminist movement, while men looked on in bewilderment and anger. The codes that had for so long guided sexual behavior, at least the public face of it, fell before the onslaught. Homosexuals—alien others reviled as queers and faggots—turned out to be our own children, who leaped out of the closet demanding acceptance. All of it leavened, if not sparked, by massive disillusionment with a government that, using tactics ranging from dissimulation to outright deception, escalated the war in Vietnam, which, even with the sacrifice of nearly sixty thousand American lives, we couldn't win.

For those who saw the events in a positive frame, these were at best liberation movements, at worst eruptions of youthful exuberance, with perhaps a touch of excess. For the others—the silent majority of the Nixon era, the blue-collar Republicans of the Reagan years, and not least the growing number of evangelical Protestants—these changes were at best disconcerting and somewhat alarming, at worst shocking violations of the moral order, of the laws of God and nature, the twentieth-century version of Sodom and Gomorrah.

It was the perfect political moment for the conservatives, who since the defeat of Barry Goldwater in 1964 had felt victimized by the "liberal media" and isolated from the political mainstream, to step in as the voice of the people, the voice that echoed their anxieties about the pace of change and called for a return to God, morality, and "family values." The airwaves bloomed with a host of personalities dedicated to getting the message across, men like Rush Limbaugh who gave voice to white male rage about women's changing roles by railing about "feminazis"; and women like Laura Schlesinger, the physiologist turned talk-show therapist, who lamented the abdication of character in modern life, talked about God's laws as if they had been handed down to her personally, and advised the troubled souls foolish enough to call in to shape up and stop whining.

As the movement grew, it gave birth to a stable of pundits and policy analysts who write for such periodicals as *Commentary, Policy Review, American Spectator,* and the *Weekly Standard* and make the rounds of the cable news networks and Sunday morning talk shows. At the same time, conservative money poured into organizations such as the American Enterprise Institute, the Heritage Foundation, and the Project for the New American Century, think tanks that support a group of right-wing writers whose job was to stir popular anger and fear into a stew that would boil over and scorch what they called the "liberal elite," each generation becoming more vitriolic until we now have Ann Coulter, who accuses liberals of treason. Before long they had framed the debate, and the initiative was theirs.

The intensity of the right's reaction, the wholesale condemnation, the moral certainty with which it was expressed, predictably led to a counter reaction on the left, although interestingly, apart from Michael Moore and Al Franken, there haven't been nearly as many easily identifiable national personalities. As the attacks from the right escalated, liberals and progressives found themselves on the defensive, and their positions, too, hardened. Pretty soon both sides had drawn a politically correct line behind which they hunkered down—a wall that, although not made of bricks and mortar, would soon separate us as completely as the Berlin Wall did the two Germanys.

I say "both sides" because it's true. But here I'm not concerned with them; I want to talk about us, about how we promulgated and enforced a politically correct line on a series of key social-cultural issues that played into right-wing charges that we were out of touch and helped to consolidate our virtual isolation from America's lower-middle and working class.

Enforced! I can almost hear the astonishment as some readers ask derisively, "Who are the enforcers? Have progressives jailed anyone for being politically incorrect?" No, of course not. But if there were no pressure to remain silent, how do we explain the many times we sat at meetings wanting to dissent but didn't for fear of being politically incorrect? Or the times we wished for a fuller, more nuanced discussion of the subject at hand but stilled our thoughts because we knew they would be unacceptable, that our commitment to the cause would be questioned?

It's possible to dismiss the idea of coercion in voluntary associations only if we don't take seriously the human need to feel a part of a community, especially in difficult and contentious times. When we feel under siege, as we have increasingly in recent years, there's an impulse to pull together, to tighten our bonds, to take comfort and affirmation in the presence of others like ourselves. This is our community—colleagues, friends, comrades with whom we share a world that frames our lives. To speak out against the "party line" is to set ourselves up as outsiders and risk being excluded. Or, if not wholly excluded, sent to the periphery, someone who suddenly becomes the "other," not out perhaps, but not quite in.

Unfortunately, our silence creates emotional and intellectual conflicts that can be costly both personally and politically, as I found out a decade ago when I published *Families on the Fault Line,* a book about working-class families. Some readers of an early draft of that work criticized my use of the word black (the designation almost all the people I spoke with used to identify themselves) instead of African American, which was then the politically correct term. Others questioned the fact that I referred to illegals (the word used by every Latino I spoke with) instead of the newly minted undocumented workers. And still others told me I should "push the delete button" on my computer before going public with my doubts about the efficacy of bilingual programs, even though these were also the concerns voiced by many of the Latino and Asian families I interviewed.

I struggled with these criticisms, fought silently with my critics and myself, and finally decided to write about the intellectual and emotional dilemmas they posed. In the final version of the book, therefore, I recounted the criticism and mused aloud about the constraints of needing to be politically correct. What obligation, I asked, do I have to honor my respondents' definitions of self and their opinions on the red flag issues of the day? What responsibility do I have to the political subtleties of the time? To my own political convictions? How do I write what my research told me was a true picture of the lives I wanted to portray and not give aid and comfort to right-wing bigots?

I leave it to others to decide how successfully I answered those questions. What I know is that going public about the problems raised by the need to be politically correct didn't endear me to my critics and left wounds that didn't heal easily.

A caveat here: I understand the impulse to keep our differences to ourselves and to vet the work we put into the public arena for fear that our words will be distorted to serve the agenda of the right. But I also know that, no matter how carefully we say our piece, we cannot protect ourselves or control the way our ideas are used—or abused. I learned that lesson firsthand in 1996 when I published *The Transcendent Child,* a book that examines how and why, despite living in families where poverty, neglect, and abuse are commonplace, some children manage to become functional adults while others, often in the same family, do not. The theory I developed to answer the question sets forth a complex of psychological qualities and social conditions that make it possible for some people to transcend a problem-filled past and develop flourishing adult lives. Not a word to cast blame on those who don't, not a syllable to suggest that their plight is due to their own failing, or because they're stupid, lazy, or unwilling to pull themselves up by their bootstraps. Yet within weeks of publication, I became the darling of right-wing radio talk shows, whose hosts insisted that this was my message, even shouting me down when I argued that it wasn't.

These real concerns notwithstanding, the consolidation of power by the political right in recent years has convinced me that by insisting on political correctness, we not only played a part in impoverishing the national discourse but, in doing so, we also marginalized ourselves politically and lost what should have been our natural constituency. Our belief that we had to hold the line lest it crumble completely, our fear that by granting any legitimacy at all to the pervasive cultural anxiety of the time we would give fuel to the enemy led us to take positions on many issues that damaged our credibility with a considerable portion of the American public.

Let's go back, for example, to the 1960s and 1970s, when the sexual, gender, and cultural revolutions were roiling American society. In each of these struggles, there was both hope and danger. The birth control pill and the sexual revolution that followed promised important breakthroughs in women's ability to express their sexuality more freely and openly.

But as with all revolutions, there were excesses and unintended consequences, among them the shift downward to younger and younger ages, until some among us were defending the right of fourteen-year-olds to be sexually active—while most remained silent.

I'm not suggesting that we should have joined the right in arguing against sex education in the schools in favor of an "abstinence only" position. Even if I believed in it, common sense tells me it wouldn't have worked in the highly sexualized society in which our teenagers live. But surely we could have spoken up publicly and agreed with thoughtful and frightened parents that most fourteen-year-olds are too immature, too prone to give way to peer pressure, to make an informed decision about sex. Never mind the argument that fourteen-year-olds in Samoa or some other island paradise manage their sexuality quite well. American kids generally do not, as witness the number of unwanted pregnancies, as well as the many stories I've heard from teenage girls about the role of peer pressure in their "decision" to become sexually active (*Erotic Wars: What Happened to the Sexual Revolution?*).

Move up a couple of decades to the 1980s when "crime in the streets" was the biggest issue in American politics. While the right argued for more police, for tougher sentences, for trying juveniles as adults, we insisted that racism and overheated media coverage were at the core of the furor, that the perception of crime didn't match the reality, and with as much fanfare as we could muster, presented statistics to prove the point. It struck me even then that we were mistaken to try to reorder perceptions with facts, partly because we failed to take account of the psychological reality that experience overwhelms statistics no matter how compelling the numbers may be, but also because the perception of crime wasn't totally illusory.

Not that there wasn't truth in our side of the argument; it just wasn't the whole truth. I believe unequivocally that racist assumptions are built into the American psyche but, in this case, they were fueled by the fact that a disproportionate number of street crimes were committed by young African Americans. The media were often irresponsible and always sensationalist in reporting crime, but they didn't make it up. Crime was on the rise; the streets in urban communities had become more dangerous; and, while most people were never themselves mugged, it was enough to know someone who had been—whether a personal acquaintance or a victim encountered on the eleven o'clock news—to create the kind of fear that was so prominent during those years.

Back then there was a saying that "A conservative is a liberal who got mugged on his way to the subway." When I first heard it, I was outraged by those flip words; now it seems to me that they weren't entirely wrong. So today I wonder if a conservative isn't a working-class guy who heard the "liberal elite" (as the right has effectively labeled us) tell him he had nothing to fear when experience told him otherwise—not just on crime but on a whole slew of issues that have turned the country into a cultural and political battlefield.

Take the family values debate. While the events of these last decades left most Americans worried about their families and longing for a return to what felt like a less tumultuous past, feminist writers told them it was all nostalgia, that the families they remembered never existed. We weren't totally wrong, but anyone who lived through those earlier times, as I did, knows also that we weren't wholly right.

Yes, the image some now hold of the family of the fifties is part fantasy, but the fifties really were a time of relative quiet in family life. Yes, if the families the right now celebrates had been so perfect, they wouldn't have given birth to the revolutionaries of the sixties, who wanted to smash the family as they knew it. Nor would the divorce rate have soared as soon as women became more economically self-sufficient. Yes, in those allegedly halcyon days many women awakened every day with what Betty Friedan so aptly labeled the "problem that has no name." But those same women also found a certain amount of gratification and safety in their families. And even those who were actively discontented (and I was among them) didn't recognize their families as the oppressively hierarchical and patriarchal institution some feminist scholars were describing. Yes, there was much to celebrate as feminists led the way in opening the doors of the occupational world and women gratefully flooded through. But there were also legitimate questions about what happens to children when both parents work full time, which we preferred not to talk about. Yes, most Americans agreed that divorce was a reasonable option when it became too hard for wives and husbands to live together, no matter what the reasons, but that didn't mean they were ready to destroy the institution of marriage itself. I have no brief for those writers who bemoan divorce and warn us that our children will be damaged forever, but our refusal to acknowledge and discuss the pitfalls in divorce for everyone in the family, fathers included, was another of those politically correct blind spots that distanced us from people we wanted to reach.

Even on abortion, that most contentious issue of all in the culture wars, we missed opportunities to build alliances. Not with the hard-core right-to-lifers, to be sure, but with the majority of women and men who might agree on a woman's right to choose, but not a child's. Our reasons for standing against legislation that required a parent to be notified before granting an abortion to a teenager (some parents would force a decision on an unwilling child, others would be abusive) weren't all wrong. But they weren't all right, either. It is, after all, in the nature of the parent-child relationship that parents impose decisions about things large and small on their sometimes unwilling children. True, the abortion decision is larger than most, and a girl forced to continue a pregnancy faces consequences that will affect not only the rest of her life but the life of the child she will bear. Nevertheless, our refusal to acknowledge the real dilemmas inherent in how and when to draw the line between parental authority and responsibility and an adolescent child's rights left us more isolated than we should have been on abortion, especially at a time when most Americans favored our side of the abortion debate.

Whether on welfare, race, or identity politics, we kept silent when we might have built bridges. We resisted talking about the role of Aid to Families with Dependent Children in the rising rate of illegitimacy in the African American community and called those who did racist. I don't say this as an advocate for the Clinton welfare reform program, which has its own serious deficiencies: not enough effective job-training; no adequate child care to allow a mother to work in peace even if she finds a job; and perhaps worst of all, no guarantee that she will keep the health care her family was entitled to under the Medicaid program once she has a job. My argument is simply that our opposition to the reform of AFDC, even after it became clear that its unintended consequences had created a whole new set of social problems, left us with little influence either with policy makers or the general public in the debate about how to change it.

On race, too, we failed to speak out at crucial moments and to face up to self-evident truths. For decades the left has argued that the antisocial behavior of significant numbers of

African American youth (dropping out of school, getting pregnant, gang behavior, drugs) is a direct result of the painful realities under which they live and the hopelessness and helplessness their plight generates. Once again, we're not wrong, but we're not wholly right either.

No doubt the prospects of African American youth have been seriously affected by the massive neglect of our public schools, very high levels of unemployment, crushing poverty, police practices that criminalize behavior that's treated like a boyish prank in white suburbs, and a long history of prejudice and discrimination. But as William Julius Wilson, a Harvard scholar who can't by any stretch be called an apologist for the right, argues, there are also behavioral causes of black poverty-decisions and choices that are not the inevitable result of social constraints but of an amalgam of culture and personal behavior that is destructive to both the individual and the community. To believe otherwise is to strip an entire population of any agency and to treat them as if they were as helpless to influence the direction of their lives as leaves tossed about in a hurricane. Well meaning, perhaps, but ultimately condescending.

As was the huge flap that arose recently, mostly among whites, when comedian Bill Cosby scolded black parents for their failure to parent and young people for their illiteracy and irresponsibility. The white liberal press, mainstream and Internet, huffed and puffed; white readers wrote letters of protest; and Barbara Ehrenreich published a stinging rebuke ("The New Cosby Kids," *New York Times,* July 8, 2004). A few weeks later, senatorial candidate Barak Obama used his platform as keynote speaker at the Democratic National Convention to say much the same, albeit in language kinder and gentler than Cosby used. "[The] government alone can't teach kids to learn . . ." Obama said, "parents have to parent . . . children can't achieve unless we raise their expectations and eradicate the slander that says a black youth with a book is acting white." To which Harvard professor Henry Louis Gates, Jr., himself an African American, virtually shouted "Amen," while noting also that black Democratic delegates were "galvanized" by Obama's words, "not just because they agreed, but because it was a home truth they'd seldom heard a politician say out loud" (*New York Times,* "Breaking the Silence," August 1, 2004).

As racial and identity politics became increasingly strident, we were right on economic issues but tone deaf to the cultural and emotional sources of white working-class fear and anger. They objected to what they saw as minority privilege, and we called them racist, which was probably true but did nothing to facilitate an alliance with them. I'm not saying that we should have backed away from our support of affirmative action, minority scholarships, and other attempts to level the playing field. And perhaps their rage and fear were so great that no bridge was possible. We'll never know because we couldn't hear their *cri de coeur.* Instead, we spoke from our own privileged position and tried to silence their resentment by reminding them that they were the beneficiaries of a long history of white privilege.

Certainly, if we consider privilege from the long view of history, whites of all classes have been (and still are) privileged when compared to African Americans and other people of color. But tell that to the white, working-class people I studied, men and women who were struggling to pay the rent and put food on the table, and you'll get an earful about what that "privilege" feels like to them.

A decade ago, I wrote about the emerging movement of European-American clubs and warned that in these groups we could see "the outlines of things to come" (*Families on the Fault Line*). The clubs themselves faded away, but the consciousness of self as "other," an idea that had been alien to whites of any class until identity politics came to dominate political life, took root and evolved into what we see today: America's white working and lower-middle class claiming for itself the status of another aggrieved group, only this time the largest in the land. And unlike earlier working-class movements of discontent, it isn't the bosses or the corporations or even the government that are the target of their anger, it's us, "the liberal elite."

This, then, is the political reality we face today—a reality that, as I have been arguing, we had a hand in creating. History, however, is useful only if we can take its lessons forward to a different future. These aren't easy truths to take in, especially for a generation that cut its political teeth on the slogan of the 1960s: If you're not part of the solution, you're part of the problem.

Friends and colleagues who read earlier drafts of this article generally agreed that the insistence on being politically correct had hobbled discourse on the left and too often kept them silent. Yet they did not see themselves as an active part of the problem. Instead, each one said something akin to "Yes, but not me." In silence, however, there is complicity, and each one of us who failed to speak, or who complained *sotto voce* to some trusted friend, has been part of the problem.

It's time to break the silence.

There's much to do in the coming years to build a set of institutions that can begin to compete with the highly organized, enormously well-funded network of newspapers, periodicals, think tanks, publishing houses, and television and radio stations the right already has in place. But no institutions will save us until we find the way to reframe the debate so that it's on our terms, not theirs. That means opening up discussion among ourselves to debate and develop positions and strategies that, while honoring our own beliefs and values, enable us to build bridges across which we can speak to those who now see us as an alien other.

It's not enough to speak in another voice, however. We must learn to listen as well, to develop a third ear so that we can hear beneath their rage to the anguish it's covering up. Only then will we find our way into the hearts and minds of those Americans who have been seduced and exploited by the radical right into "strangling their own life chances." Only then will we be able to stop asking, "Why don't they listen to us?"

# 27

# The Era of Exploitation

*BOB HERBERT*

*Bob Herbert, columnist for* The New York Times, *focuses on the federal budget proposed by President Bush in 2005. Although the details of this proposal were changed slightly by the Republican-controlled Congress, the message is clear. The plan is to reduce or eliminate programs that aid the vulnerable in society (e.g., food stamps, Medicaid, education, AIDS treatment) and to curtail environmental protection programs. And while these reductions are made, the budget contains billions in tax cuts going mostly to the affluent. Contrast these proposals with those of the New Deal of Franklin Roosevelt and the Great Society of Lyndon Johnson and you see vividly what a difference the Republican takeover means.*

Congress is in recess and the press has gone berserk over the Terri Schiavo case. So very little attention is being paid to pending budget proposals that are scandalously unfair, but that pretty accurately reflect the kind of country the U.S. has become.

President Bush believes in an "ownership" society, which means that except for the wealthy, you're on your own. The president's budget would cut funding for Medicaid, food stamps, education, transportation, health care for veterans, law enforcement, medical research and safety inspections for food and drugs. And, of course, it contains big new tax cuts for the wealthy.

These are the new American priorities. Republicans will tell you they were ratified in the last presidential election. We may be locked in a long and costly war, and federal deficits may be spiraling toward the moon, but the era of shared sacrifices is over. This is the era of entrenched exploitation. All sacrifices will be made by working people and the poor, and the vast bulk of the benefits will accrue to the rich.

F.D.R. would have stared slack-jawed at this madness. Even his grand Social Security edifice is under assault by the vandals of the G.O.P.

While the press and the public are distracted by one sensational news story after another—Terri Schiavo, Michael Jackson, steroids in baseball, etc.—the president and his party have continued their extraordinary campaign to undermine the programs that were designed to fend off destitution and provide a reasonable foundation of economic security for those not blessed with great wealth.

President Bush has proposed more than $200 billion worth of cuts in domestic discretionary programs over the next five years, and cuts of $26 billion in entitlement programs. The Center on Budget and Policy Priorities, which analyzed the president's proposal, said: "Figures in the budget show that child-care assistance would be ended for 300,000 low-income children by 2009. The food stamp cut would terminate food stamp aid for approximately 300,000 low-income people, most of whom are low-income working families with children. Reduced Medicaid funding most certainly would cause many states to cut their Medicaid programs, increasing the ranks of the uninsured."

Education funding would be cut beginning next year, and the cuts would grow larger in succeeding years. Food assistance for pregnant women, infants and children would be cut. Funding for H.I.V. and AIDS treatment would be cut by more than half a billion dollars over five years. Support for environmental protection programs would be sharply curtailed. And so on.

Conservatives insist the cuts are necessary to get the roaring federal budget deficit under control. But they have trouble keeping a straight face when they tell that story. Laden with tax cuts, the president's proposal will result in an increase, not a decrease, in the deficit. Shared sacrifice is anathema to the big-money crowd.

The House has passed a budget that is similar to the president's, except it contains even deeper cuts in programs that affect the poor. In the Senate, a handful of Republicans balked at the cuts proposed for Medicaid. Casting their votes with the Democrats, they were able to eliminate the cuts from the Senate budget proposal. The Senate also added $5.4 billion in education funding for 2006.

All the budgets contain more than $100 billion in tax cuts over the next five years, which makes a mockery of the G.O.P.'s budget-balancing rhetoric. When Congress returns from its Easter recess, the Republican leadership will try to reconcile the differences in the various proposals. Whatever happens will be bad news for ordinary Americans. Big cuts are coming.

The advances in areas like education, antipoverty programs, health services, environmental protection and food safety were achieved after struggles that, in some cases, took many decades. To slide backward now (hurting millions of people in the process) because of a desire to siphon funds from those programs and hand them over as tax cuts to the wealthiest members of our society, is obscene.

This is not a huge national story. It's just the way things are. It was Herbert Hoover who said: "You know, the only trouble with capitalism is capitalists. They're too damn greedy."

# The Role of Government
# in Achieving the Good Society

*Were our government for the* people, *we would have the best education in the world, universal health insurance, a decent way of financing elections, and a massive commitment to sources of clean energy.*

—William Sloan Coffin

*Every gun that is made, every warship launched, every rocket fired signifies in the final sense, a theft from those who hunger and are not fed, those who are cold and are not clothed. This world in arms is not spending money alone. It is spending the sweat of its laborers, the genius of its scientists, the hopes of its children. This is not a way of life at all in any true sense. Under the clouds of war, it is humanity hanging on a cross of iron.*

—President Dwight D. Eisenhower, 1963

Proponents of both the conservative and progressive persuasions would likely agree with the highly esteemed economist John Kenneth Galbraith that "the essence of the good society . . . is that every member, regardless of gender, race or ethnic origin, should have access to a rewarding life" (1996:23). What divides progressives and conservatives, of course, is how best to achieve this goal. The role of government is critical to this ideological divide.

The prevailing hostility of conservatives to the New Deal legacy of "big government" is based on two fundamental beliefs. First, they believe that the unequal distribution of economic rewards is none of the government's business. They value individualism, freedom, and a market economy. Inequality is not evil: rather it is good because it motivates people to compete and it weeds out the weak. Progressives counter that this laissez-faire approach guarantees an exaggerated inequality and leads to what economists Robert Frank and Philip Cook (1995) have called a "winner-take-all" society.

The second tenet of the conservative creed is that government efforts to reduce poverty and class inequality actually cause the very problems they seek to solve. The assumption is that social problems are the consequence of bad people making bad decisions. Consider this statement by John Goodman, president and CEO of the National Center for Policy Analysis:

*Our most serious problems are caused by the behavior of the recipients of welfare, behavior that is subsidized and sustained by the welfare state. Solutions that help people without encouraging dependency and perverse behavior can only be implemented by the private sector. . . . Virtually all of our federal welfare programs are entitlement programs—AFDC, food stamps, Medicaid, etc. This means that people qualify for relief based on financial considerations alone. Applicants for welfare are not required to show that their need for relief was caused by their own behavior. They do not have to promise to change behavior or develop a plan to become self-sufficient. (Goodman, 1996:537–538)*

Welfare dependency, in this view, is the source of poverty, illegitimacy, laziness, crime, unemployment, and other social pathologies. Conservatives agree with Charles Murray (1984) that only when poor people are confronted with a "sink or swim" world will they develop the will and the skill to stay afloat.

This book counters the conservative position, arguing that throughout U.S. history social problems have been ameliorated by progressive government policies—that is, from the top down. The U.S. welfare state, modest in comparison to Canadian, Scandinavian, and European welfare states, emerged in the 1930s as a reaction to the economic instability of the Great Depression and capitalism run amok in the 1920s. Motivated by a fear of radical unrest by the disadvantaged and disaffected (Piven and Cloward, 1993), and the need to save capitalism from its own self-destructive tendencies (economic instability, rape of the environment, worker exploitation, lack of worker and consumer safety), the creators of the New Deal under President Franklin D. Roosevelt and the Great Society under President Lyndon Johnson instituted Social Security, Medicare, the minimum wage, federal aid to education, health and nutrition programs, subsidized housing, and other services. These programs were successful, until recent cutbacks, in reducing poverty, for example, by 20 percent and elderly poverty by one-half, since President Johnson's War on Poverty.

The overriding question, then, is should we do away with the welfare state as conservatives favor, or should we take the progressive stance of making it stronger? Flowing from this fundamental question are other questions: Will dismantling the welfare state be beneficial or will it create chaos? Will reducing or eliminating the safety net to the economically disadvantaged save them or hurt them? Will it make society safer or more dangerous?

Based on our study and analysis of these questions, we believe that the answers to these questions are quite obvious. Society will be worse off rather than better off if the welfare state is dismantled. The number of people on the economic margins will rise. Homelessness will increase. Family disruption will escalate. Crime rates will swell. Public safety will become more problematic. Economic inequality, which today is the highest since the Gilded Age of the late 1890s, will continue to increase. This has implications for democracy, crime, and civil unrest. As economist Lester Thurow has asked, "How much inequality can a democracy take? The income gap is eroding the social contract. If the promise of a higher standard of living is limited to a few at the top, the rest of the citizenry, as history shows, is likely to grow disaffected, or worse" (Thurow, 1995:79).

Criminologists have shown that poverty, unemployment, and economic inequality are powerful determinants of street crime. Comparing the United States with the welfare states of Scandinavia and Europe, our rates for murder and rape are much higher. The incarceration rate in the United States is 685 per 100,000, compared to an average of 87 per 100,000 in Europe.

The more generous welfare states of Canada, Europe, and Scandinavia have compre-hensive social supports for their residents (Reid, 2004; Rifkin, 2004). All have universal health care plans. They have a much higher minimum wage than does the United States. Holidays and paid vacations are generous. Unemployment benefits far exceed those in the United States. They provide generous pensions and nursing home care for the elderly. They have paid maternity (and in some cases paternity) leave, whereas women in the United States, if they work for a company with at least fifty workers, receive *unpaid* maternity leave. They have universal, free education, from preschool through college.

These benefits are costly with income, inheritance, and sales taxes considerably higher than in the United States. The trade-off is that poverty and homelessness are rare, and the people feel relatively safe from crime and from the insecurities over income, illness, and old age. Most important, there is a large middle and working class with a much stronger feeling of community and therefore, of social solidarity, than found in the United States. This solidarity is enhanced by a much greater proportion of public moneys going to mass transit, and public spaces such as parks, bicycle paths, museums, subsidies for orchestras, and other forms of the arts.

Compared to the welfare states of Canada, Scandinavia, and Europe, the United States has the highest rate of poverty by far, a withering bond among those of different social classes, a serious racial divide, and an alarming move toward a two-tiered society. Evi-dence of this bipolar society includes a rise in private schooling and home schooling, an increase in the number of walled and gated affluent neighborhood enclaves on the one hand and ever greater segregation of the poor and especially poor racial minorities in deterio-rating neighborhoods and inferior schools on the other. The affluent tend to oppose taxes for public services because they have opted out of public institutions—schools, hospitals, parks—using instead the private equivalent for each. Why then should they care about and help to pay for improving the crumbling public infrastructure, inferior urban schools, the lack of decent mass transit, and so on? Furthermore, democracy is on the wane because money rules and because so many people opt out of the electoral process (consistently, the United States has the lowest voter turnout among the industrialized nations).

Over the past century or so the U.S. government has been instrumental at various times in regulating corporations and industries to curb abuses, in providing a safety net for those on the outside of the affluent society (who are, for the most part, in dire straits for structural reasons, not due to personal flaws) in protecting the environment, in strengthening public education, in setting aside public lands for public use, and in righting the injustices toward racial and ethnic minorities and women. These successes, mostly from the 1890s to the mid-1960s, have eroded since then with the ascent of conservatives to dominant government roles in the executive, leg-islative, and judicial branches. The subsequent policies have reduced the role of government in attempting to solve social problems. The result has been to increase the inequality gap, to add to the proportion of people including children in poverty (up 4.8 million from 2000 to 2004), and to keep 45 million people outside the health care system because they have no insurance.

## A PROGRESSIVE PLAN FOR ACHIEVING THE GOOD SOCIETY

What would be the planks of a progressive platform for achieving the good society? Let us suggest some possibilities in the areas considered in this book.

## A Reliable Safety Net

Political observer E. J. Dionne summarizes the progressive position this way: "If there is a principle that unites the left side of the political spectrum, it is a belief that an energetic government can effectively use progressive taxation to insure the poor, the unlucky and the elderly against undue hardship" (2005a:7B). The structural sources of economic hardship are low wages, unemployment, inadequate pensions, lack of health insurance coverage for expensive medical needs, and for women, divorce.

Therefore, we recommend the following:

- Retention of Social Security for ample and secure retirement benefits and for providing financial aid to children of workers who become disabled or have died (Cauthen, 2005).
- The Social Security system discriminates against low-income workers because the payroll tax is regressive. Therefore, the payroll tax needs to be changed to exempt people who earn less than, for example, $30,000 from payroll taxes. And, instead of the current cap at $90,000, raise it to, say $150,000, "so that the wealthiest among us, those with the greatest financial security, can help those with the least" (Rosen, 2005:32).
- Retain safety net programs such as Food Stamps, WIC (Women, Infants, and Children), school lunch subsidies, immunization of children, and subsidized housing.
- Institute a universal health care insurance plan for all residents.
- Raise the minimum wage to at least one-half the median wage of workers (between $7 and $8 dollars). Index this wage according to the rate of inflation and the methods used to establish the poverty line.
- Secure the earned income tax credit (EITC) for the near poor. The 2003 federal tax bill, in a progressive move, included a provision allowing families making $10,500 or more to claim a credit of $100 for every $1,000 they earn above $10,500 even if they owed little or no federal income taxes. Previously, they could only use the credit to reduce the tax they owed (Children's Defense Fund, 2004:12).

Former senator Bob Kerry has proposed a "Kid Save" plan that would give every child a savings account. Although helpful to all children, it would be especially beneficial to poor children who at present have little hope for the future. His plan is that "the government would give every newborn a $1,000 savings account, to which $500 would be added every year until the child's fifth birthday. The money accumulates and the interest compounds until the child reaches twenty-one, and then the child has a cool $20,000 to start his or her adult life. The tab would be about $15 billion a year" (roughly the cost for our military of three months in Iraq) (reported in Reich, 2002:58).

## Family Protections

The notion of "family values" has been defined by conservatives as opposition to abortion, gay marriage and other forms of nontraditional marriage, and traditional sex education in schools, promoting instead sexual abstinence before marriage. We prefer to define "family values" in economic terms such as supporting efforts that would make families stronger at a time when more and more women are in the work force. "Some politicians who speak fervently of family values leave out home economics. They talk passionately about the breakdown of American homes, but they neglect to mention the breakdown of family incomes" (Reich, 2002:106). Therefore, we propose the following:

- Paid maternity leave with guaranteed job retention upon return.
- Subsidized child care for working parents. Provide a national, universal child care subsidy for preschool children and school and recreation programs for older children to provide adult supervision after school for latchkey children.
- Universal health care insurance that provides coverage for prevention as well as treatment of health problems.
- Adequate funding of Medicare so that the special health needs of seniors, including home care and nursing home care, are provided.
- Make unemployment insurance available to anyone who loses a job.

## Reduction of Extreme Income/Wealth Disparities

The goal here is not the elimination of wealth inequality but its reduction. "Equality is not consistent with either human nature or the character and motivation of the modern economic system. As all know, people differ radically in their commitment to making money and also in their competence in doing so" (Galbraith, 1996:59). That said, the inequality gap is too great. At the extremes there is extravagant wealth at one end and homelessness and hunger at the other. That fosters resentment and social unrest. Moreover, the inequality gap separates people thus fraying the social fabric. The high taxes in the generous welfare states allow for quite wealthy individuals and families (actually, there are more millionaires in Europe than in the United States). What they have done, contrary to our system, is to bring the wealthy down a bit and raise those at the bottom significantly. In addition to many of the proposals noted previously for helping the poor, proposals to reduce income/wealth disparities include the following:

- Restore real progressivism to the tax system by closing loopholes for corporations and the wealthy.
- Increase inheritance taxes.
- Take the power of money out of politics by public financing of local, state, and federal campaigns, provide free media for debate among candidates, and eliminate all political contributions. The rationale for this proposal is that the money contributed to political parties and candidates comes disproportionately from the wealthy, who see their contributions translated into favorable legislation and administrative actions.
- Reduce the income gap between workers and their bosses. At present, the income of CEOs at the larger corporations is 500 times greater than that of the workers in those companies. In Europe the ratio averages about 30:1.

## Race and Gender Equity

The good society must ensure that no one because of race/ethnicity or gender shall be denied equal economic and educational opportunity, and equal access to a rewarding life (Galbraith, 1996:23). For race/ethnicity, this means the following:

- Constant vigilance to ensure that the guarantees for voting rights and equal access to public facilities are guaranteed.
- End all redlining and other forms of discrimination by realtors, banks, and insurance companies that artificially limit the housing opportunities for the poor and racial minorities.

- Provide job training and jobs. The unemployment rate for racial minorities is consistently twice that for whites. The government can generate jobs, for example, in child care, road building and maintenance, mass transit, waste recycling, parks and national forests management, pollution cleanup, assisting in schools and hospitals, and building or renovating affordable housing.
- Break up the de facto segregated public schools—segregated not only by race/ethnicity but also by economic stratum. Robert Reich proposes giving each child a subsidy for education with the poorer the child, the greater the subsidy. Schools would then compete for students and the subsidies that go with them. In this scheme poor students (disproportionately racial/ethnic minorities) would be in demand. This mechanism would work to break up the concentrations of poor and minority children in the same schools (Reich, 2002:69).

For women, achieving equity means the following:

- Passage of the Equal Rights Amendment, which reads: "Equality of rights under the law shall not be denied or abridged by the United States or any state on account of sex."
- Ensure that equal work translates into equal pay.
- Eliminate the bias against women in the Social Security system. For example, Social Security does not recognize unpaid housework, it pays divorced women only one-half of her former husband's benefit but only if they were married ten years or more, and retired women workers receive lower monthly benefits than retired male workers because they usually are paid less than men for work.
- Enforce Title IX and other laws pertaining to gender equity.
- Ensure government protections for a woman's right to choose regarding contraception and pregnancy.
- Prohibit discrimination against someone because she is a woman, or wants to raise a family, or has to attend to family needs (Reich, 2002:105).

### Education

Americans believe in the value of education. There is a strong commitment to everyone being able to achieve his or her potential by developing her or his talents and abilities. But for this to work we must provide an excellent education and job training for all, not only the better off (Reich, 2002:65). This experience begins with preschoolers and extends through college. The good society should incorporate the following:

- Compensatory education for preschool and school children from high-risk situations.
- The school day for all children should extend until parents return from work.
- A change in the formula for funding education (now based primarily on local property taxes) to one that equalizes the per pupil expenditures across districts and states. The current system disadvantages poor children (rundown buildings, inadequate equipment, large classes, sometimes noncertified teachers), while privileging the already privileged. Our current funding of education is backward because it results in greater funding for children of the affluent and less for children of the poor, who have greater educational deficits (Reich, 2002:68).
- Cost-free public education through college.

## Public Spaces

As the population in the United States continues to rise and metropolitan areas become more densely populated, the need for public space increases. Cities, counties, states, and the national government need to set aside and maintain space for the masses to enjoy. Although it is expensive to purchase land and maintain it, we believe that this is what the government should be involved in—that is, providing for the common good. Some proposals:

- The government should not only protect its currently held parks and wilderness areas but they should also be expanded.
- Expand the government's subsidy for a variety of public spaces—museums, zoos, public broadcasting, architectural conservation, and the arts (visual arts, music, theater, ballet, opera). This in effect is calling for a bigger role for the public sector, which, we repeat, enhances the common good.

## The Environment

There are a number of environmental concerns that must be met or the earth and its peoples will be irreparably damaged. Individuals can change their lifestyles (conserve, recycle) but governments must lead the way to make a significant positive impact on the environment. Some suggestions:

- Environmental concerns are global. We must not only cooperate with other nations to protect the earth's air, land, and water but also we must lead by example in these protections.
- Domestically, reduce the use of hydrocarbons, finding alternatives to conserve resources, protect the air we breathe, and reduce global warming. Some possibilities are to demand that automobile manufacturers meet a high miles per gallon average for their vehicles (e.g., 40 mpg); increase the gasoline tax so that gasoline would cost $4 a gallon; build safe nuclear power plants to replace the coal-burning ones; and place a high tax on carbon, which would induce more industries to move from coal to wind, hydro, solar, geothermal, and other, cleaner and renewable fuels (Friedman, 2005).
- Enact stiffer laws and penalties for regulating the environmental footprint of corporations and municipalities. This requires that the existing regulatory agencies take their mandate to enforce these laws seriously.
- The money necessary to clean up hazardous waste sites must be extracted from the offending entities (corporations, governments) and used immediately to make them environmentally safe.

## FINANCING THESE PROPOSALS

The proposals above will be costly. Financing them requires a shift in budget priorities. These are several possibilities. First, we can reduce defense spending. The United States spends more on the military than the rest of the world combined. It spends seven times more than the combined military budgets of Russia and China. Taking all expenditures related to the military in consideration (e.g., Homeland Security, Veterans Affairs), the United States spends 30.7 percent of total government spending on the military (Monkerud, 2005).

The question is, how much spending on the military is enough? We could reduce military spending by $200 to $300 billion and still have the most superior military in the world.

Second, end all of the recent tax cuts that go disproportionately to the affluent. Repealing the tax cuts for the richest 1 percent would put more than $1 trillion back in the treasury by 2010 (Sklar, 2004).

Third, tax all forms of income at the same rate. At present, wages are taxed at the highest rates whereas capital income is taxed at considerably lower rates.

A fourth source of funds would be to reduce or eliminate corporate welfare and subsidies to the wealthy. This costs Americans more than $815 billion a year, which is more than four times the cost of welfare programs for the poor (Zepezauer, 2004).

Fifth, we could increase tax revenues. Totaling federal, state, and local taxes equals about 31 percent of the gross domestic product. This is the lowest rate of any industrialized nation. In comparison, the total in the European and Scandinavian countries ranges from the upper 30s to the upper 50s.

There are also long-term savings that would accrue if a progressive plan were implemented. Research has shown, for example, that for every $1 invested in comprehensive childhood programs, $7 is saved in social costs, unemployment insurance, incarceration, and welfare.

## THE POTENTIAL FOR A NEW PROGRESSIVE ERA

The crucial question: Is there any hope of achieving the good society, with government programs and incentives working for the common good? At first a resounding "no" seems overwhelming. Foremost is the fundamental belief of U.S. citizens in individualism. We celebrate individualism, which seems to be the antithesis of cooperation, social solidarity, and acceptance of a more equitable redistribution of resources. But this actually is not the case because historically people have shown that they are willing to support a variety of legislative initiatives and public policies on behalf of the common good.

A second barrier to progressive policies is political. The federal government and many state legislatures are currently dominated by conservatives, which means that they opt for reducing or eliminating programs for the common good rather than expanding these government programs. The prevailing discourse in these political assemblies favors the extreme conservative to moderate conservative side of the political spectrum, with little, if any, significant voice from the progressive perspective. Another political barrier is that the two major political parties are financed by big business and wealthy individuals. Money rules in today's politics and that money comes, for the most part, from conservative sources.

The huge national debt, to which is added $500 billion or so annually, much of which is military spending, constricts government spending for social services, making it difficult to fund existing social programs, let alone institute new ones.

One of the necessary ingredients for a generous progressive state is the existence of a heavily unionized workforce. This condition is not present in the United States, where only about 13 percent of workers belong to unions.

There are some reasons for optimism, however. First, in the election of President Bush in 2000 he actually received 500,000 fewer votes than his Democratic opponent. Moreover, his vote count amounted to less than 25 percent of those eligible to vote. He received a majority of votes four years later but his narrow victory was clearly not much of a mandate for his conservative policies; instead, it was a vote for an incumbent in a time of war. Also, the Republicans have fifty-five of the one hundred seats in the Senate, but the states they represent have 4 million fewer inhabitants than the total in the forty-four states with Democratic senators (Dionne, 2005b). So the conservative majority is a slim one. If the nonvoters, disproportionately the poor and the near poor, racial/ethnic minorities, and urban dwellers, were mobilized by a progressive political party that spoke to their needs, the balance of power would likely shift.

Second, the current group of conservatives may take what they consider a mandate and go too far with it, thereby alienating substantial portions of the citizenry. However, there is no guarantee that if the conservatives go too far, that progressives will prevail. This can occur, but so, too, is the possibility that the conservatives will become more and more the dominant political force.

Third, looking at the lessons from history, merely 110 years ago or so, the Progressive movement began as a reaction to unchecked capitalism, the robber barons, economic exploitation, and political corruption. Out of the Progressive Era came an activist government that addressed consumer issues, workplace safety, child labor, and worker disability. The government broke up business monopolies, established a national parks system, and granted women the right to vote.

If the government fosters the continued erosion of the safety net programs of Franklin Roosevelt and Lyndon Johnson, then it may lead to a further unraveling of social solidarity and a less secure society. In short, it may lead to a search for new answers—perhaps waves of progressive government actions that characterized the Progressive Era in 1900, the New Deal in 1935, and the Great Society in 1965.

A new progressive era will work only if a political party has a program that addresses the needs of the masses. In particular, this requires progressive leaders who can articulate a vision of the good society, a sense of direction, and building a sense of community. The future of the United States depends on the welfare of all in the community in which we live, and the society of which we are a part, not only our personal accumulated wealth.

To conclude, Robert Reich ends his book, *I'll Be Short: Essentials for a Decent Working Society,* with a plea and an argument that we share:

> To become a highly productive society, we have to change our thinking about the role of government. We've become so accustomed to thinking about education, health care, and public transportation as government spending *that we don't see the obvious. In the new global economy where financial capital is footloose, these are critical public* investments. *They mark the only path to a sustained and shared prosperity. Failure to make them—and make them wisely— condemns a society to a steadily declining standard of living. The same is true for regulations protecting worker safety, guarding the environment, and preventing discrimination. These, too, are investments in our future. In other words, making these investments is both an ethical imperative and an economic necessity. (Reich, 2002:115)*

**REFERENCES**_____

Cauthen, Nancy K. (2005). "Privatizing Survivors, Abandoning Children" (March 28): http://alternet.org/story/21607.

Children's Defense Fund. (2004). *The State of America's Children, 2004.* Washington, DC.

Dionne, E. J. (2005a). "Can Bush Sustain Unity?" *Denver Post* (March 30):7B.

Dionne, E. J. (2005b). "Senate Faces Upheaval." *Denver Post* (March 23):7B.

Eitzen, D. Stanley. (1996). "Dismantling the Welfare State: Is It the Answer to America's Social Problems?" *Vital Speeches of the Day* 62 (June 15):532–536.

Frank, Robert H., and Cook, Philip J. (1995). *The Winner-Take-All Society.* New York: Free Press.

Friedman, Thomas L. (2005). "Geo-Greening by Example." *New York Times* (March 27):17.

Galbraith, John Kenneth. (1996). *The Good Society: The Humane Agenda.* Boston: Houghton Mifflin.

Goodman, John C. (1996). "Taxpayer Choice: A Solution to the Crisis of the Welfare State." *Vital Speeches of the Day* 62 (June 15):537–541.

Monkerud, Don. (2005). "U.S. Military Budget." *Z Magazine* (April):8–9.

Murray, Charles. (1984). *Losing Ground: American Social Policy, 1950–1980.* New York: Basic Books.

Piven, Frances Fox, and Cloward, Richard A. (1993). *Regulating the Poor: The Functions of Public Welfare,* updated ed. New York: Vintage/Random House.

Reich, Robert B. (2002). *I'll Be Short: Essentials for a Decent Working Society.* Boston: Beacon Press.

Reid, T. R. (2004). *The United States of Europe.* New York: Penguin Press.

Rifkin, Jeremy. (2004). *The European Dream.* New York: Jeremy P. Tarcher/Penguin.

Rosen, Ruth. (2005). "Old Women in the Cold." *The Nation* (April 11):32.

Sklar, Holly. (2004). "Wealthy Taxpayers Bank on Bush." *The Progressive Populist* (May 15):13.

Thurow, Lester. (1995). "Why Their World Might Crumble." *New York Times Magazine* (November 19):78–79.

Zepezauer, Mark. (2004). *Take the Rich Off Welfare,* expanded ed. Cambridge, MA: South End Press.

# 28

# Imagine a Country:
# Life in the New Millennium

*HOLLY SKLAR*

*Social critic Holly Sklar captures in this imaginative essay the social problems that plague the United States. The problems she cites are real and have damaging implications for the quality of life, social justice, and social solidarity. What then, do we do about them? The remaining essays in this section address that question.*

Imagine a country where one out of five children is born into poverty and wealth is being redistributed upward. Since the 1970s, the top 1 percent of households has doubled their share of the nation's wealth. The top 1 percent has close to 40 percent of the wealth—nearly the same amount as the bottom 95 percent of households.

Imagine a country where economic inequality is going back to the future circa the 1930s. The combined after-tax income of the top 1 percent of tax filers was about half that of the bottom 50 percent of tax filers in 1986. By the late 1990s, the top 1 percent had a larger share of after-tax income than the bottom 50 percent.

Imagine a country with a greed surplus and justice deficit.

Imagine a country where the poor and middle class bear the brunt of severe cutbacks in education, health, environmental programs, and other public services to close state and federal budget deficits fueled by ballooning tax giveaways for wealthy households and corporations.

It's not Argentina.

Imagine a country which demands that people work for a living while denying many a living wage.

Imagine a country where health care aides can't afford health insurance. Where people working in the food industry depend on food banks to help feed their children. Where childcare teachers don't make enough to save for their own children's education.

It's not the Philippines.

Imagine a country where productivity went up, but workers' wages went down.

In the words of the national labor department, "As the productivity of workers increases, one would expect worker compensation [wages and benefits] to experience similar gains." That's not what happened.

Since 1968, worker productivity has risen 81 percent while the average hourly wage barely budged, adjusting for inflation, and the real value of the minimum wage dropped 38 percent.

Imagine a country where the minimum wage just doesn't add up. Where minimum wage workers earn more than a third less than their counterparts earned a third of a century ago, adjusting for inflation. Where a couple with two children would have to work more than three full-time jobs at the $5.15 minimum wage to make ends meet.

It's not Mexico.

Imagine a country where some of the worst CEOs make millions more in a year than the best CEOs of earlier generations made in their lifetimes. CEOs made 45 times the pay of average production and nonsupervisory workers in 1980. They made 96 times as much in 1990, 160 times as much in 1995 and 369 times as much in 2001. Back in 1960, CEOs made an average 38 times more than schoolteachers. CEOs made 63 times as much in 1990 and 264 times as much as public school teachers in 2001.

Imagine a country that had a record-breaking ten-year economic expansion in 1991–2001, but millions of workers make wages so low they have to choose between eating or heating, health care or childcare.

A leading business magazine observed, "People who worked hard to make their companies competitive are angry at the way the profits are distributed. They think it is unfair, and they are right."

It's not England.

Imagine a country where living standards are falling for younger generations despite increased education. Since 1973, the share of workers without a high school degree has fallen by half. The share of workers with at least a four-year college degree has doubled. But the 2002 average hourly wage for production and nonsupervisory workers (the majority of the workforce) is 7.5 percent below 1973, adjusting for inflation. Median net worth (assets minus debt) dropped between 1995 and 2001 for households headed by persons under age 35 and households that don't own their own home.

About one out of four workers makes $8.70 an hour or less. That's not much more than the real value of the minimum wage of 1968 at $8.27 in inflation-adjusted dollars.

It's not Russia.

Imagine a country where for more and more people a job doesn't keep you out of poverty, it keeps you working poor. Imagine a country much richer than it was 25 years ago, but the percentage of full-time workers living in poverty has jumped 50 percent.

Imagine a country that sets the official poverty line well below the actual cost of minimally adequate housing, health care, food, and other necessities. You were not counted as poor in 2001 (latest available final data) unless you had pre-tax incomes below these thresholds: $9,214 for a person under 65, $8,494 for a person 65 and older, $11,569 for a two-person family, $14,128 for a three-person family, and $18,104 for a family of four. On average, households need more than double the official poverty threshold to meet basic needs.

Imagine a country where homelessness is on the rise, but federal funding for low-income housing is about 50 percent lower than it was in 1976, adjusting for inflation. The largest federal housing support program is the mortgage interest deduction, which disproportionately benefits higher-income families.

Imagine a country where more workers are going back to the future of sweatshops and day labor. Corporations are replacing full-time jobs with disposable "contingent workers." They include temporary employees, contract workers, and "leased" employees—some of them fired and then "rented" back at a large discount by the same company—and involuntary part-time workers, who want permanent full-time work.

It's not Spain.

How do workers increasingly forced to migrate from job to job, at low and variable wage rates, without health insurance or paid vacation, much less a pension, care for themselves and their families, pay for college, save for retirement, plan a future, build strong communities?

Imagine a country where after mass layoffs and union busting, just 13.5 percent of workers are unionized. One out of three workers were union members in 1955. Full-time workers who were union members had median 2001 weekly earnings of $718 compared with just $575 for workers not represented by unions.

Imagine a country where the concerns of working people are dismissed as "special interests" and the profit-making interests of globetrotting corporations substitute for the "national interest."

Imagine a country negotiating "free trade" agreements that help corporations trade freely on cheap labor at home and abroad.

One ad financed by the country's agency for international development showed a Salvadoran woman in front of a sewing machine. It told corporations, "You can hire her for 33 cents an hour. Rosa is more than just colorful. She and her coworkers are known for their industriousness, reliability and quick learning. They make El Salvador one of the best buys." The country that financed the ad intervened militarily to make sure El Salvador would stay a "best buy" for corporations.

It's not Canada.

Imagine a country where nearly two-thirds of women with children under age 6 and more than three-fourths of women with children ages 6–17 are in the labor force, but affordable childcare and after-school programs are scarce. Apparently, kids are expected to have three parents: Two parents with jobs to pay the bills, and another parent to be home in mid-afternoon when school lets out—as well as all summer.

Imagine a country where women working full time earn 76 cents for every dollar men earn. Women don't pay 76 cents on a man's dollar for their education, rent, food or childcare. The gender wage gap has closed just 12 cents since 1955, when women earned 64 cents for every dollar earned by men. There's still another 24 cents to go.

The average woman high school graduate who works full time from ages 25 to 65 will earn about $450,000 less than the average male high school graduate. The gap widens to $900,000 for full-time workers with bachelor's degrees. "Men with professional degrees may expect to earn almost $2 million more than their female counterparts over their worklife," says a government report.

Imagine a country where childcare workers, mostly women, generally make about as much as parking lot attendants and much less than animal trainers. Out of 700 occupations surveyed by the labor department, only 15 have lower average wages than childcare workers.

Imagine a country where most minimum wage workers are women, while 95 percent of the top-earning corporate officers at the largest 500 companies are men, as are 90 percent of the most influential positions, from CEOs to executive vice president. Less than 2 percent of corporate officers at the largest companies are women of color.

Imagine a country where discrimination against women is pervasive from the bottom to the top of the pay scale and it's not because women are on the "mommy track." In the words of a leading business magazine, "At the same level of management, the typical woman's pay is lower than her male colleague's—even when she has the exact same qualifications, works just as many years, relocates just as often, provides the main financial support for her family, takes no time off for personal reasons, and wins the same number of promotions to comparable jobs."

Imagine a country where instead of rooting out discrimination, many policy makers are busily blaming women for their disproportionate poverty. If women earned as much as similarly qualified men, poverty in single-mother households would be cut in half.

It's not Japan.

Imagine a country where the awful labeling of children as "illegitimate" has again been legitimized. Besides meaning born out of wedlock, illegitimate also means illegal, contrary to rules and logic, misbegotten, not genuine, wrong—to be a bastard. The word illegitimate has consequences. It helps make people more disposable. Single mothers and their children have become prime scapegoats for illegitimate economics.

Imagine a country where violence against women is so epidemic it is their leading cause of injury. So-called "domestic violence" accounts for more visits to hospital emergency departments than car crashes, muggings, and rapes combined. About a third of all murdered women are killed by husbands, boyfriends, and ex-partners (less than a tenth are killed by strangers). Researchers say, "Men commonly kill their female partners in response to the woman's attempt to leave an abusive relationship."

The country has no equal rights amendment.

It's not Pakistan.

Imagine a country where homicide is the second-largest killer of young people, ages 15–24; "accidents," many of them drunk driving fatalities, are first. It leads major industrialized nations in fire-arms-related deaths for children under 15. Increasingly lethal weapons designed for hunting people are produced for profit by major manufacturers and proudly defended by a politically powerful national rifle association.

Informational material from a national shooting sports foundation asks, "How old is old enough?" to have a gun, and advises parents: "Age is not the major yardstick. Some youngsters are ready to start at 10, others at 14. The only real measures are those of maturity and individual responsibility. Does your youngster follow directions well? Would you leave him alone in the house for two or three hours? Is he conscientious and reliable? Would you send him to the grocery store with a list and a $20 bill? If the answer to these questions or similar ones are 'yes' then the answer can also be 'yes' when your child asks for his first gun."

It's not France.

Imagine a country whose school system is rigged in favor of the already privileged, with lower caste children tracked by race and income into the most deficient and demoralizing schools and classrooms. Public school budgets are heavily determined by private property taxes, allowing higher income districts to spend much more than poor ones. In the state with the largest gap in 1999–2000, state and local spending per pupil in districts with the lowest child poverty rates was more than $2,152 greater than districts with the highest child poverty rates. The difference amounts to about $861,000 for a typical elementary school of 400 students—money that could be used for teachers, books, and other resources. Disparities are even wider among states, with spending in districts with enrollments of 15,000 or more ranging from $3,932 per pupil in one district to $14,244 in another.

In rich districts kids take well-stocked libraries, laboratories, and state-of-the-art computers for granted. In poor schools they are rationing out-of-date textbooks and toilet paper. Rich schools often look like country clubs—with manicured sports fields and swimming pools. Poor schools often look more like jails—with concrete grounds and grated windows. College prep courses, art, music, physical education, field trips, and foreign languages are often considered necessities for the affluent, luxuries for the poor.

Wealthier citizens argue that lack of money isn't the problem in poorer schools— family values are—until proposals are made to make school spending more equitable. Then money matters greatly for those who already have more.

It's not India.

Imagine a country whose constitution once counted black slaves as worth three-fifths of whites. Today, black per capita income is about three-fifths of whites.

Imagine a country where racial disparities take their toll from birth to death. The black infant mortality rate is more than double that of whites. Black life expectancy is nearly six years less. Black unemployment is more than twice that of whites and the black poverty rate is almost triple that of whites.

Imagine a country where the government subsidized decades of segregated suburbanization for whites while the inner cities left to people of color were treated as outsider cities—separate, unequal, and disposable. Recent studies have documented continuing discrimination in education, employment, banking, insurance, housing, and health care.

It's not South Africa.

Imagine a country where the typical non-Hispanic white household has seven times as much net worth (including home equity) as the typical household of color. From 1995 to 2001, the typical white household's net worth rose from $88,500 to $120,900 while the net worth of the typical household of color fell from $18,300 to $17,100.

Imagine a country that doesn't count you as unemployed just because you're unemployed. To be counted in the official unemployment rate you must have searched for work in the past four weeks. The government doesn't count people as "unemployed" if they are so discouraged from long and fruitless job searches they have given up looking. It doesn't count as "unemployed" those who couldn't look for work in the past month because they had no childcare, for example. If you need a full-time job, but you're working part-time—whether 1 hour or 34 hours weekly—because that's all you can find, you're counted as employed.

A leading business magazine observed, "Increasingly the labor market is filled with surplus workers who are not being counted as unemployed."

It's not Germany.

Imagine a country where there is a shortage of jobs, not a shortage of work. Millions of people need work and urgent work needs people—from creating affordable housing, to repairing bridges and building mass transit, to cleaning up pollution and converting to renewable energy, to staffing after-school programs and community centers.

Imagine a country with full prisons instead of full employment. The jail and prison population has nearly quadrupled since 1980. The nation is number one in the world when it comes to locking up its own people. In 1985, 1 in every 320 residents were incarcerated. By 2001, the figure had increased to 1 in every 146.

Imagine a country where prison labor is a growth industry and so-called "corrections" spending is the fastest growing part of state budgets. Apparently, the government would rather spend $25,000 a year to keep someone in prison than on cost-effective programs of education, community development, addiction treatment, and employment to keep them out. In the words of a national center on institutions and alternatives, this nation has "replaced the social safety net with a dragnet."

Imagine a country that has been criticized by human rights organizations for expanding, rather than abolishing, use of the death penalty—despite documented racial bias and growing evidence of innocents being sentenced to death.

It's not China.

Imagine a country that imprisons black people at a rate much higher than apartheid South Africa. One out of seven black men ages 25–29 are incarcerated. Many more are on probation or on parole. Looking just at prisons and not local jails, 10 percent of black males ages 25–29 were locked up at the end of 2001, compared with 1 percent of white males. Black non-Hispanic women are five times more likely to be imprisoned than white non-Hispanic women.

Meanwhile, nearly one out of three black men and women ages 16–19 are officially unemployed, as are one out of five ages 20–24. Remember, to be counted in the official unemployment rate you must be actively looking for a job and not finding one. "Surplus" workers are increasingly being criminalized.

Imagine a country waging a racially biased War on Drugs. More than three out of four drug users are white, according to government data, but three out of four state prisoners convicted of drug offenses are black and Latino. Racial disparities in drug and other convictions are even wider when non-Hispanic whites are distinguished more accurately from Latinos.

A study in a prominent medical journal found that drug and alcohol rates were slightly higher for pregnant white women than pregnant black women, but black women were about ten times more likely to be reported to authorities by private doctors and public health clinics—under a mandatory reporting law. Poor women were also more likely to be reported.

It is said that truth is the first casualty in war, and the War on Drugs is no exception. Contrary to stereotype, "The typical cocaine user is white, male, a high school graduate employed full time and living in a small metropolitan area or suburb," says the nation's former drug czar. A leading newspaper reports that law officers and judges say, "Although it is clear that whites sell most of the nation's cocaine and account for 80% of its consumers, it is blacks and other minorities who continue to fill up [the] courtrooms and jails, largely because, in a political climate that demands that something be done, they are the easiest people to arrest." They are the easiest to scapegoat.

It's not Australia.

Imagine a country where the cycle of unequal opportunity is intensifying. Its beneficiaries often slander those most systematically undervalued, underpaid, underemployed, underfinanced, underinsured, underrated, and otherwise underserved and undermined—as undeserving, "underclass," impoverished in moral and social values, and lacking the proper "work ethic." The oft-heard stereotype of deadbeat poor people masks the growing reality of dead-end jobs and disposable workers.

Imagine a country that abolished aid to families with dependent children while maintaining aid for dependent corporations.

Imagine a country where state and local governments are rushing to expand lotteries, video poker, and other government-promoted gambling to raise revenues, disproportionately from the poor, which they should be raising from a fair tax system.

Imagine a country whose military budget tops average Cold War levels although the break up of the Soviet Union produced friends, not foes. This nation spends almost as much on the military as the rest of the world combined and leads the world in arms exports.

Imagine a country that ranks first in the world in wealth and military power, and 34th in child mortality (under five), tied with Malaysia and well behind countries such as Singapore and South Korea. If the government were a parent it would be guilty of child abuse. Thousands of children die preventable deaths.

Imagine a country where health care is managed for healthy profit. In many countries health care is a right, but in this nation one out of six people under age 65 has no health insurance, public or private.

Healthcare is literally a matter of life and death. Lack of health insurance typically means lack of preventive health care and delayed or second-rate treatment. The uninsured are at much higher risk for chronic disease and disability, and have a 25 percent greater chance of dying (adjusting for physical, economic, and behavioral factors). Uninsured women are 49 percent more likely to die than women with insurance during the four to seven years following an initial diagnosis of breast cancer.

Imagine a country where many descendants of its first inhabitants live on reservations strip-mined of natural resources and have a higher proportion of people in poverty than any other ethnic group.

Imagine a country where 500 years of plunder and lies are masked in expressions like "Indian giver." Where the military still dubs enemy territory, "Indian country."

Imagine a country which has less than 5 percent of the world's population, but uses more than 40 percent of the world's oil resources and about 20 percent of the coal and wood. It is the number one contributor to acid rain and global warming. It has obstructed international action on the environment and climate change.

It's not Brazil.

Imagine a country where half the eligible voters don't vote. The nation's senate and house of representatives are not representative of the nation. They are overwhelmingly white, male, and millionaire.

At least 170 senators and congresspeople are millionaires. That's nearly one out of three members of the house and senate. Just 1 percent of the population they represent are millionaires.

Imagine a country where white men who are "falling down" the economic ladder are being encouraged to believe they are falling because women and people of color are climbing over them to the top or dragging them down from the bottom. That way, they will blame women and people of color rather than corporate and government policy. They will buy the myth of "reverse discrimination." Never mind that white males hold most senior management positions and continuing unreversed discrimination is well documented.

Imagine a country with a president who, even more than his father before him, "was born on third base and thought he hit a triple." The president wants to undo affirmative action. Never mind that despite all his advantages he was a mediocre student who relied on legacy affirmative action for the children of rich alumni to get into a top prep school and college. Never mind that he rode his family connections in business and politics.

Imagine a country where on top of discrimination comes insult. It's common for people of color to get none of the credit when they succeed—portrayed as undeserving beneficiaries of affirmative action and "reverse discrimination"—and all of the blame when they fail.

Imagine a country where a then presidential press secretary boasted to reporters: "You can say anything you want in a debate, and 80 million people hear it. If reporters then document that a candidate spoke untruthfully, so what? Maybe 200 people read it, or 2,000 or 20,000."

Imagine a country where politicians and judges whose views were formerly considered far right on the political spectrum now rule both houses of congress and the presidency and increasingly dominate the judiciary.

Imagine a country whose leaders misuse a fight against terrorism as camouflage for undermining democracy. Fundamental civil liberties, including the right not to be imprisoned indefinitely on the word of government officials, are being tossed aside. The attorney general attacked critics of administration policy with McCarthyite words: "To those who scare peace-loving people with phantoms of lost liberty, my message is this: Your tactics only aid terrorists for they erode our national unity . . . They give ammunition to [our] enemies and pause to [our] friends." The attorney general would burn democracy in the name of saving it.

It's not Italy.

It's the United States.

Decades ago Martin Luther King Jr. called on us to take the high road in *Where Do We Go From Here: Chaos or Community?* (Harper & Row, 1967). King wrote: "A true revolution of values will soon cause us to question the fairness and justice of many of our past and present policies. We are called to play the good Samaritan on life's roadside; but . . . one day the whole Jericho road must be transformed so that men and women will not be beaten and robbed as they make their journey through life. . . .

"A true revolution of values will soon look uneasily on the glaring contrast of poverty and wealth. . . . There is nothing but a lack of social vision to prevent us from paying an adequate wage to every American citizen whether he be a hospital worker, laundry worker, maid or day laborer. There is nothing except short-sightedness to prevent us from guaranteeing an annual minimum—and livable—income for every American family."

## SELECTED SOURCES

*Business Week,* annual reports on executive pay.
Catalyst, "2002 Census of Women Corporate Officers and Top Earners," New York.
Center for Defense Information, Washington, DC.
Center on Budget and Policy Priorities, Washington, DC.
Ira J. Chasnoff, et al., "The Prevalence of Illicit-Drug or Alcohol Use During Pregnancy and Discrepancies in Mandatory Reporting in Pinellas County, Florida," *New England Journal of Medicine,* April 26, 1990.
Citizens for Tax Justice, Washington, DC.

Cushing N. Dolbeare and Sheila Crowley, "Changing Priorities: The Federal Budget and Housing Assistance, 1976–2007" (Washington, DC: National Low Income Housing Coalition, 2002).

Economic Policy Institute, Washington, DC, *The State of Working America 2002–2003,* and other publications.

The Education Trust, *The Funding Gap: Low-Income and Minority Students Receive Fewer Dollars* (Washington, DC: August 2002).

Federal Reserve Board Division of Research and Statistics, Ana M. Aizcorbe et. al., "Recent Changes in U.S. Family Finances: Evidence from the 1998 and 2001 Survey of Consumer Finances," *Federal Reserve Bulletin,* January 2003.

Anne B. Fisher, "When Will Women Get To The Top?" *Fortune,* September 21, 1992.

Joint Economic Committee (U.S. House and Senate), Democratic Staff, "The Tale of the Top 1 Percent," January 2003.

The Kaiser Family Foundation Commission on Medicaid and Uninsured, *Sicker and Poorer: The Consequences of Being Uninsured* (Menlo Park, CA: May 2002).

Jonathan Kozol, *Savage Inequalities: Children in America's Schools* (New York: Crown Publishers, 1991).

Leadership Conference on Civil Rights, *Justice on Trial: Racial Disparities in the American Criminal Justice System* (Washington, DC: 2000).

Peter Medoff and Holly Sklar, *Streets of Hope: The Fall and Rise of an Urban Neighborhood* (Boston: South End Press, 1994).

National Academy of Sciences, Institute of Medicine, Washington, DC.

National Center on Institutions and Alternatives, *Masking the Divide: How Officially Reported Prison Statistics Distort the Racial and Ethnic Realities of Prison Growth* (Alexandria, VA: May 2001).

National Labor Committee, New York.

Holly Sklar, Laryssa Mykyta and Susan Wefald, *Raise The Floor: Wages and Policies That Work For All Of Us* (Boston: South End Press, 2002).

The Sentencing Project, Washington, DC.

United Nations Children's Fund, *The State of the World's Children 2003.*

U.S. Bureau of the Census.

U.S. Centers for Disease Control and Prevention, National Center for Health Statistics.

U.S. Department of Health and Human Services, Substance Abuse and Mental Health Services Administration, National Household Survey on Drug Abuse.

U.S Department of Justice, Bureau of Justice Statistics.

U.S. Department of Labor, Bureau of Labor Statistics.

Violence Policy Center, Washington, DC.

# 29

# A National Policy Vision for Children Achievable by 2010

*CHILDREN'S DEFENSE FUND*

*The Children's Defense Fund provides a list of goals to level the playing field somewhat by giving vulnerable children a chance for good health, safety, and a good education. The cost to achieve these goals is reasonable—$75 billion annually.*

The estimated cost of all these child investments is $75 billion annually. This is less than the cost of the war in Iraq, so far; 15 percent of the military budget, and less than the 2001–2003 tax cuts for the top 1 percent.

Children do not come in pieces but in families and communities. By 2010, CDF seeks a funded commitment to:

- Get every child ready for school through full funding of quality child care and Head Start, and new investments in universal preschool.
- Lift every child from poverty by 2010.
- Ensure every child and their parents health insurance.
- End child hunger through the expansion of food programs.
- Make sure every child can read by fourth grade and can graduate from school able to succeed at work and in life.
- Provide every child safe, quality after-school and summer programs so they can learn, serve, work, and stay out of trouble.
- Ensure every child a place called home and decent affordable housing.
- Protect all children from neglect, abuse, and other violence and ensure them the care they need.
- Ensure families leaving welfare the supports needed to be successful in the workplace, including health care, child care, education, and training.

*Source:* Children's Defense Fund, "The State of America's Children 2004" from *Children's Defense Fund, 2004*, p. xxxiii. Reprinted by permission of Children's Defense Fund.

## 30

# A Progressive Plan

### D. STANLEY EITZEN AND MAXINE BACA ZINN

*Sociologists D. Stanley Eitzen and Maxine Baca Zinn provide a number of progressive principles they feel ought to guide public policy to reduce or eliminate major social problems that plague U.S. society.*

Societies are structured. That is, they have a design that results from social policies. Since, some societal arrangements result in social problems, social policies can be applied to change or reduce or eliminate these problems. In other words, the design can be changed. To do this, we propose the following progressive principles:

1. We call for *policies and behaviors that enhance our moral obligation to our neighbors (broadly defined) and their children, to those unlike us as well as those similar to us, and to future generations.* This principle runs counter to the celebration of individualism that is so pervasive in U.S. society. But, we argue, the emphasis on individualism over community leads to exacerbated inequality; the tolerance of inferior housing, schools, and services for "others"; and public policies that are punitive to the economically disadvantaged.

There is a flaw in the individualistic credo. We cannot go it alone—our fate as individuals and as a society depends on others. Thus, it is in our individual interest to have a collective interest. As sociologist Alan Wolfe, discussing the Scandinavian countries, has put it:

> *The strength of the welfare state—indeed, the accomplishment that makes the welfare state the great success story of modern liberal democracy—is the recognition that the living conditions of people who are strangers to us are nonetheless our business. (Wolfe, 1989:133).*

2. Acceptance of the first principle leads to the second: a call for *government programs that provide for people who cannot provide for themselves.* This is a call to bring all members of society up to a minimum standard of dignity. At a minimum, this includes universal health insurance, a living wage that brings workers above the poverty line, and guaranteed and adequate pensions.

3. Acceptance of these principles leads to a third: *A special commitment to children, all children, and to implement this commitment with viable, universal programs.* In sociologist Jay Belsky's words:

*Source:* From Eitzen, D. Stanley, and Baca Zinn, Maxine, *Social Problems,* 10th edition. Published by Allyn and Bacon, Boston, MA. Copyright © 2006 Pearson Education. Reprinted by permission of the publisher.

> *The time has come for this nation to regard child care as an infrastructure issue and make the
> same kind of investment in it that we talk about making in our bridges and roads and that we
> initially made in these vital transportation systems. We need to recognize that, in the same way,
> that the massive capital investment in transportation and communication systems resulted in
> huge capital gains that we continue even to this day to realize, investment in child care can bring
> with it comparable long-term benefits. To gain insight into the costs, specifically foregone oppor-
> tunity costs of not endeavoring to improve child care and increase options for families, imagine
> for a moment an America with the automobile but without paved roads. (Belsky, 1990:11).*

Such a commitment to children involves providing prenatal and postnatal medical care,
childhood immunization, protection from exposure to toxic chemicals, adequate nutrition,
the elimination of child poverty, access to preschool and after-school programs, safe neighborhoods, and equally financed schools.

4. A call *to redistribute societal resources to lift those urban and rural areas that
are economically disadvantaged.* Some areas of the nation are especially at risk. There are
many pockets of rural poverty, such as Appalachia and the Mississippi Delta, where jobs
are few and poorly paid and poverty rates are many times higher than the national average.
These areas need federal assistance for schools, job training, and infrastructure. They need
government subsidies through tax rebates to encourage businesses to locate there and hire
local workers (the subsidies to be received when company performance conditions—jobs,
pay, and benefits to workers—are met).

The other important area of neglect is the declining inner cities, which have been abandoned by the middle classes, who have moved to the suburbs, and by corporations that have
moved their businesses (and jobs) to the suburbs, to other parts of the country, or out of the
country. The tax base in the cities has eroded, leaving declining transit systems, parks, and
services, most notably schools.

The federal government can help revitalize the cities. To date, there is no will by policy
makers to do so (especially by Republicans who receive votes and money disproportionately from suburban voters).

5. *Although some social policies should be made and administered at the local level,•
others must be largely financed, organized, and administered by the federal government.*
This principle is based on the assumption that some issues are national in scope and require
uniform standards (e.g., nutrition guidelines, immunization timetables, preschool, elementary through high school goals, the certification of teachers, and health care guarantees).
Other policies such as reducing poverty require the massive infusion of money and compensatory programs, coupled with centralized planning. This principle runs counter to the current conservative mood of Congress, which wants to return most programs to the states.

While dismantling the welfare system, the strategy has been to cut funds and to move
the programs from the federal level to the states. This trend has the effect of making benefits very uneven, as some states are relatively generous while others are much less so. The
distinguished historian Arthur Schlesinger, Jr., has said this about the role of the federal
government vis-a-vis the state governments:

> *It is a delusion to say that, because state government is closer to the people, it is more respon-
> sive to their needs and concerns. Historically it is national government that has served as the
> protector of the powerless. It is national government that affirmed the Bill of Rights against local
> vigilantism and preserved natural resources against local greed. The national government has*

*civilized industry, secured the rights of labor organizations, improved income for the farmer, and provide a decent living for the old. Above all, the national government has vindicated racial justice against local bigotry. Had the states' rights creed prevailed, the U.S. would still have slavery. And historically the national government has been more honest and efficient than state and local governments. . . . As for bureaucracy, duplication, and waste, will there be more or less if a single federal agency is to be replaced by fifty separate state agencies? (cited in Shanker, 1995:E7).*

## REFERENCES

Belsky, Jay (1990). "Infant Day Care, Child Development, and Family Policy." *Society* (July/August), pp. 10–12.

Shanker, Albert (1995). "In Defense of Government." *New York Times* (November 5), p. E7.

Wolfe, Alan (1989). *Whose Keeper? Social Science and Moral Obligation.* Berkeley, CA: University of California Press.

# 31

# Whose Money Is It? A Meditation on April 15th

*JOHN SHELBY SPONG*

*If, as we have shown, the government has a significant role in achieving the good society, then it must be funded sufficiently. This requires an attitude on the part of the citizenry that taxes are important because of the benefits to each of us and to society. In this essay John Shelby Spong, a former Episcopal bishop, makes that case forcefully.*

April 15 each year is the due date for tax payments to the Federal and State Governments based on the previous year's income. We have just gone through it. It is a day dreaded by many, looked forward to by few. Taxation is the place where citizens feel the burden of citizenship. In listening to political figures, however, one gets the impression that some of them believe that no one ought to pay any taxes. It is certainly politically popular to lower rather than to raise taxes. This nation, guided by this mentality, has moved significantly to lessen that burden in recent years. The tax rates on dividends and capital gains have both been cut substantially. The percentage of the total amount of all taxes collected from the wealthiest citizens of this nation has decreased notably in the last 50 years. The amount of inheritance tax due upon the death of those citizens, whose wealth is in the tens of millions, is on a schedule to be phased out completely over the next few years. These are popular strategies until the nation begins to understand that the quality of life is impaired when we move too far in that direction. As part of the campaign for tax cuts the claim is always made that the money collected in taxes is really 'your own money.' The government is therefore guilty of 'confiscating' your property. It is an interesting argument. It sounds fair to allow those whose money it is to retain more of it. No one seems to notice or perhaps to care that while these wonderful tax breaks have been received, the budget deficit of this country has risen to an all time high and is growing daily. That deficit does not yet include the cost of the Iraqi war, nor is there any amount included to offset the new deficit that will be established if private accounts are taken out of the Social Security system. It is in the

*Source:* Excerpt from "Whose Money Is It? A Meditation on April 15th" by John Shelby Spong from www. agoramedia.com.

juxtaposition of these realities that an enormous moral question must be raised. There is no better time to do it than while the April 15, 2005, tax due date is still fresh in our minds.

"Whose money is it?" Is there a claim that the whole society has a right to make on an individual's wealth that is the legitimate basis for taxation? Where is the line to be drawn between private wealth and public good? Is it a patriotic act to avoid legitimate taxation by sending your corporate headquarters to Bermuda? Is there not a basic legitimacy for the payment of fair and equitable taxes on the part of every citizen? Do we not realize that America is still today the least taxed country in the developed world? Is it not also the nation with the highest percentage of people without health care? Are these things not related? Does it matter?

If we receive benefits for our tax dollars that none of us would be willing to sacrifice, then are not our taxes something we owe? Can it then be said to be 'our money'? Do any of us want to live in a nation that has no parks for its citizens, that does not guarantee the quality of the water we drink, the air we breathe, the food we eat or the medicine we take? No citizen can provide these things for himself or herself and yet our individual lives are dependent on each of them. Do any of us want to live in a nation that has no federal or state roads, highways, bridges or tunnels over which or under which we may travel in our cars to pursue business or to see family and friends? Do any of us want to live in a nation that has no regulations governing airline security and no way to guarantee the safety of the planes on which we fly? Do we want to live in a nation that cannot secure its people from enemies, whether that be by providing our armed forces against those who might wish to harm us from abroad or by giving us adequate police and fire protection against people or events that might harm us internally. All of those things cost money but all of them are in my mind worth whatever they cost. Since our lives depend on our government to provide these basic services to us, are the taxes we are required to pay really 'my' money or do they represent the natural and normal cost required for our lives to be lived, a legitimate expense that guarantees to us a quality of life that we want and desire?

I, for one, do want our seniors or our parents who worked and saved all of their lives to have a government that will guarantee them a pension called Social Security, designed to provide them with a floor of security and dignity in the final years of their lives. I do want a government that will provide for me and for my family basic security from terrorists who seek to enter this nation. I do want a government that will guarantee the solvency of my savings in banks and the honesty of the financial industry that issues stocks and bonds. I do want a government that will certify that when the pump says I have received a gallon of gas that I have actually received a full gallon. I want a government that will support education, make it possible for my children to attend public schools and, if their ability allows it, to receive a university education at a cost that an average person can afford. I want a government that will encourage the unbounded human spirit to press new frontiers, to explore space, to fund the search to find cures for cancer, heart disease, diabetes and thousands of other diseases that snuff out life for many and affect the quality of life for all. I want the opportunity of choosing to live in this kind of world so should I not also expect to pay for it? Does that make my taxes, "my money?"

I believe that the taxes I pay in this country are the best bargain in my entire budget. I would not trade the benefits I receive in order to get back the taxes I pay and I think it is time for someone to say so publicly. Taxes are not "my money" that some alien government seeks to extort from one of its citizens. Taxes are the price I pay for the privilege of living in this land of freedom and opportunity. I treasure my citizenship in the United States. This does not mean that I am now, or have been in the past, supportive of every decision that a particular government of my nation might make. Individual political decisions are issues that I as a citizen can fight in the appropriate political arena. Some of those decisions are major, life-altering decisions. I think the decision not to provide health care for all is wrong. I grieve at the plight of the poor when illness strikes. I think Social Security should be fully funded not dismantled. Social Security, which was created only in 1935, kept my family afloat when my father died in 1943 and I was not 12 years old. He had paid into that fund for only eight years. Yet it supported my mother and her three young children when there was nothing else on which to depend. I also think that giving tax reductions to our wealthiest citizens while refusing to raise the minimum wage for our poorest citizens is quite simply immoral. I think the "contract with America" that removed many government restrictions that guaranteed the honesty of American business practices is what has given us the corruption found in the Enrons, the World Coms, the AIG's, the Quests and the Health Souths of recent years. I think there are some things so basic to life that they ought to be federalized, not so that they are profitable but so that the citizens may be well served. Even when I list all of my complaints about the way this nation has been and is now being administered, even as I fight and lose on some of these issues, I still would not swap America for any other nation I know in the world. Since that is so I count it an incredible privilege to pay the taxes that I am required to pay to my city, to my state and to my federal government.

Patriotism takes many forms. To me it is far more than saluting the flag or observing the Fourth of July. It is more than supporting our troops who are deployed in faraway places. Patriotism means that I place the common good of my nation on a par with my assessment of my own personal good. It means that I rejoice in my annual opportunity on April 15 to do my part to keep my nation free and strong. It means that I must constantly recognize that my security has no meaning outside the security of my nation. My well-being has no meaning outside the well being of my country. Patriotism also means opposing a militaristic foreign policy that diminishes the reputation of my country among the nations of the world. Patriotism certainly does not mean seeking to destroy the common good in order to enhance my personal worth. That is why I am always amazed at the number of our citizens, who speak as super patriots, and yet who seem to believe that patriotism does not include the willingness to pay one's share of a fair and equitable taxation program that makes it possible for this great nation to be what it is.

When I wrote my check to the Internal Revenue Service of the United States, I did so thinking of the great things that my taxes bring me. I did so as one still privileged to be critical of the political decisions of this particular government. I did so hopeful that a war in Iraq that I thought was not only disastrous but morally wrong, might still turn out to bring freedom to the Middle East, to allow a Palestinian state to be developed and may yet still guarantee the security of Israel for centuries to come. I wrote that check with the hope that politicians may yet come to understand that one does not gut the public good in order to give tax breaks to the wealthiest citizens. I did so with the conscious awareness that my taxes will inevitably have to be raised at some point in the not so far distant future to address the deficit and protect our nation's financial competence in that future. When that day comes, the patriotic thing to do will be to vote to raise those taxes. Then we will see the difference between the patriots of conviction and the patriots of rhetoric. It costs money to live in the United States. I treasure that privilege so I willingly pay the price required. April 15th was my time to give thanks for the joy of citizenship in this land!